# IN DEFENSE OF LEGAL POSITIVISM

## Law without Trimmings

MATTHEW H. KRAMER

OXFORD

UNIVERSITY PRESS

# OXFORD

UNIVERSITY PRESS

Great Clarendon Street, Oxford ox2 6DP

Oxford University Press is a department of the University of Oxford.
It furthers the University's objective of excellence in research, scholarship,
and education by publishing worldwide in

Oxford  New York

Athens  Auckland  Bangkok  Bogotá  Buenos Aires  Calcutta
Cape Town  Chennai  Dar es Salaam  Delhi  Florence  Hong Kong  Istanbul
Karachi  Kuala Lumpur  Madrid  Melbourne  Mexico City  Mumbai
Nairobi  Paris  São Paulo  Singapore  Taipei  Tokyo  Toronto  Warsaw

with associated companies in  Berlin  Ibadan

Oxford is a registered trade mark of Oxford University Press
in the UK and in certain other countries

Published in the United States
by Oxford University Press Inc., New York

British Library Cataloguing in Publication Data

Data available

Library of Congress Cataloging in Publication Data
Kramer, Matthew H., 1959–
In defense of legal positivism: law without trimmings / Matthew
H. Kramer.
p. cm.
Includes bibliographical references.
1. Legal positivism.  I. Title.
K331.K726  1999
340′.112—dc21
ISBN 0–19–826819–X

1 3 5 7 9 10 8 6 4 2

Typeset in Times by
Cambrian Typesetters, Frimley, Surrey
Printed in Great Britain
on acid-free paper by
Biddles Ltd., Guildford and King's Lynn

*To my father, Alton M. Kramer*

# *Preface*

BOTH the title and the introductory chapter of this book make clear the central purpose of the various arguments that are presented herein. Only a few minor preliminary remarks are needed in this Preface. We should note three points of terminology. First, the words 'duty' and 'obligation' are used interchangeably throughout this book. Although some other writers' analytical foci involve distinctions between those two terms, such distinctions are superfluous here; consequently, every chapter of this volume will construe 'duty' and 'obligation' as synonyms. Second, the word 'citizen' will be employed herein to refer to anyone (other than a legal/governmental official) who is subject to the sway of a legal system. The word does not refer only to a full-fledged member of a polity. Third, the phrase 'prima-facie' throughout this book will carry the sense which is specified in my final chapter. That is, the phrase amounts to a synonym for 'over-ridable' or 'defeasible.'

One further preliminary remark pertains to individuals and their families. Most of the time, this book will treat individuals and their families as units; thus, wicked legal officials who strive single-mindedly to maintain and reinforce their powerful positions will be described herein as selfishly devoted to their own interests, even though the family of each such official will undoubtedly stand to benefit from the success of his striving for power. My analyses in this book will implicitly regard the members of each such official's family as mere adjuncts of his self. His bestowal upon them of benefits derived from his privileged position is morally akin to nepotism and of course may include nepotism. That is, any concern for his family members' interests which the official displays through his conferral of benefits is greatly overshadowed by the disregard of other people's interests which he thereby exhibits and which he more generally exhibits. We can thus aptly view him as entirely devoted to his own well-being. Moreover, his concern for his family members' interests may well be thoroughly selfish, in that he may well be attempting simply to secure their loyalty and their serviceability for his purposes.

By contrast, at one or two junctures in this book where wicked officials are not under consideration, an ordinary person's concern for his familial dependents is portrayed as an attitude of moral solicitude. There is no reason to think that such concern by an ordinary person will always or typically involve a cavalier disdain for the interests of other people. Hence, any familial concern felt by such a person is not greatly overshadowed by his adoption of a ruthlessly power-hungry posture in the public domain. Moreover, there is likewise no reason to think that the ordinary person will frequently view his family members primarily as instrumentally important (for his own selfish ends) rather than as intrinsically important. In sum, we are warranted in implicitly distinguishing between the wicked official's bestowal of largesse on his relatives and the ordinary citizen's solicitude for his or her dependents. Whereas the citizen's solicitude should typically be classified as moral in tenor, the evil official's dispensation of benefits is typically part of an overall course of conduct that is principally or exclusively self-interested.

I wish to express my gratitude to the British Academy for a Research Leave Award that facilitated my writing of the final five chapters of this book. Similar gratitude is owed to Churchill College (Cambridge) and the University of Cambridge Law Faculty, where I have enjoyed excellent facilities for my writing. My warm thanks are also due to many people who have offered advice or support: Trevor Allan, Brian Bix, Richard Bronaugh, Daniel Brudney, Tom Campbell, Emilios Christodoulidis, Jules Coleman, Sarah Dalton, Antony Duff, Neil Duxbury, John Eekelaar, Gibran van Ert, Kevin Gray, Andrew Hamilton, Sarah Hill, Isaac Kramnick, David Lyons, Neil MacCormick, Sandra Marshall, Richard Parker, Nigel Simmonds, Jane Spencer, John Spencer, Hillel Steiner, Gunther Teubner, Wil Waluchow, Robin West, Kay Zakarian, Lindy Zakarian. I furthermore wish to thank heartily John Louth and Mick Belson (and their colleagues) at Oxford University Press for their highly efficient handling of my book. I am grateful as well to the Cambridge Jurisprudence students who have asked questions or made observations about the matters discussed herein. Thanks should go equally to the anonymous readers—at the Oxford University Press and at several journals—whose comments have prompted some salutary amplifications and modifications. My greatest debt is to my father, to whom I dedicate this book with love.

Some small sections of this book have been delivered as talks to the law faculties in Edinburgh and Hull, where I encountered stimulating audiences to whom I am grateful. I have published earlier versions of some portions of this book in the following journals:

*Law and Philosophy* (much of Chapter 2)
*Oxford Journal of Legal Studies* (half of Chapter 3)
*Ethics* (much of Chapter 4)
*Legal Theory* (one third of Chapter 6)
*Canadian Journal of Law & Jurisprudence* (half of Chapter 6)

I thank all of these journals for permission to republish with numerous modifications. (A slightly later version of Chapter 2 was published as the third essay in my *In the Realm of Legal and Moral Philosophy* [Basingstoke: Macmillan, 1999]. I am grateful to Macmillan for permission to republish with numerous modifications.) Each of the excerpts listed above has been very significantly revised for this book.

Cambridge, England                                              Matthew H. Kramer
January 1999

# Contents

# 1

## *Introduction*

Can wicked rulers be allied with Thee, who frame mischief by statute?

Psalm 94: 20

This book's central ambition is to defend the legal-positivist claim that law and morality are strictly separable. Certain other aspects of legal positivism will be defended as well, especially in Chapter 6; but the primary objective herein is to underscore the legal/moral distinction. Though legality and morality are of course combinable, they are likewise disjoinable. Attempts to deny as much—attempts to establish the intrinsically moral import of law—will all turn out to have run aground.

The chapters below are divided into two main parts. In the first and considerably longer of those parts, composed of five chapters, the focus lies on a number of prominent recent theories which have suggested that law is somehow indissolubly connected to morality. The principal theorists studied in those chapters are David Lyons, Lon Fuller, Joseph Raz, Michael Detmold, and Ronald Dworkin; but some careful attention is paid therein as well to John Finnis, Nigel Simmonds, Gerald Postema, Philip Soper, and Neil MacCormick. Some of these theorists— especially Lyons and Raz, but also MacCormick—are normally classified as legal positivists. However, each of them (in Lyons's case, *malgré lui*) has advanced certain theses which lead to the conclusion that propositions about law are necessarily linked to propositions about morality. Consequently, each of those theorists stands as an opponent in a book which strives to eschew that conclusion altogether.

The second chief group of chapters will begin by reviewing and amplifying some of the discussions presented in Chapters 2–6. We shall then move on to consider a number of issues that have not theretofore been broached. Throughout, the aim will be to explicate a variety of key jural concepts (such as authority, obligation, and allegiance) along legal-positivist lines, in order to show that such concepts can be retained as distinctive theoretical categories without any need for a moralized understanding of law. This task of conceptual re-elaboration will have begun in Chapters 2–6—for, although those earlier chapters are dedicated primarily to the 'negative' enterprise of confuting positions that are inimical to legal positivism, they also undertake the 'affirmative' enterprise of reconceiving some basic jural notions in a positivist manner. That is, the first half of this book sets the stage for the final three chapters not only by placing in doubt some moralized accounts of law, but also by indicating the robustness of a positivist account.

I. SOME CLARIFICATIONS AND DISTINCTIONS

Before looking ahead further to the remaining chapters of this book, we should pursue some clarification of the thesis which the book defends. What exactly is meant by the claim that law and morality are always separable? One thing clearly not meant is that law and morality are always *separate*. Separability does not entail separateness. As will be emphasized at more than one juncture in the chapters that follow, there can exist any number of contingent connections between legal requirements and moral requirements. A refusal to acknowledge the possibility of such connections would be at least as foolish and misguided as an insistence that they must actually obtain in all circumstances. What this book contends is not that legal requirements and moral requirements *must* diverge, but that legal requirements and moral requirements always *can* diverge. Necessary ties between law and morality, as opposed to contingent ties, are what legal positivism gainsays.

What, then, is meant by the claim that there are no necessary connections between law and morality? A full answer to this question lies in the analyses which make up the subsequent chapters of this book, since the answer consists in refutations of the various arguments that might seem to establish some necessary connections. Only by looking at a range of theories can we gain an informed sense of the ways in which legality and morality have appeared to be inextricably intertwined. However, some preliminary sets of distinctions will help to provide a setting or framework for the analyses that emerge in the rest of this book. To be sure, none of these sets of distinctions will come close to capturing all the intricacies of the arguments that are explored and propounded in later chapters; but the distinctions together serve as a classificatory background that can organize a lot of the major lines of thought in those arguments.

## A.  Morality Thrice Construed

In the epigraph at the opening of this chapter, and in many other pieces of writing, morality is implicitly (or explicitly) contrasted with wickedness. When presented on the basis of such a contrast—a contrast between the moral and the immoral—any assertion about the lack of necessary connections between law and morality is an assertion that the norms implemented by a legal system can be evil in their content or in their effects. The status of a regime as a legal regime does not rule out the possibility that the regime is appalling; likewise, the status of a norm as a legal norm does not exclude the possibility that its requirements are morally unacceptable. Nothing guarantees that a legal system or a law will be benign merely because it is a legal system or a law.

In other contexts, the implicit or express contrast is not between morality and evil, but between morality and factuality. Here we separate people's judgments concerning what morally ought to be and people's judgments concerning what is or was or will be. When presented on the basis of such a contrast, a claim about the lack of any necessary connections between law and morality is a claim that the process of ascertaining the law does not perforce involve moral judgments; the process of law-ascertainment can unfold as a starkly factual inquiry into the relevant sources of legal norms that have been constituted by previous legislative and adjudicative decisions. Although any particular legal system (such as the American system) can obligate and empower its officials to apply certain moral tests when identifying the law, the role of such tests is a purely contingent feature.

In still other contexts, the relevant contrast is not principally between morality and wickedness or between morality and factuality, but between morality and prudence. Here one's decisions made essentially out of concern for other people's interests are separated from one's decisions made essentially out of concern for one's own interests. When presented on the basis of this contrast—which will be fully developed in Chapter 3 and repeatedly invoked thereafter—a thesis about the lack of any necessary connections between law and morality is a thesis asserting that legal decision-making and rule-of-law observances can be based on officials' purely prudential calculations. That is, officials who care only about their own interests in securing the efficacy of their grip on power will typically have solid reasons for adhering quite consistently to the rule of law. As a consequence, the ideal of the rule of law cannot correctly be deemed an intrinsically moral ideal.

Though sketched here with the utmost terseness, each of these three overlapping conceptions of morality—morality distinguished from evil, morality distinguished from factuality, and morality distinguished from prudence—will figure prominently at various points in this book. (As will be mentioned fleetingly later in this chapter and as will become evident in Chapters 5, 6, and 7, the purview of morality can be demarcated in still further ways.) Let us focus for a moment on the first of the conceptions above. When anti-positivist stances are founded on that conception, they tend to fit the image of traditional natural-law theorizing. In other words, they lay down some standards of minimal goodness which a legal system or norm must satisfy in order to count as a genuine legal system or norm. A regime which falls short of those standards is a legal regime only in a debased and weakly formal sense.

Some analysts have suggested that the dispute between the proponents of this familiar version of the natural-law standpoint and the proponents of legal positivism is trivial, in that the differences between the two sides can be explained as a matter of verbal squabbling. We are told that the term 'law' is similar to terms such as 'doctor' or 'parent' or 'teacher'.[1] When we say that some particular man

---

[1] See e.g. Brian Bix, *Jurisprudence: Theory and Context* (Boulder: Westview Press, 1996), 72; Kent Greenawalt, 'Too Thin and Too Rich: Distinguishing Features of Legal Positivism', in Robert George (ed.), *The Autonomy of Law* (Oxford: Clarendon Press, 1996), 1, 10. Cf. Lon Fuller, *The Morality of Law* (New Haven: Yale University Press, 1969) (rev. edn.), 122.

is not a 'true doctor,' for example, we quite likely mean that—although he is formally qualified for the practice of medicine—his skill and solicitude in pursuing his practice are distressingly meager. If one opts for a broad and largely non-evaluative use of the word 'doctor,' then one will intend that word to encompass anybody who engages in the medical profession with formal qualifications;[2] by contrast, if one opts for a narrower and plainly evaluative use of the word, then one will intend it to encompass only those medical practitioners who exhibit proficiency and caringness above a certain level. The context of an utterance and the conversational manner of a speaker will usually render the meaning of the word clear. In any event, no deep philosophical issues hinge on the choice between the more expansive use and the more discriminating use. Let us happily agree as much. Should we therefore conclude that basically the same is true of the term 'law' and of the jurisprudential debates in which that term saliently figures?

In Chapter 6 we shall encounter a largely similar line of thought in the later work of Dworkin. For now, let us note the following points. First, even if a dismissive attitude were warranted in regard to the controversies between legal positivism and those natural-law theories which highlight the morality/wickedness distinction, there would remain numerous other theories which concentrate chiefly instead on the morality/factuality distinction or the morality/prudence distinction. In fact, as will become apparent in my subsequent chapters, most of the leading anti-positivist theories in recent decades have drawn far more heavily on the last two distinctions than on the divide between morality and evil. To be sure, theories in keeping with the traditional image of natural-law philosophy have certainly not disappeared altogether.[3] (Indeed, within some of the works of Fuller and Dworkin, we shall come upon certain strands of argument—albeit briefly developed strands of argument—that fit the traditional image.) None the less, the most sophisticated efforts in recent years to demonstrate necessary connections between law and morality have had little time for the notion that heinous laws are not genuine laws. Morality contrasted with wickedness, rather than with factuality or prudence, has not been the focus of those efforts.

---

[2] Of course, some degree of evaluation is needed for determining what will count as formal qualifications. For example, one will have to ponder whether people possessed of chiropractic qualifications should be designated as doctors. Still, once the range of recognized qualifications has been set, we can distinguish (on the basis of skill and solicitude) between the medical practitioners who are 'true' doctors and the medical practitioners who are merely holders of the requisite qualifications.

[3] See e.g. Deryck Beyleveld and Roger Brownsword, 'The Practical Difference Between Natural-Law Theory and Legal Positivism', 5 *Oxford Journal of Legal Studies* 1, 2 n. 1 (1985) ('In our view, iniquitous rules cannot be legally valid; and, for the record, we would not consciously speak of unjust *laws*') (emphasis in original); Michael Moore, 'Law as a Functional Kind', in Robert George (ed.), *Natural Law Theory* (Oxford: Clarendon Press, 1992), 188, 198 ('My view is Augustine's view, that the justness of a norm is *necessary* to its status as law') (emphasis in original). In Ch. 8 I examine the stance taken by Beyleveld and Brownsword, and in Ch. 9 I examine the stance taken by Moore. My treatment of Beyleveld's and Brownsword's work will be quite terse, since their overall position rests through and through on the moral philosophy of Alan Gewirth, which I have elsewhere sustainedly refuted. See Matthew Kramer, *In the Realm of Legal and Moral Philosophy* (Basingstoke: Macmillan, 1999), ch. 10.

As a second response to the question asked two paragraphs ago, we should decline to accept that the disputes between legal positivism and traditional natural-law stances—viz., disputes over a broad and non-evaluative conception of law versus a narrower and plainly evaluative conception—are trivial or arid. As will be argued at some length in Chapter 6 (and more tersely in a few of my other chapters), the aforementioned disputes might appear to be verbal squabbles but are in fact often methodological controversies relating to the appropriate touchstones for the selection of basic jurisprudential concepts. While this book calls for the term 'law' to be used broadly in jurisprudential discussions, it does so not as a sheer stipulation but in furtherance of analytical clarification and explanatory power; such a pattern of usage tends to serve the theoretical objective of ferreting out the full implications of various regimes' adherence to the rule of law. Natural-law theorists, by contrast, frequently argue for their pattern of usage not principally on analytical and explanatory grounds but on moral grounds. Hence, some of the debates between legal positivism and natural-law theory concern not only questions about theoretical foci but also methodological questions about the appropriate grounds for choosing those foci. Such debates hardly amount to sterile terminological bickering. (Of course, nothing in this paragraph is meant to suggest that all adherents of legal positivism have opted for their theoretical orientation on primarily analytical grounds or that all adherents of natural-law thought have opted for *their* theoretical orientation on primarily moral grounds. Methodological differences certainly exist within those two camps as well as between them. None the less, the methodological differences have indeed loomed large in some positivist/natural-law controversies, and they loom large in some of this book's encounters with anti-positivist theories.)

## B.  Whence Derives the Value

Another set of distinctions that can help to provide a structure for the points of contention between positivists and their opponents is connected with the specification of law's value. When theorists ascribe an intrinsic moral worthiness to law, they need to locate that worthiness in some aspect or aspects of legal governance. Three very broad dimensions of law, which are by no means mutually exclusive, have generally been invoked as the sites of law's value.

Some theorists attach particular importance to the *processes* by which the institutions of legal governance formulate and implement their authoritative norms. Regardless of the substantive contents and effects of legal norms, the procedures by which they are administered can be seen as inherently valuable. We are told that moral ideals such as due process, fair notice, formal justice, and integrity are all promoted by the workings of a genuine legal system; the promotion of those values will have occurred regardless of the relative benignity or malignity of any particular legal system's mandates. Both because of the disciplined restraint which the formal mechanisms of law impose on the people who govern, and because of the protections which those mechanisms yield for the people who are governed, the procedures that make up the operations of a legal system are intrinsically valuable. They serve to establish some degree of reciprocity between the rulers and the ruled—by sustaining a relationship of mutual obligations—and they bolster the autonomy of the ruled, who are shielded against the arbitrariness and personal grudges of officials. So, at least, argue many of the theorists who view law *qua* law as morally salutary (irrespective of its substantive tenor). As will be seen in several of my subsequent chapters, this favorable assessment of law's procedural dimension has been expressed by most opponents of legal positivism, in a variety of forms.

A second aspect of law that has sometimes been perceived as morally pregnant is the generating of concrete decisions and outcomes. (Although a laudatory concentration on this aspect of law does not have to be combined with a favorable assessment of law's procedural dimension, those two positions can go together smoothly.) Here the focus is on the 'bottom line,' the level at which a legal system's officials reach judgments concerning the matters which they are called upon to resolve. When anti-positivist theorists designate those concrete determinations of a legal system as inherently moral, and when they implicitly or explicitly define morality in a contrast with wickedness, they are putting forth a view akin to the views traditionally associated with natural-law thought. That is, they are contending that flagitious decisions by officials are not genuine legal decisions at all. According to such a stance, outcomes plainly at odds with basic principles of decency and fairness are only simulacra of legal rulings; those outcomes are exertions of sheer power, for they fail to meet the minimum standards of goodness that are satisfied by any full-fledged legal determinations. (Of course, this sort of stance can be—and has been—applied to legal systems' norms as well as to the concrete decisions that are engendered thereunder.[4])

Somewhat more plausible is an outcome-oriented theory that defines morality in a contrast with prudence rather than in a contrast with evil. Anti-positivist theorists who espouse such a doctrine are thereby maintaining that each act of official decision-making is itself morally pregnant, in that the basis for any legal decision by an official is perforce a nonprudential basis. We are assured that, even if some legal determination by an official is wicked, it necessarily bespeaks his perception that the rendering of the particular determination is morally warranted on the whole. Though the moral precepts on which he draws when reaching his judgment may be woefully misguided, they are indeed moral precepts rather than a set of prudential guidelines. To the extent that they militate in favor of the advancement of his self-interest, they do so only derivatively and not essentially. In short, the generating of legal outcomes is a fundamentally moral enterprise because the lone recognized basis for arriving at any such outcomes is an essential concern for others' interests (which amounts to a concern for making the morally correct

---

[4]  See e.g. Michael Moore, above, n. 3, at 193–5, 198.

decisions). Albeit the concrete outcomes in a legal system might be startlingly evil, they must derive from considerations that are profoundly nonprudential. A judgment based essentially on an official's own interests would not be merely a bad legal decision; rather, it would be no legal decision at all. Such, at any rate, is the claim propounded by theorists such as Detmold and Dworkin.

In addition to each legal system's procedural workings and its production of concrete results, an aspect of law that has been singled out by many opponents of jurisprudential positivism is each legal system's overall functioning. Here the focus lies not on the textured level of specific outcomes, but on the role played by a regime of law as a general institution. The upshot of that role might be seen as the securement of basic social orderliness or the provision of autonomy-enhancing regularity or the facilitation of people's pursuit of various goods, for example. However the general functions of law come to be characterized, they can strike many theorists as morally valuable; they can appear to endow any overarching regime of law with some measure of moral force simply by dint of its status as such a regime. As we shall observe in later chapters, a position of this sort has not only won the favor of anti-positivist writers but has also received close attention—not entirely unsympathetic attention—from legal positivists themselves.

We have looked, in sum, at three chief potential sources of law's putative moral weight: each legal system's operations or processes, its engendering of specific decisions, and its performance of a basic role or set of functions in human society. As should be manifest, these three possible sites of law's moral significance overlap to some extent. Unsurprisingly, then, a claim about the moral import of any one of them certainly does not exclude claims about the moral import of the other two. As should also be clear, these three dimensions of law are not exhaustive; for instance, in line with what has been fleetingly suggested above, theorists who assail jurisprudential positivism can seek to ascribe inherent moral worthiness to the norms that constitute the structure of each legal regime. None the less, although the distinctions drawn in this section are neither exhaustive nor unfailingly sharp, they form an illuminating classificatory matrix in which a diversity of theoretical stances—viz., most of the stances that are challenged in my subsequent chapters—can be placed.

## C. Official Outlooks

Time and again in this book, we shall find that anti-positivist writers have sought support for their desired conclusions by adverting to legal officials' attitudes and commitments. The outlooks associated with officials' roles are widely seized upon as fertile ground for necessary connections between law and morality. Here we should note some distinctions among the various dimensions or vectors of officials' activities. Like the previous sets of distinctions in this chapter, the highlighting of several different aspects or foci of officials' endeavors should help to underscore the complex similarities and divergences among my subsequent chapters' targets.

One key facet of the running of a legal system by officials is the relationship between them and the system's norms. That relationship, understood in connection with the division between morality and evil, will assume prominence in several of my chapters but especially in Chapter 2's sustained exploration of the matter of formal justice. There at issue is whether or not the strict implementation of a legal regime's norms by officials is perforce morally commendable (prima facie). More precisely, the relevant questions are whether or not the strict implementation of legal norms by officials is perforce morally obligatory (prima facie), and whether or not that strict implementation is perforce morally permissible (prima facie). Answers to those queries will effectively be answers to the question whether the relationship between the officials and the norms of every legal system provides a warrant for the view that the institutions of law necessarily partake of moral goodness to some degree.

The relationship between each legal regime's officials and its norms has also frequently come to the fore when challenges to positivism are founded on the distinction between morality and factuality. Wielding that distinction, some foes of positivism have declared that the process of ascertaining the existence and content of legal norms is always heavily value-laden. According to such critics, judgments concerning what-the-law-is are dependent on judgments concerning what-the-law-morally-ought-to-be. Once more, then, the posture of officials toward the norms of their legal system is a focal point for a rejection of jurisprudential positivism's insistence on the strict separability of law and morality. Much the same is true when positivism's detractors define morality in opposition to prudence. Some of those detractors have declared that legal officials' persistent effectuation of the norms of their regime must stem from the officials' devotion to the interests of the people who are subject to the sway of the norms' mandates; we are informed that, even when legal rules are unjustly biased in favor of the existing order of things, officials' own selfish interests are not served by their general faithfulness to the rules' procedural and substantive requirements. Yet again, that is, the official/norm relationship is adduced in ostensible confirmation of the thesis that the workings of law are inevitably attuned to the demands of morality.

Another salient dimension of the role of officials is their interaction with one another. They assist one another in numerous ways, not least by upbraiding and correcting one another when necessary. Their collaboration—not necessarily a very friendly collaboration—is unforgoable as a means of endowing their mandates with efficacy. The relationships among the officials of any legal system will receive particularly close scrutiny in my third chapter (most notably in the Postscript thereto), but will receive some attention in the fourth chapter and some of my other chapters as well. Chief among the queries to be considered is whether the interaction of legal officials with one another can be purely prudential or whether it must involve remonstrations and assertions that are moral in tenor. That question of prudence-versus-morality is itself divided into two main parts.

First, can the grounds or motives for officials' statements to other officials be purely prudential? That is, can there be legal systems in which the officials who make the statements do so essentially and explicitly out of concern for their own interests, rather than essentially out of concern for others' interests? Second, can the orientation of the advice or admonitions directed to the addressees of the official-to-official statements be purely prudential? That is, can there be legal systems in which those statements beckon their addressees toward certain actions or decisions by indicating that those actions or decisions will redound to the benefit of the addressees themselves? As we shall discover, the widespread belief that the answers to these questions must be negative is what lies behind a number of the attacks against legal positivism.

Still another crucial aspect of the operating of a legal system by officials is the relationship between them and the ordinary people who are subject to the system's demands and authorizations. When legal officials issue directives and render decisions, they are typically addressing themselves principally to ordinary citizens (and their lawyers). Because laws are generally enforced when necessary, the official/citizen relationship is an axis of power. However, in the eyes of many opponents of jurisprudential positivism, the official/citizen relationship is also ineluctably fraught with moral significance. If we here understand 'moral' in opposition to 'evil,' then the claim of the anti-positivist writers is that the official/citizen relationship necessarily partakes of some degree of moral worthiness—worthiness consisting in the restraints which the rule of law imposes on officials, and in the protections which it bestows upon citizens. (We have already encountered this suggestion, of course, during my previous section's sketch of the anti-positivist theories that focus on the procedural dimension of law.) If we instead understand 'moral' in opposition to 'prudential,' then the claim about the official/citizen relationship is that official statements to citizens which invoke the citizens' legal obligations are strictly nonprudential; any such statement by an official to a citizen is nonprudential in that the requirement which it expresses is not essentially based on either the official's interests or the citizen's interests. In more than one way, then, the posture of legal officials toward the people under their rule may appear to pose serious difficulties for jurisprudential positivism's thesis that the only links between morality and law are contingent.

A further key element of legal officials' endeavors is their stance toward the specific decisions that must be made in the execution of their duties. As has been outlined within my previous section's discussion of the level of concrete results in each legal system, some critics of positivism have presumed that every instance of official decision-making is a fundamentally moral judgment. In particular, most of the critics who take such a view have maintained that authoritative decisions by legal officials cannot be based essentially on considerations of self-interest—if those decisions are to count as genuine legal determinations at all. Appearing to militate just as powerfully against jurisprudential positivism (at least in the eyes of some writers) is the stance of any legal regime's officials toward the overall functioning of their regime. Here the thesis put forward in contestation of positivism is that, although legal officials may be badly misguided in their moral opinions, those officials believe that the general functioning of their system of law is morally justifiable and salutary on the whole. As a consequence, they believe that legal obligations are moral obligations by virtue of being legal obligations, and they of course believe likewise that the enterprise of sustaining the operations of their system of law is a morally worthy undertaking. These beliefs are reflected in their modes of argumentation, which presuppose or overtly incorporate standards that determine the acceptable bases for legal decisions. Those standards may be iniquitous (in evil legal systems), but they are always moral in the sense of being nonprudential.

In short, this section has singled out five cardinal foci or components of legal officials' work: their approach to the norms of their regime, their interaction with one another, their posture toward ordinary citizens, their attitudes toward specific decisions, and their assessments of the general functioning of their regime. Obviously, some of these dimensions of officials' activities overlap. Equally, the set of distinctions drawn in the present section of this chapter overlaps to a certain extent with the sets of distinctions drawn in the previous sections. All the same, given the frequency with which a host of anti-positivist theorists have fastened on various aspects of officials' roles in a quest to demonstrate that legal concepts are inextricably bound up with moral concepts, a careful attentiveness to the multiple orientations of those roles is clearly advisable. Such attentiveness can enhance one's recognition of the intricacy and diversity of the objections that have been posed against legal positivism.

## II.  A ROUGH MAP

### A.  The First Part

As has already been mentioned, the rest of this book is divided into two main groups of chapters. Each chapter in the first group is a rejoinder to one or more theorists who have deliberately or unwittingly cast doubt on the separability of law and morality. Each of those chapters will deal with some of the lines of argument that have been adumbrated in the first half of this Introduction (along with numerous other lines of argument).

Chapter 2, which concentrates on the views propounded by David Lyons concerning formal or procedural justice—justice in the administration or implementation of legal norms—is an exploration of an inadvertently anti-positivist stance taken by a proponent of legal positivism. Because Lyons is keen to accentuate the separability of law and morality, he feels obliged to argue against the notion that deviations from the law are always formally unjust. He assumes that the formal injustice of any official decision would be a prima-facie moral reason against the decision, and therefore he assumes that the separability of law and morality would be undermined if all official departures from the terms of legal norms (merely by dint of being such departures) were formal injustices. However, as will be observed, some of his central arguments against classifying all official deviations-from-the-law as formal injustices are unsound. His missteps enable us to perceive that all such deviations are indeed formally unjust. Of course, this conclusion would be troubling for legal positivism if Lyons were correct in thinking that the formal injustice of an official decision will perforce have posed an overridable moral reason against the decision. Hence, that underlying premise— his ascription of an intrinsically favorable moral status to formal justice and an intrinsically negative moral status to formal injustice—is my chief target throughout Chapter 2. As will be contended therein, officials' adherence to the terms of legal norms is not necessarily prima facie obligatory or even prima facie permissible.

Both in Lyons's own analysis of formal justice and in my critique of his analysis, the domain of morality is construed in opposition to the domain of evil.[5] In other words, the paramount point at issue is whether or not the formal injustice of any official decision is invariably an impermissible and unworthy feature thereof, prima facie. The morality/unworthiness contrast (or immorality/worthiness contrast) will also figure quite saliently in Chapter 3, which investigates Lon Fuller's attempt to attribute an inherent moral significance to the basic formal characteristics of law. At least as prominent, however, will be the distinction between morality and prudence. On the one hand, some of my arguments against Fuller and his defenders will endeavor to show that worthy moral values such as individual dignity are not necessarily promoted by the formal features of law, and that such values can indeed be seriously impaired by those features. On the other hand, my longest single argument in the third chapter seeks to show that a hearty respect by officials for the formal characteristics of law can derive from purely prudential considerations; that is, even in a legal regime where officials care about nothing except their own interests, they will have solid reasons for adhering to the formal requirements of the rule of law. Thus, in every pertinent sense, the rule of law is not an intrinsically moral ideal.

Chapter 4, a critique of Joseph Raz's conception of official statements that invoke legal obligations, is in some respects the most complicated portion of the book. Like Chapter 2, it defends legal positivism against one of the major contemporary legal positivists. Raz maintains that, when officials assert propositions which specify people's legal obligations in relation to certain matters, they are necessarily thereby affirming or appearing to affirm that people are under moral obligations in relation to those matters. According to him, that is, state-

---

[5]  As I mention in Ch. 2, Lyons also appears to assume that the values of justice and injustice are governed by the Law of Excluded Middle. That is, he appears to assume that any state of affairs in human society is unjust if it is not just, and that any state of affairs in human society is just if it is not unjust. When discussing his work, I accept this assumption *arguendo*.

ments invoking legal obligations are statements laying down or appearing to lay down moral reasons (i.e., nonprudential reasons) for action. Whereas Fuller concentrated on the interaction of officials with one another as well as on the relationship between officials and citizens, the focus here is very much on the latter relationship. My critique proceeds through a number of variants and levels of Raz's analysis, in an effort to demonstrate that the concept of legal obligation can indeed be disentangled from the concept of moral obligation. In the course of the discussion, the work of some other theorists—especially Philip Soper and Neil MacCormick—receives critical scrutiny as well. Throughout, the objective is to establish that propositions about legal duties do not perforce entail propositions about the moral obligatoriness of those duties or about the moral legitimacy of enforcing them.

More persistently than any of the other theorists whose writings are examined in this book, Michael Detmold—whose jurisprudential theorizing is studied in my fifth chapter—has trained attention on the reaching of specific decisions by legal officials. He submits that officials inevitably regard their determinations as morally justified, and that the task of legal decision-making is accordingly a task of moral (i.e., nonprudential) decision-making. Many of his lines of reasoning, then, rely implicitly or expressly on a morality/prudence opposition. However, among the points raised in my critique of Detmold's ideas is a way of demarcating the bounds of morality that is different from any of the ways expounded heretofore within this introductory chapter. The elaboration of a moral/nonmoral distinction, a distinction between (1) anyone's choices that affect the interests of other people beyond a trivial level and (2) anyone's choices that do not affect others' interests beyond such a level, can help to expose the confusion from which Detmold suffers when he attributes an intrinsic moral significance to the particular judgments of officials. His attribution is unsustainable unless it rests on a divide between the moral and the nonmoral (as opposed to a divide between morality and prudence or morality and evil). Yet, if his position is indeed founded on a moral/nonmoral dichotomy, it amounts to nothing with which any legal positivist would disagree.

The moral/nonmoral dichotomy looms large as well in one of the closing sections of Chapter 6. However, that chapter's critique of Ronald Dworkin also engages with each of the three other conceptions or aspects of morality that have been outlined in the present chapter. Because Dworkin has been the most influential foe of jurisprudential positivism during the past three decades, and because he has fired his broadsides from a number of angles, my discussion of his work is considerably longer than any of my other chapters. The first half of the discussion is a defense of the 'positive' side of legal positivists' theorizing—that is, a defense of some claims about the conventionality of each jural system's law-ascertaining criteria, and a defense of some claims about the subsumption of those criteria within an overarching array that serves as a complex and variable norm which underlies each system's law-ascertaining practices. At times in this defense of the 'affirmative' doctrines of legal positivism, the distinction between morality and factuality is quite conspicuous. That distinction likewise plays an important role in the second half of the chapter, which endeavors to parry Dworkin's thrusts against the notion that law and morality are strictly separable. In that latter half of the chapter, all of the other conceptions or facets of morality (moral versus evil, moral versus prudential, and moral versus nonmoral) also come to the fore. To a greater extent than any of the other writers whose works are investigated herein, Dworkin has pursued a multiplicity of routes in his anti-positivist arguments; my ripostes to his onslaughts are therefore bound to be wide-ranging.

The multifariousness of Dworkin's attacks against legal positivism is emblem-atic of the targets in my first group of chapters as a whole. Taken separately, none of the targeted theories has covered all of the institutional and philosophical factors that have been delineated in my current chapter's various sets of distinc-tions; taken together, however, those theories do indeed cover all or nearly all of the aforementioned factors. Although the critiques in Chapters 2–6 are not steps in a long continuous argument, and although each of those chapters can be under-stood fairly well on its own, they are quite closely related to one another in many respects (to which attention is drawn via numerous cross-references within them). While they do not amount to links in a single lengthy chain of reasoning, they do form a web of criss-crossing concerns and themes. Their cumulative effect is to vindicate legal positivism in the face of barrages deriving from all or nearly all of the theoretical foci whence anti-positivist barrages are likely to emanate.

Three partly interconnected reasons underlie my decision to devote the longer half of this book to critiques of other people's writings. First, far too much of recent jurisprudence has consisted in 'debates' that involve the construction and demolition of straw men by theorists who thus obscure the subtleties and resourcefulness of the positions which they are condemning. Therefore, although this book could have pitted itself against some general models of anti-positivist argumentation while paying hardly any attention to actual specific instances thereof, the recent precedents for such an approach are not promising. However sturdy a defense of legal positivism may be on its own terms, it will rightly be dismissed by positivism's opponents if it has badly failed to do justice to the best lines of reasoning which those opponents have devised. To try to ensure that justice is done and that the efficacy of my defense is thereby maxi-mized, this book immerses itself in the intricacies of the positions which it seeks to rebut.

A second, overlapping reason for the approach taken in Chapters 2–6 is that the cardinal thesis defended by this book—the claim that law and morality are not necessarily conjoined—is a 'negative' thesis. It is a claim concerning what does *not* have to be true, rather than a claim concerning what must be true. Now, although careful investigations of the standpoints of one's opponents are gener-ally beneficial, they are especially advisable for someone championing a negative thesis. After all, such a thesis in itself can seem quite jejune unless it is fleshed out through confrontations with doctrines that argue powerfully for a contrary verdict.[6] Only by grasping the potency of the considerations in favor of that contrary verdict, can we grasp the full import of the negative thesis which runs athwart them. To be sure, those overtopped considerations could be delineated and pondered through encounters with purely hypothetical challengers. Strictly speaking, no encounters with actual challengers are required. None the less, as is suggested by my last paragraph, there are ample grounds for thinking that the strength and richness of the positions of one's foes will be underestimated if the probing of those positions is not focused on some actual texts wherein the positions are expounded.

Third and most important among the reasons for this book's method of tackling its topic is that my critiques of specific theories are highly serviceable as platforms for the development of general conceptual analyses. Throughout Chapters 2–6, my ripostes to other writers involve the reformulation or transfiguration of fundamental jural notions. For example, my chapter on Raz sustainedly reconceives the notions of legal normativity and legal authority. Likewise, my chapter on Lyons endeavors to re-elaborate the concept of formal justice in a way that allows legal positivists to acknowledge the inherent link between such justice and the strict administration of the law. In these chapters and in the other chapters, the primary aim is not only to fend off doctrines that place positivism in question, but is also to devise a set of jural/philosophical concepts that enable positivism to account for all the phenomena which the competing doctrines might highlight. In other words, the tasks of this book (and, in particular, of Chapters 2–6) lie not only in disclosing the missteps committed by the detractors of legal positivism, but also in refining and strengthening the versatility of positivism as a theory in its own right. Though the latter task could doubtless have been performed without any detailed explorations (and refutations) of various specific attempts to establish intrinsic connections between law and morality, the execution of the task of theoretical refinement can flow very smoothly and fruitfully from such explorations. My critiques, that is, are as important for their 'affirmative' function—their function as the vehicles of conceptual re-explications—as for their 'negative' function of warding off attacks. Without them, the advisability of many of the conceptual re-explications

---

[6] Thus, for example, both Jules Coleman and Ronald Dworkin (from very different perspectives) have submitted that legal positivism's insistence on the separability of law and morality is in itself largely trivial. See Jules Coleman, 'Negative and Positive Positivism', in *Markets, Morals and the Law* (Cambridge: Cambridge University Press, 1988), 3, 12; Ronald Dworkin, 'A Reply', in Marshall Cohen (ed.), *Ronald Dworkin and Contemporary Jurisprudence* (London: Duckworth, 1984), 247, 252; Jules Coleman, 'Authority and Reason', in Robert George (ed.), *The Autonomy of Law* (Oxford: Clarendon Press, 1996), 287, 316 n. 5. However, the remarks by Coleman and Dworkin pertain to only a single version of the thesis that law and morality are separable—a version focused on the distinction between morality and factuality. A full defense of legal positivism, alert to the diversity of the attacks thereon, must range more widely.

would be much harder to pinpoint. Harder to pinpoint as well would be the paths which those re-explications should take.

## B. The Second Part

My second main group of chapters will collect and considerably amplify some of the central themes and concepts of Chapters 2–6. That concluding half of the book will also confront a number of further potential objections to legal positivism, and will expand on some of the theoretical orientations that have been touched upon in the present chapter. Although to a large degree the mode of discussion will shift from close and prolonged scrutiny of individual writers to more general reflections and analyses, the shift will not be thoroughgoing. Indeed, one of the concluding chapters—Chapter 8, which deals with the commitment or allegiance shown by legal officials to the norms of their regime—will be devoted principally to doing battle with several theorists who have contended that legal officials' posture of committedness is inherently a moral posture. Specifically targeted ripostes do not come to an end after Chapter 6. Thus, whereas the first half of this book includes quite a few general reflections and analyses as parts of its fine-grained critiques, the second half includes quite a few critiques as parts of its general reflections and analyses.

Chapter 7 begins with a recountal of a number of claims that are *not* entailed by the legal-positivist thesis affirming the separability of law and morality. On the one hand, because there are manifold routes that can be taken by efforts to demonstrate the inextricability of law and morality, a comprehensive denial of that inextricability must take manifold forms; yet, on the other hand, there are certain propositions about law/morality connections that would not be disputed by any minimally intelligent legal positivist. In the interest of clarity and accuracy, then, Chapter 7 begins by noting some of those propositions. The chapter then plumbs a law/morality nexus that has struck many analysts as an inevitable characteristic of any legal system—the link between the content of any society's legal norms and the content of the society's conventional morality. My discussion argues against the inevitability of such a link, in order to underscore the limitedness and harmlessness of the putative concessions that have been readily granted in the first half of the chapter.

Chapter 8 distills and explicates several of the key concepts that have emerged in the earlier portions of the book: concepts such as authority, obligation, normativity, and formal justice. Above all, the chapter investigates the concepts of commitment and allegiance, which characterize the posture of legal officials toward the system which they operate. As has already been noted herein, the officials' posture is often seized upon by critics of jurisprudential positivism, who maintain that the attitudes of commitment and allegiance are fundamentally moral (in the sense of being nonprudential). Although this issue arises during several of the chapters in the first half of the book, it warrants further attention on its own. Among the writers who will be confronted on this issue in Chapter 8 are Stephen Perry, Deryck Beyleveld, and John Finnis. As will be seen, each of them has gone astray by underestimating the potency of self-interest as a motivating and justifying force. Like the other major concepts that are analyzed in my eighth chapter, the concept of official commitment or allegiance is best understood in ways that reflect the separability of law and morality.

Chapter 9 addresses a set of questions that have not theretofore undergone sustained perusal within this book. It focuses on the overall place and functioning of law as a crucial institution in any society. The chapter starts by considering and rejecting Michael Moore's attempts to found a theory of natural law on the notion that law fulfills an intrinsically worthy function. Most of the chapter then ponders the implications of the fact that law plays an indispensable role in securing the basic degree of orderliness which is prerequisite to the long-term existence and indeed the medium-term existence of any society. Given some manifest features of human beings and the world in which they live—as H. L. A. Hart observed—any viable society must include legal prohibitions (prohibitions against murder, unprovoked assaults, serious vandalism, and the like) that coincide or overlap with key moral precepts. To determine what to make of this fact concerning law's general functions in society, Chapter 9 first seeks to gain a clear and precise understanding of those functions; the chapter then mulls over the extent to which those functions render obedience-to-the-law morally obligatory. As the chapter argues, the orderliness-securing role of law does not in itself engender any blanket moral obligation of obedience, not even a weak prima-facie obligation.

On the question of the morally obligatory status of legal requirements, this book will have come to a close. Having repeatedly taken steps to demonstrate that there are no jurisprudential grounds for accepting the view that law and morality are necessarily connected, this book finishes by demonstrating that there are no grounds in political philosophy for accepting such a view, either. This latter demonstration will in effect have brought us full circle, since it complements the conclusions reached in Chapter 2. In the second chapter, which looks at the problem of law-administration from the perspective of legal officials and which puts aside the matter of law's general security-engendering role in order to concentrate on questions of justice, the verdict is that a strict adherence by officials to the terms of legal norms will not invariably be either prima facie morally obligatory or prima facie morally permissible. In the ninth chapter, which looks at the problem of law-administration chiefly from the perspective of ordinary citizens and which concentrates on law's basic security-engendering functions, the verdict is that those functions do not give rise to either a blanket prima-facie moral duty of obedience for citizens or a blanket prima-facie moral duty of enforcement for officials. Viewed from all relevant angles, then, law *qua* law does not carry any inherent moral consequences. Legal positivism is impeccable within the domain of political philosophy as well as within jurisprudence.

In short, neither because of law's essential nature nor because of its general functions in society is there any dissolution of the divide between legality and morality. While contingent ties across that divide are possible and plainly abundant, they are indeed contingent rather than preordained by the status of law as law. Notwithstanding the multiplicity of the ways in which the thesis of the separability of law and morality can be assailed and has been assailed, it remains firmly intact.

PART I

*Positivism Defended*

# 2

## *Justice as Constancy*

Anyone seeking to gain a clear understanding of the relationships between law, justice, and morality must attend to numerous distinctions within each of those phenomena. Not least important is the distinction between the substantive aspects and the procedural or formal aspects of law and justice. Claims about the moral import of law will prove to be untenable if they give insufficient heed to the form/substance gap. My current discussion, which is largely a critique of a brilliant essay by David Lyons, will aim to highlight the unwisdom of approaches to the law-morality relation that generalize too sweepingly over the divide between substance and procedure.

In the aforementioned essay, which has recently been republished after first appearing more than two decades ago, Lyons attacks the view that public officials' deviations from the effectuation of applicable legal norms are perforce unjust.[1] Lyons maintains that the justice or injustice of any departures from the persistent implementation of legal requirements by the officials in charge of law-administration is a matter that varies with circumstances. From the mere fact that a judge or some other official has declined to enforce an applicable legal norm, we cannot infer that an injustice of any sort has been done; in order to arrive at such an inference validly, we have to add some premises about the specific context and implications of the nonenforcement.

In a roughly similar vein, Lyons has subsequently argued that a formal principle of justice (demanding that like cases be treated alike) is insufficient to support a judicial practice of strictly following precedents; and he has likewise argued that the mere fact that some particular decisions are required by law does not in itself create even a prima-facie substantive moral justification for the rendering of the decisions by a judge.[2] Those later arguments by Lyons will not be challenged

---

[1]   David Lyons, 'On Formal Justice', 58 *Cornell Law Review* 833 (1973) ['Formal Justice'], republished in David Lyons, *Moral Aspects of Legal Theory* (Cambridge: Cambridge University Press, 1993) [*Moral Aspects*], 13. For two recent restatements of the view which Lyons assails, see Neil MacCormick, 'Natural Law and the Separation of Law and Morals', in Robert George (ed.), *Natural Law Theory* (Oxford: Clarendon Press, 1992), 105, 122–4; and Kent Greenawalt, 'Too Thin and Too Rich: Distinguishing Features of Legal Positivism', in Robert George (ed.), *The Autonomy of Law* (Oxford: Clarendon Press, 1996), 1, 28 n. 28. Neither MacCormick nor Greenawalt takes account of Lyons's criticisms at all.

I should note that, throughout this chapter, I use the words 'formal' and 'procedural' interchangeably.

[2]   See David Lyons, 'Formal Justice and Judicial Precedent', 38 *Vanderbilt Law Review* 495 (1985), reprinted in *Moral Aspects*, above, n. 1, at 102; and David Lyons, 'Derivability, Defensibility, and the Justification of Judicial Decisions', 68 *Monist* 325 (1985), reprinted in *Moral Aspects*, above, n. 1, at 119.

at all—and will indeed be implicitly endorsed—by my present analysis. Instead, this analysis will critically investigate the contention that an official's failure to enforce an applicable legal norm does not necessarily amount to an injustice of *any* sort. Such a contention unduly blurs the divide between procedural and substantive justice. Although Lyons is hardly unaware of the procedure/substance distinction, he too frequently neglects to differentiate between procedural justifications and prima-facie substantive justifications. While an applicable legal norm requiring a certain decision does not in itself necessarily yield even a prima-facie substantive warrant for the decision, it does indeed yield a procedural warrant. Such a warrant is independent of the substantive merits of the norms and outcomes to which it pertains.

Lyons takes a number of theorists as his targets in his broadsides against the ideal of formal justice, but his most sustained encounter is with H. L. A. Hart. In some well-known passages from *The Concept of Law* (and also from a slightly earlier article), Hart maintained that a procedural form of justice consists in the application of any general rule to all of its instances.[3] Because Hart's thesis draws the fire of Lyons's most important arguments, and because the weakness of Lyons's case becomes most apparent in his onslaughts against that thesis, the last main part of my analysis will concentrate on the position espoused in *The Concept of Law*. Although Hart himself later came to have some doubts about his notion of formal justice,[4] and although the lines of reasoning which he advanced in support of his view do need some modification, his basic claim will here receive a defense. As will be contended, Lyons has failed to disclose any serious difficulties in the procedural-justice position.

Given that one chief strand of this chapter builds on a confrontation between David Lyons and H. L. A. Hart—each of whom is readily classifiable as a legal positivist—it is quite plain that the points at issue do not mark a neat division between legal positivism and natural-law theory. Instead, the controversy over procedural justice is mainly (though not exclusively) an intra-positivist dispute. Whereas a positivist such as Lyons is uncomfortable with the suggestion that a strict adherence to the law is intrinsically just, other positivists have accepted that a strict application of the law by officials does amount to a form of justice even though it does not necessarily further the attainment of justice in any substantive sense. Indeed, as will be contended here, the positivists who embrace the procedural-justice position should see it as a contribution to their project of dissolving the ostensibly inherent connections between law and morality. Precisely because

---

[3] H. L. A. Hart, *The Concept of Law* (Oxford: Clarendon Press, 1961) [*Concept*], 155–7; H. L. A. Hart, 'Positivism and the Separation of Law and Morals', 71 *Harvard Law Review* 593, 623–4 (1958), reprinted in *Essays in Jurisprudence and Philosophy* (Oxford: Clarendon Press, 1983), 49, 81.

[4] See H. L. A. Hart, 'Introduction', in *Essays in Jurisprudence and Philosophy*, above, n. 3, at 1, 18, where Hart avouched that he was uncertain about the sustainability of his claim concerning formal justice and was 'clear that my claim requires considerable modification'.

the achievement of procedural justice in the administration of law by officials is not perforce conducive (and is frequently inimical) to the substantive justice of their law-administering activities, the equation between procedural justice and the strict effectuation of applicable mandates can be acknowledged by a diehard positivist. Anyone who takes account of that equation can then insist on the following two points: (1) the mere status of norms as laws does not impose any moral obligations, even prima-facie moral obligations, upon the people whose lives are regulated by the norms; and (2) the mere status of norms as laws does not confer any moral legitimacy, even prima-facie moral legitimacy, on officials' enforcement of the norms.

I. THE JUSTICE OF PROCEDURAL JUSTICE

## A. Abstracting from Substance and Morality

Before we investigate Lyons's ripostes to Hart's arguments, we should explore how Lyons has more generally tended to characterize the ideal of procedural justice. In his descriptions of the position which he seeks to oppugn, he too frequently blurs the difference between procedural justice and justice *tout court*. For example, near the beginning of his essay, he submits that the formal-justice doctrine 'identifies conformity to law not with justice overall but with justice in the administration of the law, and thus with justice in the conduct of public officials' ('Formal Justice', 836). Now, although this comment does distinguish between administrative justice and justice overall, its final clause tends to obscure that distinction. Because public officials' conduct has both a procedural dimension and a substantive dimension, we cannot safely draw an inference about the justice of their conduct from the fact that the law has been administered justly. While we can indeed know that officials who justly administer the law have enforced legal norms in all and only those circumstances to which the norms are applicable, we cannot know whether the norms themselves are substantively acceptable. When the laws have been administered strictly, the conduct of officials is procedurally impeccable; yet if the impeccable procedures have given effect to laws that are substantively unjust, then the conduct of the officials is unjust.

We can develop this point further in connection with another observation by Lyons on the doctrine of formal justice. He writes: 'At minimum, a formalist maintains that acting within the law is a necessary condition of justice in its administration, and thus that any official deviation is an injustice. Formal justice thus implies that there is always a real moral objection to official deviation from the law' ('Formal Justice', 840). For the sake of argument, let us assume that the categories of justice and injustice are jointly exhaustive as well as mutually exclusive, and that there will not be any states of affairs in human society which fall into neither category. (In other words, the classification of 'unjust' will attach to any situation that is not just, and the classification of 'just' will apply to any situation that is not unjust.) Let us also assume that, when Lyons designates 'any official deviation' as 'an injustice', he is referring to procedural injustice only. In that case, the first sentence in this quotation is unexceptionable. Much more dubious, however, is the second sentence. As should be apparent from my last paragraph, the occurrence of procedural injustice is not necessarily objectionable—even prima facie—unless it relates to certain substantively acceptable norms.

Indeed, even in regard to some legal norms that are substantively acceptable, a practice of strict enforcement does not always partake of prima-facie moral obligatoriness and prima-facie moral legitimacy. As will be recounted in Chapter 9, there are contexts wherein compliance with some salutary legal mandates (such as anti-jaywalking laws) would not yield any beneficial effects whatsoever and would very likely produce harmful effects. In those situations, legal officials are under no obligations to enforce the applicable mandates and are probably under obligations to abstain from such enforcement—partly because of the likelihood that the enforcement would run athwart people's legitimate expectations, and partly because of the likelihood that it would bring discredit upon the law. Nevertheless, there are various other salutary legal mandates (such as laws proscribing murder and unprovoked assault) with which everybody's compliance is always morally obligatory prima facie. In connection with such mandates, a practice of strict enforcement is morally obligatory and morally legitimate prima facie. Of course, the prima-facie moral import of procedural justice in relation to such mandates can sometimes be outweighed by special demands of equity; an overall ethical calculation may lead a decision-maker to conclude that some morally obligatory legal directive ought not to be enforced in a particular situation. However, the ethical reasoning that eventuates in such a conclusion does not deny the prima-facie obligatoriness and prima-facie legitimacy of a posture of strict enforcement. On the contrary, the very need for such reasoning is occasioned by a clash between the demands of leniency and the moral considerations which call for enforcement. In the event of such a clash, the ideal of procedural justice carries moral weight that can be overtopped but not rightly disregarded.

Things are very different when the applicable legal norms are substantively unacceptable. Neither procedural justice nor procedural injustice then has any consistent moral weight. Departures from evil laws can be salutary (if the evil is thereby lessened) or pernicious (if the evil is thereby intensified); the moral status of each instance of procedural injustice will hinge on the specific character of the instance rather than on the general nature of procedural injustice. When the applicable legal norms are wicked, no prima-facie moral obligatoriness attaches to procedural justice—at least if our concern is sheer substantive fairness rather than the possible role of a practice of unswerving enforcement in shoring up a legal system against the specter of social chaos.[5] Instead of having to overcome moral reasons in favor of the implementation of a wicked law, an official's benevolent deviation therefrom is his or her only course of action that carries an affirmative moral weight.

At this point, Lyons may appear to have prevailed in his attack against the doctrine of formal justice. After all, his main aim is to confute the notion that 'there is always a moral objection to official deviation from the law' ('Formal Justice', 861). Since my own analysis has insisted that official departures from evil laws are not always morally objectionable in any way, my defense of the formal-justice position may seem fully in harmony with Lyons's critique of that position. None the less, in light of two closely related considerations, the stance adopted here is notably different from that of Lyons and is indeed an espousal of the doctrine which he assails.

First, although the decisions resulting from the procedurally just enforcement of wicked laws are neither obligatory nor legitimate to any degree, the enforcement ensures that official conduct in the administration of laws is no worse and no better than what is required by the substantive standards of fairness in the laws themselves. No person will then have experienced more unkind treatment or less unkind treatment than what is due to him under those laws. Given the substantive touchstones and prescriptions which the laws ordain, procedural justice ensures a minimum of substantive justice—a minimum that is also a maximum, of course. Because of this minimum-securing role, procedural justice differs from *unrestrained* evil. Even at its worst, it sets firm limits; it can therefore appositely be denominated as 'justice'.

To be sure, unlike the bounds imposed by God's command to the sea ('Thus far shall you come, and no farther, and here shall your proud waves be stayed' [Job 38:11]), the limits set by procedural justice are not immutable. They vary with the substantive standards that are laid down by the applicable legal norms. Nevertheless, whatever the standards in a particular context are, they form a barrier which a procedurally just government does not transgress in its harmful treatment of people. Distressingly meager though the decency secured by that barrier might be, the strict enforcement of the norms which define it will have meant that the regime of enforcement does not stoop to even greater depths.[6]

---

[5] The role of law as an indispensable source of basic social orderliness will be pondered sustainedly in Chs. 7 and 9, albeit with reference more to citizens' obligations than to officials' obligations. As can be inferred from my discussions there, the aforementioned role of law does warrant the attachment of some qualifications to the analyses in my present chapter; but the requisite qualifications are of limited practical significance. At any rate, the cabined focus of my current chapter is appropriate for the task of parrying Lyons's arguments.

[6] Worth noting here is that a law can be wicked not only if it authorizes heavy-handed *repression* but also if it extends grossly insufficient *protection* to the members of certain groups. Consider, for example, the former statute in Texas that deemed any man's slaying of his wife's paramour to be justifiable homicide; for an interesting discussion, see Joel Feinberg, *Doing and Deserving* (Princeton: Princeton University Press, 1970), 102–3.

Also worth noting here is a point that will receive considerable attention in my next chapter (and

Second, since a policy of procedural justice guarantees that no one will be treated worse *or better* than is demanded by the applicable legal norms, it can generate decisions that have no affirmative moral weight. When the applicable norms are substantively appalling, anyone called upon to enforce them will have a moral duty to engage in benevolent departures from the norms' dictates. Far from being obligatory and legitimate prima facie, a practice of strict enforcement of the wicked norms is an out-and-out violation of an official's moral duty; there are no moral reasons (in favor of the rigorous implementation of wicked mandates) which a benign deviation by an official must overcome in order to be morally justified. Although an official of course has a moral duty not to enforce a wicked mandate in situations where it is inapplicable, he does not have a moral duty—even a prima-facie moral duty—to enforce the mandate in situations where it indeed is applicable. He has a moral obligation not to go below the minimum of decency secured by procedural justice, but he also has a moral obligation not to treat that minimum as a maximum.

While the limit-imposing function of a policy of procedural justice is what warrants our classifying such a policy as justice, it causes the moral bearings of that policy to fluctuate with the substance of the norms which serve as the operative limits. In regard to some basic legal prohibitions (against murder, unprovoked assault, serious vandalism, and the like), a practice of strict enforcement does partake of prima-facie legitimacy and prima-facie obligatoriness. There are always moral reasons in favor of giving effect to the terms of such prohibitions, even if those reasons are occasionally outweighed by competing factors. In regard to other legal norms that are morally commendable or morally neutral,[7] there are not invariably any moral reasons in favor of giving effect to their terms. Yet, although such reasons do not always exist, they do frequently or typically exist. Since the laws in question are salutary or neutral, the enforcement of them tends to satisfy or engender legitimate expectations. Conversely, the nonenforcement of those laws will tend to disrupt or preclude legitimate expectations. Although such expectations will not always be present, and although interference with them may

a little bit of attention later in this chapter). Evil officials who behave in a procedurally just manner will have solid prudential reasons for doing so; when they decline to stoop to even greater depths than the laws ordain, they are not necessarily exhibiting any moral compunctions whatsoever. Instead of being motivated by moral concerns, they might be motivated solely by a desire to promote the effectiveness of their wicked regime. After all, minimum-transgressing departures from the terms of heinous laws are often inefficient as well as iniquitous.

[7] Many of the technical requirements within sundry areas of law—such as electoral or commercial law—may in themselves have no obvious moral bearing, either positive or negative. Such norms I designate as 'neutral'. (For a discussion that casts light on this point, see John Finnis, *Natural Law and Natural Rights* [Oxford: Clarendon Press, 1980], 284–6, 295.) I also classify as 'neutral' the myriad legal norms which are flawed in certain respects but which plainly fall short of being evil. Exactly where the realm of neutrality ends and the realm of wickedness begins is a substantive moral question that will not be addressed here. (It also undoubtedly is a variant of the ancient sorites problem, which is ably discussed in R. M. Sainsbury, *Paradoxes* [Cambridge: Cambridge University Press, 1988], ch. 2.)

be justified in special circumstances, officials bear a prima-facie moral obligation to adopt a policy of enforcement that avoids or minimizes the interference. In sum, in respect of some laws that are morally commendable, officials have a prima-facie moral liberty and a prima-facie moral obligation to enforce those laws strictly; in respect of various other morally commendable legal norms, officials have a prima-facie moral liberty and a prima-facie moral obligation to enforce those norms frequently or typically (rather than strictly).

A policy of procedural justice does not have a similar moral purchase when the applicable legal norms are evil. Though officials are morally obligated to abstain from treating anyone more *shabbily* than the norms prescribe, they are not morally free or obligated (even prima facie) to abstain from treating anyone more *decently*. As has already been discussed, strict procedural justice secures a minimum of decency even in connection with wicked laws; but it likewise unconscionably imposes a maximum of decency. Now, since procedural justice without its maximum-imposing role is not procedural justice at all, we must conclude that such justice does not carry a content-independent moral weight. Lyons's chief misstep thus occurs near the beginning of his essay, where we are told that 'an unjust act is wrong, morally wrong, unless it can be justified by overriding considerations. Other things being equal, injustice should not be done. But the idea that justice consists in conformity to law then implies . . . that deviation from the law is always wrong, unless it can be justified on other grounds' ('Formal Justice', 834). These comments by Lyons, which expound a presupposition that informs his whole discussion,[8] would be true if and only if they referred exclusively to substantive justice. Hence, given that the focus of his analysis is on *procedural* justice, we have to conclude that his central message in these comments is unsustainable.

Substantive justice is always morally desirable, and substantive injustice is always undesirable; with regard to substantive matters, the link between justice and morality is univocal. No such univocal link exists, however, with regard to procedural matters. Instead, as has been discussed here, the relationship between procedural justice and morality is complicated and content-dependent. Procedural justice lacks any prima-facie moral correctness when it serves to give effect to the wickedness of wicked laws. Thus, we now can see that Lyons has sought to saddle his opponents with a thesis—about the invariably affirmative moral weight attaching to procedural justice—which they can and should reject. Having spurned such a thesis, they can then continue to insist that strict conformity to the

---

[8] This presupposition also underlies the following passage from Kent Greenawalt, above, n. 1, at 12–13: 'Many positivists accept the principle that . . . "rule of law" standards have moral significance. H. L. A. Hart, for example, acknowledges in *The Concept of Law* that "a minimum of justice is necessar[il]y realized whenever human behavior is controlled by general rules publicly announced and judicially applied" and that "principles of legality" of the kind Fuller discusses are "requirements of justice". Thus, the thesis that "principles of legality" have moral content does not separate many positivists from natural lawyers.' (Footnote deleted.)

law by officials is a mode of justice. They need not worry that this insistence implies that strict conformity to the law by officials is always prima facie commendable.

What should be stressed again at this juncture is that procedural justice does indeed amount to a species of justice even though it can lack any affirmative moral weight. As has been remarked, procedural justice sets strict limits on official actions—albeit of course the substance of those limits is defined by the substance of any applicable legal norms. When the substance of the norms has been fixed, procedural justice upholds a minimum of decency and imposes a maximum of decency that must characterize the official administration of the law. Precisely these two limit-setting operations of such justice are what make it a type of justice. They erect the strict bounds that distinguish a procedurally just but substantively wicked regime from a regime that is equally wicked and procedurally untrammeled. (As will become apparent in my next chapter, this difference between the two types of regimes does not partake of any unequivocal or automatic moral significance. We should fleetingly note two points that will be greatly amplified in Chapter 3. First, insofar as a regime with procedural irregularities is morally worse than a regime without them, its inferiority lies in the substance of the irregularities rather than in their mere nature as procedural deviations. Second, the officials in the procedurally just regime may well have opted for procedural justice on starkly prudential grounds; their strict effectuation of their wicked laws can enhance the co-ordination of their overall endeavors and can ensure that citizens have maximal incentives to comply with those laws.)

Now, because the minimum-sustaining role and especially the maximum-imposing role of procedural justice are only sometimes morally benign (even prima facie), and because each of those roles is indispensably constitutive of formal justice, we have to infer that such justice is only sometimes morally benign (even prima facie). In other words, one's refusal to ascribe any intrinsic goodness to formal justice is based on one's taking notice of the very features that earmark it as a mode of justice. Because a formal constraint can be substantively undesirable, and because one's moral assessments of such a constraint must hinge on its substantive standing, one's recognition of it as a firm constraint is perfectly consistent with one's denial that it carries any prima-facie moral validity in relation to evil laws.

## B. Injustice to Whom?

In the course of arguing against the view that official departures from the terms of laws are always unjust, Lyons posits a scenario in which a law requires the extermination of all members of some racial or religious group ('Formal Justice', 846–8). A morally upright judge remains on the bench in the hope of doing some good in the bleak situation. One day, he seizes an opportunity to save a member of the persecuted group by departing from the provisions of the exterminatory law. Lyons acknowledges that the proponents of the formal-justice doctrine can accept that the judge has behaved correctly, all things considered. Nevertheless, Lyons maintains that those proponents will inevitably see the judge's law-disregarding conduct as wrong prima facie. Although they will surely feel that the wrongness of the deviation from the legal requirements is outweighed by its virtuousness, they will detect a certain degree of wrongness all the same.

Enough has been said already to indicate that classifying the judge's law-disregarding conduct as procedurally unjust does not amount to classifying it as prima facie wrong. We ought here to notice, however, a new line of analysis in Lyons's discussion:

Who . . . is to be regarded as the victim of the judge's injustice? Surely the person who is saved is not the victim. Nor does it seem plausible to maintain that those he had already sent to the extermination camps are victims of an injustice done by the act in question, because a new murder has been averted. However, someone may grasp upon the obvious difference in treatment accorded those who pass before the judge. For example, one may assume that those already sent to the camps deserved no worse treatment than the one who fared better. But even if this argument seems to be a ground for saying that injustice is done by the judge's failure to follow the law in the instant case, the argument does not show that his mere failure to follow the law constitutes an injustice, which is what the formalist contends. The charge of injustice here rests on the differences in treatment dispensed by the judge. It should be emphasized that failure to follow the law does not *necessarily* result in such differences of treatment; it does not even mean that anyone will be affected. ('Formal Justice,' 847, emphasis in original)

If we keep in mind that the relevant mode of injustice here is purely procedural— and if we keep in mind that procedural injustice can be morally legitimate and obligatory—then we shall discern two groups of people toward whom the judge's deviation from the law has been unjust.

First, as Lyons himself suggests, the previous victims of the exterminatory law have been treated worse than someone else whose fate should have been the same as theirs under the applicable law. To be sure, the *substantive* injustice committed against them lies in the extermination to which they have been subjected; but the *procedural* injustice lies in the preferential treatment of someone else whose status under the applicable law is on a par with their own. Of course, in light of the alterability of Lyons's scenario (as Lyons himself mentions), this pattern of differential treatment might not obtain. If the judge departs from the mandate of the exterminatory law on the first and only occasion on which he is supposed to apply it, then he will not have dealt more harshly under that law with anybody than with anybody else.

Still, we have to take account of a second group of people who undergo a procedural injustice when the judge unlawfully spares someone from extermination. The rescued person has been treated no worse under the genocidal law than have the people who do not belong to the persecuted group; conversely, those people have been treated no better under the genocidal law than has the rescued

person. Yet, according to the terms of the applicable legal norm, the people
outside the disfavored group should have enjoyed better treatment than the person
who has been unlawfully saved. They should not have suffered extermination (as
indeed they have not), whereas he or she should have been subjected to such a
fate. Thus, given the standards of substantive justice laid down in the applicable
law, the equally favorable treatment dispensed under that law is a procedural
injustice committed against the members of the dominant groups.

Obviously, this instance of procedural injustice does not detract at all from the
moral worthiness of the judge's action. Not only is such an injustice unequivocally legitimate, but it is also unequivocally obligatory—quite as plainly as are
similar instances of procedural injustice in connection with wicked laws. Having
shed Lyons's assumption that any formal injustice must be prima facie illegitimate, we can readily perceive that the judge has committed such an injustice
against the people in the dominant groups. And we can perceive this point while
adamantly insisting that those people have not suffered any sort of moral wrong
(not even a wrong outweighed by countervailing considerations). On the one
hand, the legally superior status of those people vis-à-vis the rescued person has
not been given effect in accordance with the exterminatory rule; and because their
legally ordained superiority to him has not received recognition, the sparing of
him amounts to a procedural injustice against them. On the other hand, the legally
superior people do not have the slightest moral entitlement to the effectuation of
their superiority (through the extermination of every member of the downtrodden
group). By committing a procedural injustice against them, the judge has carried
out his moral duty in an unequivocally legitimate manner.

In short, once we sever the putatively ineluctable connection which Lyons
draws between formal justice and morality, we have no difficulty in answering his
question about the identities of the victims of the judge's injustice. All of the
people previously sentenced by the judge to the death camps and all of the people
in the ascendant groups—groups which of course are legally protected from any
slaughter—are the victims of procedural injustice when the judge departs from
the mandate of the exterminatory law. To say as much is decidedly not to say that
all of those people or indeed any of those people will have been morally wronged
in any way by dint of the judge's deviation. Procedural justice is concerned only
with giving everyone his or her due (as defined by the substance of the applicable laws), both in his or her own right and in relation to everybody else; it is not
concerned with the moral acceptability of what is legally due to everyone.
Procedural justice abstracts from substantive moral questions by taking for
granted the prevailing substantive decisions. Hence, to classify someone as a
victim of procedural *in*justice is not necessarily to say that the person can legitimately complain about the way in which he or anyone else has been treated.

What my current line of analysis has shown, however, is that the judge's departure from the terms of the genocidal law does inevitably operate as a formal injustice against certain people. Even if that law is never enforced, and therefore even

if no one can claim to have been treated worse under that law than the rescued person *P*, the sparing of *P* is a slight to the formal status of another group of people. After all, *P* himself is treated no worse under the genocidal law than the members of the dominant groups—whose legally superior position, which consists in their own protectedness and in the unprotectedness of the members of the disfavored group, is thus not given effect. Contrary to what Lyons suggests, then, the judge's disregard of the law must indeed unavoidably infringe the formal standing of some people. There are always victims of the procedural injustice, however laudable the injustice may be, and however unworthy of sympathy are the victims.[9]

This line of analysis has helped to make clear another reason for declaring the strict application of legal norms to be a mode of justice. Let us briefly recall Aristotle's classic account of justice, which includes a section that explicates distributive justice as the apportionment of suitable shares of goods and burdens to people (*Nicomachean Ethics*, V. 3). Aristotle held that distributive justice establishes authorized proportions between human beings with regard to their shares of things, and he remarked that the grounds for determining the correct proportions—grounds such as birth or wealth or excellence—vary from one society to the next. A strict implementation of the laws assigning benefits and detriments to

---

[9] Although this section's analysis suffices to deal with Lyons's example of the genocidal law, the analysis would need to be refined if the example were suitably modified. Suppose that, instead of pondering a genocidal law which calls for horrific measures against some people and not against others, we were to ponder a statute that pointlessly requires of *everyone* some painful and degrading process of self-mutilation. Suppose further that no one ever complies with the statute (by engaging in the required self-mutilation); and suppose that the law-enforcement officials invariably ignore the noncompliance, despite the statute's specification of penalties. If the officials' failure to give effect to the statute is a procedural injustice, then who is the victim of the injustice?

The appropriate answer is that the officials' connivance at any breach of the statute by each person *X* is a procedural injustice against everyone other than *X*, notwithstanding that every breach by anyone else will likewise be overlooked. That is, *X* is the beneficiary of a procedural injustice committed against every other person, even though *X* is also a victim of procedural injustices committed in favor of the other persons. If we seek to determine whether a procedural injustice has occurred, we should not compare the actual treatment of *X* with the actual treatment of everyone else; instead, we should compare the actual treatment of *X* with the legally required treatment of *X* and the legally required treatment of everyone else. When we focus on *X*, we see that he has been treated better than is specified under the statute. We further see that the legally required treatment of *X* is the same as the legally required treatment of everyone else. Hence, the officials' connivance at *X*'s breach of the self-mutilation statute confers on *X* a degree of indulgence that is denied to everyone alike under the statute. In other words, the condonation of *X*'s transgression consists in treating *X* better than he or anyone else deserves under the terms of the statute. Such official condonation thus amounts to unequal treatment that bestows a special privilege on *X*—even though a similar condonation of every other person's transgression amounts to unequal treatment that is tilted against *X*.

In short, when we ask whether the pretermission of *X*'s noncompliance with the statute is a procedural injustice against other people, we are asking whether the pretermission endows *X* with a more favorable position than he deserves (under the terms of the statute) vis-à-vis his fellows. That question is separate from the question whether the pretermission of every other person's noncompliance involves a procedural injustice against *X* because it endows every other person with a more favorable position than he or she deserves (under the terms of the statute) vis-à-vis *X*. An affirmative answer to the latter query is fully compatible with an affirmative answer to the former query.

persons is thus essential for the realization of distributive justice as defined by a particular society. Of course, whether the standards for assignments in any specific society are genuinely just or even tolerably humane is a matter for substantive moral judgment; but, given that the laws which prescribe those standards are the society's scheme of distributive justice (in Aristotle's sense), and given that the unswerving administration of those laws is therefore necessary for the full-blown effectuation of that scheme, we should classify the unswerving administration as the procedural mode or element of distributive justice. (One can make a largely similar point in connection with the laws which lay down the standards for the triggering of corrective justice. Unless those laws are strictly enforced, a society's scheme of corrective justice will not be given full effect. We should accordingly classify the strict enforcement of such laws as the procedural mode or element of corrective justice.)

## II. LYONS *CONTRA* HART

As has been mentioned, the prime target of Lyons's attack against the notion of formal justice is H. L. A. Hart, who submitted that the principle of treating like cases alike and different cases differently is 'a central element in the idea of justice'. Hart was well aware that such a principle is an empty form that does not provide any determinate guidance until we have specified which of the resemblances and differences between people are significant. '[W]e must know when, for the purposes in hand, cases are to be regarded as alike and what differences are relevant' (*Concept*, 155). Though Hart underscored the difficulties of specifying which differences and resemblances should be deemed significant for the establishment of substantive justice, he was more confident in his approach to the ideal of procedural or administrative justice:

> In certain cases, indeed, the resemblances and differences between human beings which are relevant for the criticism of legal arrangements as just or unjust are quite obvious. This is pre-eminently the case when we are concerned not with the justice or injustice of the *law* but of its *application* in particular cases. For here the relevant resemblances and differences between individuals, to which the person who administers the law must attend, are determined by the law itself. To say that the law against murder is justly applied is to say that it is impartially applied to all those and only those who are alike in having done what the law forbids. . . . [T]he law is applied to all those and only to those who are alike in the relevant respect marked out by the law itself.    (Hart, *Concept*, 156, emphasis in original)

Lyons detects and controverts three principal lines of argument with which Hart sought to support his position concerning procedural justice. Lyons first considers the invocation of the treat-like-cases-alike precept, then focuses on an argument about the following of rules, and finally ponders some remarks about adjudicative impartiality ('Formal Justice', 849–58). With regard to the first and third of these lines of reasoning, Lyons is surely correct to be dismissive. Let us briefly explore each of those flawed arguments along with each of Lyons's responses thereto, before we turn to the much more powerful second line of reasoning.

Insofar as Hart tried to derive his doctrine of administrative justice from the treat-like-cases-alike maxim, he was plainly guilty of a non sequitur. Although any law does single out various differences and resemblances between people as significant, and although it thereby provides some substance for the empty form of the treat-like-cases-alike precept, its singling out of those differences and resemblances does not itself acquire any special significance or authority from that precept. On the one hand, there are myriad patterns of uniformity—of which any legal norm's pattern is only one—by which the principle of treating like cases alike can be fleshed out. At the same time, that abstract principle alone does not indicate which of those patterns of uniformity should be deemed relevant or authoritative. As Lyons contends: 'An official can deal with cases uniformly without following the law; that is, his conduct may fit another pattern, which does not perfectly follow the law, but requires some unauthorized actions. . . . [T]he possibility of construing legal rules as prescribing a way of "treating like cases alike" is of no help, for such rules prescribe only one of many possible patterns' ('Formal Justice', 851, emphasis deleted). In sum, by calling merely for uniformity, the treat-like-cases-alike mandate does not require the strict application of the law's particular prescriptions for uniformity. Alternative touchstones for uniformity will square equally well with that mandate.

Hart's references to the desideratum of adjudicative impartiality—only one of which has been quoted here—are likewise insufficient to ground his view of procedural justice as the unswerving enforcement of legal norms. A judge can show admirable impartiality without invariably giving effect to the terms of the laws which he is called upon to enforce. Faced with an outlandishly unbalanced legal norm $N$ that would produce exceedingly harsh results for certain people if it were enforced, a judge may well conclude that his impartial stance requires him to deviate from the law (perhaps to such an extent that he effectively nullifies $N$) in order to avert the lop-sidedness of $N$'s general implications. We find, then, that a striving for impartiality may not only *allow* a departure from the law but may actually *demand* it. Hence, someone who equates procedural justice with the unswerving effectuation of legal norms should not invoke the ideal of adjudicative impartiality in support of that equation. Albeit unswervingness and impartiality very frequently coincide, they can also diverge—which means that theses about the latter do not necessarily reinforce theses about the former.[10]

Much stronger than the first and third strands of argument in Hart's account of

---

[10] My approach to Hart's comments on impartiality has been slightly different from that of Lyons, primarily because Lyons's approach relies to some extent on claims (about procedural justice) which I have already rejected.

procedural justice is the second chief strand therein. Hart suggested that the nature of procedural justice is integrally related to the nature of rules (and of governance through rules): 'The connexion between this aspect of justice and the very notion of proceeding by rule is obviously very close. Indeed, it might be said that to apply a law justly to different cases is simply to take seriously the asser- tion that what is to be applied in different cases is the same general rule' (*Concept*, 156–7). Formal justice consists, then, in a faithful adherence to the task of applying sundry rules. This conception of formal justice clearly leaves open the moral status of each formally just decision. Whether any such decision partakes of prima-facie legitimacy is dependent on the substantive moral bearings of the rules that are unflinchingly applied.

Lyons's fundamental riposte to this second line of reasoning by Hart is as follows:

The argument turns entirely on the notion of applying a rule to particular cases; it contains no further restrictions. If the result were a principle of justice, then any deviation from any rule that one is supposed to apply would be, in itself, an unjust act. Nothing restricts this mode of argument to the conduct of public officials, or even to the law. For that reason, it seems clear that the argument must fail, for either it works for all kinds of rules, regard- less of the circumstances, or it works for none. And it clearly does not work for some. To see this, one need only select a rule the breach of which has no necessary moral signifi- cance, regardless of the circumstances. The charge of injustice carries moral weight, and if the breach of some rule does not automatically carry such weight, then it cannot be an unjust act. Suppose, then, that when I speak ungrammatically I can be said to break a rule of language. The argument would have it that I thereby commit an unjust act. But this is implausible.   ('Formal Justice', 852–3)

For the sake of argument, let us here pretermit Lyons's unduly sweeping assump- tion that '[t]he charge of [procedural] injustice carries moral weight'. Even when that assumption is not assailed any further, we can discern a basic shortcoming in Lyons's riposte—namely, his failure to distinguish between the *application* of rules in one's gauging of other people's conduct and the *following* of rules in one's own conduct.

Lyons is correct in thinking that nothing confines Hart's argument 'to the conduct of public officials, or even to the law', but he errs in believing that the argument cannot be sound if it does not extend to a situation which involves no passing of judgment by one person (or more than one person) on another. Lyons's infraction of a grammatical rule *R* cannot sensibly be characterized as procedu- rally unjust; but what can be characterized sensibly in that way is someone else's unwarranted judgment that Lyons has complied or failed to comply with *R*. While this point is true of a misrepresentation or misuse of *R* by anyone who is assess- ing Lyons's conformity thereto, it is especially pertinent when the assessment is being conducted by someone whose power or authority can attach detrimental consequences to the aspersion cast upon Lyons. Suppose that some expert on matters of English usage publicly derides Lyons's writing because it allegedly commits violations of $R$, and suppose that the writing does not in fact contain any such errors. In these circumstances, there is nothing odd about describing the expert's ridicule as unjust. Through malice or carelessness or a simple mistake, the expert has deviated from the terms of $R$ by condemning breaches of that rule which have not occurred. He or she has thus perpetrated a procedural injustice.

Let us contemplate an even more vivid example. In Chapter 12 of the Book of Judges, the Gileadites fight against the Ephraimites. Having seized the fords of the River Jordan, the Gileadite soldiers employ a now-famous test for identifying the tribal background of anyone who seeks to cross the river. They require each such person to say the word 'shibboleth', because the men of Ephraim are unable to pronounce that word correctly. Whenever a fleeing Ephraimite reveals his tribal origins by mispronouncing 'shibboleth', he is promptly put to death. Now—to embellish the story—suppose that a Gileadite soldier slays someone whose pronunciation has been perfectly correct. In that event, the soldier has committed a formal injustice (as well as a substantive injustice consisting in an excessively harsh penalty); by punishing someone for transgressing a rule which the person has in fact satisfied, the soldier fails to apply the rule strictly, and he thus engages in a procedurally unjust act.

As these examples illustrate, a charge of procedural injustice can be perfectly apposite in connection with an infringement or a putative infringement of a linguistic norm—provided that the charge pertains to the groundlessness of someone's condemnation (or exoneration) of the person who has allegedly infringed (or actually infringed) the norm. When we determine whether a procedural injustice has occurred in relation to such a norm, what matters is not the norm's morally neutral status but the misdirectedness of someone's judgment about someone else's compliance or noncompliance with the norm's requirements. In Lyons's example of his own transgression of a linguistic rule, the ridiculousness of accusations of formal injustice is due solely to the fact that no other people have passed judgment on his faux pas. It is not due at all to the nature of the rule that has been violated.

If we confine our accusations of procedural injustice to contexts in which people render judgments about other people's conformity or nonconformity with rules, and if we level our accusations at the judgments rather than at the conduct that has been judged, then our accusations will not be absurd (though they might be inaccurate). The moral status of any specific rule that is involved—for example, the morally neutral status of a typical rule of language—will have no bearing on the sensibleness of a charge of procedural injustice. Of course, one should not infer that the moral status of the relevant rule is wholly beside the point in an analysis of formal justice. As earlier parts of this chapter have contended, any particular rule's moral import has a crucial bearing on the prima-facie moral significance of a policy of applying the rule strictly. Nevertheless, that moral import does not in itself ever affect the pertinence of a claim about procedural injustice.

III.  CONCLUSION

Lyons, in short, has erred in two principal ways. He has wrongly presumed that formal justice is like substantive justice in always having an affirmative moral weight. Moreover, he has failed to keep in mind that formal justice or injustice is a characteristic of a person's verdict about some other person's violation or nonviolation of a rule, rather than a characteristic of the violation or nonviolation itself (unless, of course, the violation or nonviolation involves the passing of judgment by someone on someone else). Having cleared away these two missteps, we can see that legal positivists have nothing to fear from an acceptance of the formal-justice position propounded by Hart. That position does not commit us to any claims about the moral worthiness of strict law-enforcement *in abstracto*, nor does it commit us to any claims about the substantive moral worthiness of the legal norms around which accusations of procedural injustice may revolve.

Hence, Lyons has gone astray when he submits that Hart's view of procedural justice as a principle immanent in the very application of any rules is a major concession to the natural-law camp. Lyons writes: 'If this argument were sound it would be of special interest for supporting a traditional natural law contention, namely, that there is a significant, necessary connection between law and morals because the principle requiring adherence to legal rules would seem to be implicit in the law by virtue of the fact that every legal system contains some rules' ('Formal Justice', 852 n. 50). Having shown that procedural justice does not necessarily partake of any prima-facie moral legitimacy, and having shown that the appositeness of charges of procedural injustice does not hinge at all on the moral tenor of the norms that have allegedly been applied unjustly, this chapter has made no concessions to natural-law theory. Indeed, by emphasizing anew the potential divide between the realization of formal justice and the realization of substantive moral ideals, this chapter's revival of the doctrine of formal justice has endeavored to strengthen and extend legal positivism.

# 3

## *Scrupulousness without Scruples: a Critique of Lon Fuller and his Defenders*

Throughout the second half of the twentieth century, Lon Fuller's writings have enjoyed a prominent place in Anglo-American jurisprudence. Though Fuller contributed notably to contract law and several other areas of legal thought, he is best known among legal philosophers for his efforts to demonstrate the intrinsically moral nature of law. Devising what he labeled as 'a procedural version of natural law',[1] he maintained that certain fundamental characteristics of any genuine regime of law are morally pregnant. By developing a natural-law stance that focused principally on the formal or procedural aspects of law, Fuller participated centrally in American legal theorists' preoccupation with process-related values during the decades that followed the Second World War.[2]

Fuller's procedural version of natural law has frequently been assailed or queried, but it also has frequently attracted support. It remains a singularly elaborate effort to show the inseparability of law and morality on largely content-independent grounds. Anyone favorably disposed to legal positivism, then, is well advised to undertake a critical investigation of Fuller's account of law. Given the appealingness of Fuller's theory—an appealingness acknowledged by many of his critics[3]—a demonstration of the failure of that theory will tend to cast doubt on the very idea of a content-independent bond between law and morality.

The present chapter ponders not only the ideas advanced by Fuller himself, but also some of the defenses of him that have been mounted in recent years. Although his supporters have come up with lines of argument that go beyond his own exposition of his theory, I shall maintain that they are equally unsuccessful in establishing a necessary connection between law and morality. Their sophisticated attempts to shore up his general position have largely served to enable a

---

[1] Lon Fuller, *The Morality of Law* (New Haven: Yale University Press, 1969) (rev. edn.) [*Morality*], 96. The other main work by Fuller which I discuss in this chapter is 'Positivism and Fidelity to Law—A Reply to Professor Hart', 71 *Harvard Law Review* 593 (1958) ['Positivism'].

[2] For a good discussion of Fuller's seminal role in process-oriented jurisprudence in the United States, see Neil Duxbury, *Patterns of American Jurisprudence* (New York: Oxford University Press, 1995), 223–33.

[3] Indeed, many critics take pains to present Fuller's position in a favorable light, before attacking it. For a noteworthy example, see David Lyons, 'The Internal Morality of Law', 74 *Proceedings of the Aristotelian Society* 105 (1971). Even more interesting is that some theorists who ridicule Fuller have proved quite receptive to positions that are closely akin to his. For instance, compare Klaus Füßer, 'Farewell to "Legal Positivism": The Separation Thesis Unravelling', in Robert George (ed.), *The Autonomy of Law* (Oxford: Clarendon Press, 1996), 119–20, with ibid. 124, 131–2.

more precise specification of the position's unsoundness. As we shall see, Fuller's main problem was not his maladroitness in philosophical argumentation,[4] but his espousal of an untenable doctrine. Even when his arguments are reinforced by more powerful lines of reasoning, they prove inadequate for their purpose.

I. A CONSPECTUS

Fuller's accounts of the eight basic conditions for the existence of law are too familiar to stand in need of any lengthy rehearsal. A thumbnail sketch will suffice here for my critique. Fuller held that law does not exist unless each of the following requirements is satisfied to some degree:

(1) there must be general rules;
(2) the rules must be promulgated to the people who are required to obey them;
(3) the rules must not be retroactive;
(4) the rules must be understandable;
(5) the duties imposed by the rules must not conflict;
(6) compliance with the rules must be possible;
(7) the rules must not be changed with disorienting frequency; and
(8) there must be a congruence between the rules as formulated and the implementation of them.

When Fuller first recounted these precepts in a discussion about the possible derailment of a law-making enterprise, he presented them as threshold conditions (Fuller, *Morality*, 39). If a system of social control does not fulfill each condition to some extent, then it is not a *legal* system at all. A complete failure in regard to any of the eight precepts will entail the nonexistence of law within the society that is marked by the failure.

When Fuller slightly later unfolded his eight principles afresh, he portrayed them as ideals of excellence (*Morality*, 41–4). Once the principles have been respected sufficiently to constitute the existence of a legal system, they become aspirations more than requirements. Although no actual system can or should

---

[4] Even the staunchest defenders—apart from Peter Teachout in his worshipful 'The Soul of the Fugue: An Essay on Reading Fuller', 70 *Minnesota Law Review* 1073 (1986)—acknowledge Fuller's philosophical clumsiness. See e.g. Robert Summers, *Lon L. Fuller* (London: Edward Arnold, 1984), 11: '[Fuller's *The Morality of Law*] was not well argued in some of its essentials.' Indeed, we can detect the philosophical naïveté of Fuller's book not only in some of its major lines of argument but also in some of its details. For example, in *Morality*, 65, the Law of Noncontradiction and the Law of Identity are run together. A comparable degree of sloppiness afflicts some of the nonphilosophical aspects of his book as well. For instance, at 141, Fuller strikingly misunderstands a sentence (by Portalis) which he quotes in French. Perhaps the most irritating feature of Fuller's book, however, is the distortiveness of the remarks about legal positivism that appear on page after page. When one sees H. L. A. Hart attacked for believing that 'the existence or nonexistence of law is, from a moral point of view, a matter of indifference' (204), one feels a sense of despair and weariness.

realize all the aspirations perfectly, they serve as 'distinct standards by which excellence in legality may be tested' (*Morality*, 42). Deviations from those standards can be desirable in certain circumstances, but in ideal circumstances each of the standards would be thoroughly fulfilled.

Fuller believed that the eight precepts of legality, in either their imperative form or their aspirational form, amount to the 'internal morality of law' or the 'inner morality of law'. That is, the features of law which endow it with its very status as law are also features that endow it with an inherent moral worthiness (which may be outweighed by the substantive malignity of the norms in some particular legal system, but which obtains irrespective of that substantive malignity). A system's nature as a legal system—which necessarily involves its conformity with Fuller's principles of legality—is not a morally neutral fact.

Now, even if we accept that Fuller's eight precepts lay out necessary conditions for the existence of any legal regime, we still can wonder why those conditions should be classified as intrinsically moral. Fuller himself ventured several possible answers to this query, and he made some remarks that hinted at other answers. His champions have supplemented his own observations with a few additional responses. In the rest of this chapter, we shall probe these various efforts to establish an inextricable connection between law and morality. At the moment, my preliminary task is simply to delineate each of Fuller's posited justifications for classifying his precepts as inherently moral. (Some of his putative justifications overlap with one another quite substantially, though none of them is simply reducible to any of the others.) This opening section will also dismiss some of his ostensible justifications straightaway, in order to single out those which deserve careful attention.

At times, Fuller seemed to suggest that the sheer purposive nature of law is what underlies the moral import of his principles of legality. Because those principles structure and sustain a fundamentally purposive enterprise, they play a morally estimable role. Or, at any rate, they play such a role in relation to the general purpose of law: viz., the purpose of subjecting human conduct to the governance of rules. By indispensably furthering that general purpose, Fuller's eight precepts enjoy moral weight which may be overtopped by substantive considerations but which will not be canceled thereby.

At other junctures, Fuller suggested that his eight principles are morally pregnant because they set forth the essential characteristics of an institution that carries out benign functions (even when those functions are accompanied by evil objectives). Most notably, the fact that the institution of law secures basic social orderliness is a fact which confers moral weight on that institution's key features. 'Moral principles cannot function in a social vacuum or in a war of all against all. To live the good life requires something more than good intentions, even if they are generally shared; it requires the support of firm base lines for human interaction, something that—in modern society at least—only a sound legal system can supply' (*Morality*, 205). Even a morally unappealing regime of law will generally make people better off than they would be in circumstances of lawlessness; hence, the distinctive aspects of law—which set it apart from lawlessness—are morally commendable.

Fuller also maintained that the operations of a legal system must rest on a widespread perception of the system's moral worthiness. If legal authority is to function, it has to be 'supported by moral attitudes that accord to it the competence it claims' ('Positivism', 645). Although those moral attitudes belong to the domain of external morality (which Fuller distinguished from the internal morality of his eight precepts), their vital place in underpinning a legal system indicates that Fuller's requirements for the operations of a legal system must be morally significant. After all, because *ex hypothesi* a legal system cannot obtain in the absence of widespread moral allegiance, its very existence bespeaks its moral legitimacy in the eyes of all or most people; hence, the formal prerequisites of its existence must be morally pregnant.

In a somewhat similar vein, Fuller contended that the emergence of an admirable regime of law necessarily involves the emergence of *law*. As he submitted, 'law is a precondition of good law' (*Morality*, 155). Since the satisfaction of the eight principles is the *sine qua non* of law's existence, and since the existence of law is a *sine qua non* of the existence of good law, the eight principles are indispensable elements of law's morality.

Indeed, Fuller added, the constraints imposed by his principles tend to ensure that the substantive tenor of law is benign. When people are required to express publicly the aims toward which they seek to direct other people, they will be loath to pursue evil aims. 'It is the virtue of a legal order conscientiously constructed and administered that it exposes to public scrutiny the rules by which it acts' (*Morality*, 158). Furthermore, evil objectives are in any event less susceptible to precise formulation than are benign objectives. As Fuller strikingly declared: 'I shall have to rest on the assertion of a belief that may seem naïve, namely, that coherence and goodness have more affinity than coherence and evil' ('Positivism', 636). When racism or some other malevolent influence besmirches the law of a society, the legal norms will tend to be framed in murkily imprecise terms. Thus, because Fuller's precepts of legality require promulgation and clarity in the subjection of human conduct to the governance of rules, and because those requirements are largely at odds with the pursuit of nefarious objectives, his precepts are inherently promotive of goodness.

More interesting than any of the foregoing arguments are a few other lines of thought which Fuller advanced. Throughout *The Morality of Law* we encounter the notion of reciprocity, which Fuller invoked in support of his view that the formal prerequisites of law are intrinsically moral. He affirmed that his precepts of legality ensure that the obligations imposed on people by the law are precisely the obligations to which those people will be held. For all intents and purposes, then, officials who rule by law have undertaken to respect the confines of the mandates which they ask citizens (including themselves) to obey. 'Government says to the citizen in effect, "These are the rules we expect you to follow. If you follow them, you have our assurance that they are the rules that will be applied to your conduct" ' (*Morality*, 39–40). While demanding dutiful compliance with legal dictates, a government based on the rule of law is committed to gauging people's conduct by reference to those precise dictates. Fuller plainly viewed this governmental commitment as a moral commitment, undertaken for moral reasons. Not only does the absence of such a commitment render obedience to the law imprudent for citizens (whose dutifulness will not spare them from punishment or whose lack of dutifulness will not subject them to punishment), but it also renders unfair the government's *demands* for obedience. A government that flouts the restraints imposed on it by law's reciprocity has assumed an overweeningly imperious role.

In two closely related ways, Fuller expounded the moral import of the restraints on governmental action. In both of these lines of argument, he submitted that the rule of law acknowledges and preserves the dignity of each human being (i.e., each sane adult human being) as an agent capable of autonomous choice.[5] First, when a government treats its citizens with law-derived regularity and predictability, it allows them to know where they stand. Citizens living under the rule of law can know their obligations and can know which of their projects are permissible or impermissible. Within the confines of their established duties to others, they are free to plan and lead their lives as they please; the mandates of law are 'dependable guideposts for self-directed action' which constitute a 'sound and stable framework for [people's] interaction with one another' (*Morality*, 229, 210). By making clear what people may and may not do, law enables them to pursue their own ventures and purposes in the knowledge that they will not be unexpectedly punished by arbitrary governmental intervention. It thus provides the proper conditions for the flourishing of individual initiative.

A second way in which law gives expression to the dignity of the individual is that it holds each person responsible for his or her own deeds. Under the law, every sane adult is required to comply with legal norms and is therefore treated as a rational agent capable of controlling his or her own behavior. By calling for conformity to various demands, the law presupposes the capacity of each of its addressees for self-determination. 'To embark on the enterprise of subjecting human conduct to the governance of rules involves of necessity a commitment to the view that man is, or can become, a responsible agent, capable of understanding and following rules, and answerable for his defaults' (*Morality*, 162). Law's particular means of social control, the subjection of human conduct to the governance of rules, inevitably draws upon and acknowledges the autonomy of each

---

[5] For an exposition of Fuller that largely concurs with him on this point, see Gerald Postema, 'Implicit Law', 13 *Law and Philosophy* 361, 369–79 (1994). See also John Finnis, *Natural Law and Natural Rights* (Oxford: Clarendon Press, 1980), 272–4, 353; Michael Moore, 'Law as a Functional Kind', in Robert George (ed.), *Natural Law Theory* (Oxford: Clarendon Press, 1992), 188, 222; Joseph Raz, *The Authority of Law* (Oxford: Clarendon Press, 1979), 220–2.

individual. Without such autonomy and an attendant capacity for self-restraint on the part of each person, the governance of human beings by legal norms would not be feasible.

Fuller's argument about the connection between law and individual responsibility has been developed by some commentators along the following lines.[6] What his eight principles together do is to ensure as far as possible that the law is followable by those who are subject to it. In other words, the essential features of law are features which tend to minimize the chance that any individual will be punished for violating a prohibition of which he could not have been aware or with which he could not have complied. As far as possible, the fundamental characteristics of law engender opportunities for individuals to orient their behavior toward the duties that are incumbent on them. If a scheme of governance is grossly failing to satisfy one or more of Fuller's precepts, then it may well be punishing people for breaches of duties even when the people could not have known of the duties or could not possibly have avoided transgressions of their requirements. Only when all of Fuller's precepts are generally followed, will the chances of such unfair punishments be reduced to a minimum. Hence, his precepts encapsulate the values of fair warning and fair opportunity, in regard to the demands laid on people by the law. In short, the qualities of law which make it distinctively legal are morally significant; they prevent the unfairness that is involved in the laying down of unfollowable mandates.

And so we come to the end of this conspectus. Each of the lines of argument summarized above has professed to demonstrate the inherently moral status of Fuller's eight principles of legality. Several of those arguments (along with one or two other such arguments) will receive attention in my critique of Fuller's position. However, some of them are too flimsy to warrant any perusal. For instance, we can dismiss post-haste any suggestion that the sheer purposiveness of a legal system is sufficient to render such a system intrinsically moral.[7] Since purposes

---

[6] Fuller himself adumbrated the line of thought which I summarize here. See Fuller, *Morality*, at 39, 70 n. 29, 132. For the first sustained and explicit presentation of this line of thought, see David Lyons, above, n. 3. See also Tom Campbell, 'Obligation: Societal, Political, and Legal', in Paul Harris (ed.), *On Political Obligation* (London: Routledge, 1990), 120, 140–4; David Lyons, *Ethics and the Rule of Law* (Cambridge: Cambridge University Press, 1984), 75–8; Philip Mullock, 'The Inner Morality of Law', 84 *Ethics* 327, 329, 331 (1974); Peter Nicholson, 'The Internal Morality of Law: Fuller and His Critics', 84 *Ethics* 307, 316, 324–5 (1974); Robert Summers, above, n. 4, at 37–8. Cf. Theodore Benditt, *Law as Rule and Principle* (Hassocks: Harvester Press, 1978), 98; Kent Greenawalt, 'Too Thin and Too Rich: Distinguishing Features of Legal Positivism', in Robert George, *The Autonomy of Law* (Oxford: Clarendon Press, 1996), 1, 12–13; John Ladd, 'Law and Morality: Internalism vs. Externalism', in Sidney Hook (ed.), *Law and Philosophy* (New York: New York University Press, 1964), 61, 69–71; Paul LeBel, 'Blame This Messenger: Summers on Fuller', 83 *Michigan Law Review* 717, 723–4 (1985); Neil MacCormick, 'Natural Law and the Separation of Law and Morals', in Robert George (ed.), *Natural Law Theory* (Oxford: Clarendon Press, 1992), 105, 122–4; R. George Wright, 'Does Positivism Matter?', in Robert George (ed.), *The Autonomy of Law* (Oxford: Clarendon Press, 1996), 57, 60.

[7] For just such a suggestion, see George Breckenridge, 'Legal Positivism and the Natural Law: The Controversy between Professor Hart and Professor Fuller', 18 *Vanderbilt Law Review* 945, 961

and the pursuit of purposes can be immoral or amoral as well as morally admirable, the attribute of purposiveness *in abstracto* does not suffice to imbue an institution with any degree of moral legitimacy.

Even if we flesh out the notion of purposiveness in connection with the law by stating that the purpose of any legal system is to subject human conduct to the governance of rules, we shall not yet have said anything about the substance of this or that particular set of rules; and so we shall not yet know whether the specified rules are morally estimable or not. As H. L. A. Hart declared, '[o]nly if the purpose of subjecting human conduct to the governance of rules, no matter what their content, were itself . . . an ultimate value, would there be any case for classing the principles of rule-making as a morality' ('Fuller', 351). To be sure, the general purpose of law as characterized by Fuller will be investigated at length in this chapter. We shall indeed have to look more carefully not only at that purpose's complications, but also at Hart's criticism of Fuller's observations on this topic. None the less, we can straightaway be confident that the bare notion of subjecting human conduct to the governance of rules is insufficient to establish a necessary connection between law and morality.

Perhaps the most evident way of expanding on the moral significance of the basic workings of law is to note the law's role in enabling and consolidating the orderliness that is essential for the fruitful interaction and coexistence of human beings. As has been mentioned, Fuller himself sought to stress this point when he highlighted the effects of law in bringing about the governance of rules. However, his remarks about the stabilizing function of law will attract little attention in the present chapter—not because they are flatly and manifestly wrong, but because that function will be explored at length in Chapters 7 and 9. Every legal positivist would readily agree that law is indispensable for the securing of basic social peace and co-ordination; H. L. A. Hart's famous discussion of the 'minimum content of natural law' is merely one notable example of the positivist position.[8] Nevertheless, as will become plain in my later discussions of this matter, the essen-

---

(1965): 'With Fuller's view of law as a purposive enterprise, even a procedural aspect could not be devoid of substantive moral content.' See also ibid. 963, where a similar suggestion is made in a long quotation from Lon Fuller, 'American Legal Philosophy at Mid-Century', 6 *Journal of Legal Education* 457, 472 (1954). For a largely similar position, see Douglas Sturm, 'Lon Fuller's Multidimensional Natural Law Theory', 18 *Stanford Law Review* 612, 630–1 (1966). For criticism of Fuller on this point, see e.g. Theodore Benditt, above, n. 6, at 98–9; Tom Campbell, *The Legal Theory of Ethical Positivism* (Aldershot: Dartmouth Publishing, 1996), 119–20; H. L. A. Hart, 'Lon L. Fuller: The Morality of Law', in *Essays in Jurisprudence and Philosophy* (Oxford: Clarendon Press, 1983), 343, 350–1 ['Fuller']; Graham Hughes, 'The Existence of a Legal System', 35 *New York University Law Review* 1001, 1023–4 (1960); Graham Hughes, 'Positivists and Natural Lawyers', 17 *Stanford Law Review* 547, 558 (1965). For analyses contending that Fuller has been misunderstood on this point, see Peter Nicholson, above, n. 6, at 317–19; Robert Summers, above, n. 4, at 22, 26–7, 33–4.

[8]  See H. L. A. Hart, *The Concept of Law* (Oxford: Clarendon Press, 1961), 187–95. In Ch. 9 below, I contend that Hart's minimum-content argument does not lead to the conclusion that the law in any society imposes a universally borne and comprehensively applicable prima-facie moral obligation of obedience. Hart would very likely have agreed; see Frederick Schauer, 'Fuller's Internal Point of View', 13 *Law and Philosophy* 285, 291–2 n. 15 (1994).

tial role of law in sustaining societal orderliness and co-ordination does not in any way belie the legal-positivist insistence on the separability of law and morality.

Also unexamined herein is the claim that law is a precondition of good law. Though such a claim is unexceptionable, it is also exceedingly feeble as a means of positing an intrinsic connection between law and morality. One could just as well observe that law is a precondition of wicked law, and conclude that there is an intrinsic connection between law and *im*morality. Neither in Fuller's claim nor in my inverted variant of his claim has an inherent connection been demonstrated. To say simply that $X$ is a precondition of $X$-plus-some-quality-$Y$ does not in itself establish that $X$ partakes of $Y$.

Equally undeserving of lengthy investigation is Fuller's assertion that the public ascertainability of norms in a legal system will tend to deter officials from pursuing disreputable objectives. In response to such an assertion we should first take note of some apt comments by Hart:

> It is . . . quite generally true that a regime bent on monstrous policies will often want the cover of secrecy and vague, indefinable laws if it is not certain of general support for its policies or finds it necessary to conciliate external opinion. But this is a matter of the varying popularity and strength of governments, not of any necessary incompatibility between government according to the principles of legality and wicked ends.   ('Fuller', 353)

In addition to taking account of Hart's riposte, we should here glance at a fact that will later be explored in depth—the fact that evil regimes may find law an indispensable vehicle for their heinous ends. Not only can the workings of law fail to discourage wickedness, but they can be crucially serviceable for wicked objectives. In short, although Fuller's faith in the salutary effects of the promulgation of laws is doubtless warranted in certain circumstances, it can prove completely unfounded in other circumstances.

A final salient point that will go largely undiscussed in this chapter is Fuller's thesis about the insusceptibility of evil aims to clear and precise formulation. Such a thesis is implausible on its face, and it gains little support from what Fuller wrote about it. In 'Positivism and Fidelity to Law' he simply asserted a link between coherence and goodness, without argument ('Positivism', 636); he was correct to think that such an assertion would seem naïve. In *The Morality of Law* he did make a passing effort to substantiate his assertion empirically, by pointing to some examples of regimes that have encountered difficulties when trying to formulate and apply laws that distinguish among people on the basis of race (*Morality*, 159–62). At most, however, such examples may go some way toward showing that racist aims—as opposed to evil aims generally—do not lend themselves to being expressed in terms with clear-cut applications. Moreover, the examples are not wholly persuasive even in regard to racism. Fuller may well have overstated the problems of definition to which he pointed,[9] and he very likely exaggerated the

---

[9] For example, the anomalies in the application of South Africa's racist laws were at least partly due to the inconsistent definitions of racial categories among various statutes.

significance of borderline cases (which are extremely interesting to legal scholars, but which occur alongside multitudes of easy cases). On the whole, then, Hart was doubtless correct again when he retorted that Fuller 'shows only that the principle that laws must be clearly and intelligibly framed is incompatible with the pursuit of vaguely defined substantive aims, whether they are morally good or evil. In particular, [he] does not show . . . that clear rules are not "ethically neutral" between good and evil substantive aims. There is therefore no special incompatibility between clear laws and evil' ('Fuller', 352).[10]

## II. A TROUBLESOME AMBIGUITY

Let us now probe the more impressive lines of reasoning which Fuller propounded. To find an apposite means of entry for my critical rejoinders, we should return to the matter of law's basic purpose. As any reader of *The Morality of Law* becomes aware, Fuller submitted that the fundamental purpose of law consists in subjecting human conduct to the governance of rules. We should begin by noticing an ambiguity in this statement of law's chief function. On the one hand, the statement can be taken to mean that law operates to channel and guide behavior by addressing the demands and prescriptions of its rules directly to the people who are subject to them. On the other hand, the statement can be taken to mean simply that law operates to impose order and regularity on human interaction by providing clear and precise guidelines for dispute-resolution. Under the latter interpretation of law's function, the norms of a legal system might be addressed only to officials rather than to both officials and citizens. Let us briefly consider this second interpretation of the purpose of law, before we explore more lengthily the first interpretation.

The difference between the two understandings of law's role does not pertain to the *form* of legal norms. As John Finnis has observed, most laws are framed in an indicative propositional mode rather than in a prescriptive or imperative mode.[11] From the form alone, we cannot tell who the immediate addressees of the law are. Instead of pertaining to the form of legal norms, then, the difference between the two conceptions of law's Fullerian purpose relates to the focus of promulgation. Under the second conception, the set of people to whom legal norms are directly promulgated can be officials plus citizens, but can equally well be officials only. If the latter situation obtains, then the basic function of law will not occur through the direct presentation of citizens with formulated norms. It will occur, rather, through the law-enforcing activities of officials who give effect

---

[10] For some further critical discussion of this aspect of Fuller's thought, see Frederick Schauer, above, n. 8, at 295–8.
[11] John Finnis, above, n. 5, at 282–3, 314, 315–16. See also A. M. Honoré, 'Real Laws', in P. M. S. Hacker and Joseph Raz (eds), *Law, Morality, and Society* (Oxford: Clarendon Press, 1977), 99, 117–18.

to a scheme of substantive and procedural guidelines for authoritative dispute-resolution. Though law perforce involves the regulation of behavior through the laying down of norms and the setting of standards—viz., the subjection of human conduct to the governance of rules—it does not necessarily involve making those norms and standards known to citizens by means other than the patterns of official approval and disapproval that implement the norms and the standards. Conflict-terminating judgments, as opposed to promulgation, can be the chief vehicle for the expression of legal requirements. So long as officials are provided with a matrix of norms that enable them to impose regularity and order on their society by resolving disputes methodically, and so long as they adhere quite firmly to those operative norms when gauging the merits of people's claims, their regime can aptly be classified as a regime of law. Whether the prevailing norms are communicated to citizens directly in published form, or are communicated only through instances of official punishment and tolerance, is of secondary importance.

In short, once the central purpose of law is understood to be concerned first and foremost with the securing of social peace through the establishment of precise rules for dispute-resolution, the Fullerian principle of promulgation can fall by the wayside. In a society where the rules are promulgated directly to officials only, the citizens will of course be able to infer the content of the rules by studying the patterns of the decisions which authoritatively settle disputes; but citizens' knowledge of the law is then wholly derivative of officials' knowledge and behavior. Direct promulgation to citizens—promulgation of the sort on which Fuller insisted—can be altogether absent from a rigorously rule-governed system of social control. All the same, because the official deliberations and determinations within such a system are strictly in accordance with its procedural and substantive norms that direct the authoritative regulation of behavior, those deliberations and determinations are the workings of a legal regime.

Given the second conception of law's fundamental purpose, an insistence on promulgation is not the only casualty among Fuller's eight precepts of legality. Also dropping away to a considerable extent is the precept concerning impossibility. If the overriding objective of a legal system is to resolve disagreements by reference to rules, then the unfollowability of substantive rules is acceptable so long as those rules help to realize that overriding objective. To be sure, some unsatisfiable laws will not facilitate the resolution of disputes at all. A mandate requiring people to remove themselves from the Milky Way Galaxy is one of the many such pointless laws that might be imagined. Nevertheless, other unfulfillable directives could well play a powerful role in enabling the termination of disputes.

Consider, for instance, a law providing that any adult who is shorter than six feet in natural height must grow taller or lose certain entitlements *vis-à-vis* each person whose natural height is greater than six feet. If the basic purpose of law is to channel and guide behavior, then the demand for greater height is not only invidious but also largely futile (save perhaps with regard to some people who may undertake exercises or eat more heartily during childhood in order to increase their chances of growing beyond six feet in height). However, if the basic purpose of law is to resolve disputes conclusively in a strictly rule-governed fashion, then the dictate on height may prove highly serviceable.

Of course, one should acknowledge that a mandate which specifically requires an adult to grow taller is somewhat ridiculous in ordinary circumstances. One should acknowledge as well that any legal system devoted chiefly to the authoritative settlement of conflicts will doubtless include numerous followable directives, which can gradually help to avert the eruption of conflicts (as the tenor of each followable directive becomes manifest through the patterns of official law-enforcement activity). None the less, unfollowable mandates that are far less strange than the rule about people's heights can easily be imagined. And, although a legal regime that is concerned primarily with the containment of disputes will indeed lay down many followable directives, its efficient operations can also involve as many unfollowable directives as are promotive of the enterprise of containing disputes. When the presentation of law's demands to citizens is perceived as one of the ancillary functions of a legal system—a function that occurs solely through the resolution of conflicts by the enforcement of those demands—the fulfillability of the demands is likewise consigned to an ancillary status.[12]

Hence, insofar as the general purpose of law is seen to consist in the imposition of a rule-ordained order through the snuffing out of disputes, two of Fuller's eight earmarks of legality are dispensable to quite a considerable degree. To be sure, the imposition of a rule-ordained order will involve the regulation and co-ordination of citizens' interaction; but such regulation and co-ordination can be entirely derivative of the co-ordination of *officials'* decisions. In a legal system of the sort described by my last several paragraphs, the primary mission does indeed lie in channeling and guiding the judgments of *officials* as they endeavor to secure social peace in a manner that is substantively and procedurally regularized. To the extent that the direct promulgation of laws to citizens and the ability of citizens to satisfy the law's demands are inessential for the advancement of the officials'

---

[12] Of course, Fuller himself acknowledged a place for unfulfillable legal behests, in his discussion of 'laws requiring the impossible' (*Morality*, 70–9). Particularly interesting (and somewhat poorly argued) is the following passage:

Law has here been considered as 'the enterprise of subjecting human conduct to the governance of rules.' Yet when men act under mistake or through inadvertence they obviously do not and cannot pattern their actions after the law; no one studies the law of quasi contracts to learn what he should do in moments when he does not quite know what he is doing. The solution of this difficulty is fairly obvious. To preserve the integrity of a system of legal relations set by advertence there is need for a supplementary system of rules for healing the effects of inadvertence. (ibid. 74)

My current discussion has sought to show that the followability of laws by citizens can be a secondary concern *throughout* a legal system, rather than only in some supplementary areas thereof.

task, the promulgation and the satisfiability are inessential for the existence of a legal system. In principle, the wholesale absence of those two features would be compatible with the emergence and continuation of such a system.

What this discussion reveals is the hazardousness of Fuller's effort to encapsulate the general purpose of law. As the price of coming up with a fairly uncontroversial statement of law's central function, Fuller had to remain at a dauntingly high level of abstraction—such a high level, indeed, that his statement of the function can plausibly be construed in a way which runs athwart his more detailed explication of law's basic characteristics.[13] As we have seen, the subjection of human conduct to the governance of rules can occur without the direct presentation of rules to citizens; it can occur through the presentation of rules (to citizens) in only the mediated form of official decisions about the rules' applications, and therefore it need not tally with Fuller's insistence on promulgation. Likewise, since the enterprise of subjecting human conduct to the governance of rules can focus principally on the systematic clearing up of disputes and only secondarily on the guiding of citizens' behavior, it can depart from the Fullerian precept concerning compliability and can do so as often as is serviceable for the task of dispute-resolution. In sum, when Fuller attempted to single out law's purpose, he offered a formulation under which the followability of rules by citizens can quite easily be regarded as an ancillary concern. He thereby characterized law in a way that can clash with some of his own preconditions for the existence of law.

### III. FULLER'S CONCEPTION OF THE PURPOSE OF LAW: SOME PRELIMINARY POINTS

Having explored the second of the two interpretations of the general purpose which Fuller ascribed to law, we should now return to the first interpretation. Under this alternative conception of law's central function, the followability of legal norms by citizens is moved to the fore. This conception, which Fuller doubtless had in mind at virtually every juncture, is closely akin to the traditional notion of the rule of law. For a pithy and representative expression of that notion, we can turn to John Rawls: 'A legal system is a coercive order of public rules addressed to rational persons for the purpose of regulating their conduct and providing the framework for social cooperation.'[14] Here the direct addressees of the rules in a legal system are not only the officials but also the citizens. Legal norms channel and guide behavior by presenting citizens directly with behests

---

[13] Along with other commentators, H. L. A. Hart pointed out a further problem that derives from the high abstraction of Fuller's pronouncements on the purpose of law: 'This large conception of law, admittedly and unashamedly, includes the rules of clubs, churches, schools, "and a hundred and one other forms of human association" ' ('Fuller', 343). I am not quite as troubled by this aspect of Fuller's theory as are some of his other critics. (On this point, I am in agreement with Roger Cotterrell, *The Politics of Jurisprudence* [London and Edinburgh: Butterworths, 1989], 138.)

[14] John Rawls, *A Theory of Justice* (Cambridge, Mass.: Harvard University Press, 1971), 235.

and prescriptions, via the promulgation of the norms. A rule-ordained scheme of
life is established through the operation of laws as direct instructions to citizens,
even more than through the instances of official enforcement of the laws.
Dispute-resolution is of course a key function of any legal system, but it proceeds
against a background of extensive and direct guidance to potential disputants. We
here no longer perceive dispute-resolution as the paramount or virtually exclusive
point of law, in relation to which the followability of legal rules can be very
frequently sacrificed as a subordinate consideration.

As has just been remarked, Fuller appeared quite clearly to subscribe to this
more conventional conception of law's purpose, when he expounded the inner
morality of law. Before we look again at his arguments about that inner morality,
however, we should consider three aspects of the purpose of law as he understood
it. First, *pace* Fuller, legal positivists can happily take account of the purpose
which he attributed to law. Positivist denials of necessary connections between
law and morality are perfectly consistent with the view that the central function
of law is to subject human conduct to the governance of rules (by promulgating
legal rules directly to citizens). When Fuller persistently sneered at legal positivism for its blindness to the purpose of law, he was knocking down a straw man.
Although legal positivists have tended to concentrate their attention on the structural configurations and components of legal regimes, they can perfectly well
recognize the functional or dynamic facets of any such regimes. A keen alertness
to law's formality does not preclude alertness to its operational systematicity.
Hence, a legal positivist can and should be aware of the effects that flow from
law's systematic workings—effects consisting in the channeling and guiding of
behavior. As Hart affirmed: '[I]nvestigations into the structure of legal systems
and inquiries . . . designed to draw out the implications of law as a form of purposive activity are not rivals but complementary forms of jurisprudence' ('Fuller',
344).

To be sure, legal positivists may feel more comfortable in talking about the
general function or role of law than in talking about its general purpose. But such
a terminological preference does not really derive from any tenets of positivism.
It derives, rather, from a sensitivity to the potential gaps between the intentions of
individuals and the consequences of their actions. Although the general function
of law may indeed be in harmony with the designs of the officials and citizens
who sustain law's workings, there is no guarantee of such harmony—with respect
to law or indeed (*mutatis mutandis*) with respect to any human institutions or
undertakings. We are therefore probably well advised to speak of law's chief
function or role, rather than of its purpose; such a manner of speaking will avoid
glossing over the potential disjunction between what is individually envisioned
and what is collectively accomplished.[15] Still, however we choose to label the
general function of law, we should of course recognize that a legal system does

---

[15]  Cf. Gerald Postema, above, n. 5, at 381–2.

indeed operate over time and does indeed produce distinctive effects. We should also recognize that the general operations and effects of a typical legal regime (in contrast with many of its *specific* operations and effects) are ordinarily consentaneous with the intentions of the participants in the regime.

A second point to be noted here about Fuller's conception of the purpose of law is that Hart was undoubtedly drawing on that conception when he famously argued that Fuller's so-called internal morality of law is merely a set of conditions for the efficient carrying out of law's purpose ('Fuller', 350–1, 357). Hart's designation of Fuller's eight precepts as conditions of efficacy has recurrently come under fire,[16] not least from Fuller himself:

[N]ote the fundamental obscurity of my critics' position. Just what do they have in mind when they speak of efficacy? It is not hard to see what is meant by efficacy when you are trying to kill a man with poison; if he ends up dead, you have succeeded; if he is still alive and able to strike back, you have failed. But how do we apply the notion of efficacy to the creation and administration of a thing as complex as a whole legal system? (*Morality*, 202)

Fuller's riposte to Hart has found favor with other analysts. Consider, for example, the following passage from one of the most sophisticated discussions of Fuller's jurisprudence:

We are now in a position to see the fallacy that is involved in treating Fuller's eight principles as mere principles of efficacy. For us to speak meaningfully of efficacy, it must be possible to distinguish means from ends. Thus, there could be principles of effective poisoning because there is a definite end in view (a dead victim) and certain steps calculated to achieve that end (the right dose). But Fuller's eight principles are not related in this way to any independent end. (Simmonds, *Issues*, 121)

Now, although Fuller's precepts indeed do not necessarily promote any *independent* end, they do generally promote an end that is *intrinsic* to law. That end, naturally, is the subjection of human conduct to the governance of rules. When Hart characterized the Fullerian principles as merely principles of 'efficiency for a purpose' ('Fuller', 350), the purpose to which he referred was the very purpose which Fuller himself imputed to law. We can ascertain as much at a slightly later juncture in Hart's analysis, where we are told of 'the activity of controlling men

---

[16] For examples of such criticism, see Brian Bix, *Jurisprudence: Theory and Context* (Boulder, Colo.: Westview Press, 1996), 83; Charles Covell, *The Defence of Natural Law* (New York: St. Martin's Press, 1992), 53; J. W. Harris, *Legal Philosophies* (London: Butterworths, 1980), 132–4; Neil MacCormick, above, n. 6, at 122–4; Peter Nicholson, above, n. 6, at 312, 322–3; Nigel Simmonds, *Central Issues in Jurisprudence* (London: Sweet & Maxwell, 1986) [*Issues*], 119–21, 123; Robert Summers, above, n. 4, at 37. For analyses broadly similar to Hart's, see Paul LeBel, above, n. 6, at 723–4; Anthony Lisska, *Aquinas's Theory of Natural Law* (Oxford: Oxford University Press, 1996), 21–4; David Lyons, above, n. 6, at 77–8; Margaret Jane Radin, 'Reconsidering the Rule of Law', 69 *Boston University Law Review* 781, 784–7 (1989); Robert Summers, 'Professor Fuller on Morality and Law', 18 *Journal of Legal Education* 1, 14, 26 (1965). Cf. Jeremy Waldron, 'Why Law—Efficacy, Freedom, or Fidelity?', 13 *Law and Philosophy* 259, 261–2 (1994).

by rules and the principles designed to maximize its efficiency' ('Fuller', 357). Hart was not positing any goal outside the overall process of law-creation and law-administration; he was accepting Fuller's contention that the end of law consists in functioning as a system of rules (i.e., in bringing people's conduct under the sway of the rules). Apropos of that general end—an end which involves the control of human conduct *by rules*, rather than simply the control of human conduct—Fuller with his eight precepts did in fact lay down conditions of efficacy, in that most deviations from those precepts impair the realization of law's dominion.[17] Distinct from each of the fundamental qualities of law, and not guaranteed to be achieved by the presence of all of them, the subjection of human conduct to the governance of rules is an ongoing pursuit that cannot gain effective hold except by way of those qualities. There is indeed a means/end distinction here, even though the end is immanent in the very legal systems that are composed of the means. (It is immanent in those systems because it amounts to the operation of each system as such.)

Yet, although Hart could view Fuller's principles as instrumental guidelines without presupposing any goal external to the functioning of law as law, he should also have perceived them as conceptual or constitutive conditions for the existence of a legal regime.[18] Here we come to the third of my preliminary points about Fuller's conception of law's purpose. When the defining enterprise of law (the enterprise of subjecting human conduct to the governance of rules) is seen as involving the direct presentation of legal demands and prescriptions to citizens for their compliance, Fuller's eight precepts are related to that enterprise not only instrumentally but also integrally. Though various departures from each precept may not in themselves mark the demise of a legal system (even if they detract from the efficacy of its functioning as a regime of operative rules), a thoroughgoing failure to satisfy one or more of the precepts will result not in an inefficient legal system but in the outright absence of such a system. If a mode of governance is based on general rules not at all or hardly at all, for example, then it is not governance by law. Much the same can be said in connection with the rest of Fuller's principles.

Consider, for instance, the upshot of a comprehensive failure to comply with

---

[17] Throughout this discussion (and indeed throughout the rest of this book), I am construing law's end or purpose in the way that Fuller himself construed it. That is, I am assuming that the enterprise of subjecting human conduct to the governance of rules must involve the direct presentation of law's requirements and prescriptions to citizens.

[18] This point has occasionally been discerned by other analysts. See e.g. Ronald Dworkin, 'Philosophy, Morality, and Law—Observations Prompted by Professor Fuller's Novel Claim', 113 *University of Pennsylvania Law Review* 668, 683–6 (1965) ['Philosophy']; R. A. Duff, 'Legal Obligation and the Moral Nature of Law', 25 (n.s.) *Juridical Review* 61, 74 (1980) [Duff, 'Obligation']. (Duff, however, fails to see that a characterization of Fuller's principles as principles of efficiency is quite legitimate.) For a skeptical treatment of the conceptual or constitutive status of Fuller's precepts, see James Boyle, 'Legal Realism and the Social Contract: Fuller's Public Jurisprudence of Form, Private Jurisprudence of Substance', 78 *Cornell Law Review* 371, 372, 375–8, 396–7 (1993).

the principle of nonretroactivity. Fuller himself conveyed quite vividly the bizarreness of such a failure ('Positivism', 650–1), and he aptly submitted that it would be incompatible with the very *existence* of legal norms rather than merely with their *effectiveness*. After all, if every ostensible norm is purely retroactive, then at every moment there are no prospectively applicable norms at all—and so there is no law on any point, from one moment to the next. Anyone who wishes to be apprised of the legality or illegality of her actions will find no guidance whatsoever until the time for guidance has passed. Hence, when a society is governed in a manner that involves few or no forward-looking rules, it is a society devoid of law. At any time $t$, in such a society, people's conduct will be largely or wholly unregulated by any rules existent at $t$; accordingly, the role of law in channeling and steering behavior through the subjection of human conduct to the governance of rules is altogether missing.

In the current context, the most problematic entry among Fuller's principles is the requirement of nonconflicting duties. Although Fuller expressed this requirement as a principle pertaining to contradictions, his subsequent discussion reveals that he actually had in mind the undesirability of *conflicting* duties. To grasp why the precept concerning such duties cannot be accommodated entirely smoothly within the present discussion, we should take a quick look at the difference between contradictions and conflicts.

A contradiction obtains when the existence (or nonexistence) of some situation entails the nonexistence (or existence) of some other situation and vice versa. If a person $X$ enjoys a legal liberty to do $\varphi$, for example, then necessarily he is not under a legal duty to abstain from doing $\varphi$; and if he is under a legal duty to abstain from doing $\varphi$, then necessarily he does not enjoy a legal liberty to do $\varphi$. The liberty and the duty cannot coexist. By contrast, the coexistence of conflicting duties—the coexistence of $X$'s duty to do $\varphi$ and his duty to abstain from doing $\varphi$—does not violate any laws of logic. $X$ can indeed be under an obligation to do something which he is obligated not to do. Though the simultaneous *fulfillment* of the two conflicting duties would of course violate the Law of Noncontradiction, the duties themselves can lie upon $X$ in concert.

Now, one might presume that Fuller's precept relating to noncontradictoriness would indeed be focused on out-and-out contradictions. After all, a legal system in which every rule is contradicted by another rule cannot properly guide and channel the behavior of citizens or officials at all—since it declares to people that they are legally required to do certain things, while it also declares to them that they are legally free to forbear from doing those things. People are then no better informed about their jural entitlements than if the legal rules of their society were written in incomprehensible gibberish. Hence, a total failure or virtually total failure in regard to the requirement of noncontradictoriness will result not in a poor legal system but in no legal system whatsoever. A conceptually deducible condition for the existence of law will be missing. Hence, if Fuller's disapproval of contradictions had been targeted at genuine contradictions, it would have fit very neatly into his jurisprudential scheme.

In fact, however, Fuller was referring principally or exclusively to *conflicting* duties when he expressed disapproval of contradictions. He was worried about situations in which someone has both a duty to do φ and a duty not to do φ. We therefore have to ask whether a legal system can function as such if situations of this sort are pervasive. If every duty borne by each person $X$ is in conflict with another duty borne by $X$, will an ostensible legal system be devoid of operative force in much the same way as when it teems with contradictions?

Given that conflicting duties can coexist and that the pervasive presence of such duties in a legal system will therefore not render the system's scheme of regulation unintelligible, they will not necessarily prevent the system from functioning as such. Crucial here are the penalties that attach to breaches of duties. If the penalty incurred for a breach of $X$'s duty to do φ is much stiffer or lighter than the penalty for a breach of his duty not to do φ, then $X$ will have a strong incentive to comply with one duty as opposed to the other; and if every pair of conflicting duties is marked by a similar disparity in the applicable remedies, then the legal system which imposes the conflicting duties will probably manage to function as a legal system by guiding and channeling behavior on the basis of rules. If, on the other hand, every pair of conflicting duties is marked by a balance (or near-balance) in the applicable remedies, then no one will have a legally created incentive to choose any particular course of action in preference to a contrary course. In that event, a legal system suffused with conflicting duties will do nothing or virtually nothing to guide and channel people's behavior, and it will therefore not obtain as a legal system. In light of the possibility of these circumstances, Fuller's principle against conflicting duties—when suitably modified to take account of what has just been said here about penalties—sets forth a conceptually deducible condition for the very existence of a legal regime. A complete failure to satisfy that condition will mean that the system of governance in which the failure occurs is not a system of law.

### IV. WHENCE COMES THE MORALITY? A FIRST LOOK

This chapter has just expounded the following three points: legal positivists, who view any system of law as a system of norms, can readily acknowledge the central function which Fuller ascribed to law; Fuller's eight principles articulate requirements which are instrumentally related to law's general function; and those requirements are related to law likewise as conceptually derivable preconditions for its existence. We now must consider whether Fuller was warranted in believing that the requirements expressed in his principles constitute an inner morality of law. Here we return to the variations on the theme of law's reciprocity.[19]

---

[19] On the general theme of law's reciprocity in Fuller's work, see Trevor Allan, 'Citizenship and Obligation: Civil Disobedience and Civil Dissent', 55 *Cambridge Law Journal* 89, 94–5 (1996);

In the first of those variations we are told that the law respects individual dignity and initiative by letting people know quite precisely what they may and may not do. As a consequence of making clear which projects are permissible and which projects are forbidden, a regime of law enables each person to plan her life with a confident awareness that governmental officials will not arbitrarily clamp down on her undertakings. A sense of security against unpredictable meddling is what Fuller's eight requirements bring about. By endowing individuals with such security, those requirements advance the ideal of self-determination. And thus they perform an intrinsically moral function, even in a wicked system of law.[20]

When we subsequently explore the other variations on the theme of reciprocity, we shall devote close attention to certain aspects of the argument that has just been sketched. For now, let us concentrate on three overlapping difficulties in that argument. First, the argument overlooks the fact that uncertainty in the law can play a choice-expanding role as well as a choice-inhibiting role. An example will help to illuminate this point. Suppose that a society's legal system includes numerous mandates that regulate people's lives to a stifling extent. Among those mandates, let us assume, is a law clearly specifying the way in which shoelaces must be tied. Despite Fullerian admonitions about the need for congruence between the enacted law and the administered law, the shoelace-tying dictate is only occasionally enforced. The sporadic enforcement of the dictate engenders uncertainty among people about the extent to which they can get away with tying their laces in styles that are not legally countenanced; but it induces many people to take their chances by adopting just such styles. After some prissy busybodies repeatedly complain that the intermittent enforcement of the law encourages the proliferation of aesthetically displeasing shoelace patterns, the government announces that it will henceforth unflaggingly implement the shoelace-tying restriction. When a policy of strict enforcement does indeed ensue, people lose their uncertainty about the extent to which they can get away with unorthodox styles of lacing—yet they have hardly thereby undergone an enhancement of their autonomy. Although they have retained the autonomy-bolstering certainty which

Deryck Beyleveld and Roger Brownsword, 'The Practical Difference Between Natural-Law Theory and Legal Positivism', 5 *Oxford Journal of Legal Studies* 1, 29 (1985); Brian Bix, above, n. 16, at 80; James Boyle, above, n. 18, at 377, 392–7; Daniel Brudney, 'Two Links of Law and Morality', 103 *Ethics* 280, 284 (1993); Roger Cotterrell, above, n. 13, at 140, 148–9; Charles Covell, above, n. 16, at 50–2; Duff, 'Obligation', 75–8, 80, 82; J. W. Harris, above, n. 16, at 133–4; Peter Nicholson, above, n. 6, at 314, 323–4; Gerald Postema, above, n. 5, at 367–87; Noel Reynolds, 'Grounding the Rule of Law', 2 *Ratio Juris* 1, 14–15 (1989); Simmonds, *Issues*, 124–5; Robert Summers, above, n. 4, at 38; Jeremy Waldron, above, n. 16, at 277–82. For some of the key remarks by Fuller himself, see Fuller, *Morality*, 39–40, 138–40, 192–5, 207–10, 214–23, 233–4. For a slightly different view of law's reciprocity, see John Finnis, above, n. 5, at 272–3.

[20] For a recountal of this argument, see Jeremy Waldron, above, n. 16, at 266. Cf. Joseph Raz, above, n. 5, at 220, 221–2. One of Waldron's criticisms of the argument is broadly similar to the second of my principal criticisms thereof. See ibid. 268–9. (And cf. James Boyle, above, n. 18, at 390–1; Kenneth Winston, 'Legislators and Liberty', 13 *Law and Philosophy* 389, 398 [1994].) However, Waldron goes on to commend a modified version of Fuller's position. See Jeremy Waldron, above, n. 16, at 275–84. Considerably more skeptical is James Boyle, above, n. 18, at 392–4.

they formerly enjoyed (i.e., the certainty that they will not be punished for tying their laces in orthodox patterns), they have lost some autonomy-bolstering *uncer-*tainty.

Quite clearly, the point of the foregoing example is not confined to restrictions on the lacing of shoes. Let us assume for the moment that the only threats to autonomy stem from governmental action. In that case, we should observe that compliance with Fuller's principles not only tends to make plain where punitive measures will end, but also tends to make plain where such measures will begin. Whenever uncertainty about the likelihood of governmental intervention is portrayed as autonomy-retarding, it is implicitly or explicitly contrasted with people's confidence that the government will forbear from intervening in some area(s) of their lives. Contrariwise, when the uncertainty about governmental intervention is contrasted with people's confidence that the government will indeed intervene in some area(s) of their lives, the uncertainty should be seen as autonomy-promotive; it leaves people a measure of leeway that is denied to them when their government enforces restrictive mandates tirelessly. If uncertainty of this latter type is eliminated in sundry areas of life by the strict enforcement of the laws that suffocatingly regulate those areas, then the damage to each person's latitude for self-determination can be considerable. In short, an assessment of Fuller's principles as autonomy-nurturing or autonomy-dampening must hinge on the nature of the baseline that is relied upon for the tacit or express comparison that underpins the assessment. An evaluation of those principles *in abstracto* is illusive.

A second difficulty in the argument for the autonomy-promotive role of the settled expectations which ensue from Fuller's precepts is that threats to auton-omy do not stem solely from governmental action. If a policy of strict law-admin-istration enables people to be confident that their government will not intervene in some areas of their lives, then they know that they themselves are free in those areas to impinge on the well-being and activities of one another. Some people will undoubtedly enjoy an increased degree of self-determination as a result, but others may lose more than they gain when uncertainty about the government's forbearance from intervention is removed. If apprehension about the possibility of governmental action deters some people from oppressing others, then a change to a policy of strict noninterference by the government will mean that the victims of the newly unleashed oppression suffer a diminution of their latitude to pursue their own projects. In other words, even when a reduction of uncertainty involves an assurance that the government will stay out of people's lives in certain respects, we cannot automatically conclude that the effect will be generally promotive of autonomy. Once again, pronouncements at an abstract level must give way to context-specific judgments.

To discern a third shortcoming in the argument that was outlined four para-graphs ago, we should look at a powerful version of that argument presented by Nigel Simmonds:

The fact that the rule of law is compatible with injustice does not demonstrate that it is not a genuine moral value. Imagine two régimes, A and B, both equally guilty of violating human rights of various kinds; régime A operates by clearly declared rules, consistently and scrupulously enforced, while régime B operates with the aid of retrospective legislation, unlawful acts of violence by officials, secret trials, secret laws, and so forth. Is there any moral value attaching to régime A's commitment to the rule of law? Clearly there is. Where the government acts in accordance with the eight principles it makes its behaviour both public and predictable. This means that the citizen who wishes to avoid official interference knows just how far he can go without meeting that interference; this provides the degree of order and regularity which is the necessary framework for purposeful and creative activity.   (*Issues*, 123)

In the course of evaluating Simmonds's reasoning, let us consider ten sorts of legal regimes:

|   |   |   |
|---|---|---|
| *A* | Good law, no procedural deviations | 1 |
| *B* | Good law, malign procedural deviations | 2 |
| *C* | Quite good law, no procedural deviations | 2 |
| *D* | Quite good law, benign procedural deviations | 1 |
| *E* | Quite good law, malign procedural deviations | 3 |
| *F* | Quite evil law, no procedural deviations | 3 |
| *G* | Quite evil law, benign procedural deviations | 2 |
| *H* | Quite evil law, malign procedural deviations | 4 |
| *I* | Evil law, no procedural deviations | 4 |
| *J* | Evil law, benign procedural deviations | 3 |

In this roster—which manifestly does not form an exhaustive list of the myriad possible types of regimes—the number at the end of each entry indicates the level of human-rights abuses committed by each regime. A score of '1' denotes an especially low level of such abuses, whereas a score of '4' denotes an especially high level. We are therefore now in a position to scrutinize Simmonds's claims about governments that are 'equally guilty of violating human rights of various kinds'.

In the roster above, government *A* and government *D* are equally guilty of human-rights abuses (at a very low level). Yet the overall posture of *A* is clearly morally preferable to the overall posture of *D*. Much the same can be said about government *C* and government *G*; those two governments are equally guilty of human-rights violations, but *C* on the whole is clearly morally preferable to *G*. A similar point applies to governments *F* and *J*. Should we conclude, then, that Simmonds is correct in his contentions about the inherent moral value of conformity to Fuller's principles?

An affirmative answer to this question would be ill-advised, since we can readily come up with a much better explanation of the superiority of *A* over *D* (and of *C* over *G*, and of *F* over *J*). What renders government *D* morally inferior to government *A* is not that the former government has deviated from procedural or substantive norms, but that it has enacted laws which officially endorse some harsh positions and which potentially or actually create anxiety. In other words, the moral divergence between government $D$ and government $A$ lies not in the differing degrees of their adherence to Fuller's precepts, but in the differing degrees to which their formulated laws countenance evil and thereby give grounds for concern among citizens. Because the laws of $D$ give expression to some immoral stances that are not similarly approved by the laws of $A$, the former government's overall record is more tainted than the latter government's—even though its departures from Fullerian principles keep its human-rights violations as few in number as those committed by $A$.

Let us now compare regimes $B$ and $C$. Those two governments are equally guilty of human-rights violations, yet an observer might feel that $C$ on the whole is morally superior to $B$. Much the same can be said about $F$ in relation to $E$, and about $I$ in relation to $H$. Hence, we must once again ask whether the sheer occurrence of notable deviations from Fullerian principles is morally blameworthy. Given that $B$'s formulated laws are better than $C$'s, and given that the number of actual human-rights violations is the same for each government, the only apparent source of $B$'s possible inferiority to $C$ lies in $B$'s departures from Fullerian precepts. Has Simmonds's view been borne out, then?

Once again, an affirmative answer would be ill-advised. The key factor in the example of $B$ and $C$ is not that $B$ has engaged in procedural deviations, but that $B$'s deviations have been malign. Although those malign deviations do not push the number of $B$'s human-rights abuses past the level of such abuses committed by $C$, they run athwart legitimate expectations that have actually or potentially been engendered by $B$'s good scheme of law. Crucial here is that the relevant expectations are legitimate. Had government $B$ dashed *il*legitimate expectations by engaging in benign departures from Fuller's precepts, it would scarcely have rendered itself morally worse in the process. However, what $B$ has done is to encourage the formation of *legitimate* beliefs which it then undermines.[21] Consequently, the system of law established by $B$ may be morally inferior to $C$'s system, since the latter system does not tend to stimulate the development of legitimate outlooks which are then belied. Even though the two systems are on a par in regard to their human-rights violations, $B$'s system is sullied by its tendency to foster morally proper expectations which prove to be groundless. That additional taint arises not from $B$'s procedural deviations *qua* deviations, but from $B$'s procedural deviations *qua malign* deviations. (Of course, $B$'s moral inferiority to $C$ is debatable. $B$'s cultivating and undercutting of legitimate expectations may be outweighed by $C$'s countenancing of evil in the formulation [as well as the implementation] of its legal norms. In any event, regardless of which government we deem to be morally inferior, our verdict

---

[21]  My point here does not depend on the actual emergence of the beliefs that are undermined. I am focusing on the fact that the emergence of those beliefs is *encouraged* by the terms of some of government $B$'s laws.

will not hinge on the bare fact of a regime's adherence or lack of adherence to Fullerian precepts; we have to look beyond such a content-independent consideration.)

Hence, Simmonds's contentions about the intrinsically moral import of Fuller's principles are not sustainable. When we compare regimes which are dissimilar in the frequency of their deviations from Fullerian principles but which are equally good or bad in their levels of human-rights abuses, we find that any moral disparities between the regimes are not due to the dissimilar levels of their procedural deviations. Either the substantive tenor of the deviations is crucial (as was true in my comparison between *B* and *C*), or the substantive tenor of the enacted law in each regime is decisive (as was true in my comparison between *A* and *D*). Transgressions of Fullerian precepts, merely in their content-independent status as such transgressions, do not determine the relative moral positions of regimes. Substantive factors determine those relative positions.

## V. WHENCE COMES THE MORALITY? A SECOND LOOK

Let us now turn to the second principal way in which Fuller drew a connection between law's reciprocity and the dignity of the individual. He contended that governance by law entails an acknowledgment of each citizen's capacity for autonomous decision-making. By issuing demands and prescriptions which people are expected to heed, and by holding people accountable for their noncompliance with those demands and prescriptions, the law pays tribute to each sane adult's status as an agent who is capable of deliberation and choice. Hence, the general constitutive features of law, encapsulated in Fuller's eight precepts, form an institution that inherently recognizes the responsibility and dignity of everyone to whom the norms of the institution are addressed. Law's constitutive features should therefore be classified as an inner morality.[22]

The problem with this ascription of intrinsic moral worthiness to the Fullerian principles is that either the ascription proves too much or it is unacceptably provincial. On the one hand, perhaps we are being asked to believe that legal mandates pay tribute to each person's dignity as an agent simply by dint of letting each person ultimately decide whether to comply with the mandates or to suffer the consequences of noncompliance. By issuing demands and prescriptions that

---

[22]  For some analyses that take a positive view of Fuller's arguments along these lines, see George Breckenridge, above, n. 7, at 958; Duff, 'Obligation', 75–85; Gerald Postema, above, n. 5, at 369–70; Simmonds, *Issues*, 120–4; Kenneth Winston, 'Introduction', in Lon Fuller, *The Principles of Social Order* (Durham, NC: Duke University Press, 1981), 11, 37–40; R. George Wright, above, n. 6, at 63. Cf. Trevor Allan, above, n. 19; Trevor Allan, 'Procedural Fairness and the Duty of Respect', 18 *Oxford Journal of Legal Studies* 497, 504–5 (1998); Joseph Raz, above, n. 5, at 221–2. For some criticism of Fuller's arguments, see Daniel Brudney, above, n. 19, at 284–5; Dworkin, 'Philosophy', 673; Philip Soper, 'Choosing a Legal Theory on Moral Grounds', in Jules Coleman and Ellen Frankel Paul (eds), *Philosophy and Law* (Oxford: Blackwell, 1987), 31, 47; Robert Summers, above, n. 16, at 26.

are to be followed, legal dictates in their normal operations rely on the ability of citizens to follow them (even though that ability is not always exercised). Those dictates hence involve a morally laden recognition of each individual's capacity for deliberation and self-restraint. Such, at least, seems to be the view in Fuller's statement—quoted earlier—that 'the enterprise of subjecting human conduct to the governance of rules involves of necessity a commitment to the view that man is, or can become, a responsible agent, capable of understanding and following rules, and answerable for his defaults' (*Morality*, 162).

Now, what is so objectionable about this summarized line of reasoning is that it leads to the conclusion that a bank robber's orders to his victims will have paid tribute in a morally laden way to the agency of the victims by letting them ulti- mately decide whether to obey the orders or be shot. Insofar as a robber carries out a heist by issuing commands rather than by merely grabbing booty without any assistance from cowed employees, he has acknowledged that his victims are capable of rational deliberation and choice. Similarly, when an assailant holds a knife near the throat of his victim and informs her that he will take her wallet or her life, he is trading upon her capacity for rational decision-making and is treat- ing her as an agent who will be held accountable if she makes the wrong decision. Much the same can be said about a kidnapper who sends a ransom note to the spouse of the person whom he has abducted. He is presupposing that the spouse has the ability to decide whether to comply with the terms of the note or suffer the consequences of noncompliance. In each of these scenarios the wrongdoer has not simply shoved or dragged someone around, without relying at all on the volitionality and autonomy of the human being whom he is exploiting; nor has he sought to manipulate the psyche of his victim subliminally. In each scenario, rather, the very issuance of commands by the wrongdoer has attested to his belief in the rational agency of his victim—a quality which the wrongdoer sees as a vehicle for the achievement of his own ends. Yet who would maintain that those commands involve any moral respect or concern for the victim?

To be sure, the distinction between agency-acknowledging behests and agency-disregarding shoves is not always entirely clear-cut. At one juncture in the movie *Schindler's List*, for example, a German soldier bellows at his terrified victims with such ferocity that their obedience to his orders is more like a reflex action than like a rational choice. Nevertheless, one can imagine countless instances of wrongdoing where the culprits issue commands which do plainly presuppose that their victims are agents who are capable of arriving at rational determinations. My preceding paragraph broaches three such instances. In any of those situations, the miscreant's recognition of the agency of his victim does not carry any moral force. To presume otherwise is to conflate the notion of agency or autonomy *qua* cognitive fact with the notion of agency or autonomy *qua* moral/political ideal. The former notion deals with the sheer ability of a person to deliberate and to make choices; the latter notion, by contrast, pertains to deliber- ation and the making of choices under circumstances where a person's will is not unduly coerced or cabined by someone else. A person $X$'s acknowledgment of someone else's autonomy in the former sense does not commit $X$ to an endorsement of the value of autonomy in the latter sense. A bank robber or some other wrongdoer can recognize and exploit the agency of his victims for his own purposes, but he scarcely will accept that he has to give them substantial leeway in deciding how they will act. In refusing to embrace the moral/political value of autonomy, he is guilty of no logical or analytical error—though, of course, he is guilty of an egregious moral fault.

Legal rules do normally trade on each citizen's agency or autonomy in the cognitive sense; they normally present requirements and prescriptions that are to be heeded by persons who are capable of choosing to heed them. But this general attestation to the cognitive autonomy of each citizen does not entail a commitment to the moral/political ideal of autonomy. Autonomy of the former sort can be the typical vehicle for an enterprise that gives short shrift to autonomy of the latter sort. Legal rules remain legal rules even if they stiflingly constrict the civil and political liberties of citizens, and even if they establish harsh penalties for anyone who chooses to step out of line. Thus, to the extent that Fuller's claims about the necessary connection between law and individual self-determination are defensible, they must be referring to self-determination *qua* cognitive condition rather than to self-determination *qua* moral/political objective. Any connection between legality and autonomy in the moral/political sense is contingent rather than inherent. Accordingly, the law's general acknowledgment of each citizen's agency does not carry any intrinsic moral force. Only insofar as such an acknowledgment is combined with a substantive policy of extending broad leeway to individuals for the making of their various choices, does that acknowledgment incorporate a respect for the dignity of the individual (in a full-blooded political sense). Shorn of that substantive moral/political policy—a policy which is a strictly contingent feature of a legal system—the law's recognition of the agency of citizens may in itself be no more admirable than a bank robber's or kidnapper's similar recognition of the agency of his victims.

Of course, unlike a typical order issued by a bank robber or a kidnapper, a typical norm in a legal system extends to a general class of situations rather than to only one particular situation. The generality of legal rules, highlighted in Fuller's first precept, might strike some observers as a distinctive tribute to the rational autonomy of the law's addressees.[23] After all, such generality obliges individuals not only to ascertain what each law requires, but also to ascertain when it is applicable. Instead of receiving minute-by-minute instructions from governmental officials, each human being has to infer such instructions from the general norms that cover broad arrays of actions. Each human being is therefore responsible for working out the correct applications of those norms.

Now, even if we overlook the salient role of lawyers in offering expert advice

---

[23] For just such a view, see Gerald Postema, above, n. 5, at 370–1, 376–7.

and assistance to individuals who cannot themselves grasp the implications of various legal rules, we should reject the notion that the generality of such rules is in itself a mark of respect for individual self-direction. In the first place, an outright villain might indeed issue general commands rather than situation-specific orders. For example, a kidnapper might decline to release his victim unless the victim's family and friends abstain from certain modes of behavior for a year or two. (Recall that the mandates of John Austin's gunman-writ-large sovereign were general both in the scope of their address and in the scope of their coverage.[24]) Second, although the generality of a rule may indeed serve as an acknowledgment of the cognitive autonomy of the rule's addressees, the question whether it serves to uphold the moral/political ideal of autonomy is a query that cannot be answered without reference to the substance of the rule. Rules can be expansively general while harshly choking the liberty of the people who are subject to them. Third, as will be emphasized in the next main section of this chapter, the generality of each rule is a feature that can be adopted by officials for purely prudential reasons. Though the grounds for the generality do not *have* to be purely prudential, they always *can* be so; and if they are indeed purely prudential, they deprive the generality of its status as an expression or indication of moral concern.

In sum, to the extent that Fuller's postulated connection between legality and individual dignity was based on the fact that law typically operates through the capacity of citizens for rational decision-making, the connection proves unsustainable. Suppose, however, that Fuller instead meant to suggest that a regime of law—simply by dint of being a genuine regime of law—must indeed uphold the moral/political ideal of individual autonomy. He did sometimes appear to imply as much, especially in the second edition of *The Morality of Law*. For instance, he proclaimed: '[I]f the law is intended to permit a man to conduct his own affairs subject to an obligation to observe certain restraints imposed by superior authority, this implies that he will not be told at each turn what to do; law furnishes a baseline for self-directed action, not a detailed set of instructions for accomplishing specific objectives.' He added: '[L]aw is not, like management, a matter of directing other persons how to accomplish tasks set by a superior, but is basically a matter of providing the citizenry with a sound and stable framework for their interactions with one another, the role of government being that of standing as a guardian of the integrity of this system' (*Morality*, 210). If Fuller in these passages and similar passages was not flagrantly guilty of the *non sequiturs* that have been criticized in my last several paragraphs, and if he was not merely dwelling on the manifest fact that governance by law involves general rules, then he must have been assuming that any genuine legal system preserves an extensive degree of freedom for individuals.[25]

---

[24] See H. L. A. Hart, above, n. 8, at 21–2.
[25] That Fuller advocated the preservation of such freedom is not in doubt. See e.g. Kenneth Winston, above, n. 20, at 412–13.

So understood, Fuller's position does not rest on a *non sequitur*, but it is start-lingly provincial. It refuses to attach the designation of 'legal system' to any such system that is illiberal, and it thereby engages in an arbitrary and heavy-handed stipulation. By declining to encompass any morally unworthy systems of gover-nance within one's conception of law, one can of course validly conclude that law partakes of an intrinsic moral significance; yet one then is playing a stipulative game that is not worth the candle. A narrow and tendentious conception of law does not become persuasive by being buttressed with sterile *ipse dixits*. If an illib-eral scheme of governance exhibits all the formal features of a legal system that are encapsulated in Fuller's eight precepts, then the illiberality of the scheme is hardly in itself an adequate reason for withholding the tag of 'law'.

Why did Fuller occasionally indulge (or come close to indulging) in the wooden stipulation that has just been decried? Perhaps, like many other American legal thinkers, he succumbed to the temptation to build a jurisprudential theory out of the central elements of American constitutional law. A variety of provisions in the American Constitution effectively lay down tests that must be met by any valid law in the United States. Some of those tests are formal, and some—includ-ing tests that relate to civil liberties—are substantive. Because a failure to surmount the Constitution's substantive hurdles will invalidate a law as surely as a failure to surmount the formal hurdles, those two broad types of touchstones for legal validity can seem to be on a par (as indeed they by and large are, *within the American system*). And because some of the Constitution's formal requirements are roughly similar to requirements expressed in Fuller's eight principles, its formal requirements and its substantive requirements alike can come to be regarded as fundamental aspects of law generally, rather than just as key aspects of *American* law. Perhaps Fuller was sometimes engaged not in general jurispru-dential reflections but in a theoretical exposition of the law of his native land.[26]

VI.  WHENCE COMES THE MORALITY? A FINAL LOOK

We come finally to the most important of the arguments that may seem to support Fuller's classification of his principles as the internal morality of law. As was outlined earlier, the focus here lies on the role of those principles in securing the followability of laws. When a regime has satisfied the Fullerian conditions for the existence of a legal system, it has gone as far as is reasonably possible toward providing everyone with a fair opportunity to conform to applicable mandates and prescriptions. Such a regime gives fair notice of what it expects and requires of people, and it does not lay upon them requirements which they cannot possibly fulfill. It thereby helps to ensure that any noncompliance with its behests and

---

[26]  For a largely similar point about Fuller in a somewhat different context, see Richard Posner, *The Problems of Jurisprudence* (Cambridge: Harvard University Press, 1990), 230.

prescriptions is attributable to the fault of the citizen rather than to the oversights of officials. As a consequence, the punitive mechanisms of such a regime will normally be brought to bear against someone only when he or she has gone astray in ways that are genuinely his or her responsibility.

Before we ponder the merits of this latest argument that has been advanced on behalf of Fuller, we ought to take note of a point that should be obvious. The relevant question here is not whether Fuller's precepts *can* have the moral significance that has just been ascribed to them; the relevant question, rather, is whether they *inevitably* have such significance. In other words, what is at issue here is a matter of *inherent* moral worthiness. If a regime adheres scrupulously to the Fullerian precepts, does it *ipso facto* occupy the moral posture which my last paragraph has delineated? A negative answer to this query is wholly consistent with the view that a strict adherence to the Fullerian principles will very frequently rest on moral underpinnings and partake of moral significance. Fuller sometimes wrote as if his legal-positivist opponents denied that his principles could ever be endowed with a profound moral import. 'Why, then, are my critics so intent on maintaining the view that the principles of legality represent nothing more than maxims of efficiency for the attainment of governmental aims?' (*Morality*, 214.) In fact, no sensible positivist would deny that a government can abide by the principles of legality for moral reasons and in furtherance of moral ideals. Such a situation does indeed obtain in liberal democracies such as the United States and the United Kingdom. To gainsay the intrinsic moral worthiness of compliance with Fuller's principles is not to gainsay the fact that compliance with those principles is indeed often morally worthy. When pondering the relationship between law and morality, a positivist should not attempt to show what has to be true of every legal system; a positivist should instead attempt to show what does *not* have to be true of every such system.[27]

To grasp why conformity to Fuller's principles does not have any intrinsic moral significance, we should consider the status of normative propositions generally. My discussion here builds on part of my opening chapter, and will be repeatedly invoked in subsequent portions of this book. Since we shall be exploring Fuller's principles from the perspective of the officials who opt to abide by them, we should examine a first-person statement of a normative proposition. Let us begin, then, by taking the following declaration: 'I ought to stop smoking.' Though such a statement is clearly normative, we cannot yet tell whether the normativity (the 'ought') is prudential or moral. To ascertain the character of the normativity, we have to inquire into the grounds or reasons for the utterance of the statement. On the one hand, the person who makes the statement may have

---

[27] In Jules Coleman's terms, I am here advocating negative positivism in preference to positive positivism. Cf. Jules Coleman, 'Negative and Positive Positivism', in *Markets, Morals, and the Law* (Cambridge: Cambridge University Press, 1988), 3. However, I am doing so only in regard to the relationship between law and morality. I do not question the fruitfulness of positive positivism in other respects; indeed, the first half of Ch. 6 below defends positive positivism at length.

based it solely on the pursuit of objectives such as better health, greater energy, fresher breath, unstained teeth, and more available pocket money for other personal expenditures. On the other hand, the statement may have been based solely on the pursuit of objectives such as a lessening of one's tendency to burden other people by becoming physically incapacitated, a freeing up of health-care resources that can thus go to meet the needs of other people, and an enhancement of one's ability to engage in services for one's community. Or, of course, the proposition about smoking may have been asserted for reasons that combine various factors from the two foregoing lists. If all the grounds for the utterance are contained in the first list of objectives or are similarly oriented toward one's own interests, then the normative statement is prudential through and through. Alternatively, if all the grounds for the utterance are contained in the second list of objectives or are similarly oriented toward other people's well-being, then the normative statement is fundamentally moral. And, obviously, if the grounds for the utterance combine solicitude for oneself and solicitude for others, then the tenor of the normative statement is both prudential and moral.

Of key importance here is that the normativity of an assertion does not in itself endow the assertion with any moral standing whatsoever. Only insofar as the reasons for an asserted statement are essentially focused on the interests of people other than the assertor, does the statement partake of any moral force.[28] (Of course, if the assertor defines his own interests partly by reference to other people's well-being, then the essential focus on their well-being will serve also to further his own interests.) A bald normative proposition such as 'I ought to stop smoking', in isolation from the grounds for its being stated, is neither moral nor prudential; its sheer normativity becomes focused, as moral or as prudential or as both moral and prudential, only when it is attached to those grounds.

Officials' actions and discourse give effect to various normative propositions, which can be presented here (from the perspective of the officials) as first-person normative statements. If a regime abides by the Fullerian principles, then its officials are guided in their behavior by such propositions as 'We ought to govern by general rules' and 'We ought to promulgate the rules to the people who are required to comply with them' and 'We ought usually to eschew retroactive rules'. Now, manifestly, those propositions and the statements which express them are normative; but, until we know the reasons for the officials' adherence to those normative propositions, we have no basis for knowing whether that

---

[28]  When the reasons for the assertion include the aim of furthering-other-people's-interests-for-the-sake-of-furthering-their-interests, the focus on their interests is 'essential'. That is, such an aim does not derive from any ulterior interests of the assertor (apart from interests—such as a concern for acting in a morally proper fashion—which are themselves defined solely by reference to the well-being of others). To be sure, as will be maintained shortly, the possibility of the absence of an essential focus on the well-being of others by officials who act in accordance with Fuller's precepts is not sufficient for a refutation of Fuller's position. What also must be shown is that the prudential reasons for the officials' abiding by his precepts are not confined to the advantages of *appearing* to act morally.

adherence partakes of any moral orientation. Only inasmuch as the sheer normativity of those propositions is focused through their being connected to the
reasons for officials' acceptance of them, does the normativity have a moral or
prudential character (or a character compounded of morality and prudence).
Hence, if officials accept the Fullerian principles for purely prudential reasons,
the conformity of their regime to those principles does not endow the regime
with any moral orientation And thus the designation of those principles as law's
'inner morality' is inapt.

Might officials abide by Fuller's precepts for purely prudential reasons?
Plainly, there is a logical possibility that they could; but is there any more than a
bare possibility? Some commentators have submitted that a largely negative
answer is appropriate here. John Finnis, for example, has declared:

A tyranny devoted to pernicious ends has no self-sufficient *reason* to submit itself to the
discipline of operating consistently through the demanding processes of law, granted that
the rational point of such self-discipline is the very value of reciprocity, fairness, and
respect for persons which the tyrant, *ex hypothesi*, holds in contempt. . . . None of [the
three principal] types of tyranny can find in its objectives any rationale for adherence
(other than tactical and superficial) to the disciplines of legality. For such regimes are in
business for determinate results, not to help persons constitute them*selves* in community.[29]

Nigel Simmonds has expressed such a view even more pungently:

The fact is that compliance with the eight principles is logically consistent with the pursuit
of evil aims in very much the same way that armed robbery is logically consistent with a
scrupulous concern for paying one's debts. They are indeed logically consistent, but they
are very unlikely to be found together. An evil régime which is likely to meet opposition
from its subjects will not choose to operate through the rule of law. An evil régime that has
the massive support of its populace (say, because it persecutes only a small minority group)
may find it easier to comply with the eight principles; but even here such compliance
would be problematic.   (*Issues*, 123)

A slightly earlier passage from Simmonds's text proceeds along basically similar
lines: 'If social control is merely a matter of preventing widespread violence and
revolutionary dissent, it is unlikely that Fuller's eight principles will be a good
guide to the most effective techniques. A regime of terror where officials act
unpredictably or on the basis of secret directives is much more likely to succeed
in quelling opposition' (*Issues*, 119). Fuller himself took much the same view:
'Does Hart mean merely that it is possible, by stretching the imagination, to
conceive the case of an evil monarch who pursues the most iniquitous ends but at

---

[29]   John Finnis, above, n. 5, at 273–4 (emphasis in original). For some views that are more or less
similar, see George Breckenridge, above, n. 7, at 954, 960; Duff, 'Obligation', 75–7; J. W. Harris,
above, n. 16, at 132–3; Noel Reynolds, above, n. 19, at 12; Jeremy Waldron, 'The Rule of Law in
Contemporary Liberal Theory', 2 *Ratio Juris* 79, 93 (1989); Jeremy Waldron, above, n. 16, at 263–4.
For some views to the contrary, see George Anastaplo, 'Natural Right and the American Lawyer: An
Appreciation of Professor Fuller', 1965 *Wisconsin Law Review* 322, 331–2 (1965); Hart, 'Fuller',
351–3. More equivocal are Brian Bix, above, n. 16, at 83–4; Peter Nicholson, above, n. 6, at 321–2.

all times preserves a genuine respect for the principles of legality? If so, the observation seems out of place in a book that aims at bringing "the concept of law" into closer relation with life' (*Morality*, 154).

In short, Fuller and his supporters contend that officials who act for purely prudential reasons will be decidedly uninclined to adhere steadily to the eight Fullerian principles. Before we evaluate this contention, we should take note of Finnis's suggestion that any actual adherence to Fuller's principles by evil regimes will probably be 'tactical and superficial'. This suggestion alerts us to what must be shown for a refutation of Fuller's insistence on the moral character of his principles. Such a refutation will not succeed merely by demonstrating that evil regimes can have ample prudential grounds for electing to abide by the Fullerian precepts; what equally must be shown is that the conformity to those precepts is not perforce tied in any way to their putative moral significance. If the officials in an evil regime comply with Fuller's requirements solely because they want to avert the indignation of the populace by appearing to act morally, then, although their conduct is not morally worthy, it is tied to the perceived worthiness of the requirements. When one behaves in a certain way because one wishes to seem to be behaving solicitously, one thereby concedes that the mode of behavior in question is plausibly regarded as solicitous. Hypocrisy is the homage that vice pays to virtue. Hence, if officials adhere to Fuller's principles solely for the sake of appearing to take account of citizens' interests, their pattern of conduct will lend support to the characterization of those principles as morally pregnant— even though the conduct itself is purely prudential.[30]

To clarify this point, let us return briefly to the example of the smoker who renounces his habit. Suppose that a person $X$ has decided to act upon the proposition 'I ought to stop smoking'. If his only reason for abandoning the habit of smoking is the enhancement of his reputation by appearing to show solicitude for the interests of others, then his decision—though purely prudential—is a testament to the moral significance of the proposition on which he acts. In such circumstances, we are not justified in inferring (from the purely prudential character of his conduct) that the proposition 'I ought to stop smoking' has no intrinsic moral force. Indeed, if the only credible prudential ground for desisting from smoking were the desire for plaudits that has motivated $X$, we could safely conclude that the aforementioned proposition does partake of an inherent moral worthiness.

We know of course that there are numerous other prudential reasons that can prompt a decision to give up smoking; and thus we know that the proposition 'I ought to stop smoking' is not intrinsically moral. Can we say the same about officials' adherence to the Fullerian principles? Fuller and his defenders maintain that there is little more than a bare possibility that such adherence will occur for prudential reasons (except when it serves tactically to mollify

---

[30]  Cf. Daniel Brudney, above, n. 19, at 301.

the ethical indignation of the populace). To see why their position is unconvincing, we should keep in view a major role of law that has been stressed by
Fuller himself and by most of his supporters—the role of law in co-ordinating
social and economic and political life. The myriad activities of an evil regime
need to be co-ordinated and structured, at least as much as the myriad activities of a liberal-democratic regime. Officials have to direct and channel the
behavior of citizens, and they likewise have to co-ordinate their own multitudinous efforts.

Even if a regime is wicked, it will normally have to abide by the Fullerian
precepts quite perseveringly if it is to give effect to its wicked designs over the
long term. It will have to induce citizens to facilitate (grudgingly or willingly) the
accomplishment of its aims, and thus it will have to steer and constrain their
conduct in ways that are very likely to involve compliance with Fuller's requirements. We can best grasp the importance of those requirements if we first
consider their applicability on a small scale—an applicability that will obtain *a
fortiori* on the much larger and more complicated scale of a national regime.
Suppose that a group of gunmen have subjected a number of people to their
control. Although the gunmen might initially (and perhaps intermittently thereafter) deem it advisable to engage in the sorts of random violence to which
Simmonds adverts, they will not be able to direct their victims' behavior effectively unless they issue commands that accord with Fuller's principles to a
considerable extent. They undoubtedly will continue to inflict violence and will
impose harsh demands that serve only their own interests; but, if the violence
which they inflict is persistently random, and if the demands which they impose
are unintelligible or otherwise unfollowable, they will severely reduce the effica-
ciousness of their efforts to channel the behavior of their victims along the paths
which the gunmen themselves desire. While the followability of directives is a
moral desideratum for liberal democracies, it is a practical desideratum for evil
men who seek to accomplish their wicked objectives by ordering their victims to
act in certain ways and perform certain tasks. If the gunmen issue instructions that
are not very clear, for example, they will impede the rapid implementation of
those instructions. To get their wishes translated into actions (by their victims),
they need to express their wishes in followable behests. In other words, not only
is a striving for followability quite compatible with ruthless coerciveness; even
more important, the followability is essential for the effective steering of behavior that will bring about the nefarious ends which are being sought in a ruthlessly
coercive manner.

Fuller himself went a long way toward acknowledging these points when he
discussed managerial direction, which he contrasted with the rule of law
(*Morality*, 207–16). Having stated that managers direct the conduct of their
subordinates in order to advance the purposes which the managers lay down,
Fuller then readily granted that five of his eight principles are highly serviceable
for this one-way projection of power. He explained:

If the superior is to secure what he wants through the instrumentality of the subordinate he must, first of all, communicate his wishes, or 'promulgate' them by giving the subordinate a chance to know what they are. . . . His directives must also be reasonably clear, free from contradiction, possible of execution and not changed so often as to frustrate the efforts of the subordinate to act on them. Carelessness in these matters may seriously impair the 'efficacy' of the managerial enterprise.   (*Morality*, 208)

These comments by Fuller apply as well, *mutatis mutandis*, to the behests of officials in a wicked regime who view the members of the public as mere instruments (cognitively autonomous instruments) to be exploited and manipulated in furtherance of the regime's aims.

Somewhat strangely, Fuller contended that his other three requirements—generality, nonretroactivity, and congruence between formulated and implemented rules—are not straightforwardly applicable to the managerial setting (*Morality*, 208–9). Though his view on this point is exceedingly dubious, it need not be challenged here; instead, we should explore why those three remaining requirements are clearly applicable to an evil regime of governance. An investigation of this matter can perhaps most fruitfully proceed by highlighting some of the differences between the circumstances of a small group of gunmen and the circumstances of officials in a vile regime.

When gunmen gain dominion over a group of people, their ascendance is typically quite limited in space and time. They normally exercise their power over areas considerably less expansive than the territory of a state, and they themselves are usually far less numerous than a state's officials; furthermore, very often their power over any particular set of victims does not last much longer than (say) the duration of a bank robbery. Their instructions to their victims are thus typically situation-specific rather than general. They have no need to issue commands of broad applicability and extensive durability, since they can fully realize their purposes through behests that are much more narrowly focused. They likewise usually will have no cause to resort to retroactive dictates, because their dominion over any specific group of victims is normally so ephemeral. Similarly, the brevity of that dominion largely relieves the gunmen from having to concern themselves with preserving any long-term incentives for submission to their dictates. Thus, if they finish a robbery by shooting their compliant victims, they will very likely not have made their own future heists more difficult by reducing incentives for compliance with their orders. (Of course, if the gunmen's murderous actions are known to their next group of victims, the problem of diminished incentives will indeed emerge.)

On each of these counts, officials in a wicked government are positioned quite differently from the gunmen.[31] A legal system typically stretches over an expanse of territory on which occur myriad sets of circumstances, and the sway of the

---

[31] Of clear relevance throughout this portion of my present discussion is H. L. A. Hart, above, n. 8, at 20–4.

system typically lasts indefinitely (or, at any rate, for a period measured in years rather than in minutes). Hence, virtually any legal system, be it benign or heinous, must rely on general norms in addition to situation-specific directives. There are ample prudential grounds for the use of general norms; the costs of eschewing such norms, costs arising from the vast numbers of on-the-spot officials who would have to be hired to issue situation-specific imperatives, would be unbearably immense. (And in any event—in line with what I shall presently emphasize—the on-the-spot officials' actions would themselves have to be guided by general norms, or else a regime of governance would not be sufficiently co-ordinated to pursue any long-term objectives.) In short, because the sway of a government is typically quite extensive in its spatial and temporal scope, and because a government must therefore deal with a multitude of problems in a wide variety of circumstances, it must make use of general norms in its operations. Benevolent regimes have to effectuate their aims through such norms, but so do malevolent regimes—for purely prudential reasons.

In a like vein, the durability and expansiveness of a typical government's dominion create a strong likelihood that retroactive norms will occasionally be deemed advisable by wicked rulers. Although a despotic government is *ex hypothesi* untroubled by the need to correct or avert injustices, it indeed will endeavor to correct or avert developments that are inexpedient from its own perspective. From time to time, officials in an evil regime may well decide that a certain policy should be modified retrospectively as well as prospectively. An evil government will resort to such a device whenever the perceived advantages clearly outweigh the perceived disadvantages (which may include a possible reduction in the incentives for compliance with the government's dictates). Indeed, Fuller himself drew attention to a retroactive change carried out by one of the most monstrous of all regimes: the Soviet Union's retroactive introduction of the death penalty, during the early 1960s, for certain economic crimes (*Morality*, 202–3).

However, a despotic government will probably avoid the *frequent* enactment of retrospective laws. It will do so not because of any moral compunctions, but because of a need to sustain incentives for the heeding of its mandates. More broadly, there will usually be incentive-encouraging reasons for the despotic regime to maintain quite a strict congruence between its vile laws-as-promulgated and its vile laws-as-enforced. After all, if people often undergo punishment even when they have conformed closely to the prevailing legal norms, or if they often do not undergo any punishment even when they have plainly violated those norms, the inducements for them to abide by those norms will be markedly sapped. Fuller recognized this point straightforwardly: '[I]f the citizen knew in advance that in dealing with him government would pay no attention to its own declared rules, he would have little incentive himself to abide by them' (*Morality*, 217). Because systems of governance typically exist for long periods rather than for brief stretches of interaction, officials are well advised to promote lasting prudential incentives for law-abidingness. And given that such incentives are greatly impaired when the penalties imposed on people are largely unrelated to their compliance or noncompliance with applicable laws, a regime that wishes to advance its aims efficaciously will have solid prudential reasons for keeping a consistency between its laws-as-enacted and its laws-as-implemented. This point applies especially forcefully to evil regimes, which ofttimes cannot rely on any sense of moral commitment among citizens that might induce them to be law-abiding. Benevolent regimes, by contrast, are not so heavily dependent on the fostering of prudential incentives for conformity with their laws.

Of course, the sort of *unpredictable* terror mentioned by Simmonds may for a certain period be serviceable at the outset of a brutal regime, and it may likewise be serviceable if it is employed occasionally thenceforward (or if it is employed often but only against some narrowly defined group[s] of people). Furthermore, one scarcely should overlook the fact that some appalling regimes have indulged in such terror on a very wide scale for periods of months.[32] None the less, there will typically be ample prudential reasons for wicked rulers to govern in accordance with Fuller's precepts. Instead of departing frequently from those precepts, the rulers can normally further their own interests most effectively if they adhere to those formal precepts while laying down mandates that are substantively flagitious. Adherence to Fuller's principles is therefore devoid of *intrinsic* moral significance.

If we consider another way in which the circumstances of gunmen usually differ from the circumstances of officials in an evil government, we shall discern another major prudential reason for such officials to cleave to the Fullerian principles. Whereas a group of gunmen not belonging to an organized crime syndicate will probably amount to no more than a few people, a full-fledged legal system composed of legislative and administrative and judicial institutions may encompass thousands or even millions of officials. Unless there obtain numerous general norms to co-ordinate the operations of those officials, their operations will be spectacularly inefficient and perhaps impossible. And unless those norms are structured and implemented in accordance with Fuller's precepts to a large degree, they will not enable the necessary co-ordination. The relevant norms include not only the procedural rules and standards that pertain directly to the mechanisms of government, but also the substantive imperatives and prescriptions that are applied by officials to the doings of citizens. If the latter set of norms is grossly deficient in regard to Fuller's principles, then various official measures may be as disastrously unco-ordinated and erratic as they would be if procedural rules and standards were grossly defi-

---

[32] One of the most rebarbative examples is well described by Geoffrey Hosking: '[F]or the totality of the [Soviet] population 1936–8 was a nightmare, during which no one, save Stalin himself, could be certain of not being woken in the small hours of the night by a knock at the door, dragged out of bed and snatched away from family and friends, usually for ever. Since there was neither rhyme nor reason to the process, no one could be sure of not attracting the next accusation in the capricious chain' (*A History of the Soviet Union* [London: Fontana Press, 1985], 195–6).

cient. Unlike a small group of gunmen, then, the throngs of officials in a full-blown government are bound to be woefully at cross-purposes unless their actions are organized by a scheme of procedural and substantive norms. In the absence of such a scheme, a government will be staggeringly inefficient.[33]

In short, given that officials in a wicked regime must co-ordinate their own endeavors while they achieve their aims through the direction of citizens' behavior, and given that the co-ordination of their efforts will almost certainly involve a normative structure that fulfills the eight Fullerian requirements to a considerable extent, a steady adherence to those requirements can commend itself to monstrous regimes on purely prudential grounds. Such adherence and such requirements, accordingly, do not partake of any intrinsic moral significance. Evil officials can exhibit a genuine commitment to Fuller's precepts for self-interested reasons; and those self-interested reasons need not be parasitic on moral reasons (as would be true if the sole self-interested reason consisted in an effort to appear virtuous). Like the proposition 'I ought to stop smoking', the Fullerian principles are not in themselves morally pregnant. Their moral status varies with the circumstances in which they are operative.

## VII. A POSTSCRIPT: TWO ADDENDA

To bolster the argument that has just been presented, this chapter now briefly investigates a couple of lines of analysis propounded (respectively) by two of the most incisive writers on Fuller. The first of these lines of analysis, advanced by Ronald Dworkin in a critique of Fuller more than three decades ago, may seem to be a creditable alternative to my own distinction between prudential normativity and moral normativity; as will be contended, however, Dworkin's approach is unable to deal adequately with scenarios that can readily be handled by the approach adopted herein. We then shall ponder some remarks by R. A. Duff on the acceptance of norms. Contrary to what Duff suggests—and in line with what has been argued herein—officials can accept legal norms and Fuller's principles for purely prudential reasons.

1. Having expressed doubts about the moral character of Fuller's precepts, Dworkin then assumes *arguendo* that those precepts are indeed inherently moral. He goes on to draw a distinction between *complying* and *coinciding* with a moral principle. He expounds that distinction as follows:

This is not the place to attempt a full exposition of the circumstances under which behavior that *coincides with* a principle can be regarded as in compliance with it. Broadly,

---

[33] In one of the long passages quoted above, Nigel Simmonds may have had in mind the need for co-ordination of officials' actions; he submits that such actions might be based on 'secret directives' (*Issues*, 119). Insofar as Simmonds is implying that the regularization of a government's workings can occur through procedural and substantive norms that are promulgated only to officials, he is broaching a possibility that was explored in section II of this chapter.

however, such behavior does not constitute compliance with a moral principle when that principle would not, if offered, constitute a moral reason counting *in favor of* the behavior. When we report that a person has observed a moral principle, we make a moral *claim* about what he has done, although we do not necessarily claim—this depends on other factors—that he acted out of respect for the principle, or that he deserves any praise for having done it, or even (since *other* moral principles may count against his act) that he ought to have done it. ('Philosophy', 675, emphasis in original)

By bringing the compliance/coincidence distinction to bear on several tersely stated examples, Dworkin reveals that that distinction is plainly akin to my morality/prudence dichotomy. He indicates, for instance, that someone who keeps a promise out of fear of the promisee can be said to have complied with a moral principle in favor of promise-keeping. Under my approach, a fear-induced keeping of one's promise will usually (though not invariably) amount to a situation that bespeaks the moral significance of the promise-keeping principle. After all, the potential wrath of the promisee is usually in part a product of his or her sense that the promisor is morally obligated to fulfill the undertaking which has passed between them; hence, the promisor's prudential ground for abiding by his undertaking is an offshoot of a moral ground. In sum, just as the promisor's conduct falls on the compliance side of the compliance/coincidence division, it falls on the moral side of the morality/prudence dichotomy (not by being moral in itself but by being derivative of a moral principle).

Should we conclude, then, that Dworkin's distinction can suitably handle the same array of situations as my own distinction? Even with regard to some variants of the promissory scenario that has just been sketched, the answer has to be negative; when the promisor's prudential ground for keeping his promise is not parasitic on a moral ground, his conduct falls squarely on the prudential half of the morality/prudence divide. However, the appropriateness of a negative answer to the foregoing question will become still more manifest if we turn our attention to a different scenario. Consider, thus, a car thief who offers to return his stolen vehicles to their owners in exchange for ransom money. After having been paid for each car, he refrains from the pleasurable activity of wrecking it. He forbears from destruction not because he has any moral compunctions about such an enjoyable deed, and not because he wishes to appear morally enlightened in any way, but simply because he wants to maintain incentives for people to come up with ransom money in the future. If he ruins automobiles even after having been paid for their release, he may substantially reduce the likelihood that the owners of cars which he steals henceforth will part with cash for the return of their property. They may feel that, since their payments will prove unavailing, they ought not to waste their money on a futile purpose. Their prudential incentives to yield to the thief's behests will have dissipated. If the thief does provoke such reactions in the future by demolishing vehicles now, he will have acted against his own interests. Hence, purely in order to protect his interest in receiving future ransom payments, he preserves in good condition the cars which he has currently stolen; and he does so without presuming that he will appear virtuous at all.

How should we assess the thief's abstention from ruining the cars? My own approach leads us to the verdict that the thief has restrained himself for purely prudential reasons, which are not derivative of moral reasons. His behavior enables us to see that the proposition 'I ought not to destroy the property of some-one who accedes to my bidding' does not invariably partake of moral signifi-cance. Dworkin's approach, by contrast, leads us to the conclusion that the thief has *complied* with a moral principle against demolishing others' goods. After all, if we apply Dworkin's test, that principle does indeed constitute a moral reason counting in favor of the miscreant's decision to forbear from damaging the stolen vehicles. In sum, Dworkin's compliance/coincidence distinction is less service-able for highlighting the subtleties of practical reasoning than is my morality/prudence distinction.

2. In the course of an important essay that includes a sympathetic but critical discussion of Fuller, Duff seeks to explain what is involved in the acceptance of rules generally and of legal rules specifically ('Obligation', 68–73, 76–7, 79–87). He submits that someone who genuinely accepts a rule must grasp and endorse the values that are internal to it. For instance, someone who truly *accepts* a moral norm—instead of merely *following* it—must be morally committed thereto. A genuine acceptance of legal rules, then, must involve an endorsement of the values that are internal to such rules. Those values, Duff argues, center on the notion of the common good (which, he readily acknowledges, can be understood in many different ways). Ergo, somebody who accepts the norms of a legal system must view and commend them on the whole as serving the common weal.

Much of Duff's analysis is marred by some of the *faux pas*—especially the slippage between cognitive autonomy and moral/political autonomy—that have already been exposed in my critique of Fuller. However, Duff's account of the acceptance of rules deserves fresh attention here. We should initially notice a point which is not denied at all by Duff but which is not explicitly acknowledged by him, either. The values internal to various rules need not be moral values; and thus, even if we allow *arguendo* that one's acceptance of a rule entails one's endorsement of the values internal thereto, we need not allow that one's accep-tance is typically a posture of moral commitment. Numerous rules, such as rules of language and rules of games (especially solitary games), involve values that are plainly nonmoral. Suppose, for instance, that a person X is undertaking a cross-word puzzle. If X accepts the rules of the puzzle in order to enjoy the challenge which it poses, he has thereby endorsed the objective of intellectual stimulation which is internal to those rules—but he will hardly have thereby taken a moral stance. In short, being committed to rules on their own terms does not entail being morally committed to them. Acceptance does not necessarily occur as a moral commitment except when the values internal to rules are themselves morally pregnant.

Given that the sheer acceptance of rules (with a consequent endorsement of their values) is not in itself a moral posture, we have to ask about the ethical significance of specified types of rules before we can know whether one's acceptance of those rules is perforce fraught with such a significance. Throughout, Duff assumes that social practices such as etiquette and law consist of norms that cannot truly be accepted on prudential grounds. Though such norms might be *followed* by someone purely out of self-interest, a genuine *embrace* of them and of their intrinsic values is inevitably nonprudential. In regard to etiquette, for example, Duff declares: '[A]lthough the rules of etiquette (and of morality) can and do change, the values which are internal to these practices set logical constraints on the kinds of reason which can justify such changes, and exclude considerations of self-interest as inappropriate and irrelevant. But if convenience and profit are inappropriate as reasons for changing the rules of etiquette, they must equally be inappropriate as reasons for accepting those rules: a concern for etiquette is not a concern for ease or profit' ('Obligation', 71). He takes a similar position when discussing the nature of law: '[A]n acceptance of a legal system and its rules . . . requires an understanding of, and concern for, the values implicit in the law which is incompatible with a purely self-interested or habitual relationship to it' ('Obligation', 77). If Duff were correct on this point, then officials in any genuine legal system could not be moved by purely prudential considerations to embrace Fuller's precepts.

Let us examine first the status of etiquette. Duff does not maintain that the values internal to etiquette are moral values, but he insists that they are indeed nonprudential. He contends that a purely self-interested attitude toward the requirements of etiquette is 'defective by the standards of the practice itself' ('Obligation', 72). Such a contention exhibits an unalertness to the possibility of a full-blown system of etiquette established purely on the basis of self-interest. Consider the following scenario. A number of people meet regularly for meals, and each of them supports the implementation or continuation of a scheme of etiquette to further his own interest in being spared the disgustingness and disorder of the untrammeled boorishness of his fellows. Incentives for compliance with the scheme consist in the revulsion and ostracism—and perhaps even harsher reactions—that are provoked by transgressions. (The people who inflict such penalties are not burdened by so doing, because the penalties express natural impulses of aversion.) Hence, not only is the underlying justification for the scheme purely prudential, but the motivational reasons for each instance of compliance are likewise so.

Now, given that the concrete incentives for conformity as well as the basic rationale of such an arrangement are prudential, each person will have few reasons to forbear from committing transgressions that are unworrisome for their perpetrator because they are almost certain to go undetected by his or her fellows. (Of course, there will probably still be prudential reasons for abstaining from *some* such instances of coarse conduct. After all, a person might disgust herself if she were to act in a highly repellent manner. Besides, she may have tailored her conduct to the requirements of etiquette so often that she can satisfy some of those requirements with greater facility than she can violate them. Insofar as compliance becomes 'second nature', it is no longer a burden—a burden that has to be shouldered for the sake of avoiding other people's revulsion.) Let us suppose that each person does indeed engage in certain types of boorishness while no one else is looking, and that each conforms to the code of etiquette at virtually all other times. Is such a pattern of behavior inconsistent with a genuine acceptance of the rules of the code by everyone? To answer affirmatively would be to beg the question by presuming that rules of etiquette cannot be truly accepted on the basis of self-interest. Such an answer would complacently take for granted the very point that is here being impugned.

If both the fundamental justification for a scheme of etiquette and the immediate reasons for adherence thereto are wholly prudential, then the rules of the scheme and the values internal to those rules are likewise prudential. Thus, we scarcely should be surprised to discover that people who *accept* such a scheme will comply with its rules only to the extent that the compliance furthers their interests. By allowing their interests to determine the measure of their obedience, people are acting in accordance with the concerns—prudential concerns—that are internal to the rules. Indeed, if people did not focus on prudential considerations when deciding whether they should sometimes cease to abide by the requirements of etiquette (within the scheme postulated above), they would be departing from the internal significance of those requirements. To adhere faithfully to the fundamental tenor and values of those requirements, one's decisions about compliance with their terms must proceed as self-interested judgments.

Perhaps a defender of Duff would stipulate that no set of norms for the regulation of people's manners can count as a code of etiquette if its underlying rationale and its specific grounds for obedience are wholly prudential. But such a stipulation would be a sterile dogma that would go no way toward countering my sketch of just such a set of norms. In regulating people's manners, those norms perform the essential function of any scheme of etiquette; an effort by defenders of Duff to withhold the label of 'etiquette' from those norms would therefore be an *ad hoc* maneuver to shore up an unsound theory. Such a question-begging move would turn his position into a wooden fiat concerning the application of labels.

Let us now consider the acceptance of legal rules. *Officials'* acceptance of such rules is my focus here—chiefly because *officials'* acceptance of Fuller's principles has been my focus throughout this chapter, but also because a legal system can exist even if *citizens* merely abstain from breaking the law and do not genuinely accept its mandates.[34] That the underlying reasons for officials' acceptance of legal

---

[34] On this last-mentioned point, see H. L. A. Hart, above, n. 8, at 109–14. Duff, of course, does not concur with Hart's view on this point—because he feels that Hart's position cannot adequately distinguish between authority and sheer power, or between obligation and sheer coercion. In fact, however, legal positivism draws a straightforward distinction between those concepts, through a focus

norms can be purely prudential is a central theme of the present chapter. Hence, we only have to ask here about the *specific* incentives for officials' adherence to those norms (in a regime untouched by moral compunctions). Clearly, the principal incentives for their adherence will lie partly in the natural desire of each of them to promote the vibrancy of a system through which he or she occupies a privileged position, and partly in the desire of each to avoid the authoritative disapproval that is incurred by maverick officials who deviate from what is expected and required of them.[35] (Such disapproval may be expressed by officials within one branch of government or by officials among the different branches. It can range from mere criticism to much harsher measures.) In turn, the immediate incentives for each official's manifestation of disapproval will lie in two main sources: (1) natural and thoroughly self-interested feelings of irritation at any waywardness that threatens the smooth working of a system through which the officials enjoy their privileged statuses; and (2) each official's concern that a failure to express apposite disapproval will itself trigger disapproval from his fellow officials. Thus, not only can officials' acceptance of legal norms rest on a *general* basis that is unalloyedly prudential, but each official's evidencing of his acceptance—via conformity to the norms, censure of others' deviations, and acknowledgment of censure directed against his own deviations—can be based on *concrete* reasons that are likewise rooted purely in self-interest.

An analogy may help to illuminate this discussion.[36] Suppose that a cartel is set up, and that the members of the cartel make clear their unhappiness whenever

on prevailing norms. Because my next chapter will expatiate on this matter, only a few words are needed here.

If someone is legally obligated to act in a certain way, then she is required to do so *by a norm or set of norms* emanating from a legally determinative provenance. When the person is simply coerced to act in the specified way, by contrast, there is not any prevailing norm (derived from a legally determinative provenance) to which the coercion is a means of giving effect. Similarly, if someone acts with legal authority, then she is acting *under a norm or set of norms* (stemming from a legally determinative provenance) by which she is entitled to direct other people's behavior in certain ways. To be sure, the sundry norms of a legal system ultimately derive from its Rule of Recognition, of which the existence is a matter of fact. Within each system, nevertheless, the distinction between authority and stark power—and between obligation and stark coercion—is quite clear-cut.

Duff also goes astray in this area as a result of his conflation of prescriptions and imperatives. That conflation, which lies beyond the scope of the present discussion, will be assailed throughout my next chapter.

[35] As Gregory Kavka ingeniously showed in his discussion of 'perfect tyranny', the first of these two sources of incentives is dispensable; however, as he likewise stressed, a regime that draws support from only the second of these sources is bound to be unstable (Kavka, *Hobbesian Moral and Political Theory* [Princeton: Princeton University Press, 1986], 254–66). Cf. John Finnis, 'Comment', in Ruth Gavison (ed.), *Issues in Contemporary Legal Philosophy* (Oxford: Clarendon Press, 1987), 62, 68, 70; Rolf Sartorius, 'Positivism and the Foundations of Legal Authority', ibid. 43, 51–2.

[36] For earlier and more laconic versions of this analogy—an analogy which I shall discuss further in Ch. 8—see Matthew H. Kramer, 'The Rule of Misrecognition in the Hart of Jurisprudence', 8 *Oxford Journal of Legal Studies* 401, 426–7 n. 100 (1988); id., *Legal Theory, Political Theory, and Deconstruction* (Bloomington: Indiana University Press, 1991), 291 n. 54. For an example of the position which I am seeking here to refute, see Jeffrey Goldsworthy, 'The Self-Destruction of Legal Positivism', 10 *Oxford Journal of Legal Studies* 449, 458 (1990).

anyone departs from the terms on which they have agreed. On the one hand, their criticisms (and other punitive measures) might derive from moral wrath and might be articulated as moral censure. The participants in the cartel might feel that a recalcitrant member is flouting the Golden Rule in relation to themselves, and they might upbraid him for neglecting his moral duties to them. On the other hand, the criticisms might very likely derive from prudential considerations and might be expressed accordingly. The members of the cartel might worry that their arrangement will not function properly—and will indeed be in danger of breaking down completely—unless each of them persistently adheres to it. In that event, their criticisms of one another for any deviations from the requirements of their arrangement will focus on their shared interest in the sustainment of their cartel. Instead of reproaching an uncooperative member for behaving immorally, they will chide him for being foolish. The concerns that impel their remonstrations, as well as the terms of the remonstrations themselves, are prudential through and through. (Obviously, the point made in this paragraph about the cartel's members will apply not only to their censure of any breaches of the cartel's guidelines, but also—*mutatis mutandis*—to each member's normal sense of commitment to the guidelines. To be sure, each participant may believe that he should abide by the cartel's requirements in order to fulfill a moral duty which he owes to the other participants. More likely, however, is that each will abide by the requirements on the basis of prudential factors: i.e., because compliance is necessary if the highly profitable cartel is to be sustained, and because compliance is necessary if the wrath of one's fellow participants is to be avoided.)

Of course, the participants in a real cartel may be moved by some combination of moral and prudential considerations. Their collaboration need not be either purely moral or purely prudential in character. Once we turn our attention to legal systems, moreover, we find an even greater likelihood that the conduct of officials will be impelled by a mixture of prudential and moral factors. However, what has been shown herein is that officials' conduct *can* be purely prudential (in a stronger sense of 'can' than bare logical possibility). When the officials in a benevolent regime accept Fuller's principles along with the substantive norms of their regime, they are very likely doing so because they wish to treat citizens fairly (and presumably also for other reasons); but when the officials in a *wicked* regime accept the Fullerian principles along with the substantive norms of their regime, they may well be doing so only for prudential reasons. They can scrupulously adhere to those principles in order to effectuate more smoothly the evil designs which the substantive norms embody. An unfortunate blindness to the plausibility of this situation—a blindness to this situation of scrupulousness without scruples—is what Duff and Fuller have in common.

# 4

## Requirements, Reasons, and Raz:
## Legal Positivism and Legal Duties

During the last three decades, Joseph Raz has developed a number of important themes in jurisprudence and political philosophy. His work has branched out in many directions, but he continues to explore some of the central issues that have preoccupied him since his earliest major writings. The present chapter examines just one aspect of Raz's work, an aspect that is of special interest to anyone who seeks to defend legal positivism. Raz has argued that judges' statements of legal obligations—by dint of being such statements—are perforce statements of moral obligations as well. Even when a particular assertion declaring the existence of some legal duty is made by someone with no actual commitment to the moral bindingness of the duty, the assertion carries on its face the implication that the duty is indeed morally binding. When judges and other officials affirm propositions concerning legal obligations, they *ipso facto* affirm or appear to affirm propositions concerning moral obligations for compliance therewith.

Raz, then, maintains that the meaning of the word 'obligation' in legal contexts is inseparable from the meaning of that word in moral contexts. Such a position is not easily squared with legal positivism—even when allowance is made for uncommitted statements, erroneous statements, and insincere statements—and indeed this matter constituted one of the chief points of contention between Raz and his mentor H. L. A. Hart.[1] After a few preliminary remarks, the

---

[1] Hart presented his objections in his *Essays on Bentham* (Oxford: Clarendon Press, 1982) [*Bentham*], 153–61, 262–8; and in his *Essays in Jurisprudence and Philosophy* (Oxford: Clarendon Press, 1983) [*Jurisprudence*], 9–10. Hart was responding to the following three works by Raz: *Practical Reason and Norms* (London: Hutchinson Press, 1975) [PRN], 123–9, 146–8, 162–77; *The Authority of Law* (Oxford: Clarendon Press, 1979) [AL], 153–7; and *The Concept of a Legal System* (Oxford: Clarendon Press, 1980) (2nd edn.) [CLS], 234–8. (My own citations to PRN are to the second edition, published in 1990 by the Princeton University Press.) Raz has most directly responded to Hart in 'Hart on Moral Rights and Legal Duties', 4 *Oxford Journal of Legal Studies* 123, 129–31 (1984) ['Moral Rights']. For some secondary works that take largely or wholly favorable views of Raz's stance on this matter, see Steven Burton, 'Law as Practical Reason', 62 *Southern California Law Review* 747, 769–71 (1989); William Edmundson, 'Legitimate Authority Without Political Obligation', 17 *Law and Philosophy* 43, 44, 56–8, 60 (1998); J. D. Goldsworthy, 'Detmold's "The Unity of Law and Morality"', 12 *Monash University Law Review* 8, 17–18 (1986); Jeffrey Goldsworthy, 'The Self-Destruction of Legal Positivism', 10 *Oxford Journal of Legal Studies* 449, 453–60, 461–2 (1990) ['Self-Destruction']; Leslie Green, 'Law, Legitimacy, and Consent', 62 *Southern California Law Review* 795, 797–800 (1989); Andrei Marmor, *Interpretation and Legal Theory* (Oxford: Clarendon Press, 1992), 45–7; Michael Moore, 'Authority, Law, and Razian Reasons', 62 *Southern California Law Review* 827, 837–8, 840 (1989); Stephen Perry, 'Interpretation and Methodology in Legal Theory', in Andrei Marmor (ed.), *Law and Interpretation* (Oxford:

present chapter will begin by recounting the debate between Hart and Raz. We shall then consider in greater depth the line of argument to which Hart was responding; and we shall likewise examine some alternative lines of argument with which Raz has sought to support his position. On the whole, this chapter will side with Hart against Raz, albeit with some important modifications and amplifications of Hart's ripostes. As will be submitted, there are both similarities and differences between the meaning of 'obligation' in legal settings and the meaning of that term in moral settings. Though the similarities are far from unimportant, the differences are momentous.

This critique of Raz's stance will reject some of his specific claims and will impugn his account of legal pronouncements. Certain of his theses which are directly connected to that account will therefore also be challenged (at least implicitly and in part). However, most of Raz's theoretical framework is not in question here. Nothing in this chapter casts doubt on his overall model of practical reason or on his powerful arguments about the absence of a general obligation to obey the law, for example. My critique is an effort to resist the undue extension of his theoretical framework rather than to assail that framework itself.

Still, although many elements of Raz's thought go unquestioned here, the points actually at issue are of central importance to present-day legal philosophy. Specifically, the aim of this chapter is to resist any elaboration of Raz's ideas that would appear to close off the potential for a gap between statements of legal obligation and statements of moral obligation. Because the elimination of the potential for that gap would be devastating to legal positivism,[2] a challenge to Raz's conception of jural statements is essential for the task of defending an alternative to natural-law theory. Hence, by showing the tenability of the stance which

Clarendon Press, 1995), 97, 115–16, 126–8; Gerald Postema, 'The Normativity of Law', in Ruth Gavison (ed.), *Issues in Contemporary Legal Philosophy* (Oxford: Clarendon Press, 1987) ['Normativity'], 81, 88–93; Gerald Postema, 'Law's Autonomy and Public Practical Reason', in Robert George (ed.), *The Autonomy of Law* (Oxford: Clarendon Press, 1996) ['Autonomy'], 79, 84. For a much more wary treatment, see J. W. Harris, *Legal Philosophies* (London: Butterworths, 1997) (2nd edn.), 124–7.

Other works by Raz to which I refer in this chapter are 'The Morality of Obedience', 83 *Michigan Law Review* 732 (1985) ['Obedience']; 'The Purity of the Pure Theory', in Richard Tur and William Twining (eds), *Essays on Kelsen* (Oxford: Clarendon Press, 1986) ['Purity'], 79; *The Morality of Freedom* (Oxford: Clarendon Press, 1986) [MF]; *Ethics in the Public Domain* (Oxford: Clarendon Press, 1994) [EPD]; 'Intention in Interpretation', in Robert George (ed.), *The Autonomy of Law* (Oxford: Clarendon Press, 1996) ['Intention'], 249.

Lest there be some unclarity, I should note that the Razian thesis which I oppose in this chapter is a thesis about the meaning of any obligation-asserting legal statement. Like Raz, I focus on that question of meaning rather than on the sorts of conversational implicatures explored by H. P. Grice.

[2] Although I shall not here investigate the dire consequences of Raz's stance for legal positivism, I should mention that those consequences are explored in Goldsworthy, 'Self-Destruction', 473–8. While (in my view) Goldsworthy's argument stands in need of some modifications, it goes a long way toward showing that Raz gravely threatens his own version of legal positivism when he insists that statements of legal obligations are statements of moral obligations. (For some of the most explicit instances of Raz's insistence on this point, see AL, 37–9, 158–9.)

Raz purports to have refuted, this chapter seeks to reaffirm a positivist answer to questions about the nature of law.

Two preliminary caveats are advisable here. First, my critique of Raz does not attempt to demonstrate that a certain feature has to be present in every legal system. It tries to demonstrate, rather, that a certain feature does *not* have to be present in every legal system; in other words, I try to demonstrate that some legal systems can be marked by the absence of that feature. More precisely, there is no suggestion in this chapter that statements of legal obligations *cannot* be statements of moral obligations as well. Instead, all that is contended is that statements of the former sort are not *perforce* statements of the latter sort. To argue that legal norms can be stark imperatives (as opposed to prescriptions) is not to argue—in the manner of nineteenth-century jurisprudential positivism—that legal norms are *always* stark imperatives. Likewise, when this chapter submits that legal norms in themselves (in isolation from the sanctions attached to them) do not necessarily serve or profess to serve as reasons for compliance on the part of their addressees, it does not thereby submit that such norms in themselves can never serve or profess to serve as such reasons.

Second, a couple of points of terminology need to be clarified straightaway. (One or two further points of terminology will be clarified later.) Albeit Raz uses the term 'norm' in a manner connected with his overall account of practical reason, that term will be used more broadly here. It will cover not only general prescriptions (concerning how people *ought* to behave), but also general imperatives (concerning how people *must* behave). A norm is any general directive that lays down a standard with which conformity is required and against which people's conduct can be assessed. Never strictly confined to a single event or situation, and therefore always applicable or potentially applicable to similar events or situations, a norm can be formulated at varying degrees of generality. It can be a rule, a principle, a doctrine, a regulation, a broad decree, or some other sort of touchstone for guiding and appraising human conduct—conduct which the norm is designed to channel by rendering certain acts or omissions mandatory.

The last paragraph may seem to suggest that all norms are duty-imposing. On the one hand, given that this chapter mounts a critique of Raz's conception of legal obligations, the norms which establish legal duties do indeed receive most of my scrutiny herein. On the other hand, I certainly do not mean to imply that all legal norms are duty-imposing. Many such norms confer legal liberties, powers, or immunities—either instead of imposing legal duties or in addition to doing so. That such norms do not attract too much attention in this chapter is of course fully consistent with a recognition of their vital importance in numerous other contexts.

Finally, as the Preface to this book has stated, and as might be inferred from my pattern of usage so far in this chapter, the terms 'duty' and 'obligation' will be employed interchangeably throughout. Although some analytical purposes can render advisable the drawing of a distinction between those words, the arguments below do not require any such demarcation. What this chapter highlights is a distinction between two types of duties (and thus between two types of obligations) rather than between duties and obligations.

### I. RAZ *CONTRA* HART

H. L. A. Hart responded in the early 1980s to Raz's conception of officials' statements. While clearly in sympathy with many aspects of Raz's jurisprudence, Hart balked at the suggestion that 'obligation' carries the same meaning in legal and moral settings. He correctly maintained that Raz has reached such a conclusion through a reason-focused approach to legal and moral discourse. That approach proceeds along the following lines (summarized very tersely here). When jural officials declare that a legal norm requires people to act in a certain way, they are declaring that people ought to act in the specified way. Now, because every 'ought' statement in favor of a person $X$'s adopting a certain mode of conduct is logically equivalent to a statement asserting the existence of one or more reasons for $X$ to adopt that mode of conduct,[3] the pronouncements of legal officials explicitly or implicitly assert that people have reasons to act in the ways that are specified by the prevailing laws. Statements of legal obligations are statements implicitly or explicitly affirming the existence of reasons for people to engage in the acts which the obligations require or to eschew the acts which the obligations forbid. Those reasons must be interest-independent, since the obligations themselves are interest-independent; that is, because legal duties frequently require individuals to act against their own interests and preferred objectives, the reasons-for-action presented by those duties must be independent of those interests and objectives. If legal duties consisted only in prudential reasons-for-action—reasons essentially tied to the interests of the people for whom they are reasons—then they could not amount to the sorts of requirements which legal duties very often are. (Of course, the laws that establish duties typically back them up with sanctions of various sorts. The avoidance of such sanctions will almost always be a prudential reason for complying with those laws. But the focus here is on the requirements of the laws themselves in isolation from the penalties that are attached to them. We are inquiring into the fundamental tenor of statements that invoke legal norms in their own right; we are not inquiring into the tenor of statements that concern the punishments inflicted when the demands of legal norms go unfulfilled.) Thus, statements of legal duties are statements of interest-independent reasons for people to behave in accordance with the terms of the duties. In short, such statements expressly or

---

[3] Of course, *mutatis mutandis*, a parallel point is true of 'ought' statements *against* the adoption of a certain mode of conduct by $X$. For Raz's most sustained discussion of the logical equivalence between 'ought' statements and reason-asserting statements, see PRN, 29–32. I fully agree with Raz on this matter, as should be evident from Matthew Kramer, *In the Realm of Legal and Moral Philosophy* (Basingstoke: Macmillan, 1999), ch. 10.

implicitly assert *moral* reasons for people to conduct themselves in particular ways.[4]

In response to this ostensible demonstration of the moral tenor of legal pronouncements, Hart was willing to accept *arguendo* Raz's overall account of moral reasoning. However, he dissented from the notion that legal decision-making is relevantly similar to such reasoning. He retorted as follows:

I find little reason to accept . . . a cognitive interpretation of legal duty in terms of objective reasons or the identity of meaning of 'obligation' in legal and moral contexts which this would secure. Far better adapted to the legal case is a different, non-cognitive theory of duty according to which committed statements asserting that others have a duty do not refer to actions which they have a categorical reason to do but, as the etymology of "duty" and indeed 'ought' suggests, such statements refer to actions which are due from or owed by the subjects having the duty, in the sense that they may be properly demanded or exacted from them. On this footing, to say that an individual has a legal obligation to act in a certain way is to say that such action may be properly demanded or extracted from him according to legal rules or principles regulating such demands. (Hart, *Bentham*, 159–60)

As Hart made clear when expanding on these remarks, judges can and often do maintain that particular laws impose moral obligations. He contended merely that such a stance (or the pretense of such a stance) is far from unavoidable for judges and other officials: 'I have only argued that when judges or others make committed statements of legal obligation it is not the case that they must necessarily believe or pretend to believe that they are referring to a species of moral obligation' (*Bentham*, 161).

Raz has replied to Hart by underscoring afresh the soundness of the reason-focused perspective on legal duties. Because statements asserting that each person ought to do φ are logically equivalent to statements asserting that each person has

---

[4] This Razian argument rests on the assumption that interest-independent reasons are always moral reasons, which are thus contrasted with prudential reasons. Raz has sometimes suggested that certain commitments cannot be properly described as either moral or prudential, and that they likewise cannot be properly described as both moral *and* prudential. For an account of friendship along these lines, see AL, 253–6. Cf. MF, 33. Other scholars have appeared to take the view that certain institutional and social duties are neither moral nor prudential. See e.g. Steven Burton, above, n. 1, at 770.

My own position on this question is supportive of the analysis—the analysis of obligation-asserting legal statements—which I am attributing to Raz (and which I shall shortly oppugn, on other grounds). In my view, morality and prudence exhaust the realm of reasons. Other commitments and considerations, such as familial and institutional requirements, can be classified as moral or prudential or both moral and prudential. Numerous though the varieties of moral reasons and prudential reasons and moral/prudential reasons are, they do not make up additional basic categories. (A contrary position leads to exceedingly odd consequences. For example, Steven Burton seems [ibid.] to have committed one or both of two missteps. On the one hand, he appears to saddle Hart with a cognitive approach to statements asserting legal duties, notwithstanding Hart's own repeated characterizations of his approach as non-cognitive. On the other hand, Burton appears to conflate the reasons-for-action of legal officials [the law's addressors] with the reasons-for-action of ordinary citizens [the law's addressees]. However, I should mention that Burton later quite clearly avoids the second of these missteps; see ibid. 774.)

one or more reasons to do φ, such statements must pertain to moral considerations or to considerations of each addressee's interests. An addressor's interests cannot themselves support pronouncements concerning how other people ought to act. A person *X* cannot correctly say that you ought to adopt a certain mode of conduct simply because it will be in his interest; in order to sustain his prescription, *X* will additionally have to claim that you have a moral responsibility to promote his interests, or that your welfare is linked to his own. Thus, given that officials' pronouncements concerning legal duties are pronouncements concerning how people ought to behave, and given that those pronouncements therefore affirm that people have reasons to behave in the prescribed ways, and given that the requirements of legal duties are interest-independent, the reasons-for-action affirmed by official pronouncements must be moral reasons. Raz observes that Hart sought to escape this conclusion by denying the step in the argument where statements of legal duties are deemed to be statements of reasons-for-action. Raz rejoins: 'This sudden Kelsenian twist to Hart's view of legal duties implies that duty-imposing laws are instructions (or perhaps merely permissions) to courts to apply sanctions or remedies against people who are guilty of breach of duty. Hart himself feels uncomfortable with the conclusion he has reached . . . as well he might. For if he is right then it follows either that it is not wrong to fail to fulfil one's duty or that acting wrongly is not something one has a reason not to do' ('Moral Rights', 131). Having advanced this riposte, Raz recapitulates his well-known views about law's claim to moral authoritativeness: 'The decisive argument concerning the meaning of statements of legal duties is that the law claims for itself moral force. No system is a system of law unless it includes a claim of legitimacy, of moral authority. That means that it claims that legal requirements are morally binding, that is that legal obligations are real (moral) obligations arising out of the law' ('Moral Rights', 131).

II. THE DEBATE JOINED

In the discussions below, we shall look further at the Hart/Raz dispute and especially at certain strands of Raz's rejoinder. Henceforth, however, this chapter joins the debate instead of merely recounting it. As will become apparent, the debate hinges on the question whether obligation-asserting legal statements must present themselves as reason-asserting statements. We shall be considering the chief lines of argument which Raz has adduced in favor of his position. This chapter begins its critical scrutiny by probing the set of theses on which Hart concentrated his attack; most of Raz's other arguments are variously designed to bolster that set of theses.

## A. From Prescriptions to Imperatives

Let us first briefly note that, even if norms were inevitably prescriptive and therefore even if statements invoking norms were inevitably statements of prescriptions,

Raz's conception of legal obligations would stand in need of some modifications. To be sure, prescriptions (i.e., practical 'ought' judgments) do set forth or presuppose reasons-for-action, be they moral or prudential. Hence, to address someone with a practical 'ought' judgment is indeed to contend—perhaps falsely or insincerely—that the person has either a moral reason or a prudential reason for behaving as the judgment prescribes. However, the requirements of legal norms are not necessarily interest-independent for each individual; and thus the inherently prescriptive tenor of those norms would not perforce consist in their laying down or presupposing (or appearing to lay down or presuppose) *moral* reasons-for-action. Statements of legal duties would not perforce be, or purport to be, statements of moral duties. After all, officials can establish some legal mandates that are aimed nonderivatively at promoting the interests of each person to whom the mandates are addressed. In that event, the reasons-for-action presented by those mandates are prudential rather than moral.

In short, even when the prescriptive tenor of legal mandates goes unquestioned, Raz's conception of statements which assert legal obligations is not invulnerable. Raz has not shown that *all* such statements would affirm or presuppose moral reasons-for-action. He has shown only that *many* such statements would do so; other obligation-asserting statements could affirm or presuppose prudential reasons-for-action. Still, we are well advised not to make too much of this point. Although some prescriptive obligation-asserting statements would set forth prudential reasons-for-action, those statements would be expressive of moral concern (i.e., nonprudential concern) on the part of officials. When a regime lays down mandates that are essentially directed at advancing the interests of every citizen, the statements invoking those mandates convey the sort of concern which a parent exhibits when ordering his or her children not to go near the street. Thus, if all obligation-asserting statements were prescriptive, they either would express moral reasons-for-action or would express moral solicitude. In either case, that is, legal statements would be moral statements. Hart was quite correct, then, in thinking that a defense of jurisprudential positivism necessitates a partial rejection of Raz's reason-focused analysis of legal norms.

Instead of following Hart in his reference to the etymology of 'ought', however, we should shift our attention to an altogether different auxiliary—the auxiliary 'must'. Whereas Raz regards legal norms as intrinsically prescriptive, they are in fact only contingently so. Some such norms are imperatives rather than prescriptions; their requirements are 'must' demands rather than 'ought' judgments.[5] Unlike practical 'ought' judgments, the 'must' demands of imperatives do not necessarily lay down or presuppose reasons-for-action for their *addressees*

---

[5] I have clearly benefited from reading D. N. MacCormick, 'Legal Obligation and the Imperative Fallacy', in A. W. B. Simpson (ed.), *Oxford Essays in Jurisprudence* (Second Series) (Oxford: Clarendon Press, 1973) [MacCormick, 'Legal Obligation'], 100. However, a number of my specific analyses are very different from those of MacCormick, and in some respects my general aims are the opposite of his.

(though the *addressors* of such demands undoubtedly have reasons for issuing them).

Before exploring the prescription/imperative distinction in greater depth, we should return for a moment to the question of the meaning of 'obligation' in moral and legal contexts. In one important respect, the meaning of that word remains constant when we move from the realm of morality to the realm of legality. That is, both in the phrase 'moral obligation' and in the phrase 'legal obligation', the word denotes a requirement imposed by a norm or set of norms. However, we discover a crucial shift in the word's meaning when we ascertain the nature of the norms which impose the requirements; the requirements of moral norms are always prescriptions that constitute reasons-for-action for their addressees, whereas the requirements of legal norms can be stark imperatives that do not in themselves (i.e., in isolation from attached penalties) constitute such reasons-for-action. We have encountered a shift or potential shift from the sway of 'ought' to the sway of 'must'.

Now, in the ordinary sense of 'imperative', some imperatives are of course themselves moral injunctions.[6] 'Thou shalt not kill', for example, is both an imperative and a moral prescription. Throughout this chapter, however, the word 'imperative' will be used more narrowly to indicate only those general commands that are not morally pregnant. As understood here, imperatives in themselves (i.e., in isolation from any sanctions) do not perforce lay down or presuppose reasons for their addressees to act in accordance with their terms. By definition they do not set forth or presuppose moral reasons, and—given that many imperatives require actions which are not in the interests of their addressees—they do not necessarily set forth or presuppose prudential reasons.

Of course, some imperatives require actions that are promotive of their addressees' interests. An older brother might command a younger brother: 'Shut the door, I'm cold!' If the younger brother is also cold, then he has a prudential reason (apart from the avoidance of a beating) to do as his older sibling has instructed him. Other imperatives, however, are not promotive of their addressees' interests. When a gunman commands his victim to hand over her money, her only prudential reason for doing so is to avoid being shot. In isolation from the gunman's threat, the handing over of money is not something which the victim has a reason to do. Thus, although imperatives can be in harmony with their addressees' interests, they can likewise be at odds therewith.

The interest-independence of imperatives stems from the fact that they are products of the overwhelming superiority—the actual superiority or the presumed superiority—of the addressors over the addressees. Because of this overwhelming superiority, the addressors of imperatives will themselves frequently have no

---

[6] Indeed, Stuart Hampshire has contended that all especially strong moral prohibitions are best formulated as 'must' demands. See Stuart Hampshire, *Two Theories of Morality* (Oxford: Oxford University Press, 1977), 16–17.

prudential reasons to cater to the interests of the addressees, and will be able to disregard any moral reasons for solicitude. Their dictates will therefore be only contingently promotive of the addressees' objectives and projects. In what does the overwhelming superiority consist? Within a discussion of law, of course, the factor that should be singled out is coercive might; for the most part, this chapter will take for granted that such a factor lies behind legal imperatives. But, even given that any overwhelming superiority based on moral worthiness is excluded from consideration here (because of my deliberately narrow conception of imperatives), we should note that factors other than overpowering strength can loom large in some contexts. For example, an exceptionally beautiful woman may so captivate her admirers that she enjoys over them the sort of superiority which impels them to do her bidding. (In Turgenev's great short story 'First Love', for instance, the protagonist unhesitatingly jumps off a high wall in obedience to a behest from the young woman who has infatuated him.) Much the same can be true of an exceptionally handsome man or an exceptionally skillful athlete.

Neil MacCormick has pertinently captured the basic structure of the overwhelming superiority that underlies effective interest-independent imperatives: '*A* has . . . power to, and is prepared to, inflict undesired harm on *B* without present risk of equal or similarly undesirable retaliation; there is at least some range of acts which *B* is prepared to do, however unwillingly, in order to avoid suffering the harm which *A* can inflict; and *A* and *B* both know all this, or at least suppose it to be the case' ('Legal Obligation', 106–7). An imperative is thus 'an utterance which the speaker intends his addressee to take as expressing a will that the addressee do some act in recognition of the speaker's superiority' ('Legal Obligation', 108). (Although typically the person issuing the imperative will harbor an actual intention of the sort which MacCormick describes, 'it is sufficient if *A* knows, or ought to realize, or thinks it likely that *B* will take him to have the relevant intention' ['Legal Obligation', 105 n. 11].)

As has been remarked in passing, the overwhelming superiority that serves as the basis for imperatives can be putative rather than actual. A person *X* can quite intelligibly issue a command to other people even if he enjoys no actual superiority over them. Though *X* is presumptuous in such circumstances, his dictate is not meaningless. Still, unless the others are deluded about *X*'s actual position, or unless his command happens to be in harmony with what they perceive as their interests, they will almost certainly not put his directive into effect. Actual superiority, rather than purported superiority, is prerequisite to the general efficacy of interest-independent commands. (Of course, if the addressees of *X*'s presumptuous command are submissive because they are deluded about his position, then *X* enjoys an actual superiority over them—albeit a superiority based on their misconceptions rather than on any factor which *X* has explicitly or implicitly invoked.)

Before re-examining Raz's conception of legal duties in light of this discussion of imperatives, we should ponder one more feature of the imperative/prescription distinction. Clearly, the surface form or mood of a statement is not always decisive in regard to the imperative or prescriptive tenor of the requirement which the statement articulates. Many sentences with imperative forms—for instance, many warnings such as 'Look out for the sliding rocks!'—will in most circumstances have the semantic content of prescriptions. Conversely, some sentences with prescriptive forms may be used as deliberately understated ways of articulating imperatives. Thus, although 'ought' is normally the auxiliary of prescriptions and 'must' is normally the auxiliary of imperatives, and although the surface form of a statement will often be a reliable indicator of its prescriptive or imperative tenor, the key to the prescription/imperative distinction lies not in the grammatical mood but in the kind of requirement which a statement expresses. If a requirement is grounded in morality or essentially in the interests of the addressee, then the formulation expressing it is a prescription; contrariwise, if a requirement is grounded not in morality and not essentially in the interests of the addressee but essentially or exclusively in the interests of the addressor, then the formulation expressing it is an imperative.

Let us return now to Raz's reason-focused conception of legal obligations. His chief argument involves the claim that duty-imposing legal norms prescribe certain interest-independent patterns of behavior to individuals, and that the norms therefore lay down or presuppose (or appear to lay down or presuppose) interest-independent reasons for the individuals to act in the specified ways. Statements invoking legal duties are therefore statements actually or ostensibly invoking interest-independent reasons-for-action—which means that they are statements actually or ostensibly invoking moral reasons-for-action. So runs the gist of Raz's argument. The premise which will be denied here is that legal norms are always actually or putatively prescriptive; though such norms can indeed be prescriptions, they can likewise be stark imperatives (in my sense of 'imperatives'). Legal obligations, which are the requirements established by duty-imposing legal norms, can be grounded essentially or exclusively in the interests of the officials who issue and apply the norms. In such circumstances, the addressees of the norms have no moral reasons and no prudential reasons (i.e., no punishment-unrelated prudential reasons) to behave in accordance with the norms' requirements.

As was explained a moment ago, we cannot tell whether legal norms are imperatives or prescriptions by looking merely at the grammar or vocabulary of their formulations. (Worthy of a passing remark, however, is the fact that—especially in statutes—the imperative auxiliaries 'shall' and 'must' get employed frequently.) Nor can we determine whether legal requirements are prescriptions or imperatives by asking if they are commonly designated as 'obligations'. After all, the very matter in question here is whether a term such as 'obligation' or 'duty' carries the same meaning in legal and moral contexts. As has already been submitted, each of those terms does bear a uniform meaning across moral and legal contexts in that it denotes a requirement imposed by the applicable norms.

Whether the uniformity extends further, however, is exactly the point of contention which this chapter seeks to address. Raz maintains that the uniformity does extend further because the tenor of statements which assert legal duties is perforce prescriptive in much the same way as the tenor of statements which assert moral duties. He has attempted to shore up his position with some sophisticated arguments which we shall explore presently. For now, we need only note that one cannot sustain Raz's view by simply pointing to legal officials' use of deontic terms such as 'obligation' and 'duty'. Any such terminological observation would patently beg the question.

Instead of focusing on superficial matters of terminology or grammar, we must inquire about the role of legal norms in the reasoning of their addressors and their addressees. Let us take another look at the key sentence from Raz's rejoinder to Hart: 'For if [Hart] is right then it follows either that it is not wrong to fail to fulfil one's duty or that acting wrongly is not something one has a reason not to do' ('Moral Rights', 131). In fact, Hart's position does not entail either of these disjuncts as Raz formulates them, though it does entail a suitably modified version of the first disjunct. A defender of Hart need not and should not maintain that a failure to fulfill one's legal duty is never morally wrong. Hart plainly did not oblige himself to deny that there can be circumstances wherein the fulfillment of one's legal duty is morally obligatory. All that the Hartian analyst should insist is that a failure to fulfill one's legal duty can in various other circumstances be morally permissible (i.e., 'not wrong') and can be regarded as morally permissible even by someone who perceives the legal duty as a legal duty.

In the preceding paragraph I have assumed that Raz wields the terms 'wrong' and 'wrongly' to refer to *moral* unacceptability. If instead he has used those terms to refer to strictly *legal* unacceptability, then Hart's position entails a suitably modified version of Raz's second disjunct. Acting in violation of the requirements of legal norms can be something which a person has no reason—i.e., no punishment-unrelated reason—to forbear from doing. Consider the country of Despotia, where the governmental officials sustain their own lavish lifestyles by imposing legal obligations on the citizens to pay crushingly heavy taxes. Perhaps the payment of taxes up to some modest level is morally obligatory for each Despotian citizen; but the payment of extortionate taxes beyond that level is neither morally obligatory nor promotive of any citizen's interests. Thus, apart from considerations of staving off the infliction of penalties, each citizen in Despotia has no reason to forbear from committing the legal wrong of disregarding his or her duty to contribute to the public revenues above a certain level.

Supporters of Raz would presumably respond by contending that the Despotian officials cannot assert both that the citizens are under legal obligations to pay extravagant levels of taxes and that the citizens have no moral reasons to pay. Officials cannot affirm that legal norms which impose legal duties are stark imperatives. Now, unless this posited response is no more than a flagrant begging of the question, it has to derive from lines of argument which we have not yet probed. After all, this chapter has hitherto confronted only one main Razian argument—the argument that officials who invoke legal duties are perforce implicitly or explicitly invoking interest-independent reasons-for-action. Serious doubts about that argument have emerged. In countries like Despotia, some of the norms which establish legal requirements are imperatives rather than prescriptions. That is, in isolation from penalties, those norms do not constitute or reflect any reasons for their addressees to abide by the requirements which the norms ordain. Moreover, the Despotian officials do not mince words when they invoke the directives which they enforce. Their assertions of those directives amount to variations on a circular theme: 'You [the addressees] must do these things because the prevailing norms enjoin you to do them.' Thus, since the requirements imposed by the Despotian regime will be characterized by officials and other people as legal duties, the pronouncements that affirm legal duties in such circumstances do not necessarily advert or profess to advert to any moral reasons-for-action. Instead, those pronouncements in those circumstances can invoke demands as sheer demands. If Raz aims to expose the inconceivability or untenability of this pattern of official discourse, he will have to offer arguments beyond those which we have already plumbed. He has indeed propounded such arguments, to which we now turn.

## B. Justification or Motivation

Among the ways in which Raz has sought to defend his stance is his pointing to the justificatory tenor of the statements whereby officials invoke legal obligations. When legal officials (especially judges) have to resolve disputes between people, and similarly when officials have to decide whether or not people should be punished for behaving in certain ways, they explain their decisions by reference to the legal duties which the relevant people have borne. These explanations of official decisions are not purely informational or theoretical; rather, they are practical and justificatory, in that they attempt to show that the mechanisms of governmental coercion—which implement the officials' determinations—are being applied in a morally legitimate fashion. Because judges and other officials have to reach decisions that significantly impinge on people's lives and well-being, they cannot purport to be involved in an innocuous activity (such as the making of jigsaw puzzles) that stands in little or no need of justification. They have to present their determinations as morally legitimate and indeed as morally obligatory, in order to vindicate the far-reaching effects of those determinations on other people. Precisely for this justificatory purpose they cite relevant legal duties as the bases for their holdings. By contending that their holdings give effect to those duties, the officials establish or appear to establish the morality of what they have done. Yet this apparent conferral of moral authority rests on a supposition that the legal duties themselves are morally pregnant; unless the duties are deemed to be morally binding, the mere fact that decisions give effect to them will not be seen as carrying any moral significance. Hence, given that judges and other officials explain their decisions in order to justify them, and given that their explanations refer centrally to legal duties, the officials must actually or ostensibly regard the duties as moral obligations.

If the argument just outlined were successful, then the reason-focused approach to statements of legal obligations would quite clearly be sound. As Raz observes: 'While one can accept the law as a guide for one's own behaviour for reasons of one's own personal preferences or of self-interest one cannot adduce one's preferences or one's self-interest by themselves as a *justification* for holding that other people must, or have a duty to, act in a certain way' ('Purity', 92–3, emphasis added). Gerald Postema develops this point:

[Defenders of Raz's position] argue that it is a necessary feature of law that it claims authority over officials and citizens, and that it plays an important role in the justifications of decisions and actions offered by official[s] and citizens. For this to be true, they argue, self-identified participants in legal practice must believe that legal norms, regarded separately or collectively as a system, have some sort of moral justification—that the separate and special practical significance of legal norms is rooted in broader moral aims and values served by them, or by the system of norms of which they are a part. ('Autonomy', 84, footnotes omitted)

Here as elsewhere, of course, Raz avoids the mistake of confusing a claim-to-legitimacy with legitimacy itself. Though (according to him) a judge or any other official necessarily portrays legal obligations as morally significant by dint of invoking them in order to justify decisions, the portrayals and the justifications may often be inaccurate. Raz's view of statements of legal obligations is quite wisely concerned with the tenor of such statements rather than with their truthfulness. None the less, his appeal to the justificatory role of official discourse cannot withstand scrutiny—because it fails to apply to the very regimes wherein legal duties are most frequently and straightforwardly the products of imperatives.

As should be plain from my third chapter, the officials in an evil regime might not concern themselves with morally justifying their decisions when they pass judgments on a variety of issues. They might instead be preoccupied with reinforcing incentives for compliance with their regime's wicked laws. The officials may well explain their heinous decisions by reference to people's legal obligations, but their purpose in doing so will not necessarily be to demonstrate the decisions' moral warrantedness; rather, their purpose might be to make clear that violations of applicable legal requirements will indeed trigger punishments and that punishments are not inflicted on anyone who abstains from such violations. In emphasizing the connection between the breaching of duties and the incurring of penalties, the officials need not be motivated by a desire to establish that their rulings are fair. They may simply want to sustain people's incentives for conformity to the law's evil demands. After all, if the imposition of punishments is seen as bearing very little relation to the legal culpability or innocence of each person—in other words, if there is a widespread perception that sanctions are often levied against people who have behaved as the law requires, or if there is a widespread perception that sanctions are frequently not levied against people who have failed to fulfill the law's demands—then the inclination of the law's addressees to abide by its requirements will dwindle. If people presume that they will often undergo penalties notwithstanding the lawfulness of their conduct, or if they presume that they will often escape penalties notwithstanding the *un*lawfulness of their conduct, then a crucial motivation for their adherence to the terms of wicked laws will have been undercut. Thus, faced with the task of providing strong inducements for people to behave in accordance with the prevailing legal norms, the officials who administer those norms in a malevolent regime are well advised to explain their decisions by reference to citizens' legal duties. Highlighting the correlation between nonfulfillment-of-duty and subjection-to-punishment is the means of promoting a pattern of incentives that will secure the efficacious functioning of a scheme of imperatives.

Hence, even if we allow that publicly accessible explanations of official decisions are an integral feature of anything that counts as a full-fledged legal system, we should recognize that the explanations need not be presented as moral justifications. Both the actual purpose and the avowed purpose of the explanations can consist in the reinforcement of incentives for submission to evil dictates, rather than in the ascription of fairness to the decisions that apply those dictates. Of course, even within a monstrous legal regime, there is nothing inevitable about an eschewal of moral justifications; the people who run such a regime may well attempt to clothe their decisions in the garb of fairness, even while they also endeavor in a sterner fashion to foster appropriate motivations for compliance with their commands (along the lines described in my last paragraph). Slim is the likelihood, indeed, that every official will invariably forgo the ideological advantages of moral justifications. Much more likely is that at least some officials will explain at least some of their decisions in ways that serve to engender an appearance of fairness. Nevertheless, the pursuit of such an appearance is a matter of political shrewdness rather than of conceptual necessity. Nothing rules out the mode of official explanation that was sketched in my last paragraph—i.e., official explanation as the stark reinforcement of incentives for law-abiding behavior, with no pretensions to moral worthiness. Officials certainly *can* opt to account for their decisions in that nonjustificatory spirit, and at least some officials in wicked legal systems very likely *do* account for many of their decisions in such a manner. At any rate, whether or not the official statements of legal obligations in monstrous regimes are frequently marked by an absence of moral pretensions (and by an unembellished focus on the shoring up of proper incentives for citizens to obey the law), the very fact that those statements *can* quite intelligibly be free of such pretensions is sufficient to dispel the notion that officials who explain their judgments through references to legal duties are perforce thereby announcing moral duties. Instead of implicitly or expressly characterizing legal norms as moral prescriptions, officials can be striving to ensure the efficacy of such norms as imperatives.[7]

## C. Raw Evil and Legal Evil

My response to the argument about moral justification may seem to run aground on another line of argument which Raz has advanced. Like many other jurisprudential theorists,[8] he has suggested that a denial of the ineluctably moral tenor of legal discourse is tantamount to a denial of the distinction between law and the brute coercion of gangsters. This suggestion recurrently surfaces in his writings. In *The Authority of Law*, for example, he proclaims: 'A person needs more than power (as influence) to have *de facto* authority. He must either claim that he has

---

[7] Correctly observing that Hart's jurisprudential method consists in elaborating the central or standard case of a legal system, Jeffrey Goldsworthy has maintained that 'a small ruling caste oppressing, with no claim of right, a larger helot caste, is a borderline case [of a legal system]'. He accordingly asserts that anyone who portrays the claim-to-moral-authority as an inessential feature of law has thereby 'mistake[n] one of Hart's secondary interests (the classification of borderline cases) for his primary interest in elucidating the inter-relationships between law, coercion and morality in the central case. To focus on very unusual and extreme borderline cases in analysing those inter-relationships must lead to distortion' ('Self-Destruction', 459). This argument misconstrues the upshot of Hart's method. Hart characterized the central or standard case of a legal system as an institutional structure consisting in a combination of primary and secondary norms (including norms of recognition, change, adjudication, and punishment). Borderline cases—such as international law or the law of primitive tribal communities—are societal or intersocietal arrangements which exhibit some but not all of the attributes of the central case. At no point did Hart suggest that a claim-to-moral-authority is an integral feature of the central case of a legal system. On the contrary, while certainly accepting that any standard legal regime involves authoritativeness, he declined to accept that such a regime must present itself as *morally* authoritative. Hence, a regime which does not so present itself but which does consist in a full-fledged combination of primary and secondary norms will not be a borderline case at all within Hart's model; instead, it will be one instance of the central case. For the jurisprudential positivist, a regime of the sort which I have described is clearly a legal system, notwithstanding that it is equally clearly a wicked legal system.

Pertinent here is Hart's rejection of John Finnis's insistence on treating moral commitment as an integral element in the central or focal case of the internal perspective of officials. See Hart, *Jurisprudence*, 11–12. (For Finnis's view, which I shall discuss in my eighth chapter, see John Finnis, *Natural Law and Natural Rights* [Oxford: Clarendon Press, 1980], 13–16, 234–7; John Finnis, 'Comment', in Ruth Gavison [ed.], *Issues in Contemporary Legal Philosophy* [Oxford: Clarendon Press, 1987], 62, 67–9.) Though Hart did not explicitly extend his remarks to deal with claims-to-moral-authoritativeness along with moral commitment itself, such an extension is very much in keeping with the tenor of his riposte.

[8] See e.g. Robert Alexy, 'On Necessary Relations Between Law and Morality', 2 *Ratio Juris* 167, 176–7 (1989); Andrei Marmor, above, n. 1, at 114; E. Philip Soper, 'Legal Theory and the Obligation of a Judge: The Hart/Dworkin Dispute', in Marshall Cohen (ed.), *Ronald Dworkin and Contemporary Jurisprudence* (London: Duckworth, 1984), 3, 22; Philip Soper, *A Theory of Law* (Cambridge, Mass.: Harvard University Press, 1984), 55–6, 117–25 *et passim*. Cf. Trevor Allan, 'Citizenship and Obligation: Civil Disobedience and Civil Dissent', 55 *Cambridge Law Journal* 89, 96–7 (1996); Michael Detmold, *The Unity of Law and Morality* (London: Routledge & Kegan Paul, 1984), 56–60, 158–9; Ronald Dworkin, *Taking Rights Seriously* (Cambridge, Mass.: Harvard University Press, 1978), 18–20. When focused on moral authority rather than only on a claim thereto, this position goes back to Cicero and Augustine.

legitimate authority or be held by others to have legitimate authority. There is an important difference, for example, between the brute use of force to get one's way and the same done with a claim of right. Only the latter can qualify as an effective or *de facto* authority' (AL, 9). A similar declaration occurs later in the same book: '[T]he law—unlike the threats of the highwayman—claims to itself legitimacy. The law presents itself as justified and demands not only the obedience but the allegiance of its subjects' (AL, 158). Much the same view appears in *The Morality of Freedom*:

Nor do I doubt that all political authorities must and do resort to extensive use of and reliance on coercive and other threats. Yet it is clear that all legal authorities do much more. They claim to impose duties and to confer rights. Courts of Law find offenders and violators guilty or liable for wrongdoing.

None of these and similar claims has much to do with threatening people. To threaten is not to impose a duty, nor is it to claim that one does. None of this shows that legal authorities have a right to rule, which implies an obligation to obey. But it reminds us of the familiar fact that they claim such a right, i.e. they are *de facto* authorities because they claim a right to rule as well as because they succeed in establishing and maintaining their rule. (MF, 26)

Raz sounds the same theme at several junctures in *Ethics in the Public Domain*. For instance, he contends:

[T]hough [an] alleged authoritative instruction may be wrongly conceived and misguided, it must represent the judgment of the alleged authority on the reasons which apply to its subjects, or at least it must be presented as the authority's judgment. Otherwise it cannot be an authoritative instruction. It fails not because it is a bad instruction, but because it is not an instruction of the right kind. It may be an instruction given for some other occasion, or in jest, or an order or threat of a gangster who cares for and considers only his own good. Strictly speaking, to be capable of being authoritative a directive or a rule has actually to express its author's view on what its subjects should do. (EPD, 203)

In a similar vein is the assertion that '[t]he significance of [the law's claim to authority] is . . . in its distinctive moral aspect, which brings special considerations to bear on the determination of a correct moral attitude to authoritative institutions. This is a point missed . . . by those who regard the law as a gunman situation writ large' (EPD, 221). Raz again adopts this stance in the following passage: 'By normal usage mere *de facto* authorities, authorities who rule over their subjects but do not have a right to rule, are included among authorities. Many have seen this as proof that an authority cannot be distinguished from a gunman by reference to a right to rule, for both may lack it. This is a *non sequitur*. While both may lack it, *de facto* authorities are characterized by their claim to have it. . . . [I]t is the claim of legitimacy that is a condition of the possession of *de facto* authority' (EPD, 341 n. 2).

In all of these passages, to be sure, Raz has carefully avoided conflating the claim-to-moral-authority with moral authority itself. He acknowledges and indeed emphasizes the potential for a gap between what is professed and what is actual. None the less, he has erred in repeatedly insisting that an evil legal regime must claim to be morally authoritative if it is to qualify as a legal regime at all (by dint of being distinguishable from the nakedly coercive sway of a gunman). A claim-to-moral-authoritativeness is extrinsic, for the decisive difference between law and raw coercion lies not in any such claim but in the sway of norms. Whereas the ascendance of a gunman over his victims typically involves situation-specific orders rather than any general decrees or standards, a regime of law must involve the reign and application of general norms if it is to be properly classifiable as a regime of law.

To explore this thesis further, we should first glancingly note the distinction between the interaction of officials among themselves and the interaction of officials with ordinary citizens. Within a legal system, the first sort of interaction unavoidably includes 'ought' judgments.[9] When officials address one another in the course of assessing and co-ordinating their respective decisions, they inevitably issue prescriptions (sometimes in combination with imperatives, handed down from a regime's upper echelons to its lower echelons). However, even when the prescriptions are delivered as reproaches, they are not necessarily moral in their tenor. That is, any criticisms and exhortations addressed by officials to one another can be explicitly based on the interests of the officials to whom the criticisms and exhortations are directed—as well as on the interests of the officials from whom the criticisms and exhortations emanate. In other words, the tenor of the normative interaction among officials can be starkly prudential rather than moral.[10] I shall not develop or substantiate this point here, partly because I have argued for it at length in Chapter 3, and partly because my focus in this chapter lies on the interaction between officials and ordinary citizens.

Very different from the interaction of officials among themselves is the interaction between officials and citizens. Intercourse of the former kind, as has just been remarked, inevitably includes prescriptions (although the prescriptions can

[9]   Even within the 'perfect tyranny' brilliantly expounded by Gregory Kavka (whose analysis is cited above, Ch. 3 n. 35), prescriptions will inevitably be issued by officials to one another—from the bottom up, or among officials of equal status, or sometimes even from the top down. (I should observe, incidentally, that Raz several times commits a misstep that has been exposed as such by Kavka's discussion of perfect tyranny. See e.g. 'Obedience', 736–7; AL, 28–9, 158.)

[10]   For some failures to recognize this point, see 'Intention', 261; EPD, 207; Goldsworthy, 'Self-Destruction', 458; Neil MacCormick, 'Natural Law and the Separation of Law and Morals', in Robert George (ed.), *Natural Law Theory* (Oxford: Clarendon Press, 1992) ['Natural Law'], 105, 114; Gerald Postema, 'Coordination and Convention at the Foundations of Law', 11 *Journal of Legal Studies* 165, 197–200 (1982); Postema, 'Normativity', 97–8, 99; Philip Soper, 'Law's Normative Claims', in Robert George (ed.), *The Autonomy of Law* (Oxford: Clarendon Press, 1996) ['Normative Claims'], 215, 218–20. (This point is overlooked even in Jules Coleman, 'On the Relationship Between Law and Morality', 2 *Ratio Juris* 66, 71–2 [1989]. Coleman denies that the normative interaction among officials necessarily involves duties of critical morality, but he presumes that it does perforce involve duties of conventional morality.) The importance of the prudence/morality distinction tends to be submerged by Raz when he defines 'morality' so broadly as 'to include binding normative considerations of any kind' (EPD, 254).

be mixed with imperatives and can be strictly prudential). By contrast, the relationship between officials and citizens can be one of stark imperatives and obedience. Both the prevailing legal norms and the applications of those norms can lay down requirements that are neither morally obligatory nor in the interests of the norms' addressees. In such circumstances, the only reason for each citizen to comply with the norms is a fear of punishment; the norms in themselves, considered apart from the sanctions attached to them, do not present people with any reasons for compliance.

How, then, does a wicked regime that issues stark imperatives to citizens differ from a gunman who issues orders to his victims? Like the gunman, after all, the officials in such a regime make demands that are solely in their own interests. As has already been suggested, the key difference pertains to the means by which the demands are articulated and imposed. Here we return to a topic investigated in Chapter 3, from a slightly different angle. Whereas a gunman almost always issues his orders to a highly limited set of people for a highly limited stretch of time, a system of governance that counts as a full-fledged legal regime will have imposed its requirements through various sorts of norms (statutes, regulations, general decrees, judicial principles, and so forth) that typically apply to indefinitely numerous people for long periods of time. Those norms together cover a far, far wider range of behavior than do the usual instructions of a gunman.

Legal norms are nearly always designed to steer the behavior of citizens along certain paths, and they serve as the touchstones for specific decisions by officials concerning alleged violations of the norms' requirements. To be sure, a gunman also seeks to direct the behavior of his victims, and he probably tends to base his treatment of them on their conformance or nonconformance with his behests. But (as has just been mentioned) the gunman's direction of his victims' behavior is typically much more limited in its scope and much less systematic or regularized in its occurrence. The dictates uttered during a heist by a gunman are narrowly focused on certain specific instances of conduct to be undertaken by a small group of people who are temporarily in proximity with him; moreover, those dictates are hardly ever intended to be applicable to the victims after the brief period during which the heist is carried out. Laws, by contrast, extend to general classes of people and to general modes of conduct, and they typically last for long periods (often for indefinitely long periods). All or most laws have the general applicability and standing durability of norms. A gunman's instructions, on the other hand, are almost always occasion-specific through and through, and are thus devoid of some of the indispensable qualities—the generality and the durability—of norms.

Furthermore, because the formulation and implementation of the gunman's orders are far less systematic than the formulation and implementation of legal norms, the likelihood of a close correspondence between the stage of formulation and the stage of implementation is considerably greater in a legal system than in a heist. Unless a gunman intends to prey on future victims who will probably recognize him and who will know about his treatment of his current victims, he may well elect to shoot his current victims despite their having submitted to his bidding and despite his having suggested that he would let them go in the event of such submission. *Ex hypothesi*, he does not have to worry about impairing the incentives for his future victims to submit. A legal regime, even a monstrous legal regime, is quite different. As we earlier observed, officials have to be concerned about the effects of their current actions on the motivations of people in the future. If a legal system is known to depart frequently from the terms of its own norms by punishing lawful conduct or by conniving at *un*lawfulness, then citizens' incentives for compliance with the norms will greatly diminish. Hence, given that wicked rulers will doubtless want their malevolent laws to operate effectively, they will have good grounds for insisting that the laws be enforced in accordance with the terms thereof. A policy of strict enforcement is what best sustains incentives for obedience. Thus, law's continuousness helps to ensure its regularity—which means that one distinctive feature of law (i.e., one feature that differentiates legal norms from a gunman's commands) helps to ensure the existence of another indispensable feature.

Of course, an organized-crime syndicate such as the Mafia might well exert control over most aspects of life in a certain region, with dictates that are just as broadly applicable and lasting as the mandates of a veritable legal system. Moreover, for reasons similar to those recounted in the last paragraph, the Mafia's enforcers could seek to shore up incentives for obedience by giving effect to their organization's decrees in ways that adhere closely to the decrees' terms. Suppose that such an organized-crime regime—characterized by generality, durability, and regularity—does in fact prevail in some region alongside a more benign system of governance. Are we forced to conclude that the gangsters are legal officials who formulate and implement laws? And are we therefore forced to conclude that two conflicting legal systems reign over a single portion of territory?

This chapter is not the place for a long discussion of the degree of efficacy that must be achieved by a scheme of governance before it is properly classifiable as the legal system that obtains in a particular area. Suffice it to say that the relatively benign regime mentioned in my last paragraph (henceforth labeled as 'Regime *R*') must enjoy very little efficacy in the region where the organized-crime syndicate has attained wide-ranging control over people's lives. What is of crucial importance here is not whether the syndicate should be designated as a legal regime—a question that would oblige us to ponder the matter of efficacy—but whether such a designation should be withheld simply because the syndicate does not lay claim to moral worthiness. As this chapter has contended, a claim to moral legitimacy or authoritativeness is not a decisive factor; instead, the key factors are the generality and durability of the Mafia's norms, and the institutional regularity of the application of those norms.[11] If the Mafia's system of exerting far-reaching control over people's lives does indeed very substantially partake of the key qualities just listed, and if it also meets some relevant test for efficacy (whatever that test might be), then it ought to be classified as a legal system. Or, at any rate, the appropriateness of such a classification should not be denied merely because the Mafia's officials make no pretensions to moral admirability. In other words, we should view the respective positions of Regime *R* and the Mafia in much the same way that we would view the positions of competing factions within a country where a unified legal system has disintegrated (perhaps Yugoslavia or Somalia during the early 1990s, for instance). If each faction establishes its ascendance in its own regions by regulating all arenas of life via a matrix of norms that exhibits the indispensable characteristics of generality, durability, and regularity, then the question whether one or another faction operates the legal system in some particular stretch of territory is largely or entirely a question about the efficacy of the faction's sway therein. The absence of a claim to moral authority or legitimacy by the functionaries on either side is not determinative.

Though the notion of an organized-crime syndicate as a legal regime may initially seem outlandish, the strangeness of the notion derives chiefly from the unlikelihood that such a syndicate will indeed establish a system of social control that exhibits the essential features of law. Gangsters do not usually rule over virtually all aspects of social and individual life in a given region; and, even if they do manage to gain comprehensive control, they are likely to retain such power for too brief a period to develop a full-blown legal regime with its formal and institutional characteristics. Gangsters *qua* gangsters are in violation of the laws of an existent legal system, and are therefore bound to face considerable difficulties if they try to establish a legal system of their own that holds sway over numerous people other than the gangsters themselves. However, in the event that those difficulties are overcome by a criminal syndicate that exerts a comprehensive reign over the populace of some territory via norms that are general and durable and regularly applied, the evil reign of the syndicate should be designated as a legal regime irrespective of its being accompanied or unaccompanied by a claim-to-moral-worthiness. (Note, incidentally, that, even when gangsters do not rule over the public at large, they might well institute a system of norms to regulate the

---

[11]   These factors are, of course, three of Lon Fuller's eight main conditions for the existence of a legal system; the other five of Fuller's conditions would typically be satisfied even by a gunman's situation-specific orders. Also relevant, naturally, is the breadth of the range of issues to which the Mafia's norms pertain. Unless those norms encompass most aspects of human life, they do not together constitute a full-blown legal system. (Here and elsewhere, of course, I am not suggesting that a full-blown legal system must closely monitor and minutely regulate all or most spheres of human interaction. The comprehensive or nearly comprehensive reach of such a system can consist in the sort of regulatory control established by a laissez-faire regime that secures the workings of free markets through the elaboration and implementation of private-law norms. On the importance of such regulatory control, see Matthew Kramer, above, n. 3, at ch. 7.)

sundry relations and interactions among themselves. Their intra-group matrix of norms might well partake of the exhaustiveness, generality, durability, and regularity that are the hallmarks of law. Still, the question whether such a scheme of regulation should be classified as a legal system is not a question which I alone have to face. After all, the scheme of regulation internal to a criminal syndicate—as opposed to the scheme of regulation imposed by the syndicate on others—will probably in some instances involve claims to moral legitimacy.)

Now, readers of H. L. A. Hart's work will have recognized the qualities that have been singled out here as distinctive of legal systems. When reconstructing (and then criticizing) John Austin's theory of law, Hart readily acknowledged that Austin's model of the legal sovereign as a gunman-writ-large did not overlook all the differences between legal norms and a gunman's dictates.[12] Austin fully grasped that legal norms are general, in that they typically apply to general classes of persons and pertain to general types of conduct. He also was well aware that legal norms have a lasting or durable force, which differentiates them from the ephemerally operative orders of a gunman. He furthermore highlighted the importance of regularity in the application of the law, by which he meant specifically the likelihood that sanctions would be inflicted in response to violations of the law's commands. Austin's views on the supremacy and independence of the legal sovereign, moreover, are very roughly akin to my thesis that the regulatory sway of a full-fledged legal system must encompass most aspects of life (even if that regulatory sway is not actively exercised in regard to some aspects). In these significant respects, the analysis in the present section of this chapter resembles Austin's approach to law. Does a response to Raz, then, necessitate a return to Austin—and a return to the many shortcomings in Austin's jurisprudence?

Quite plainly, there are some Austinian elements in my attempt to distinguish wicked legal systems from naked coercion. But the discussion here has in fact remained as warily distant from Austin's account as did Hart himself. Not much has been said here about the nature of the legal sovereign, and certainly nothing has been said that would constitute an endorsement of Austin's portrayal of the sovereign. Even more important, I have introduced a few key caveats in order to disown some of Austin's worst missteps. For example, a warning near the outset of this chapter stressed that my focus on duty-imposing norms is not to be taken as an indication that other sorts of norms—norms which confer liberties, powers, or immunities—are perceived here as unimportant or derivative. My concentration on one type of norm simply reflects the fact that my target in this chapter is

---

[12] See H. L. A. Hart, *The Concept of Law* (Oxford: Clarendon Press, 1961) [*Concept*], 20–5. For Austin's own exposition, see John Austin, *The Province of Jurisprudence Determined* (Cambridge: Cambridge University Press, 1995) (Wilfrid Rumble ed.), 25–9. The position actually taken by Austin in regard to law's generality was slightly different from the position which Hart ascribed to him. However, the basic similarity between the actual position and the attributed position is evident in the following pronouncement: 'Most of the laws established by political superiors are, therefore, *general* in a twofold manner: as enjoining or forbidding generally acts of kinds or sorts; and as binding the whole community, or, at least, whole classes of its members' (ibid. 29, emphasis in original).

a conception of legal obligations (or of statements asserting legal obligations). Unlike Austin, the discussion here does not presume that the realm of law is exhausted by the norms which impose such obligations.

Similarly, Austin's own conception of obligations has certainly not received approval in this chapter. When a theory defines 'legal obligation' by reference to the likelihood of one's undergoing punishment for a failure to abide by a legal mandate, the account becomes susceptible to all the objections posed by Hart against Bentham and Austin (*Bentham*, 131–6; *Concept*, 81–3, 86–8). By contrast, my conception of obligations as requirements imposed by legal norms—requirements which may be imperative or prescriptive in their tenor—is Hartian rather than Austinian. Time and again, indeed, this chapter has emphasized that it is inquiring into the nature of obligations in isolation from the penalties that are appurtenant to them.

To exist as a functional regime of law, a legal system has to give effect to a large proportion of its norms on most relevant occasions; but virtually any such system will include some norms that are not very often enforced when violated. Whereas an Austinian theorist must submit that no legal obligations are imposed by norms that are seldom implemented, my approach to this matter enables us to see that those norms do indeed impose such obligations (albeit largely uneffectuated obligations).[13] Like the myriad legal obligations that are regularly given effect, the relatively few obligations that infrequently or never get enforced are established directly or indirectly by general precepts. Those precepts can abide as such, regardless of the extent to which they are implemented. Hence—given my conception of legal obligations—even a regime of stark imperatives will always leave open the potential for situations where having legal obligations to perform $\phi$ does not involve any likelihood of being obliged to perform $\phi$. A complete failure to acknowledge any such situations is one of the trademarks of Austinianism.

What is equally significant, this chapter has explicitly (albeit briefly) taken into account the foremost variety of discourse which Austin neglected—the prescriptive discourse of officials who are addressing one another. (My preceding chapter has of course sustainedly highlighted that prescriptive discourse.) Like Hobbes, Austin too often wrote about legal/governmental institutions as if each overall matrix of such institutions were a monolith. An anthropomorphic view of a legal system as an overarching person is bound to obscure the vital role of exhortative and argumentative exchanges among the people who operate the system. Hart's comments on jurisprudential personifications of legal systems are highly pertinent:

---

[13] Obligations can be uneffectuated either because they are left unenforced (although they are enforceable), or because they are unenforceable. In the former situation, a power-of-enforcement exists but is largely or wholly unwielded; in the latter situation, no power-of-enforcement exists. My present discussion does not need to distinguish between these two possibilities.

[W]e can push out of sight the whole official side to law and forgo the description of the use of rules made in legislation and adjudication, and instead, think of the whole official world as one person (the 'sovereign') issuing orders, through various agents or mouth-pieces, which are habitually obeyed by the citizen. But this is either no more than a convenient shorthand for complex facts which still await description, or a disastrously confusing piece of mythology.   (*Concept*, 110)

In the present section of this chapter, the distinction between statements addressed by officials to one another and statements addressed by officials to citizens is crucial. As has been contended, that distinction marks the divide between a domain in which prescriptive statements are inevitable and a domain in which officials' directives can be pure imperatives. By collapsing the former domain into the latter, and by neglecting to explore the character of officials' interchanges with one another, Austin did indeed largely obfuscate the immensely important role of prescriptive assertions in the application of legal norms by officials. This chapter has not committed a similar mistake.

A final point of distinction between my approach and that of Austin is closely related to what has just been said. For Austin, legal sovereignty and thus legal authority consisted in laying down orders backed by threats of overwhelming force, in being habitually obeyed, and in habitually obeying no one. The conception of authority operative in this chapter is much more complicated, for it eschews the disastrously confusing view of the state as a single man writ large. Legal authority is in part the legally recognized power (and liberty) to change or create or effectu-ate the entitlements which the law confers; and it is in part the legally enforceable right to the obedience of the law's addressees. My description of the general norma-tive power as 'legally recognized' is meant to cover two points.[14] First, the effects of the power are taken into account by officials when they assess one another's actions with reference to the prevailing norms. That is, the touchstones which offi-cials invoke for gauging the correctness or incorrectness of their fellow officials' decisions will adjust in response to appropriate exercises of norm-creating or norm-altering prerogatives, which in turn are ultimately dependent on the general author-itative power of the system in which they operate. Second, the effects of the exercising of such prerogatives are likewise taken into account by officials when they pass judgment on the activities and disputes of citizens. Whether the norms on which the officials rely are imperatives or prescriptions (in regard to the citizens whose actions are judged), the applicability of those norms as the relevant bases for assessing people's behavior is determined by the norm-creating and norm-modify-ing and norm-implementing prerogatives of officials—which, again, are ultimately dependent on the general authoritative power of the officials' regime.

---

[14]  Whenever I refer to a power in this discussion, I am referring to a normative power—a norm-based capacity to change or introduce or implement norms—rather than to a physical or other non-normative power. (I should also mention that I have used the term 'right' in a morally neutral sense; I employ that term to refer to the legal protection bestowed upon one person by the imposition of a legal duty upon another. Such protection may or may not be morally estimable, in any particular situation.)

When legal authority is so understood (in a manner that departs significantly from Austin), we can safely say that the law does necessarily claim authority in its workings.[15] *Pace* Raz, however, the claim to authority is not perforce a claim to moral authority. My account of authority squares perfectly well with a legal system in which the following two conditions obtain: (1) the discourse among officials is starkly prudential, in that the criticisms and justifications exchanged by officials in connection with their decisions are based overtly on the need to maintain the smoothly co-ordinated functioning of a system from which every official derives benefits; and (2) the norms invoked as the relevant standards for judging the conduct of citizens are sheer imperatives, and are invoked only to reinforce incentives-for-compliance rather than to establish the fairness of the decisions that apply the norms. In other words, my account of authority squares perfectly well with a legal system which not only lacks moral worthiness but which makes no pretensions to such worthiness. An absence of moral pretensions is of course not a necessary feature of legal systems, and is undoubtedly an extremely uncommon feature. But there are no conceptual impediments to the existence of a legal regime that is marked by just such an absence.

A legal system that does indeed lay down substantive norms which are sheer imperatives (and which are presented as such) will still be a fundamentally norm-structured regime. Its sway therefore differs crucially from the raw violence of a highwayman with his situation-specific orders. To some extent, the notable dissimilarities between the imperative-issuing regime and the highwayman reflect the dissimilarities between an Austinian sovereign and a highwayman; one should not forget that Austin's model of law included the indispensable features of generality, durability, and—in a somewhat distorted form—regularity. In addition, however, the differences between a legal system that enacts stark imperatives and a gunman who utters his orders are reflective of the differences between Austin's conception of law and my own conception. Most of the shortcomings in Austin's model are due to his insufficient attentiveness to the normativity of law. For example, as has been mentioned, his theory largely obscures the inevitable and prominent role of prescriptions in the criticisms and justifications and exhortations that are addressed by officials to one another. Once these weaknesses of Austin's jurisprudence have been removed, the divergences between a wicked legal regime (brimming with imperatives) and a gunman become all the more apparent.

## D. Feeling Good about Oneself

Raz has occasionally pursued a different tack in support of his view concerning the moral tenor of statements which assert legal obligations. Here we need to

---

[15] At the same time, one should not overlook the fact that the law's demands for conformity with its requirements are of differing degrees of intensity. For an illuminating discussion, see Kent Greenawalt, *Conflicts of Law and Morality* (Oxford: Clarendon Press, 1987), ch. 2.

distinguish between two aspects of moral authority: moral legitimacy or propriety and moral bindingness. (The terminology here is mine, not Raz's.) A legal norm is morally *legitimate* insofar as it does not require or authorize conduct that violates anyone's moral rights. A legal norm is morally *binding* insofar as its addressees are morally obligated to comply with its requirements or to acquiesce in what it authorizes.

If a directive is legitimate, then the formulation and implementation of it do not involve the commission of any moral wrongs. To maintain that officials have set forth a morally legitimate norm is to maintain that they were morally at liberty to engage in such a course of action. If a directive is binding, then the formulation and implementation of it impose obligations on the people who are subject to it. To maintain that officials have set forth a morally binding norm is to maintain that its addressees are not morally at liberty to disregard its demands.

Having separated these two aspects of moral authority, we can see that Raz has concerned himself chiefly with the second aspect when propounding his notion of law's claim-to-authority. Most of the time, his thesis about law's moral pretensions is a thesis about the law's claim to be morally binding. In his view, statements asserting legal obligations are statements which assert or profess to assert moral *obligations*. Occasionally, however, Raz appears to take a different and somewhat milder approach by emphasizing the first aspect of moral authority—the aspect of moral permissibility—rather than the second.

This different emphasis is most clearly present (though not indisputably so) in two quite recent works. In *Ethics in the Public Domain*, Raz declares:

I am taking it to be a necessary truth . . . that whatever people do they do because they believe it to be good or valuable, however misguided and even reckless their beliefs may be. Given that the courts are manned by people who will act only in ways they perceive to be valuable, principles of adjudication will not be viable, will not be followed by the courts, unless they can reasonably be thought to be morally acceptable, even though the thought may be misguided.   (EPD, 317–18, footnote omitted)

In a footnote to the first sentence of this quotation, Raz adds: 'Even *akratic* actions are undertaken because of the good perceived in them. They are *akratic* because the agent believes that on balance it is against reason to engage in them, not because they are done for no reason at all' (EPD, 317 n. 11). (He does then acknowledge that 'the principle is overstated in the text and has to be modified to allow for pathological cases', but he remarks that '[t]his . . . need not detain us here' [EPD, 317 n. 11].) A similar view surfaces in a recent essay by Raz on legal interpretation. There he contends that, 'barring *akrasia*, [any deliberate human act] is done in the belief that the act is not against reason' ('Intention', 262).

These quoted passages are by no means entirely clear-cut. Perhaps Raz is not distinguishing between the permissibility and the bindingness of authoritative decisions, and perhaps he regards his comments in these extracts as encompassing both of those aspects of such decisions. Still, to some extent the extracts do appear to presuppose such a distinction—with a focus on the side of permissibility. If so, then Raz has aligned himself with Philip Soper, who has argued in some of his recent work that the essential claim of any legal system is 'that the State does no wrong (is not morally culpable) in acting on (enforcing) the norms which, in good faith, it believes are necessary to govern society.'[16]

Soper has abandoned his former conviction that legal officials inevitably profess to hold a moral right to citizens' obedience; he now distinguishes the claim-to-bindingness from the claim-to-legitimacy, and submits that only the latter claim is an intrinsic feature of law. His principal argument in support of his current position begins by pointing out that the officials who put the law into effect are thereby performing acts which affect the basic interests of other people. Soper declares that 'a morally conscientious agent will commit such acts only in the belief that they are justified. Only if one thought that the law did not purport to be a morally conscientious agent (if it purported, for example, to be no more than a "gunman writ large") could one fail to see that the practice of law belongs in the same category of other social practices that claim to be morally defensible' ('Normative Claims', 219). Soper explains his reasoning, which he takes to be uncontroversial:

The insight that underlies this observation is, of course, not peculiar to law: governments do not enact 'Administration of Injustice Acts', but neither do parents announce 'Unjust Demands for Bedtime' or friends or neighbours proffer 'Silly Advice for Improving your Garden'. The point is simply the truism about human behaviour that conscientious people (unless they are engaging in some odd joke of the Monty Python sort) do not offer advice, much less issue demands or take action that affects others, unless they implicitly believe that what they are doing—advising, acting, ordering—is based on morally defensible (sincerely held) beliefs about what it is permissible or right to do. ('Normative Claims', 220)

In a note to this passage, Soper adds that a choice by an official to create and enforce a norm 'while still denying that he approved of the norm . . . would at best be strange, at worst "pragmatically self-defeating" or "logically inconsistent" ' ('Normative Claims', 241–2 n. 10).

Before we turn to the main shortcomings of the argument that is encapsulated in these extracts, we should pause to consider one way in which Soper has unnecessarily weakened his case. As Raz has observed in quite a different context ('Obedience', 740), Soper does not always take sufficient account of the difference between beliefs and purported beliefs. Especially in the second (and longest)

---

[16] Philip Soper, 'Legal Systems, Normative Systems, and the Paradoxes of Positivism', 8 *Canadian Journal of Law & Jurisprudence* 363, 375 (1995). This position also figures prominently in Soper, 'Normative Claims'. For similar stances, see Robert Alexy, above, n. 8, at 177–82; MacCormick, 'Natural Law', 110–18; Postema, 'Normativity', 92–3. For the suggestion that moral permissibility is a necessary condition for *legitimate* authority (a suggestion with which I fully agree, as my choice of terminology indicates), see e.g. Kent Greenawalt, above, n. 15, at 53–4; Rolf Sartorius, 'Positivism and the Foundations of Legal Authority', in Ruth Gavison (ed.), *Issues in Contemporary Legal Philosophy* (Oxford: Clarendon Press, 1987), 43, 55–6; M. B. E. Smith, 'Is There a Prima Facie Obligation to Obey the Law?', 82 *Yale Law Journal* 950, 975–6 (1973).

of the three passages by Soper that have just been quoted, he presumes that legal officials must actually believe in the claim-to-legitimacy which he attributes to the law and to them. To be sure, the first quotation deals with what legal officials purport or claim to believe, rather than with what they do indeed believe; but the second quotation goes too far toward suggesting that the relevant issue is one of actual beliefs rather than of professed beliefs. This confusion becomes manifest shortly afterward, when Soper seeks to rebut the notion that the law's claim-to-legitimacy is irreconcilable with legal positivism's insistence on the separability of law and morality. He retorts: '[T]hat conscientious persons believe they act correctly does not prove that they do, and this distinction between what is claimed (or believed) and what is the case is all that the modern positivist needs for his continued denial of a necessary connection between law and morality' ('Normative Claims', 220). This retort is correct as far as it goes, but it does not go nearly far enough. It employs 'claimed' and 'believed' as if they were virtually interchangeable, and it thereby obfuscates the potential for a gap between what is believed and what is claimed. Such a gap is at least as important as the division between what is claimed and what is the case.

Soper has needlessly weakened his stance by sometimes slighting the distinction between actual beliefs and purported beliefs. His neglect of that distinction obliges him repeatedly to compare legal officials to morally conscientious people—for example, in his remark that a legal system's 'claims about its actions . . . are no different from those of any ordinary conscientious individual' ('Normative Claims', 221). Given that the claim-to-legitimacy is a claim to moral acceptability, and given that Soper sometimes implies that such a claim in a genuine legal system has to be sincere (i.e., a matter of actual beliefs rather than of merely professed beliefs), he has placed himself in the position of having to portray legal officials as morally earnest. Now, since anyone who wishes to contest the thesis of an inherent claim-to-legitimacy is almost certain to focus on the posture of some wicked legal systems, Soper's obscuring of the claim/belief divide has given the aforementioned thesis the appearance of flagrantly begging the question—because the thesis seems to exclude regimes that are staffed by officials who lack all moral scruples, and because it thus seems to rule out such regimes dogmatically as genuine legal systems. That appearance of natural-law dogmatism dissipates, however, once we take proper notice of the claim/belief divide. Officials who implicitly or explicitly stake a claim-to-legitimacy might not believe in the moral legitimacy of their actions at all; they might simply wish to avail themselves deceitfully of an aura of legitimacy. To recognize this point is to recognize that Soper's thesis concerning the claim-to-legitimacy will indeed be potentially applicable to regimes staffed by men who harbor no moral compunctions. Hence, to construe his thesis most favorably and to confront it in its strongest form, we should not overlook the gap between claimed beliefs and actual beliefs. In other words, we should grasp that even the villainous officials who undeceivedly apprehend the immorality of their nefarious legal system may deem it advisable to bedeck their enterprise with the mantle of putative legitimacy.

If we take Soper's thesis to be about a claimed belief (rather than an actual belief) in the legitimacy of one's actions, should we agree that the thesis has singled out a characteristic of every genuine legal system? A negative answer is in order here. Soper's argument in support of his position wrongly assumes that someone who does not claim to be acting legitimately is thereby necessarily claiming to be acting *il*legitimately. Even if we agree that any genuine legal system is exceedingly unlikely to advance a claim of the latter sort, we are not obliged to accept that such a system must be explicitly or implicitly advancing a claim of the former sort. Officials in a vile regime may simply display complete indifference to questions about the moral legitimacy or illegitimacy of their actions. Here the analogy between such officials and a group of gunmen is illuminating, despite the imperfections of that analogy in several other respects. The gunmen are exceedingly unlikely to announce: 'We hereby issue a reprehensibly unjust demand for your money!' But the improbability of this self-accusatory assertion—whether the assertion be compunctious or openly cynical—should not lead us to infer that the gunmen's orders explicitly or implicitly profess to be morally worthy. Instead, the gunmen and their behests will very likely exhibit a thoroughgoing lack of concern with the moral status of their conduct. Suppose that the leader of the gunmen proclaims: 'Hand over your money now!' Such an utterance does not portray itself as unjust. Should we therefore conclude that it implicitly portrays itself as just? To discern in this imperative utterance an implicit moral self-commendation is to attribute to the gunmen a degree of moral alertness which they probably *do* not possess and certainly *need* not possess. If the immorality of their conduct were pointed out to them by one of their victims, they would very likely not respond by denying the charge. Their response, rather, would be 'So what?!' Their dictates to their victims carry (or, at any rate, might well carry) the moral indifference of the 'So what' response, rather than the pretended moral sensitivity of an implicit claim-to-legitimacy.

Officials in a wicked legal regime may show the same unconcern about even purporting to be morally conscientious. On the one hand, as has already been discussed herein, the officials face some constraints and pressures which gunmen typically do not face. The persistence and regularity of the officials' interaction with citizens are not usually characteristic of a gunman's interaction with his victims. As a result, the officials may feel a greater need than do gunmen to depict their own actions as morally acceptable. On the other hand, there is no basis for thinking that officials in a monstrous regime will invariably feel a need to commend their actions in such a fashion. Though they are exceedingly unlikely to label the norms of their regime candidly as flagitious, they may simply exhibit indifference to the moral status of those norms. To be sure, a reticent disdain for the whole question of the morality or immorality of their institutions and decisions is not the only posture which evil officials might adopt; but it is certainly not an outlandish posture, which can never be attributed to them without ludicrousness. Hence, by failing to distinguish adequately between expressing-moral-disapproval and not-expressing-moral-approval, and thus by supposing that the only alternative to an expression of moral disapproval is an expression of moral approval, Soper has wrongly concluded that we must ascribe to any official utterance an implicit or explicit seal of moral self-approbation. We should recognize the possibility (a credible possibility) of a contrary state of affairs. A heinous legal system might not make any claim-to-legitimacy, precisely because the absence of such a claim can be due to contemptuous indifference rather than to an overt disavowal.

Soper makes a partly comparable error in the passage (quoted above) where he highlights the ostensible absurdity of a situation in which an official discretionarily adopts a norm while disclaiming any endorsement of it. Two chief missteps and a third slightly less important misstep plague that passage. First, even if we leave aside the fact that a self-hating person can quite coherently engage in a freely chosen course of action which he or she detests,[17] we should grasp that Soper has committed an *ignoratio elenchi*. In the context of his argument, he is discussing a situation wherein an official freely chooses a norm *N* which she regards as *morally* dubious. Such a situation leaves plenty of room for the official to regard *N* as highly desirable and valuable in other respects. If the official believes that her choice of that particular norm will be doubtful morally but extremely serviceable prudentially, then she may very well choose freely to adopt *N*. That course of action will involve no moral endorsement of *N* by the official, but will indeed involve her endorsement of it—a self-interested endorsement, which overcomes any moral inhibitions that might stand in the way. By conflating moral approval and approval generally, Soper wrongly implies that a stance devoid of moral approval must be devoid of approval *tout court*. Quite the contrary; when someone freely elects a state of affairs which she regards as morally illegitimate, the usual factor driving the choice is that she favors the state of affairs for prudential reasons (i.e., for the furtherance of one or more of her interests). Hence, when an official frankly acknowledges the immorality of a norm which she voluntarily chooses, she has not thereby denied that she approves of the norm.

A second *faux pas* in Soper's remark about the official's choice is similar to the *faux pas* in his observations about the unwillingness of people to label their own actions as reprehensible. Even when an official who freely embraces a norm *N* is cognizant of its immorality and is inclined to avoid mendacity, she is

---

[17] For an elaboration of this point, see Matthew Kramer, above, n. 3, at ch. 1. Cf. Ronald Dworkin, 'Objectivity and Truth: You'd Better Believe It', 25 *Philosophy & Public Affairs* 87, 116 (1996) (emphasis added): 'Given what we take judgments about wrongful conduct to mean, we therefore withhold their attribution unless we find it plausible to suppose that the agent would be moved to some degree to avoid the act he deems wrongful quite independently of other motives he might have for avoiding it, *at least absent circumstances that show weakness of the will or emotional disorder.*'

not thereby logically committed to denying that she morally approves of *N*. Instead, the official may deal with questions of the immorality or morality of her conduct by contemptuously ignoring them. Instead of either falsely affirming her moral endorsement of *N* or truthfully denying such an endorsement, the official may brush aside any discussion of the moral status of the norm which she has embraced. A curtly dismissive wave of the hand, rather than a negative shake of the head, may be the gesture which the official deems to be most suitable. (Of course, in a liberal democracy where officials are required to justify their decisions publicly, a brusquely dismissive wave of the hand will not suffice. An official who is aware of the injustice of his decision will very likely have to resort to mendacious affirmations of its justness. But my focus throughout this chapter is on monstrously illiberal regimes, rather than on liberal-democratic states. Indeed, one way of encapsulating the basic theme of my arguments herein is as follows: the benevolent features that characterize liberal-democratic legal systems are absent from some other sorts of legal systems, and should therefore not be designated as essential for the existence and functioning of law.)

A third error in Soper's comment is also worth a brief mention. Soper neglects to distinguish adequately between a norm and a choice of a norm. A legal official might view some particular norm *N* both as immoral and as unpromotive of his own interests, but might choose *N* anyway because he views the *choice* of that norm as a prudent move. Suppose, for instance, that an official opts for a tax-imposing norm *T* that is unfairly biased in favor of the rich. If the official is himself not very affluent, then he has chosen a norm which not only is immoral but which also harms his own interests (i.e., his interests in minimizing his burden of taxation). None the less, his *choice* of *T*—as opposed to *T* itself—may redound to his benefit. By making such a choice, he may cunningly ingratiate himself with certain wealthy people; perhaps they will help to secure his position as an official, or perhaps they will bestow other favors upon him. Whatever be the exact outcome, the official can plainly have reasons to opt freely for *T* while disapproving of *T* itself on both moral and prudential grounds.

In short, on the basis of this discussion of Soper, we can see that Neil MacCormick commits a twofold mistake when he asserts that 'there would be a pragmatic self-contradiction involved if a legislature enacted a Bill expressly purporting to be for the implementation of unjust discrimination' ('Natural Law', 112). MacCormick's first and somewhat less important error lies in deeming the envisioned enactment to be pragmatically self-contradictory, as if it were akin to the utterance 'I am not currently saying anything' (or 'I am currently speaking a sentence that is not true', which is thoroughly paradoxical when spoken). Though a legislature's branding of its own mandates as morally unjust would doubtless be strange and probably imprudent, it would certainly not be incoherent or self-subverting. It would merely amount to the attribution of a moral status—the status of moral unjustness—to a legal enactment. Of course, if 'unjust' is taken to refer to *legal* injustice, and if MacCormick is recounting a scenario in which the legislature declares its own mandate to be legally impermissible, then indeed the enactment will be pragmatically self-subverting.[18] In that event, however, MacCormick is guilty of an *ignoratio elenchi*. No one disputes that legislatures implicitly or explicitly deem their own properly passed enactments to be *legally* permissible; the point at issue, rather, is whether they perforce implicitly or explicitly deem their enactments to be *morally* permissible. If we construe the term 'unjust' by reference to the relevant point of contention, then, MacCormick has gone astray in characterizing the posited enactment as pragmatically self-contradictory.

A second and somewhat more important error by MacCormick is his apparent assumption that the only alternative to wicked officials' commendation of their enactments as just is their acknowledgment of the enactments' injustice.[19] Though such an acknowledgment by evil men is indeed extremely improbable, the absence of it need not indicate their (sincere or insincere) moral commendation of their doings. Instead, they may be brusquely ignoring the whole question of the moral status of any norms which they have introduced. Thus, even if MacCormick were correct in thinking that a legislative bill's proclamation of its own injustice would be pragmatically self-contradictory, he would not have shown that every such bill must rest on a tacit or express affirmation of its own justness. Some legislative enactments might be endowed with that sort of affirmation implicitly or explicitly, but other such enactments might embody a frosty indifference toward the matter of their own legitimacy or illegitimacy.

Once again, then, we should not presume that the lack of moral self-denunciation amounts to moral self-approbation. Evil officials in a vile regime who decline to avow the wickedness of their measures have not thereby logically committed themselves to the view that those measures are morally worthy. Their silence on the topic can be the silence of utter unconcern, rather than the silence of a feigned or sincere conviction of moral correctness.

### E. A Concluding Rebuttal: Attention to Specificity

One other argument by Raz emerges most clearly in the course of his rejoinder to Hart. The key passage, quite concessionary in tone, is as follows:

---

[18] I am assuming that the members of the legislature view their enactments as legal enactments. An anonymous reader for the journal *Ethics* has alerted me to the possibility that people who act as legislators might not see themselves as such and might not see their institution as a law-making body (because they subscribe to a misguided jurisprudential theory). In such circumstances, the legislators would not regard their enactments as legal enactments, and would therefore not take for granted the enactments' *legal* legitimacy. However, they would still see their operative enactments as partaking of *some* sort of normativity, and thus they would still take for granted some sort of legitimacy (which, of course, would not necessarily be moral legitimacy). Perhaps, for example, the legislators would classify their operative norms as 'schmegal' norms. In that event, they would presuppose the 'schmegal' legitimacy of those norms.

[19] For another example of this error, see Robert Alexy, above, n. 8, at 178–80.

It is possible that while judges believe that legal obligations are morally binding this is not what they say when they assert the validity of obligations according to law. It may be that all they state is that certain relations exist between certain people and certain legal sources or laws. Their belief that those relations give rise to a (moral) obligation may be quite separate and may not be part of what they actually say when asserting obligations according to the law. But such an interpretation seems contrived and artificial.    ('Moral Rights', 131)

As I have argued throughout this chapter, judges do not necessarily believe or purport to believe that legal obligations are morally binding. None the less, let us look closely at Raz's remarks and consider them in connection with benevolent regimes (or other regimes) wherein the officials do regard legal duties as morally obligatory.

Raz appears correct in submitting that the benevolent officials' statements of legal duties cannot typically be disentangled from their credence in the moral bindingness of the duties. When a judge announces that someone is obligated to comply with a legal mandate, and when the judge views the mandate as morally obligatory for any people to whom it applies, he very likely does not see himself as making a statement about a purely legal requirement—a requirement that might or might not partake of moral significance. Rather, the judge presumes to be making a statement about a requirement which is morally binding and which derives its moral weight partly or wholly from its status as a legal duty. A legal obligation considered apart from its moral obligatoriness will very likely not play a role in the judge's reasoning or pronouncements. Yet, given that any efforts in these circumstances to separate the judge's claim about the legally binding force of a duty from his claim about the morally binding force thereof are apt to be artificial and contrived, a friendlier attitude toward Raz's conception of legal duties may seem warranted. After all, Raz has firmly maintained that a judge's view of the legal obligatoriness of a requirement cannot be asserted without a tacit or explicit assertion of the requirement's moral obligatoriness. Since Raz's position is borne out by the situation described in the present paragraph, we should perhaps wonder whether his stance is sound in a wide array of other contexts as well.

To dispel any impression that Raz's position is sweepingly applicable to all official statements of legal obligations, this discussion should distinguish between law in general and specific systems of law. Such a distinction brings with it a further distinction between statements about law generally and statements about the law in some particular system.[20] When a judge or any other official

---

[20] This distinction is repeatedly drawn in Philip Soper, above, n. 16; and in Soper, 'Normative Claims'. However, my own discussion departs significantly from Soper's analyses, which presume that every legal system is indeed characterized by a claim-to-moral-authoritativeness. Soper contends merely that such a claim typically arises from officials' focusing on the substance of their own regime rather than from their focusing on the nature of law generally. Though such a contention is unexceptionable as far as it goes, it leaves in place the key tenet of Raz's position: the notion that a claim-to-moral-authoritativeness is indeed an integral element of every legal system.

asserts the existence of a legal duty, he is not typically presupposing anything about the moral status of legal duties generally; instead, he is presupposing something about the moral status of the duties in his particular system. If he regards or pretends to regard a duty in that system as morally binding (perhaps because of the content or significance of the duty itself, or perhaps because of the duty's place in a legal regime which the judge deems to be morally binding as a whole), then his invocation of the duty is the expression of a moral judgment as well as a legal judgment. But the inextricability of the moral judgment and the legal judgment in such a situation does not obtain when we move to legal settings wherein judges do not believe or pretend to believe that the obligations which they enforce are morally worthy. (That exactly such settings are possible is, of course, what this whole chapter has sought to demonstrate.)

When a judge implicitly or expressly engages in moral censure of someone for failing to abide by a legal obligation, he is not usually putting forward a jurisprudential thesis about the nature of legal obligations generally. Rather, he is usually putting forward a much narrower thesis. He may be setting forth a claim about the particular obligation to which he is giving effect, or he may be making a wider claim about the moral tenor of all the obligations that are imposed by the particular legal system within which he works. Still more broadly, he may be taking a view about the moral bindingness of duties imposed by legal regimes of a certain type (e.g., liberal-democratic regimes, where citizens directly or indirectly participate in the creation of laws). Only rarely will a judge have ascended to a jurisprudential level of abstraction, where his upbraiding of someone for a breach of duty is based on a thesis about the general nature of law and legal duties. Such a level of abstraction is hardly ever necessary. Moreover, it is rarely advisable—since a judge ordinarily has little aptitude for philosophical speculation far above a duty-specific or system-specific level. A judge typically trains his scrutiny not on law, but on the law.

Hence, quite understandable is the inseparability of the affirmative legal assessment and the affirmative moral assessment that are involved in an official's application of a perceivedly benevolent legal obligation. That inseparability reflects the following two facts: the obligation being applied or the legal system establishing the obligation is regarded (sincerely or insincerely) as morally worthy; and the official who applies the obligation does so with a focus on its specific substance or on the specific substance of the regime imposing it, rather than with an abstract focus on the obligation as an instance of legal obligations generally. In other words, given that the official who treats a legal duty $D$ as a moral requirement has taken that stance because he esteems $D$ as morally binding in itself or because he esteems the moral worthiness of the system in which $D$ has a place, he does not take into account $D$'s legal status without taking into account its moral status. Because his focus lies on the specific tenor of a requirement or regime which he regards as morally admirable, he does not separate the matter of legal bindingness from the matter of moral bindingness. From his perspective of moral commitment, those two matters are indivisible—at the concrete level with which he is concerned.

Of course, nothing debars a morally committed judge from ascending to a jurisprudential level of abstraction at which he can grasp that the matters of legal bindingness and moral bindingness are distinct even within his own regime. But Raz is undoubtedly correct in thinking that judges do not usually pursue such a level of abstraction. If we were to analyze legal reasoning in a way that depicts the typical judge as a sophisticated jurisprudential thinker, our findings would indeed be artificial and contrived. Much more troubling for Raz, however, is a quite different way in which an affirmation of legal bindingness and an affirmation of moral bindingness can become disjoinable. Instead of positing a credulity-straining regime of philosopher-judges who draw fine jurisprudential distinctions, we should think about a much more credible situation in which the officials who operate a monstrous legal regime do not affirm or pretend to affirm the moral bindingness of the requirements that are imposed by their norms. (Again, the quite credible possibility of such a situation is exactly what this chapter has endeavored to show.)

To be sure, no more than a judge who believes or purports to believe in the moral obligatoriness of the legal duties which he enforces, will the officials in an unconcealedly wicked regime be likely to focus on the general nature of law rather than on the specific substance of the law in their own system. We certainly have no grounds for thinking that evil judges will be more adept philosophers of law than benevolent judges. But, when the officials in a wicked legal system disjoin legal obligatoriness from moral obligatoriness, they do so not by abstracting from the substance of their regime but precisely by remaining focused on that substance. They do not believe that their norms are morally binding, and they need not profess to believe as much. Though they very likely do not go so far as to proclaim the immorality of the norms which they enforce, they may well exhibit arrant indifference toward questions about the moral status of those norms (by leaving such questions unaddressed). When these officials invoke the vile norms of their system to explain their decisions, they do so—or may often do so—exclusively in order to reinforce incentives-for-compliance, rather than to justify the decisions as fair. Hence, evil officials in these circumstances make statements of legal obligations without committing themselves implicitly or explicitly to the notion that the legal obligations are moral obligations. Because they concentrate on the specific legal requirements of their regime while carrying out their responsibilities, and because they do not purport to look upon those requirements as morally legitimate or binding, their assertions of the legal force of those requirements do not carry any implications about the moral force thereof.

In short, the argument by Raz in the passage most recently quoted above would be troubling only if he had established the truth of its initial premise—the premise which submits that legal officials must believe or profess to believe that the legal requirements which they invoke and enforce are morally binding.

However, because this chapter has exposed the unsustainability of that premise, we can see that Raz's argument is at best a demonstration of a point that applies only when the officials do indeed harbor or profess to harbor the belief just mentioned. At most, that is, the argument shows that officials who believe or claim to believe in the moral authoritativeness of their legal system's duties do not distinguish between legal obligatoriness and moral obligatoriness when they give effect to those duties. Such a conclusion, plainly, does not extend to situations in which officials neither affirm nor purport to affirm the moral authoritativeness of the requirements which they implement. A line of reasoning applicable to benevolent or ostensibly benevolent legal regimes is not applicable to legal regimes that are undisguisedly wicked. In other words, the comments by Raz examined in this section are ineffective for their purpose unless his foregoing arguments have managed to prove that officials' statements of legal obligations are perforce statements of moral obligations. The burden of the present chapter has been to reveal that any such view of officials' statements is untenable.

# 5

# *The Law in Action: a Study in Good and Evil*

The most widely read book by Michael Detmold carries the subtitle '*A Refutation of Legal Positivism*'.[1] Hence, my sustained defense of legal positivism should not ignore Detmold's work altogether. Indeed, notwithstanding that a lot of his missteps are basically similar to the missteps committed by other opponents of positivism, a separate chapter on his work is warranted—because his point of view is quite distinctive in certain respects, and because some of his errors (when corrected) are illuminating.

Before examining several instances of Detmold's arguments, we should note *en passant* that a number of his arguments and assertions will not receive any attention herein. On the one hand, to be sure, many elements of his book are ignored in my present chapter simply because they do not bear upon the chief points of contention which I wish to pursue. Some of those unexplored elements—some of the remarks on Joseph Raz and Ronald Dworkin, for example—are not devoid of insights (though the significance of the insights is overstated by Detmold). On the other hand, quite a few aspects of *The Unity of Law and Morality* are disregarded here precisely because they do not merit serious attention. Detmold frequently indulges in philosophically undisciplined flights of rhetoric. Confronted with the numerous passages in which he counsels respect for the mystery of the existence of the world, any readers who are not of a mystical disposition will very likely feel dissatisfaction.[2] We shall leave those passages aside, without further ado.

Here we shall peruse only those strands of Detmold's thought that relate to his project of undermining the legal-positivist insistence on the separability of law and morality. We shall begin by looking very briefly at a few shopworn anti-posi-

---

[1]  Michael Detmold, *The Unity of Law and Morality: A Refutation of Legal Positivism* (London: Routledge & Kegan Paul, 1984) [ULM]. Detmold's anti-positivist stance is less prominent, though not entirely absent, in his later writings: 'Law as Practical Reason', 48 *Cambridge Law Journal* 436 (1989) ['Practical Reason']; *Courts and Administrators* (London: Weidenfeld and Nicolson, 1989) [CA]. For some telling criticisms of Detmold's 1989 book, see T. R. S. Allan, 'Book Review', 49 *Cambridge Law Journal* 135 (1990). (One objectionable feature which Allan does not mention is Detmold's persistent running together of cognitive-volitional autonomy and political-legal autonomy.)

[2]  For some negative reactions to this facet of Detmold's thought, ranging from amusement to thorough hostility, see Brian Bix, 'Recent Publication', 22 *Harvard Journal on Legislation* 620, 621 (1985); J. D. Goldsworthy, 'Detmold's "The Unity of Law and Morality" ', 12 *Monash University Law Review* 9, 23–4 (1986) ['Unity']; John Robinson, 'Book Reviewed', 31 *American Journal of Jurisprudence* 173 (1986); N. E. Simmonds, 'Book Review', 4 *Legal Studies* 343, 345–6 (1984); Richard Susskind, 'Detmold's Refutation of Positivism and the Computer Judge', 49 *Modern Law Review* 125, 126–7 (1986); David Wood, 'Review', 63 *Australasian Journal of Philosophy* 562 (1985). More favorably disposed toward Detmold are Zenon Bankowski, 'Review', 49 *Modern Law Review* 138 (1986); Andrew Tettenborn, 'Book Review', 44 *Cambridge Law Journal* 144 (1985).

tivist canards to which Detmold has unfortunately subscribed. Thereafter, we shall investigate some of his more subtle missteps.

I. THE USUAL SUSPICIONS

1. Throughout his book, Detmold maintains that legal positivists cleave to a belief in the *separation* of law and morality. Such a characterization of the legal-positivist stance suggests that the upholders of that stance deny the possibility of a convergence between legal norms and moral norms. In fact, legal positivists insist only on the *separability* of law and morality. As I have remarked in my previous chapters, positivists do not contend that legal norms and moral norms are necessarily divergent; they contend, rather, that legal norms and moral norms are not necessarily consentaneous. Instead of submitting that law and morality must always be separate, the positivist submits that they *can* be separate. No legal positivist gainsays the existence of contingent connections—widespread connections—between legal requirements and moral requirements. What the positivist gainsays is the idea that such connections are preordained or that they exist by dint of the very nature of legality. The separability of the legal realm and the moral realm, as opposed to their ineluctable separation, is the condition which the positivist seeks to highlight.

2. A second canard which Detmold apparently endorses is the notion that legal positivism calls for a slavish adherence to the letter of the norms in any particular legal system. (This notion is closely related to a deeper misconception concerning moral responsibility, which we shall explore presently. It is also very closely related to the hackneyed and utterly baseless allegation that legal positivism tends to be serviceable for tyranny.[3]) In fact, jurisprudential positivism does not prescribe any particular mode of adjudication; it certainly does not prescribe a blind fidelity to absurd or iniquitous requirements laid down by statutes or other sources of law. To be sure, a few positivists—most notably Raz—contend that legal norms as legal norms have to be ascertainable without recourse to moral considerations. However, the positivists of that stripe have sharply distinguished between a theory of law and a theory of adjudication. They readily acknowledge that an appropriate process of adjudication will often be informed by moral values, which are extra-legal but which are not thereby excluded as decisional touchstones for judges.

3. Another falsehood propagated by Detmold is that all legal positivists are like Raz in thinking that moral principles can never amount to sources of law. We are told, for example, that 'according to legal positivism, [a judge] cannot ever

---

[3] For one of the many junctures at which Detmold broaches this unfounded allegation, see 'Practical Reason', 455. Such an allegation was also frequently hurled by Lon Fuller, whose own flirtation with Nazism—recounted in N. E. H. Hull, *Roscoe Pound & Karl Llewellyn* (Chicago: University of Chicago Press, 1997), 244–5—was therefore particularly reprehensible.

say in the single case "this statute because of its iniquity is not the law" ' (ULM, 258). In fact, as will be reaffirmed in Chapter 6, most legal positivists are inclusive rather than exclusive in their approach to this matter.[4] That is, while they proclaim that moral principles are never *perforce* among the factors that govern and impel the ascertainment of laws, they accept that such principles can indeed be among those factors in particular legal systems; and, what is most important, they accept that the moral principles in such circumstances are legal bases for legal decisions. Everything hinges on the Rule of Recognition—the set of criteria for the ascertainment of legal norms—to which a particular regime adheres. If a moral test forms part of the Rule of Recognition in a specific legal system (the American legal system, for instance), then the precepts involved in the test are sources of law for that regime. Though such a state of affairs is not inevitable, it is always possible. When it does exist, most jurisprudential positivists feel no unease about saying that the wickedness of a formally impeccable enactment will have deprived the enactment of its status as a law.

4. Another misconception sometimes peddled by Detmold is that legal positivism plays down or even disregards the normative character of law. (This misconception is related to a more profound misunderstanding of normativity itself—a neglect of the distinction between prudential normativity and moral normativity—which we shall plumb shortly.) Although he allows that H. L. A. Hart was generally not an 'extreme' positivist bent on construing legal statements as purely descriptive, Detmold purports to detect the extreme position in a passage from Hart's *The Concept of Law*. In that passage, Hart had observed that an official who applies criteria for the ascertainment of laws does not usually state explicitly that her fellow officials regard those criteria as authoritative. Instead, she will tend to assume implicitly that just such a situation obtains. Detmold pounces: 'It was important for Hart's positivism that [the official's] assumptions be paradigmatically assumptions of fact, not of bindingness' (ULM, 51). He elaborates: 'Hart's lawyer makes the . . . assumption of the *fact* that there is a rule, but not the assumption . . . of bindingness' (ULM, 52, emphasis in original). Exactly how Detmold has arrived at this strange interpretation is quite unclear. Hart was certainly not denying that the officials who apply the Rule of Recognition will have made some normative assumptions about the rule's bindingness. Indeed, such normative assumptions constitute the officials' 'critical reflective attitude', in which their acceptance of the Rule of Recognition consists. Hart highlighted the existence of this attitude, and he then pointed out that it is closely linked to certain factual assumptions—assumptions that are typically left unvoiced, as he sought to indicate in the passage on which Detmold has seized. Far from suggesting that the officials' factual assumptions crowd out or obviate their critical reflective attitude, Hart was detailing the set of interconnected factual premises and normative premises in their outlook.

---

[4] For a fine statement of this position, see W. J. Waluchow, *Inclusive Legal Positivism* (Oxford: Clarendon Press, 1994).

II. EVIL INTENTIONS

Having dealt briskly with a few of the fallacies in *The Unity of Law and Morality*,[5] this chapter now more lengthily addresses some of the subtler and profounder errors therein. Detmold's anti-positivist barrage is not limited to familiar misrepresentations of positivist theses. It also contains some more thought-provoking arguments that have to be parried by a defender of the legal-positivist stance.

## A. Detmold's Case against Legal Positivism

To understand properly the tenor of Detmold's attack against the thesis that law and morality are separable, we must grasp his general conception of law. As Jeffrey Goldsworthy has aptly commented: 'At the root of Detmold's various arguments is his conception of law as an activity rather than an inert system of norms' ('Unity', 25). Detmold views law as a practical arena in which decisions are reached and actions are taken. He does not really distinguish between law and the workings of a legal system, for he perceives law as consisting essentially in those workings. '[I]t is natural to think of the rule of law as the rule of a process rather than the rule of an entity, the law' (CA, 109). Nor does Detmold draw any clear distinction between legal norms and their applications to concrete situations. For him, the content and import of legal norms emerge as the norms are brought to bear on particular disputes and problems. Law is primarily or exclusively law-in-its-specific-applications.[6]

   Thus, when Detmold writes about the thesis that law and morality are separable, he is arguing on the basis of a jurisprudential model that prioritizes the practical or systemic aspect of law over its structural aspect. His anti-positivist challenge, accordingly, proceeds against the notion that judges' decisions and actions are separable from moral commitments. Detmold does not wish to claim, of course, that judicial decisions and actions are invariably morally worthy. He fully recognizes the manifest fact that judges (like other human beings) can arrive at moral decisions that are erroneous or even grotesque. His point, rather, is that legal decisions by judicial officials are ineluctably moral decisions. When a judge

---

[5] I should here point out another misconception. Detmold appears to believe that the Cretan-Liar Paradox—the paradox created when a Cretan announces that all Cretans lie about everything—is attributable to Zeno of Elea. See ULM, 137, 227. Detmold also sometimes confuses the structure of the Liar Paradox with that of undecidability. See 'Practical Reason', 453. For a full account of the distinction between paradoxicalness and undecidability, see Matthew H. Kramer, *Hobbes and the Paradoxes of Political Origins* (Basingstoke: Macmillan, 1997), 14–18.

[6] At any rate, this view of law is espoused by Detmold in the portions of his book on which I shall focus. In the last couple of chapters of his text, he adopts quite a different view—a view that is not easily squared with the account in his earlier chapters. For some telling criticism of this shift in Detmold's conception of law, see Goldsworthy, 'Unity', 12 n. 10, 14–17.

opts for a certain holding in preference to a contrary holding, she tacitly or expressly commits herself to the view that the favored holding is morally legiti-mate. Whether her moral sense is sound or unsound—that is, whether or not her holding is actually legitimate—her choice of her holding is expressive of her belief in its moral acceptability. Law, then, amounts to an array of moral judg-ments by officials. Ergo, the positivist insistence on the strict separability of law and morality is untenable.

Detmold seeks to elucidate his position by asking his readers to ponder the following statement, which might be made by a judge who is pronouncing her sentence in a criminal case:

(A) The prisoner ought to hang, but it is not the case (morally) that the pris-oner ought to hang.   (ULM, 23)

Detmold contends that the statement is an out-and-out contradiction. Given that every legal judgment is a moral judgment, the first portion of the statement negates the second portion. Hence, the two portions together cannot be propounded by a judge who wishes to avoid utter incoherence.

Detmold considers some ways in which the foregoing statement might be reformulated by jurisprudential positivists, who of course will hope to dispel its apparent contradictoriness. He first broaches the following possibility:

(B) *Prima facie* the prisoner ought to hang, but it is not the case (morally) that the prisoner ought to hang.   (ULM, 24)

Detmold takes exception to this version of the original statement because the first portion of it cannot justify more than a prima-facie sentence, 'which is no sentence at all' (ULM, 24). Since a judge who pronounces a sentence is implic-itly or explicitly committed to the view that the passing of the sentence is a morally legitimate action, the first portion of statement (B)—the portion in which the judge expresses the justification for his sentence—must assert a decisive moral conclusion about the sentence's warrantedness. A prima-facie conclusion is not to the purpose; it expresses indecision, and thus cannot serve as the basis for a genuine judicial determination. Exactly because anyone arriving at such a determination must harbor a conviction in the moral propriety thereof, the act of affirming the determination is incompatible with the moral tergiversation in the first half of statement (B). Or so Detmold reasons.

He goes on to consider some alternative renderings of the judge's statement:

(C1) The fact is that according to the law of (a given community) the prisoner ought to hang, but it is not the case (morally) that the prisoner ought to hang.

(C2) According to the law the prisoner ought to hang, but it is not the case (morally) that the prisoner ought to hang.   (ULM, 24)

Detmold avows that the first of these new renderings does not contain any contra-diction, but he maintains that it likewise does not express any commitment to the view that the death sentence for the prisoner is justified. '[T]he mere external existence of a norm can by itself justify no practical decision' (ULM, 24). Because a judge who imposes a death sentence must be acting out of a sentiment that such a decision is morally justified on the whole, and because the initial portion of (C1) does not in itself express any sentiment of that sort, the imposition of the sentence cannot be articulated by means of (C1) *sans plus*.

The second of the new renderings is equally futile. On the one hand, the words 'according to the law' might qualify the moral force of the first half of (C2) in much the same way as the words 'prima facie' within the first half of (B). If so, the difficulties explored in connection with (B) are difficulties for (C2) as well. On the other hand, the words 'according to the law' might not qualify the moral force of the first half of (C2)—in which case the contradiction between the two portions of (C2) is starkly apparent.

Detmold then introduces a rendering of the judge's statement that draws upon the work of Raz, who has delineated a 'detached' perspective from which legal norms and other norms can be viewed. The new rendering is as follows:

(C3)  From the legal point of view the prisoner ought to hang, but it is not the case morally that the prisoner ought to hang.   (ULM, 25)

Detmold maintains that the initial portion of this rendering cannot serve to articulate the judge's pronouncement of a sentence, because it does not justify the sentence. Precisely because the detached perspective is indeed detached, it does not capture the judge's commitment to the view that the imposition of the death sentence is morally warranted. The initial portion of (C3) has left open the question of moral legitimacy, and it therefore does not give voice to the judge's belief in the propriety of her act of sentencing—a belief which the judge must harbor if she indeed engages in that act.

As Detmold observes, Raz has sought to illustrate the detached perspective by adducing the example of an anarchist who becomes a judge. Raz supposes that the anarchist will adhere to the terms of the prevailing legal norms on most occasions. She will thereby continue to occupy a position from which she may be able to inflict considerable damage on governmental institutions in the rare cases where she can depart from the terms of the law. In response to this example from Raz, Detmold endeavors to cast doubt on the following version of the judge's pronouncement of the death sentence:

(D)  The prisoner ought to hang (in order to increase the potential for reforming the system), but it is not the case (morally) that the prisoner ought to hang.   (ULM, 26)

Detmold submits that the first portion of (D), with its instrumentalist tenor, does not express any justification for a conclusive sentence. At most, it conveys a justification for a sentence that 'would be . . . conditional on the pursuit of the impostor judge's end, and a conditional sentence of that sort would be as objectionable and as null as a *prima facie* sentence, and for similar reasons' (ULM, 26). Thus, although the new rendering of the judge's sentence does not contain a contradiction, it likewise does not amount to a genuine articulation of the sentence. Like the previous renderings, it fails to combine noncontradictoriness with adequateness; each formulation either has involved an outright contradiction or has fallen short of capturing the state of moral committedness that would underlie the judge's pronouncement of the sentence.

Detmold thus professes to have shown the inseparability of law and morality by having shown that legal decisions and actions are always moral decisions and actions. A judge who arrives at a legal determination such as the handing down of a sentence will regard that determination as morally acceptable on the whole; were she not of that view, she would have arrived at a contrary determination. Hence, each of the decisions that constitute the law is a moral judgment grounded in a conviction of moral worthiness.

## B. Detmold's Case Countered

Before the remainder of this chapter launches a volley of connected ripostes to Detmold's arguments, we should quickly glance at two possible retorts that will not be pursued here. First, critics of Detmold might well protest about his neglect of the structural dimension of law, a neglect that is due to his almost exclusive focus on law's practical or active dimension. Since many legal positivists who write about the law/morality divide have thought of law principally as a structure of norms—norms that can have legal force yet be lacking in moral worth—Detmold appears to be talking past his jurisprudential opponents rather than engaging them in a debate. Second, specifically in connection with Detmold's treatment of the detached perspective outlined by Raz, we can notice a conflation of the pragmatics and the semantics of judicial statements. Raz's notion of detachedness relates to the pragmatic implications of judicial discourse (i.e., to the implications of participation in such discourse), yet Detmold construes the notion as if it were a semantic thesis (i.e., a thesis about the meanings of the statements that might be drawn upon in such discourse).

The chief drawback of each of the two foregoing retorts is that each of them leaves in place the most firmly anti-positivist strand of Detmold's theory. Were legal positivists to criticize Detmold solely because he slights the existence of law as a matrix of norms, they would very likely give the impression that the practical workings of law do indeed perforce have the moral significance which he attributes to them. This chapter does not countenance any such concession (or even the appearance of such a concession). A necessary conjunction between morality and law-in-its-applications would be devastating for jurisprudential positivism, even if no such conjunction could be established between morality and law-as-a-scheme-of-norms.

Similarly, a correction of Detmold's misunderstanding of Raz's comments on the detached perspective would in itself simply lend support to Raz's own position:

a position which, as my last chapter has indicated, is deeply at odds with legal positivism in some key respects. Consequently, the present chapter will not fight any battles on Raz's behalf, and will instead seek to challenge some theses espoused by both Raz and Detmold—as well as some other theses that are peculiarly Detmold's. A misreading of Raz is not the most serious of Detmold's lapses.

Detmold's prime error lies in his failure to apprehend that the reasons for judges' actions and decisions—like the reasons for any other people's actions and decisions—can be prudential through and through. Judges can base their actions on moral reasons, but they can likewise base their actions on reasons of unalloyed self-interest. As a result, the statements with which they express their decisions and actions do not necessarily carry any implications of moral committedness. Detmold does his best to push aside this basic fact of judicial and moral life; but, as we shall see, his efforts are unavailing.

We can begin by asking exactly what Detmold means when he insists that the first portion of (A)—and the first portion of each variant of (A)—must 'justify' the death sentence which the judge imposes. If Detmold is contending that the first portion of the statement cannot be adequate unless it expresses a *moral* justification for the application of the death sentence, then his demonstration of a clash between the two halves of the statement is stipulatively assured and is therefore trivial. If he is indeed adopting this stipulative position, then he is not really confronting legal positivism at all; instead, he is merely charting the implications of some anti-positivist dogmas to which he himself subscribes. Though Detmold is of course at liberty to stare into an intellectual mirror, he ought not to seize upon his own reflection as proof of the unsoundness of jurisprudential positivism.

Legal positivists can agree with Detmold that the first half of the judge's pronouncement of the death sentence must bespeak a reason that justifies the sentence. However, they should certainly not accept that the reason must be moral rather than prudential. (The distinction between moral reasons and prudential reasons has been drawn in previous chapters, and thus it need not be explicated afresh here.) When a judge affirms that 'the prisoner ought to be hanged', the term 'ought' can be purely prudential; that is, it can be expressive solely of a desire by the judge to promote her own interests. Perhaps, for example, she regards the death sentence as warranted because it will help to reinforce people's incentives for compliance with the onerous requirements that are laid down by a legal system in which she occupies a privileged position. Or perhaps she feels that the imposition of the sentence is advisable because her colleagues expect it of her and because they will question her competence if she declines to have the prisoner hanged. Whatever be the exact grounds for her decision to hand down the death sentence, those grounds might pertain essentially to her own interests and might not pertain essentially to anyone else's interests. In other words, her decision and the reasons for her decision might not partake of any moral concern whatsoever.

Detmold has to deny that the decisions and actions of legal officials can be devoid of moral concern. After all, he maintains that those decisions are fundamentally moral judgments. He attempts to shore up his position through a number of argumentative tacks, none of which is successful. His basic assumption is that people always view their own actions and decisions as morally correct. Even if they act in wicked or selfish ways—even if they are giving effect to the most atrocious Nazi policies, or even if they are tycoons pursuing their own material interests with breathtaking avarice—they must believe that their conduct is morally legitimate. However mistaken the belief in moral legitimacy may sometimes be, it must obtain; if people believed otherwise, they would act otherwise.

Now, some legal positivists might be inclined to acquiesce in Detmold's thesis about people's perceptions of the moral acceptability of their own conduct—since his thesis does *not* suggest that the conduct will inevitably be morally worthy. None the less, his stance should be resisted; it posits too firm a connection between legal decision-making and moral decision-making. Indeed, Detmold's thesis can be tellingly controverted in two main ways.

First, as has been argued at length in my chapter on Raz, the officials in a nefarious legal system may be wholly indifferent to the question of the moral status of their actions. Instead of presuming (perversely) that their wicked judgments show a proper degree of concern for the interests of others, they may remain firmly uninterested in gauging whether they have shown proper concern or not. Like gangsters who respond with brusquely indifferent shrugs (rather than with denials) when they are upbraided by their victims for the immorality of their conduct, the officials in an evil regime of law may give no thought to the moral worthiness or unworthiness of what they do. Each official may carry out his functions in pursuit of his own self-interest without pausing to consider whether those functions and that pursuit are morally legitimate or not.

In other words, we need to distinguish between two types of moral obtuseness: an obtuseness (viz., self-deception) that leads a person to regard his own wicked actions as ethically acceptable, and an obtuseness (viz., moral apathy) that blinds a person to the question whether his own wicked actions are ethically acceptable or not. If a heinous decision is reached by a self-deceiving person, then the expression of that decision does carry a commitment to the view that the decision is legitimate. By contrast, if a heinous decision is reached by a person who is staunchly indifferent to moral concerns, the expression of the decision does not carry any commitment to the view that the decision is legitimate. Like other people, the indifferent person acts on the basis of all-things-considered judgments; but, unlike other people (including other evil people), she effectively excludes moral considerations from the category of 'all things considered'.

A second grave difficulty plagues Detmold's thesis about people's perceptions of their own actions. Not only can legal officials be thoroughly uninterested in the moral status of their decisions, but, even if they are sufficiently astute to recognize the decisions' moral unacceptability, they will not necessarily change their minds. They might be weak-willed and might accordingly allow their pursuit of their own interests to override any moral compunctions. Having

enough discernment to grasp the wickedness of their own judgments and directives, they might none the less keep issuing those judgments and directives
because their moral qualms give way to weighty considerations of self-interest.
Perhaps over the long term these officials find it hard to live with themselves, or
perhaps not; in any event, each of them can perfectly well manage to hand down
evil decisions in spite of being divided between his sense of what is good for
himself and his sense of what is right.

Detmold is hardly unaware that he needs to address the possibility of weak-
willed officials. Indeed, he discusses that possibility at more than one juncture.[7]
He attempts to rule it out by contending that all reasons for action are moral
reasons and that people consequently always behave on the basis of considerations which they deem to be more significant morally than any competing considerations. Detmold begins with the following definition of 'moral judgment': '[A]
conclusive judgment about life, liberty, property and the like (matters of importance, certainly including all the matters of law) is a moral judgment' (ULM, 34).
He acknowledges that this definition in this context is bound to strike his opponents as ludicrous: '[M]uch may be thought to turn on this definition of "moral".
We are arguing against the separation of law and morals; but the argument will be
no more useful or interesting than its definitions. The definition we have proposed
may be thought to have begged the whole question' (ULM, 34–5). Detmold
lashes out against his would-be mockers: 'One of the most muddling things in
moral philosophy is the idea that the word "moral" refers to a limited area of practical thought; for instance, when it is said that there are moral reasons for action
and other sorts of reasons as well' (ULM, 35). He endeavors to substantiate his
view by asking his readers to imagine a situation in which he and two other
people (Robert and Harold) are drifting in an open boat. Detmold supposes that
he has possession of the only provisions on board, and that there is not enough
food for more than one person:

There is a moral decision to be made here. It seems clear that my whole decision is the
moral decision, and not just the decision between Robert and Harold (if it were just the
decision between Robert and Harold, then when judging my own claim I would be deciding between morality and self-interest). To refer to my whole decision is the way the word
'moral' is conventionally used: the extent to which self-interest should be allowed weight
against the interests of others is taken to be almost paradigmatically a moral question. If
such a decision is the moral decision then I cannot contrast moral reasons (in favour of
Robert and Harold) with self-regarding reasons. Either all the reasons are moral reasons,
because they all go into the moral decision, or none are.   (ULM, 35)

---

[7] In his first discussion of this matter, he suggests that legal positivism amounts to 'an analysis
which requires judges to be seen paradigmatically as moral backsliders' (ULM, 31). The word 'paradigmatically' should be 'potentially'; having chosen the former word, Detmold here errs in much the
same way as when he claims that legal positivists believe in the 'separation' of law and morality. Legal
positivism's insistence on the separability of law and morality is a thesis about what *can* be, not a
thesis about what *must* be or even a thesis about what typically *is*.

Detmold's stance here is untenable. It improperly trades upon a fact which my introductory chapter highlights: the fact that the term 'moral' can carry various senses when used in jurisprudential and other philosophical discussions. Two of those senses are directly relevant here. On the one hand, the term 'moral' can be attached to any decision that effects a trade-off between the nontrivial interests of some person(s) and the nontrivial interests of some other person(s)—even if the decision-maker thoroughly favors his or her own interests at the expense of everyone else's. When used thus, 'moral' is contrasted with 'nonmoral'. On the other hand, the term can be confined to decisions that exhibit some degree of nonderivative concern by the decision-maker for the well-being of other people. When used thus, 'moral' is contrasted with 'prudential'. Moral grounds for one's actions pertain essentially to the advancement of others' well-being, whereas prudential grounds for one's actions pertain essentially to the advancement of one's own well-being.

When jurisprudential positivists propound their thesis about the separability of law and morality, they are using the term 'moral'—and its cognates—in the second, narrower way sketched above (as well as in certain other ways explicated in Chapter 1). They are maintaining, in part, that the decisions of legal officials can stem from purely prudential considerations. They are thus maintaining that those decisions need not be moral, in the narrower sense of 'moral'. However, jurisprudential positivists would hardly submit that official decisions need not be moral in the first, broader sense sketched above. Given a definition of 'morality' sufficiently broad to encompass all the nontrivial self-regarding factors along with all the nontrivial other-regarding factors that bear on people's relationships with one another, all or virtually all legal decisions will be moral decisions. Who could think otherwise? If Detmold really feels that he is countering legal positivism when he employs his expansive definition of 'moral' to assert the unity of law and morality, then he has fundamentally misunderstood the target of his ire. He is shadow-boxing against some fanciful foe.

Pertinent here is a point made earlier in this book. No jurisprudential positivist would deny that moral categories are suitable for the evaluation of law and legal decisions. Law differs from rocks and sunsets and ordinary pencils in this important respect (as well as in other respects, of course). Just about any legal decision can be appositely assessed for its conformity or lack of conformity with moral standards, because the making of a legal decision determines the extent of someone's enforceable responsibilities to someone else. Whereas asking about the moral goodness or evil of a rock is nonsensical, asking about the moral goodness or evil of legal precepts and legal determinations is perfectly apt.[8] Every

---

[8]   Recall here H. L. A. Hart's exasperation at Lon Fuller's superfluous insistence that law 'is "not simply a datum of nature" '. Hart retorted: 'Surely this last phrase merely darkens counsel. . . . The author's use of this opaque philosophical phrase suggests that those who, like myself, attempt to analyse the notion of legislative powers in terms of rules are committed to eliminating from their analysis any reference to anything but the inanimate' (H. L. A. Hart, 'Lon L. Fuller, *The Morality of Law*', in *Essays in Jurisprudence and Philosophy* [Oxford: Clarendon Press, 1983], 343, 359).

jurisprudential positivist would accept as much; the positivist thesis about the separability of legal norms and moral norms is emphatically not a claim about the insusceptibility of law to moral appraisal.

The thesis of separability is focused instead on morality in narrower senses. It conveys three principal points. First, it maintains that laws and legal decisions can be laws and legal decisions regardless of whether they satisfy any tests of moral worthiness. Second, it maintains that the process of ascertaining the law in a particular jural regime might raise and address only factual questions as opposed to evaluative questions. Third, it maintains that the people who make laws and legal decisions can do so for purely prudential reasons. Especially in connection with the last-mentioned point (about officials' reasons-for-action), Detmold muddies the issue by repeatedly conflating the notions of moral commitment and moral responsibility. Early in his book he affirms the following two tenets, which he perceives as anti-positivist:

(*a*)  [L]egal decisions entail a claim to their moral justification.

(*b*)  [L]egal decisions are made with moral responsibility for what they require.   (ULM, 31)

Now, the first of these tenets does indeed come under attack from legal positivism, in ways that have already been pursued herein. By contrast, the second tenet is not inconsistent at all with positivism. No jurisprudential positivist would deny that legal officials are morally responsible for the actions and decisions in which they engage. Every positivist would readily accept that officials' determinations produce major impacts on people's lives, and that the officials are thus morally answerable—even if not legally answerable—for those determinations. (In liberal democracies, of course, one relevant consideration when we gauge the moral quality of the officials' decisions and actions is the importance of securing a clear and fairly stable set of norms for the liberal-democratic regulation of societal interaction.) Indeed, the moral responsibility of officials for their decisions is exactly what jurisprudential positivists such as Hart have been aiming to highlight when they declare that legal requiredness does not entail moral requiredness.

None the less, Detmold repeatedly traduces jurisprudential positivists by alleging that they seek to remove any moral burdens from the shoulders of legal officials. For example, we are told that positivists believe that you as an official 'have no responsibility for the happiness of your dying parent by virtue of the judgments that you make' (ULM, 49). Similarly, Detmold asserts that 'it is positivism which claims that a judge can make a legal judgment separated from moral considerations; it is positivism which allows (indeed requires) a judge to say: it is the law which makes this decision, not me' (ULM, 154).

These baseless accusations by Detmold derive from his frequent disregard of the distinction between moral commitment and moral responsibility. Consider, for instance, the following passage:

The positivistic conception of law . . . tends to see judges as computers; as, at least in clear cases, simply certifying what in fact the law is on certain facts, without necessary moral *commitment*. Now, such a state of affairs could be instituted: real computers could be substituted for judges, and their 'decisions' would obviously entail no moral justification. But this would be insufficient to establish the positivistic conception. The single-case *responsibility* would fall totally to those charged to execute the law. (ULM, 257, emphasis added)

Much the same slippage, between a focus on commitment and a focus on responsibility, occurs in the following comment: 'Legal positivism . . . disguises the audacity of rules by holding that the logical character of judgment under rules is such that one can make it without being committed to that judgment in any ultimate moral sense. On this view nothing conclusive is done by our taking a rule: no moral question is importantly prejudiced' (ULM, 21). Jurisprudential positivists do indeed avouch that someone who renders a legal decision is not necessarily committed to the claim that that decision is morally correct. However, positivists certainly do not avouch that someone who renders a legal decision or adopts a legal norm is free of moral responsibility therefor. No positivists would ever contend that an official's moral stature is unaffected by her rendering of such a decision or her adoption of such a norm. In affirming that people are not perforce committed to the view that their actions are morally legitimate, while also affirming that they are morally responsible for their actions, the legal positivist insists both that officials can act for purely prudential reasons and that their acting for purely prudential reasons is generally an evil course of conduct for which the relevant officials are culpable.

Having distinguished between the condition of moral commitment and the condition of moral accountability, and having separated the narrower from the broader sense of 'morality', this chapter has undone Detmold's attempt to deny that weakness of the will is possible. Detmold himself appears to anticipate that his argument against the possibility of *akrasia* will not win favor; he seeks to fend off defeat by declaring that a rejection of his argument will reduce the position of his opponents to triviality. 'If a more limited definition of moral judgment is taken then weakness of the will is clearly possible, but trivially so' (ULM, 122). At an earlier stage of his book, in quite a concessionary passage, Detmold sets forth his counterattack at greater length: '[I]t might be said that the argument of this chapter establishes that legal judgment is final or conclusive judgment, but not that it is [necessarily] moral judgment. Some version of the thesis of the separa[bility] of law and morals might then be saved. But it would have no point' (ULM, 36). He elaborates: 'To say that the certification of something as legally required is not to certify that it is morally required is, if "moral" is [defined in its narrower sense], no more interesting than to say that such a certification is not necessarily politically sound, or prudent, or necessarily in accordance with the principles of the Oddfellows, or with some other compartment of thought' (ULM, 37).

The response to Detmold here is quite simple. No one has ever seriously argued that all legal norms merely by dint of their status as legal norms are in accordance with the principles of the Oddfellows. Nor has anyone ever seriously contended that all legal norms merely by dint of their status as legal norms are promotive of the interests of their addressors or their addressees. Nor has anybody ever seriously suggested that the authoritative statements of legal obligations by officials necessarily imply that those obligations are in accordance with the principles of the Oddfellows or are promotive of the officials' interests (or of citizens' interests). By contrast, many sophisticated arguments have been put forth to establish just such claims about the relationship between law and morality. Whereas nobody has endeavored to demonstrate an intrinsic connection between legality and the Oddfellows' principles, numerous theorists have attempted to reveal such a connection between legality and morality. Jurisprudential positivists are not tilting at windmills or belaboring obvious points. Far from spouting mere truisms, positivists are defending a thesis that has often been oppugned with great subtlety.

## C. A Final Rejoinder

Only one argument by Detmold remains to be parried.[9] As has already been recounted, he dismisses the sixth rendering of the judge's pronouncement of the death sentence—version (D)—because he feels that the initial half of that rendering does not amount to a justification of any genuine sentence. If a furtively anarchistic judge affirms that 'the prisoner ought to hang (in order to increase the potential for undermining the system)', then the only sentence supported by the judge's affirmation is 'one conditional on the pursuit of the impostor judge's end, and a conditional sentence of that sort would be as objectionable and as null as a *prima facie* sentence, and for similar reasons' (ULM, 26). Detmold's mistake here is especially odd in light of his own emphasis on the particularity and practicality of the judge's pronouncement. Were that pronouncement the articulation of a general norm embracing a class of cases, then Detmold's response to (D) would perhaps be germane. In fact, however, as Detmold himself emphasizes, the judge in pronouncing the death sentence is decreeing that particular measures be taken against a particular person. Instead of laying down a norm to deal with the cases of prisoners generally, the judge is issuing a situation-specific order which disposes of the case of one particular prisoner.

Given that the judge is a surreptitious anarchist who enforces laws solely in order to retain her position for the effectuation of her subversive ends, and given that she has handed down a death sentence for the particular prisoner whose case is covered by (D), she has decided that the enforcement of some law through the hanging of this specific prisoner is serviceable for her ultimate ends. Of course,

---

[9]  I shall not examine Detmold's suggestion that jurisprudential positivism's insistence on the strict separability of law and morality will leave us unable to distinguish between legal obligations and a highwayman's demands (ULM, 57–8, 59–60). I have already rebutted such a line of reasoning, in my chapter on Raz. (The similarity between the stances of Raz and Detmold on this matter is indicative of their common source of inspiration in the work of Hans Kelsen.)

if she decides that a similar sentence in some future case will not be serviceable for her aims, she will not then render such a sentence. But her current pronouncement of the death sentence pertains exclusively to the case before her rather than to any cases that might arise in the future. In this case now before her, she has decided that the hanging of the prisoner will redound to the benefit of her anarchistic aspirations; hence, the efficacy or appositeness of (D) is not weakened at all by the fact that 'the only sentence it could justify would be one conditional on the pursuit of the impostor judge's end'. Because the pronouncement of the death sentence disposes exclusively of the present case, and because the imposition of such a sentence in this particular case is deemed by the judge to be a means of furthering her ideals, the fact that her basis for imposing the sentence will not warrant a similar sentence in some future cases (where it will not further her ideals) is simply beside the point.

In short, Detmold is no more successful in his discussion of the anarchistic judge than in any of his other anti-positivist onslaughts. Even when his premises are not patently unsustainable, they do not yield the conclusions which he draws from them. Having aspired to show the unity of law and morality, he has not succeeded in landing any blows against a model of law without trimmings.

# 6

## *Also among the Prophets: Some Rejoinders to Ronald Dworkin's Attacks on Legal Positivism*

Anyone engaged in a defense of legal positivism should hesitate before seeking to counter the anti-positivist volleys in Ronald Dworkin's jurisprudential writings. Although Dworkin has professed to do battle with positivism in order to clear the way for his own theoretical project, he has based his criticisms on a conception of the appropriate aims and methods of jurisprudence that is strikingly at variance with the positivist conception. Hence, the debates between Dworkin and his opponents create the impression of being missed connections more often than responsive encounters.[1]

Doubtless, the blame for the aridity of some of the aforementioned debates does not lie entirely on one side or the other. All the same, Dworkin himself bears a substantial share of responsibility for this situation of people talking past one another. In defiance of his own methodological precepts concerning interpretive generosity, he has frequently attributed certain theses to positivists which no members of their camp would accept. Because his accounts of the general ambitions and specific claims of legal positivism are sometimes bemusingly distortive, his genuinely important challenges can become obscured. Anyone who endeavors to parry or defuse those challenges must disentangle them from the caricatures that accompany them.

Dworkin has not done justice to several distinctions that figure prominently in the legal-positivist tradition. Among the most important of these are the following: (1) law versus the law; (2) theory versus practice; (3) observer versus participant; (4) detachment versus commitment; (5) prudential commitment versus

---

[1]  Despair concerning this point suffuses the 'Postscript' to the second edition of H. L. A. Hart's *The Concept of Law* (Oxford: Clarendon Press, 1994) ['Postscript'], 238. (All other references to *The Concept of Law* [*Concept*] are to the first edition, which was published by the Clarendon Press in 1961.) See also Brian Bix, *Jurisprudence: Theory and Context* (Boulder, Colo.: Westview Press, 1996), 97–9; Nigel Simmonds, 'Why Conventionalism Does not Collapse into Pragmatism', 49 *Cambridge Law Journal* 63 (1990); Philip Soper, 'Dworkin's Domain', 100 *Harvard Law Review* 1166, 1167–8, 1170–5 (1987).

The principal writings by Dworkin which I consider in this chapter are *Taking Rights Seriously* (Cambridge, Mass.: Harvard University Press, 1978) [TRS]; 'A Reply by Ronald Dworkin', in Marshall Cohen (ed.), *Ronald Dworkin and Contemporary Jurisprudence* (London: Duckworth, 1984) ['Reply'], 247; *Law's Empire* (London: Fontana, 1986) [LE]; 'Legal Theory and the Problem of Sense', in Ruth Gavison (ed.), *Issues in Contemporary Legal Philosophy* (Oxford: Clarendon Press, 1987) ['Theory'], 9; 'Objectivity and Truth: You'd Better Believe It', 25 *Philosophy & Public Affairs* 87 (1996) ['Objectivity']. (The overall book edited by Ruth Gavison will hereinafter be cited as Gavison, *Issues*; and the overall book edited by Marshall Cohen will be cited as Cohen, *Dworkin*.)

moral commitment. Though all of these distinctions will be explored in the course of this chapter, the first of them is a source of especially serious misgivings about the likelihood of fruitful controversies between Dworkin and his legal-positivist opponents. Whereas jurisprudential positivists attempt to elaborate the basic features of legal systems generally, Dworkin is principally interested in elaborating and justifying the foremost features of the American legal system (and the English legal system, to a lesser extent). As a consequence, any retorts by positivists to Dworkin's strictures—any retorts highlighting possible characteristics of law that are largely or wholly absent from the American legal regime—can seem misdirected or heavy-handed.

The difficulty just recounted is aggravated by the fact that Dworkin declines to distinguish clearly between the jurisprudential explication of the concept of law and the theoretical explication of the workings of a particular legal system. Although he concentrates chiefly on the latter, he frequently adverts to it in terms more suitable for the former. As quite a few commentators have remarked,[2] Dworkin swerves back and forth between speaking about *law* and speaking about *the law*; that is, he equivocates between speaking about a general type of institution and speaking about one instance of that general type. Problematic in itself, his equivocation is particularly troublesome because it pertains to a disjunction that separates his own theoretical enterprise from the enterprise of the positivists (in that the positivists concern themselves with law whereas Dworkin concerns himself with the law). Dworkin can lead us unwarily into thinking that many of his remarks have more of a bearing on the claims of legal positivism than they in fact do.

None the less, despite the potential pitfalls in a confrontation with Dworkin, the task is well worth the effort. Given the overall importance of his work, and given the anti-positivist flavor of many of his well-known writings, no defense of jurisprudential positivism can afford to ignore him. Moreover, even if his work as a whole were less prominent and impressive than it is, some of his onslaughts against positivism have an independent significance. Albeit many of his accusations are misguided, several of them are highly perceptive and are therefore occasions for the clarification or amplification of some key positivist doctrines. Preoccupied though Dworkin may be with the theoretical explication of one specific regime of law, he has made a number of claims that are endowed with a jurisprudential breadth. Those claims stand or fall as general philosophical theses (relating to law), rather than merely as observations about the American legal system. Partaking of a comprehensive sweep, they are direct challenges to the philosophical theory propounded by legal positivists—who must therefore show that Dworkin's theses can be rebutted or absorbed.

---

[2] See e.g. John Finnis, 'On Reason and Authority in *Law's Empire*', 6 *Law and Philosophy* 357, 367–8 (1987); Ruth Gavison, 'Comment', in Gavison, *Issues*, at 21, 25–7; H. L. A. Hart, 'Comment', ibid. 35, 36–40 ['Comment']; Hart, 'Postscript', 246–7. Cf. Steven Burton, 'Ronald Dworkin and Legal Positivism', 73 *Iowa Law Review* 109–13, 128–9 (1987); P. H. Nowell-Smith, 'Dworkin V. Hart Appealed: A Meta-ethical Inquiry', 13 *Metaphilosophy* 1, 9–10 (1982).

My focus in the present chapter will lie principally on *Law's Empire*, published by Dworkin in 1986; but I shall also have to turn to some of his earlier work and later work for certain crucial elements of his position. This chapter is divided into two main parts, each of which contains a number of sections. We shall look first at Dworkin's assault on the notion that legal norms in any particular system are ascertained by reference to some overarching set of criteria, which H. L. A. Hart dubbed the 'Rule of Recognition'. More sustainedly than in any of my previous chapters, the first half of this chapter gives attention to aspects of legal positivism beyond an insistence on the separability of law and morality. We temporarily move, that is, from 'negative' positivism to 'positive' positivism. Then the second half of the chapter returns to negative positivism, as it probes Dworkin's cardinal premise—his premise that legality and morality are deeply and inextricably connected. Dworkin views both legal theory and legal decision-making as enterprises of moral justification, for reasons that will be subjected herein to critical scrutiny.

## I. COMING TO GRIPS WITH THE LAW

### A. Accounting for Disagreement

In continuation of a tactic adopted in *Taking Rights Seriously*, Dworkin devotes many of the early pages in *Law's Empire* to the presentation of some difficult cases from American and English law (LE, 15–30). He recounts the cases in order to bring out vividly the inadequacy of Hart's contention that a Rule of Recognition governs the ascertainment of legal norms in each regime of law. Specifically, Dworkin aims to reveal that the American and English legal systems throw up cases that are marked by disagreements of a sort which Hart could not accommodate in his theory.

According to Dworkin, the positivist model of law can take account of only certain types of disagreements among judges. Within such a model (or so Dworkin maintains), judicial officials are portrayed as being thoroughly in agreement on the fundamental standards that should guide their inquiries about the existence and content of legal norms. In easy cases and in hard cases, the officials adhere to the same set of criteria for ascertaining the law. In hard cases, however, where there are no relevant norms or where the content of the relevant norms is unclear, the officials have to extend the law rather than find it—precisely because their shared criteria for identifying and interpreting the law do not yield determinate answers in such circumstances. The uniformity of those criteria among the judges is what accounts for the convergence of the judges' assessments in easy cases; conversely, the divergence of their assessments in hard cases is due to the fact that the clear-cut guidance furnished by the shared criteria will have run out at the same point for everyone.

In the positivist model of law as understood by Dworkin, the disagreements among judges that earmark hard cases are of only two types. First, judges can engage explicitly or implicitly in normative disputation concerning what the law should become (rather than what it is). When faced with sets of facts that cannot be readily subsumed under existing doctrinal categories, or when faced with the prospect of absurd results from the straightforward application of those categories, judges argue with one another about the most appropriate ways in which the categories should be developed and refined.

An especially influential account of the origins of most disagreements of this first sort is the famous seventh chapter—on the 'open texture' of language—in Hart's *The Concept of Law*. According to Dworkin, the Hartian positivist sees the clashes of opinions among judges in hard cases as 'borderline' disputes (LE, 39–46). That is, such clashes derive from the vagueness or ambiguity of the words that are used in the formulations of legal norms. Because of the clefts between abstract terms and concrete circumstances, and because of the multiple meanings that attach to some words, judges inevitably encounter situations to which the language of the operative legal norms does not apply plainly or unequivocally. When any such situations arise, judges must undertake the task of linguistic clarification and elaboration. For example, they must decide whether a 'no vehicles in the park' ordinance extends to skateboards, and whether a law dealing with houses is applicable to palaces and huts. In short, when judicial officials differ with one another in hard cases, they are arguing normatively about the borderline applications of terms. They are not arguing about the overarching Rule of Recognition which specifies that the laws containing those terms are the relevant norms to be implemented.

A second variety of disagreement that can be acknowledged by the positivists—as described by Dworkin—is empirical controversy. Judges may disagree not about the bearing of the law on certain facts, but about the facts themselves. Alternatively, they might conceivably disagree in their answers to the empirical question whether some particular law has been created in accordance with the required procedures. In that event, they are arguing about matters of fact rather than about the criteria in the Rule of Recognition (or even about the required procedures for legislation).

Having maintained that legal positivists understand the contentiousness of hard cases in these ways, Dworkin of course rejects their approach.[3] He declares that the judges in the hard cases from the American and English legal systems were differing with one another about the existing law and were not focusing

---

[3] For some accounts of Dworkin's position, see Andrei Marmor, *Interpretation and Legal Theory* (Oxford: Clarendon Press, 1992), 3–9; Charles Silver, 'Elmer's Case: A Legal Positivist Replies to Dworkin', 6 *Law and Philosophy* 381, 386–7 (1987); John Stick, 'Literary Imperialism: Assessing the Results of Dworkin's Interpretive Turn in *Law's Empire*', 34 *UCLA Law Review* 371, 376–81 (1986). For Dworkin's earlier attack on Hart's notion of the Rule of Recognition, see esp. TRS, chs. 2 & 3.

merely on the law as it ought to be. Likewise, they were not embroiled in terminological quibbles or in conflicts relating to ambiguously rehearsed facts. Even more obviously, they did not take divergent views on the empirical question whether legislative procedures had been followed. Instead, Dworkin proclaims, they were involved in theoretical or criterial disagreements pertaining to the basic standards that guide the officials of a legal system as they ascertain the existence and content of valid laws.

Although theoretical disagreements relate to factual situations and to the materials of the law, they are not empirical; they cannot be resolved through the accumulation of data. Theoretical disagreements are fundamentally moral because the criteria at issue within them are fundamentally moral. All the same, such disagreements revolve around what the law is—as much as around what the law ought to be, and indeed by dint of revolving around what the law ought to be. Judges debating with one another when deciding hard cases are usually seeking to expound the law as it exists, yet each judge is also taking a moral stance by implicitly or explicitly espousing a set of principles (a set of criteria for ascertaining the law) that will present the law in its morally best light. Disagreements among judicial officials in hard cases are disagreements about such principles. While the orientation of such disagreements is profoundly moral, the answers to the moral questions posed are also answers to questions concerning the existent law.

According to Dworkin, then, legal positivists are deeply mistaken in their approach to hard cases and in their whole conception of the Rule of Recognition. They err by separating the task of law-validation (or law-ascertainment) from the task of moral justification. They further err by presuming that the task of law-validation is accomplished via a common point of reference consisting in a set of shared criteria that make up a Rule of Recognition. Such are Dworkin's accusations. In the second half of this chapter, we shall examine his claims about moral justification; for now, we shall concentrate on his claim that the legal-positivist model of the Rule of Recognition is somehow belied by the occurrence of theoretical disagreements.

## B. Two Preliminary Criticisms

1. Before responding to Dworkin's broad attack, this chapter will briefly highlight two specific instances of highly dubious argumentation therein. The first of these relates to what Dworkin labels as 'pivotal cases'. At the first couple of junctures when he uses that designation, he is referring to the hard cases in which the divergences among judges' criteria for ascertaining the law become manifest. He carefully distinguishes such cases from what he labels as 'borderline cases', where people who are at one in their adherence to a set of classificatory standards are at odds in judging whether those standards have been satisfied by some particular state of affairs. Dworkin of course attributes to the legal positivists a focus

on borderline squabbling, the sort of squabbling which they allegedly view as characteristic of hard cases. A pivotal case is very different from any borderline quibbles, for it exposes divergences among judges at the level of basic principles and not merely at the level where those principles are applied. Fundamental starting points are at issue, as much as concrete conclusions.

The various judges and lawyers who argued our sample cases did not think they were defending marginal or borderline claims. Their disagreements about legislation and precedent were fundamental. . . . They disagreed about what makes a proposition of law true not just at the margin but in the core as well. Our sample cases were understood by those who argued about them in courtrooms and classrooms and law reviews as *pivotal cases* testing fundamental principles, not as borderline cases calling for some more or less arbitrary line to be drawn.   (LE, 42–3, emphasis added)

Pivotal cases, in short, are cases whose difficulty brings theoretical disagreements to the surface. What becomes apparent in such situations is that judges ascertaining the law adhere to disparate sets of fundamental criteria and do not simply opt for divergent applications of shared criteria. According to Dworkin, the legal positivists badly misrepresent the nature of these pivotal cases and cannot satisfactorily account for them at all.

Just a few pages after drawing this 'distinction between borderline cases and testing or pivotal cases' (LE, 41), Dworkin attaches a very different meaning to the phrase 'pivotal case'. When discussing the notion that officials adhere to common criteria for ascertaining the law, he submits that such a notion rests on 'a certain picture of what disagreement is like and when it is possible' (LE, 45). He recounts that picture as follows:

You and I can sensibly discuss how many books I have on my shelf, for example, only if we both agree, at least roughly, about what a book is. We can disagree over borderline cases: I may call something a slim book that you would call a pamphlet. But we cannot disagree over what I called *pivotal cases*. If you do not count my copy of *Moby-Dick* as a book because in your view novels are not books, any disagreement is bound to be senseless.   (LE, 45, emphasis on 'pivotal cases' added)

Having previously used 'pivotal cases' to designate especially tricky circumstances that elicit open theoretical disagreements among judges, Dworkin here employs the phrase in virtually an opposite manner. He uses it in much the same way as he later uses the term 'paradigms'—to indicate concrete phenomena that are so easily handled by the prevailing schemes of classification as to be wholly unproductive of controversy in all ordinary settings (LE, 72–3). Indeed, he seems to be going even further and to be using the word 'pivotal' in roughly the same way as he later uses the term 'preinterpretive' (LE, 65–6). That is, far from being notably controversial, pivotal cases are portrayed in the passage above as the elementary materials of a practice that are entirely taken for granted as such. Were there no consensus on those pivotal cases, there would not be any basis for profitable discussion.

Why is this terminological slippage important? By sliding from one mode of usage to the other, Dworkin tends to give the impression—probably quite unwittingly—that his attack on legal positivism is more far-reaching than it is. After all, in the first chapter of *Law's Empire*, he maintains that positivists fall far short of providing a satisfactory account of pivotal cases, i.e., hard cases. Of course, he goes on in subsequent chapters to suggest that the defects in the positivist treatment of hard cases are indicative of broader misapprehensions and failings; but the observations in his opening chapter by themselves tell merely against the positivists' approach to hard cases. Thus, when Dworkin suddenly switches directions by using the phrase 'pivotal cases' in order to denote the basic materials of a practice, he may lull his readers into thinking that he has landed a much more devastating blow than he has. If jurisprudential positivism were unable to account for the elementary components of legal systems, it would be a sorry doctrine indeed. Insofar as the terminological shift by Dworkin conveys the impression that he has shown or endeavored to show positivism's inadequacy in exactly this respect—that is, insofar as his shift encourages the belief that he has demonstrated or sought to demonstrate that positivists cannot take cognizance of legal systems' basic constituents—it has greatly exaggerated the reach of his opening chapter's attack.

2. Another dubious line of thought in the early pages of *Law's Empire* is even more puzzling. Dworkin repeatedly contends that, according to Hart, the criteria that compose the Rule of Recognition in any society must be accepted by the general public as well as by the officials who run the society's legal system (LE, 34–5, 429; TRS, 21, 42, 43; 'Theory', 11). In a single paragraph from the first chapter of *Law's Empire*, for example, we encounter the following statements:

[Hart] said that the true grounds of law lie in the acceptance *by the community as a whole* of a fundamental master rule. . . . So propositions of law are true . . . in virtue of social conventions that represent *the community's* acceptance of a scheme of rules. . . . [T]he proposition that the speed limit in California is 55 is true just because . . . *the people of California* have accepted, and continue to accept, the scheme of authority deployed in the state and national constitutions. . . . For Hart, [an accurate proposition about British law] is true because the rule of recognition accepted *by the British people* makes judges' declarations law.   (LE, 34, emphases added)

In fact, as has been remarked already in this book, Hart expressly disclaimed the view that citizens as well as officials must accept the criteria that make up the Rule of Recognition in a viable legal system. Indeed, he ridiculed as starkly implausible the notion that most members of the public in a complex society will grasp and accept the criteria of recognition. He readily observed that many people will have only a fuzzy sense of the standards to which officials adhere in the course of ascertaining the law (Hart, *Concept*, 59–60, 110–11).[4]

---

[4]  Dworkin comes close to a correct apprehension of this matter in LE, 431 n. 2, where he writes that the Hartian Rule of Recognition is 'accepted by almost everyone, or at least by almost all judges and other lawyers'.

Dworkin compounds his mistake when he asks what constitutes acceptance of the Rule of Recognition. He notes that many officials in a vile regime may give effect to the dictates of their superiors chiefly or exclusively out of concern for their own safety. He queries whether their fear-impelled compliance with the Rule of Recognition amounts to their acceptance of it. He submits:

If so, then the difference between Hart's theory and Austin's becomes elusive, because there would then be no difference between a group of people accepting a rule of recognition and simply falling into a self-conscious pattern of obedience out of fear. If not, if acceptance requires more than mere obedience, then it seems to follow that there was no law in Nazi Germany.   (LE, 35)

Dworkin has again gone astray by paying insufficient attention to the theory which he is condemning.

As has been mentioned in some of my earlier chapters, Hart distinguished carefully between obedience and acceptance (*Concept*, 109–14). Though each of those postures involves compliance, acceptance also involves commitment or supportiveness—expressed as a critical reflective attitude—whereas mere obedience does not. Every official or nearly every official in a viable legal system must accept all or most of the criteria in the Rule of Recognition plus all or most of the norms validated by those criteria. Officials have to adopt a critical reflective attitude toward the requirements laid down in those criteria and norms, if their system is to be sustainable; by contrast, ordinary citizens might display nothing more than obedience thereto. Yet, as Hart emphasized, the unforgoability of officials' acceptance of the Rule of Recognition in a functional legal system does not by itself allow any inferences about the motives for their acceptance (*Concept*, 198–9). So long as the officials engage in the sort of conduct that bespeaks commitment or supportiveness, they are engaging in the sort of conduct that is essential for the operativeness of their legal system. The precise reasons for their engaging in that conduct are variable and are largely or wholly beside the point (at least if our only concern is to inquire whether the conditions for the existence of a legal system are fulfilled). Hence, Dworkin's observations about the fear-induced behavior of some officials in Nazi Germany are not disconcerting for a supporter of Hart.

### C. Upholding the Rule of Recognition: A First Step

As has been seen, Dworkin's prime purpose in adducing an array of hard cases during the first chapter of *Law's Empire* is to maintain that the differences of opinion which occur in such cases are theoretical disagreements—disagreements of a sort that supposedly cannot be acknowledged by legal positivists. What is revealed is that divergences among judges within a particular legal system occur not just in relation to specific outcomes (borderline outcomes), but also in relation to the fundamental criteria that guide the judges' decisions about the existence and content of legal norms. This situation of criterial discord ostensibly belies the positivist account of law, wherein the officials of each legal system are said to accept a Rule of Recognition that serves as a shared point of reference for their law-ascertaining and law-applying activities.

Let us begin by noting that, even if Dworkin's presentation of hard cases is accurate as far as it goes, it does not in fact establish that judges differ with one another at the criterial level in *easy* cases (which constitute the vast majority of cases, including most of the potential cases that never reach the courtroom at all). Of course, Dworkin does not imply that criterial divergences become manifest in easy cases; because such cases are dispatched without multiple concurring and dissenting opinions, there is no opportunity therein for any criterial divergences to surface. However, he insists that such divergences do obtain in easy cases as much as in hard cases, albeit without coming to the fore. Though the theoretical disagreements among judges in easy cases remain submerged, they lurk beneath the surface. Precisely in this respect, 'easy cases are . . . only special cases of hard ones' (LE, 266).

Yet the recountal of hard cases in the first chapter of *Law's Empire*—to which Dworkin adverts at numerous junctures in his subsequent chapters—does not in itself go any way toward showing that judges adhere to different sets of criteria when ascertaining the law in easy cases. Any validly drawn conclusion about easy cases must derive from some other source. Having apprehended the open theoretical disagreements in hard cases, we cannot straightaway infer that they are paralleled by latent theoretical disagreements in routine cases. Moreover, given that no theoretical disagreements gain expression in routine cases, Dworkin cannot rely solely on the texts of official judgments as the basis for his position.

Perhaps the point at issue here can be settled through some sort of empirical study that would pose questions to judges about their standards for ascertaining the existence and content of legal norms in easy cases. If judges are sophisticatedly self-conscious about those standards as they decide easy cases—even though they do not write any separate opinions in such cases—then each judge can answer the aforementioned questions through straightforward introspection. A resolution of the point at issue here would be just as plainly empirical as any resolution of a dispute that hinges on people's recollections of their conscious attitudes.

More likely, however, is that most judges as they deal with easy cases do not have any detailed sense of the theoretical criteria that underlie their handling of those cases. Their replies to a questionnaire will thus be elaborations and interpretations of their attitudes (previously subconscious attitudes), rather than sheer recollections. In that event, however, their replies will not necessarily be definitive. Other interpretations of their behavior in easy cases can legitimately emerge. Let us recall the method of *Law's Empire*, where Dworkin endeavors to interpret the practice of legal decision-making rather than the attitudes of the participants in that practice. He affirms that 'it is essential to the structure of [a practice such as legal decision-making] that interpreting the practice be treated as different from understanding what . . . participants mean by the statements they make in its operation' (LE, 55), and he asserts that 'a social practice creates and assumes a crucial distinction between interpreting the acts and thoughts of participants one by one . . . and interpreting the practice itself, that is, interpreting what they do collectively' (LE, 63). Interpretation, as opposed to the gathering of data through questionnaires, is the relevant task here. In other words, the task of fleshing out the subconscious presuppositions of various judges in easy cases is a task that requires an interpretive understanding of the overall practice of adjudication. Because of the likelihood that many judges' presuppositions in easy cases are indeed subconscious, the judges themselves do not have privileged access thereto. Their answers to questions about those presuppositions must vie with other credible answers, which will likewise be interpretations. Thus, instead of awaiting the distribution of questionnaires to judges,[5] we may confine ourselves to the various data—the judicial opinions and decisions—for which Dworkin seeks to account. He has to establish that an interpretation of those data which posits a continuity between difficult cases and straightforward cases is superior to an interpretation which posits a discontinuity.

Now, interpretive jousting would doubtless be unnecessary if there were not any plausible reasons for thinking that judges might switch from one set of law-ascertaining criteria to another when moving from easy cases to hard cases. If there were indeed no such reasons, Dworkin could rely on the overt theoretical disagreements in hard cases as clear-cut evidence of subterraneous theoretical disagreements in easy cases. Unfortunately for him, however, it is far from incredible that a judge might be impelled by one set of considerations in straight-forward cases and by quite another set in difficult cases. Such a disjuncture is indeed quite likely.

Let us ponder a variant of one of the examples included in Dworkin's summary of some hard cases. Suppose that all the judges within a legal system *L* adhere in easy cases to the principle that the language of any statute should be construed in its ordinary sense only. Suppose further that a difficult case arises in *L*, as the ordinary wording of a statute will yield an absurd result when applied to some particular problem. Some judges stand by their normal position and do not allow the ridiculous result to deflect them from their reliance on the everyday meaning of the statute's language. Other judges depart from their usual focus on everyday meanings and address themselves instead to the broader intentions of the legislature (which militate against the ludicrous outcome that would ensue from a reliance on the everyday meanings). In routine cases, these relatively imaginative judicial officials do not tacitly or expressly advert to the law-making

---

[5] At any rate, even if all or most judges as they deal with easy cases do have a detailed sense of the law-ascertaining criteria that guide their decisions therein, and thus even if the distribution of questionnaires to the judges is appropriate, we can usefully engage in some general speculations about the likely findings of those questionnaires.

body's wider intentions; rather, in such cases, they join with their fellow officials in concentrating only on the ordinary significance of the statutory wording. In extraordinary cases, however, they feel that a shift of focus is both obligatory and permissible. Because some of their colleagues feel otherwise, the extraordinary cases are marked by theoretical disagreements.

In the scenario just sketched—a scenario that is far from outlandish—the law-ascertaining decisions of the judges in $L$ are governed by a common point of reference in easy cases. Only in difficult cases do some of the judges find themselves at odds with others, at the level of outcomes and at the level of criteria. Hence, if someone were to take note of the criterial divergences that emerge during the difficult cases in $L$, and if he or she concluded that those divergences are present (though very often submerged) in all of $L$'s cases, the conclusion would be invalid and false. With regard to a substantial majority of the actual and potential cases, there can be a solid criterial consensus among $L$'s judges.

A champion of Dworkin's ideas might respond to this analysis in either of two ways. First, he or she might maintain that my last couple of paragraphs have inappositely characterized the criteria to which the judges in $L$ adhere. Instead of cleaving to one set of criteria for easy cases and another set for hard cases, the relatively imaginative judges in $L$ accept the following bifurcated principle in easy cases and hard cases alike: 'Give effect to the ordinary meaning of statutory language, except in those cases where doing so would lead to absurd results.' The less imaginative judges in $L$ accept only the first half of this principle, in easy cases and hard cases alike. Hence, there are indeed criterial divergences among $L$'s judges in straightforward cases as well as in difficult cases (though of course the divergences do not become manifest in the straightforward cases). So a supporter of Dworkin might argue.

Such a retort founders, for it collapses Dworkin's stance into that of legal positivism. Dworkin himself contends that the positivists submit the following explanation of the disharmony among judges in hard cases: 'Each [judge] uses a slightly different version of the [Rule of Recognition], and the differences become manifest in . . . special cases' (LE, 39). If Dworkin's attempt to highlight the criterial disagreements among judges in any regime were nothing more than an insistence that the various judges' law-ascertaining standards overlap very significantly while diverging on peripheral matters, then his putative critique of positivism would be an outright reaffirmation thereof. A bifurcated-principle riposte made on his behalf is in fact a capitulation.

Supporters of Dworkin might therefore pursue a second and more subtle tack. They will still wish to declare of course that theoretical disagreements among $L$'s judges are present in easy cases as well as in hard cases. At this stage, however, their claim is not that the imaginative judges of $L$ subscribe to a bifurcated principle while the other judges of $L$ subscribe to a simple principle; their claim, rather, is that the imaginative judges endorse the simple principle for easy cases only because they endorse the touchstone that is encapsulated in the second half of the bifurcated principle. In other words, the imaginative judges in easy cases attach ordinary meanings to any statutory wording because they feel that the broader intentions of the legislature require this mode of interpretation in such cases. The focus on the everyday sense of language is a product of the primary focus on the broader aspirations of the law-making body. In routine cases as much as in tricky cases, then, the judges in *L* differ with one another about the fundamental standards for the application of laws. The less imaginative judges take ordinary linguistic usage to be decisive, whereas the more imaginative judges receive their guidance from the overall aspirations of the legislature. Although the judges' approaches coincide practically in straightforward cases, they diverge practically in difficult cases and diverge theoretically in all cases.

This second postulated rejoinder is more robustly and subtly Dworkinian than the first rejoinder (so long as the broader aspirations of the legislature are understood as transcending the intentions and aspirations of any of the individual legislators). Supporters of Dworkin would hope to argue that their interpretation of the judicial decisions and opinions in *L* is superior—superior on moral grounds—to my positivist interpretation. This chapter will later explore Dworkin's views on the connections between law and morality. For now, our inquiries are whether the Dworkinian interpretation is analytically preferable to my own interpretation and whether the two interpretations are clearly distinguishable. The discussion here will quickly lead into my broader defense of the positivist conception of the Rule of Recognition.

Both the Dworkinian account of *L* and my positivist account—in either its original version or its bifurcated-principle version—are consistent with the relevant data. Each of the accounts can be said to fit. However, the Dworkinian account attains its plausibility as an accurate exposition only by imitating or following the positivist account. The Dworkinian approach has to come to grips with the fact that most cases in *L* do not give rise to any overt theoretical disagreements. Advocates of that approach acknowledge the lack of controversy by allowing that the imaginative and unimaginative judges alike reach decisions in easy cases through a reliance on the ordinary meanings of statutory language. But the Dworkinians then seek to contrast their own approach with that of the positivists by insisting that the attentiveness of the imaginative judges to ordinary patterns of usage in easy cases is itself derivative of the rationale which those judges invoke when faced with difficult cases. However, this extra layer of exposition by the Dworkinians is emphatically not required by the data, for the positivist exposition handles all the data without it. Running afoul of Occam's Razor, the superfluous overlay of Dworkinian interpretation does not yield a model that accounts any better for *L*'s judicial decisions and opinions than does positivism's more austere model. (To be sure, Dworkinians would commend their approach as preferable because it incorporates a different conception of the consensus that prevails in *L*'s easy cases. We shall consider this point shortly.)

Should the legal positivists who explicate the pattern of decisions in *L* feel obliged to reject the Dworkinian interpretation altogether? The appropriate answer here is plainly negative, since the positivists can perfectly well avouch that the underpinnings for the imaginative judges' decisions in easy cases might be in line with what the Dworkinians maintain. If the Dworkinian insistence on the presence of criterial divergences in *L*'s easy cases is nothing more than a claim about the aforementioned underpinnings—a claim that *L*'s imaginative judges focus on everyday meanings in easy cases out of a concern for the legislature's broader aspirations, whereas the unimaginative judges focus on everyday meanings without any concern for such aspirations—then the Dworkinians are stating nothing which the positivists must repudiate. A positivist who offers an account of *L* will endeavor to provide an analysis that captures the pattern of consensus in easy cases and disagreement in hard cases. Such an analysis can and should leave entirely open any questions relating to the ulterior concerns and motives of the officials whose judgments are under consideration. As has already been mentioned in this chapter, Hart himself expressly left open such questions (*Concept*, 198–9). While accepting that the Dworkinian account of *L* is one possible elucidation of the imaginative judges' behavior in easy cases, positivists can of course still emphasize that in such cases the imaginative judges and unimaginative judges adhere to a common point of reference. In sum, a legal positivist should regard the Dworkinian interpretation as one possible extension of his or her own analysis—an extension not dictated by the data but not at odds with them, either.

## D. Upholding the Rule of Recognition: A Second Step

This section of my chapter initiates a more wide-ranging defense of the Rule-of-Recognition thesis against Dworkin's onslaughts.[6] In *Law's Empire*, Dworkin's prime tack is to expose theoretical disagreements in the law and to exploit those disagreements as a launching pad for his interpretive approach to jurisprudence. My present discussion will attempt to defuse his arguments about theoretical disagreements and to raise some queries about the interpretive approach.

Let us first clarify the objectives which Dworkin is pursuing. When he lays bare the theoretical disagreements in a number of hard cases, and when he goes

---

[6] For some of the many previous ripostes to Dworkin on this point, see, e.g., Michael Bayles, 'Hart vs. Dworkin', 10 *Law and Philosophy* 349, 353–61 (1991); Jules Coleman, 'Negative and Positive Positivism', in *Markets, Morals and the Law* (Cambridge: Cambridge University Press, 1988), 3, 12–27; id., 'On the Relationship Between Law and Morality', 2 *Ratio Juris* 66, 72–5 (1989); id., 'Authority and Reason', in Robert George (ed.), *The Autonomy of Law* (Oxford: Clarendon Press, 1996), 287, 289–96; Hart, 'Postscript', 254–9; Charles Silver, above, n. 3, at 387–90. Also clearly relevant are some of the remarks in Gerald Postema, ' "Protestant" Interpretation and Social Practices', 6 *Law and Philosophy* 283, 300, 301, 315–16 (1987). Throughout this discussion I take the Hartian view that each legal system has one overall Rule of Recognition made up of numerous criteria (some of which might not be clearly ranked). I do not see any reason to stipulate that some criteria are separate Rules of Recognition. For such a stipulation, see Joseph Raz, *The Authority of Law* (Oxford: Clarendon Press, 1979), 95–6.

on to say that such disagreements are present (though very often unactivated and thus obscured) in all cases, he is not suggesting that easy cases are unusual or that concrete legal outcomes are seldom predictable. To be sure, he once or twice tosses off comments that may seem to bespeak such a view. Near the very beginning of *Law's Empire*, for example, he writes that 'the more we learn about law, the more we grow convinced that nothing important about it is wholly uncontroversial' (LE, 10). Even in this incautious statement, the words 'important' and 'wholly' indicate that Dworkin is hardly denying the occurrence of routine cases. Still more indicative of his cognizance of such cases is a passage from *Taking Rights Seriously* in which he actually seeks to highlight the role of controversy in the law. There he denies that 'disagreements among judges [are] limited only to extraordinary and rare cases', but he immediately expands on this observation by claiming that 'disagreements among judges of this sort are very frequent, and indeed can be found whenever appellate tribunals attempt to decide difficult or controversial cases' (TRS, 62). Difficult and controversial cases in appellate tribunals are undoubtedly quite frequent, as is attested by the thickness of the casebooks in various doctrinal areas of the law; none the less, they form only a very small proportion of each such area's actual and potential cases (most of which never come before a trial court, much less before an appellate tribunal). Someone who underscores the frequency of judicial disagreements by pointing to their presence in difficult and controversial appellate cases is presumably aware that the implications of vast swaths of the law do not provoke any interesting disagreements—or indeed any disagreements, period. Likewise, when asserting that '[l]awyers . . . often call for changing even settled practice in midgame' (LE, 138), Dworkin propounds a narrative of jural change which makes clear that the ostensibly dramatic departures within the American and English legal systems are typically the culminations of gradual processes of evolution in the settled regions of the law (LE, 136–9).

Some key elements of Dworkin's theory in *Law's Empire* tend to confirm what has just been said here. My current chapter has already adverted to his discussion of paradigms. As Dworkin himself contends, '[t]he interpretive attitude needs paradigms to function effectively' (LE, 138). Equally to the point are his efforts to assure his readers that his model of law-as-integrity can account for the occurrence of easy cases. In some passages that will be carefully studied later in this chapter, he declares that his model of law is fully consistent with the fact that the legal consequences of myriad actual or potential situations are so straightforward that 'we need not ask questions when we already know the answer' (LE, 266). Perhaps even more telling is the prominence of the touchstone of 'fit' within Dworkin's interpretive approach. That touchstone is what separates interpretation from invention, and is one of the two principal dimensions of the jurisprudential theory which Dworkin commends. It is central to his ideals of integrity and fairness, as we shall presently see. Yet the touchstone of fit would have no purchase if the law were largely unsettled from one moment to the next. When Dworkin writes that an interpreter 'needs convictions about how far the justification he proposes at the interpretive stage must fit the standing features of the practice to count as an interpretation of it rather than the invention of something new' (LE, 67), the existence of numerous 'standing features' is taken for granted.

Dworkin is quite right to acknowledge that any viable legal system must be characterized by a substantial degree of settledness and regularity.[7] If in a certain society the implications of a very large proportion of the prevailing legal norms are indeterminate not only in controversial appellate cases but also in the every-day workings of the law, then no full-fledged legal system exists within that society. Though any jural regime is bound to include a number of aspects that are unsettled or open-ended, the sheer operativeness of any such regime as a jural regime entails a considerable measure of predictability and routineness. If serious controversy is typical rather than exceptional—that is, if the legal consequences of people's multitudinous actions are ordinarily (rather than occasionally) 'up in the air' and truly murky—then 'lawlessness' is the correct designation for such a state of affairs.

We should now re-evaluate the significance of Dworkin's highlighting of overt theoretical disagreements in hard cases. Let us concede *arguendo* that the criterial divergences which become exposed in such cases are also present (subterraneously) in easy cases. How damaging to legal positivism is such a concession, if it be a concession? The short answer to this question is that Dworkin's attentiveness to hard cases should be welcomed as salutary rather than resisted as threatening. His work, set within its proper limits, can serve to refine the insights of positivism rather than to undermine them.

Although some other critics of Dworkin have likewise sought to defuse his anti-positivist broadsides by accommodating them within positivism,[8] this maneuver has not been sufficiently connected to an emphasis on the routineness of the law's quotidian functioning. Once we apprehend the extent to which the ordinary workings of a legal system must be regularized if the system is to be viable as a regime of law—an extent which varies from system to system, but which is always considerable—we can see that Dworkin's attack on the Rule of Recognition is untroubling for the positivist. Criterial divergences among judges may indeed exist in straightforward cases as well as in difficult cases, but they

---

[7] I need not altogether deny Frederick Schauer's claim that, within a Dworkinian world, legal rules quite frequently give way to their underlying reasons when there are serious clashes between the two. See Frederick Schauer, 'The Jurisprudence of Reasons', 85 *Michigan Law Review* 847 (1987). I need only contend that circumstances involving such clashes—circumstances likely to generate difficult appellate cases—are vastly outnumbered by the myriad circumstances in which such clashes do not occur. Schauer would probably agree. While avouching that '[a]s a descriptive enterprise, [Dworkin's work] seems much more accurately to characterize the nature of much of appellate adjudication than did its positivist opponents', he doubts 'whether [Dworkin's jurisprudence] accurately characterizes the idea of law itself' (ibid. at 870).

[8] For an early example, see E. Philip Soper, 'Legal Theory and the Obligation of a Judge: The Hart/Dworkin Dispute', in Cohen, *Dworkin*, at 3, 16–19.

exist against a background of extensive commonality. The sorts of criterial divergences which Dworkin recounts in his hard cases are important but fairly superficial. For example, when judges disagree over the question whether the ordinary meanings of statutory language or the broader intentions of the legislature should be deemed decisive, they are hardly disagreeing about the wider question whether the legislature's enactments lay down authoritative standards. Similarly, when judges disagree about the extent to which various considerations of policy can be invoked to distinguish precedents, they are hardly disagreeing about the wider question whether precedents not plausibly distinguishable are generally binding.

Of course, the firm agreement on the deeper criteria comprised in the Rule of Recognition would be hollow if judges continually clashed with one another about the proper application of those criteria. A consensus on abstract precepts is consistent with chaos at a practical level.[9] However, the chief reason for my drawing attention to the officials' consensus on the more profound layers of the Rule of Recognition is that such a consensus is almost certainly necessary (though not sufficient) for officials' agreement at the level that matters most: the level of concrete outcomes, the 'bottom line'.

Though the regularity essential for the very existence of a legal system as such does pertain to the rationales for specific decisions, it pertains even more importantly to those decisions themselves. If most jural officials in a regime *R* disagreed with one another most of the time about the concrete legal implications of people's actions, their treatment of those actions would be erratic and chaotic rather than norm-governed. Their regime would not be a regime of law, where behavior is generally subsumed under the regulating and guiding sway of norms. To see the force of this point, we should ponder an example involving routine behavior such as one's strolling down a pathway. Suppose that some of *R*'s officials feel that anybody's strolling down a particular pathway between 2:00 and 3:00 is mandatory and permissible; while a roughly equal number of the other officials feel that it is permissible and not mandatory; while a roughly equal number of others feel that it is forbidden and not mandatory; while a roughly equal number of others feel that it is forbidden and mandatory;[10] while still others feel that issues relating to strolling down the pathway are nonjusticiable. Suppose further that the officials disagree just as dizzyingly about the concrete legal implications of most of the other routine actions (and unusual actions) in which people might engage. In these circumstances, *R* is not a regime of law at all. It is not a regime in which officials as a group handle the effectuation of norms with substantial regularity and consistency. It is instead an arena of official factions,

---

[9] This point (in a different context) is emphasized in Matthew H. Kramer, *Hobbes and the Paradoxes of Political Origins* (Basingstoke: Macmillan, 1997), 99–122.

[10] An action can be both mandatory and forbidden. A person can have both a duty to φ and a duty to abstain from φ-ing; what cannot be true is that a person has both a duty to φ and a *liberty* to abstain from φ-ing.

within which the populace is subjected to a bewilderingly higgledy-piggledy array of contrary signals and interventions.

This example has been deliberately unrealistic and indeed extravagant in order to bring out vividly a key feature of any actual legal system: the routineness and patternedness of the system's workings at the level of concrete results. Through vast stretches of people's lives within any such system, the legal consequences of most facets of their behavior are clear-cut. To be sure, every jural system exhibits unsettledness and fluidity, to a greater or lesser degree. No such system can provide for all contingencies in a manner that obviates any development of its norms, even in the unlikely event that an absence of development would be regarded as desirable. To some extent, then, the generation of particular outcomes in any regime of law is less than perfectly regularized and predictable. None the less, insofar as an operative system of law exists and functions, the specific legal implications of people's conduct in a multitude of domains do typically partake of regularity and predictability in great measure.

Dworkin himself is hardly unaware of the centripetal forces that are inevitably present in any viable legal system. He writes: 'Every community has paradigms of law, propositions that in practice cannot be challenged without suggesting either corruption or ignorance. Any American or British judge who denied that the traffic code was part of the law would be replaced, and this fact discourages radical interpretations' (LE, 88). He further states: 'Law would founder if the various interpretive theories in play in court and classroom diverged too much in any one generation. Perhaps a shared sense of that danger provides yet another reason why they do not' (LE, 88–9). A legal system operates as a set of institutions that establish and administer authoritative norms. If such a system exists—in contrast with a chaotically unco-ordinated tug-of-war by vying factions—the officials therein must converge to a very considerable degree in their perceptions concerning the particular outcomes that are required by the prevailing norms.

How, then, do the centripetal forces at work in any legal system bear upon Dworkin's attack against the positivists' belief in a Rule of Recognition? As we have observed, his attempt to refute that belief is centered on his charting of theoretical disagreements in hard cases. Such disagreements, Dworkin presumes, are present even in easy cases where they fail to surface. We now can see, however, that our acceptance of this conclusion does no harm at all to the positivist conception of law. Though criterial divergences may always be present, they cannot go beyond the point where they would bring about substantial indeterminacy and erraticism in the law at the level of concrete results. At any rate, they cannot go beyond that point if the officials are to maintain a functional legal system. Widespread though the criterial divergences among the officials may be, the practical impact of those divergences—their tendency to produce a welter of discordant opinions about the specific jural consequences of people's behavior—must be quite limited. If a legal system is to endure as such, the rivalry among judicial perspectives will be cabined by the need for most officials to agree on the 'bottom line' in most circumstances.

In this connection, recall my earlier discussion of the hard cases where imaginative and unimaginative judges are embroiled in controversies over the correct way of dealing with statutory language. As was stated there, Dworkinians would probably claim that the imaginative judges orient themselves toward the broader intentions of the legislature in routine cases as well as in knotty cases. What gives that claim its credibility is the fact that it does not overlook or gainsay the routineness of the routine cases. It acknowledges that the imaginative and unimaginative judges agree heartily on the appropriate *results* in easy cases; more precisely, in regard to any such case, it assimilates the specific substance of the legislature's underlying intentions (on which the imaginative judges rely) and the specific substance of ordinary linguistic usage (on which the unimaginative judges rely). By presuming that the general intentions of the legislature for the application of statutes in straightforward cases will center on the everyday significance of the wording in the statutes' provisions, the Dworkinian view accepts that the imaginative judges and unimaginative judges concur firmly with one another in easy cases at the level of the 'bottom line'. The criterial divergences that separate the imaginative from the unimaginative do not prevent a judicial consensus on the apposite concrete outcomes of easy cases. Abiding theoretical disagreements are structured in ways that enable unanimity concerning the disposition of myriad cases. No colorable theory of law could deny as much. Only because the Dworkinians' approach acknowledges the consensus among judges on the proper outcomes of most potential or actual cases, do Dworkinian claims about the constant presence of criterial divergences enjoy any plausibility.

Theoretical disagreements among judges in any viable legal system are thus subordinate not only to the deeper layers in the Rule of Recognition, but also to the pressures for regularity in the detailed implementation of the law. Moreover, these two forms of subordination are closely linked. As was remarked earlier, a state of virtual unanimity among judges on the fundaments in the Rule of Recognition is almost certainly necessary for a very substantial measure of agreement among them on the concrete applications of the law. Hence, given that a legal system is not sustainable as such unless officials are indeed in accord with one another to a considerable extent about the law's specific implications, it is likewise not sustainable unless the officials are unanimous or virtually unanimous in their acceptance of the precepts that make up the bedrock of the Rule of Recognition. Criterial divergences among officials obtain against the background of the officials' unanimity on the foremost criteria in the Rule of Recognition; and the intensity and range of the divergences will be limited as far as is necessary for the preservation of a large degree of regularity in the day-to-day administration of the law. Such will be true, that is, if the legal system containing the divergences is to endure as a functional legal system.

Accordingly, Dworkin's alertness to theoretical disagreements in hard cases can be welcomed by legal positivists. On the one hand, his pointing out of such disagreements is undoubtedly salutary, for it serves to counter the notion that the officials who run an operative legal regime must be in harmony with one another about all or nearly all the criteria that compose the Rule of Recognition. Within many legal systems, and certainly within the American and English legal systems, there is quite a bit of room for disaccordance at the criterial level. On the other hand, despite the importance of the criterial divergences (and despite their prominence in casebooks consisting almost entirely of appellate opinions), they are perfectly compatible with the healthy existence of a Rule of Recognition. So long as the disunity remains within the confines that have been sketched here, it does not impair the vitality of a legal system. Judges who differ with one another about some of the criteria in the Rule of Recognition can and do concur with one another about the most significant criteria therein and about the practical legal consequences of most instances of conduct.

In other words, officials' acceptance of the Rule of Recognition—a key element in the positivist model of law—does not perforce (or even typically) involve their unanimity on all the guidelines or precepts which that Rule comprises. If every official or almost every official subscribes to the paramount criteria in the Rule of Recognition, and if officials generally converge in their assessments of the concrete legal implications of most events, then their disagreements over a number of subordinate criteria do not negate their acceptance of the Rule of Recognition as described by legal positivists. Those disagreements are consistent with the unity and sustainability of a legal regime. To be sure, positivists can learn (and have learned) from Dworkin to ponder more carefully the potential for disharmony among officials in regard to the ascertainment of legal norms; however, there is no reason to think that the presence of such disharmony necessitates the abandonment of the positivist account of law.

### E.  Upholding the Rule of Recognition: A Third Step

Supporters of Dworkin may feel that my arguments so far have overlooked the principal arrow in his anti-positivist quiver. We must therefore now consider a distinction which he originally drew in the third chapter of *Taking Rights Seriously* and which he has presented afresh in *Law's Empire*. (My discussion will focus on the later treatment, in LE, 136–9, 145–6.) Is the positivist account of law belied by the distinction between a consensus of conviction and a consensus based on convention?

A consensus of conviction exists when people converge in their judgments about appropriate behavior but do not count the fact of their convergence as an essential ground for reaching those judgments. A consensus based on convention exists when people do indeed look upon the fact of their general agreement as an essential reason for arriving at the judgments on which they agree. A typical example of the former sort of consensus is the widespread acceptance of the proposition that the torture of babies is wrong; a typical example of the latter sort of consensus is a community's acceptance of the proposition that anyone using an automobile should ordinarily drive on the left-hand side of the road rather than on the right.

Dworkin contends that the convergent behavior and attitudes of officials are better understood as matters of conviction than as matters of convention. Now, before we look more closely at his arguments, we should briefly note a few preliminary caveats. First, although his distinction between conviction and convention is powerfully and subtly drawn, it is more problematic than it initially appears—largely because of the point which Thomas Hobbes so piquantly expressed when he wrote that 'he that should be modest, and tractable, and performe all he promises, in such time, and place, where no man els[e] should do so, should but make himselfe a prey to others, and procure his own certain ruine, contrary to the ground of all Lawes of Nature, which tend to Natures preservation'.[11] By reflecting on Hobbes's observation, we can see that the cogency of many basic moral and prudential propositions does hinge on a general acceptance of those propositions by one's fellows. Dworkin broaches this point (LE, 145–6), but his response to it is rather feeble. Still, we need not here pursue this matter any further. Whatever may be the limitations of the conviction/convention dichotomy, it clearly retains a significant amount of force. As Hart readily conceded ('Postscript', 255–6), a *comprehensive* conventionalist account of moral obligations would be exceedingly unpersuasive. Much the same can be said about a comprehensive conventionalist account of prudential precepts.

Second, as might be apparent from what has just been said, the current topic— the question of conventions versus convictions—does not pertain solely to legal systems that are steeped in moral concern for citizens' well-being. It pertains equally to regimes in which the officials act purely out of devotion to their own interests. Prudential stances and judgments, as much as moral stances and judgments, can form the independent convictions that are here contrasted with conventions as the bases for the task of ascertaining the law. To be sure, because of a preoccupation with the American legal system (a system which is morally worthy on the whole and which involves judicial argumentation that is expressly moral), Dworkin focuses exclusively on moral convictions. For the purposes of

[11] Thomas Hobbes, *Leviathan* (Cambridge: Cambridge University Press, 1991) (Richard Tuck ed.), 110. Hobbes's pithily stated point is more lengthily propounded (without reference to Hobbes) in William Boardman, 'Coordination and the Moral Obligation to Obey the Law', 97 *Ethics* 546, 552–3 (1987). As elegantly concise as Hobbes is the Book of Isaiah: 'Justice is turned back, and righteousness stands afar off; for truth has fallen in the public squares, and uprightness cannot enter. Truth is lacking, and he who departs from evil makes himself a prey' (Isaiah 59: 14–15).

For another snag in the conviction/convention dichotomy, see Nigel Simmonds, above, n. 1, at 77–9. Cf. John Stick, above, n. 3, at 412–13. I should note, incidentally, that I shall herein be using the terms 'conventionalist' and 'conventionalism' only with reference to the convention/conviction dichotomy, rather than with all the connotations attached to those terms in the fourth chapter of *Law's Empire*.

the present section of this chapter, there is no need to challenge him on that point. However, in anticipation of the second half of this chapter, we should grasp that the authoritative decisions whose status we seek to pin down—as products of independent convictions or as products of conventions—can be thoroughly prudential in their tenor and motivation.

Third, Dworkin sometimes expounds his distinction in a misleading manner. Most notably, when fleshing out the conventionalist view, he writes: 'Perhaps lawyers and judges accept [a paradigmatic] proposition as true by convention, which means true just because everyone else accepts it, the way chess players all accept that a king can move only one square at a time' (LE, 136). Dworkin's analogy between a judge and a chess player is infelicitous, for the proper parallel is between a judge and a scorer—or some other adjudicative official—in a chess tournament. The *players* in such a tournament are the counterparts of ordinary citizens in real life, who have no authority to change the law on their own. (Of course, a chess scorer normally has no authority to change the rules of chess; but, likewise, a judge normally has no authority to change the terms of a statute. Moreover, just as a judge has leeway to interpret a statute on debatable points of application, so a scorer has leeway to interpret the rules of chess insofar as their applications are unclear. On any matters left open by the rules of chess, a scorer can fix the prevailing standards through his own patterns of decisions, and he can adjust those decisions if he becomes convinced of the wisdom of such a move.)

Important though the points covered in these preliminary comments may be, the central weakness in Dworkin's attack on the conventionalist model of law is his ungenerosity. Dworkin appears to think that the proponents of the conventionalist approach have somehow failed to notice the prominent role of self-reflective argumentation in the legal institutions of England and the United States. He insists that the conventionalists are committed by their theory to an analogy between law and chess, which he perceives as an activity informed by a 'crisp distinction . . . between arguments about and arguments within the rules' (LE, 137–8). According to Dworkin, chess is a game in which the fixing of rules for tournaments is sharply separate from anything that takes place in the tournaments themselves.[12] Within the tournaments, arguments about the rules—as opposed to arguments about the subsuming of certain situations under the rules—are simply out of place. Hence, given that the conventionalists as portrayed by Dworkin are saddled with a belief in the close affinities between law and chess, they must further believe that the arguments made during legal cases do not ever propose changes in legal norms; and they must likewise believe that judicial officials lack authority to make such changes in the course of deciding particular cases. '[A]ny substantive attack on [a legal] proposition will be out of order within the context of adjudication, just as an attack on the wisdom of the rules of chess is out of

[12] For a somewhat more nuanced view of chess, see TRS, 101–5.

order within a game' (LE, 136). Yet, as Dworkin establishes, the beliefs which he attributes to conventionalists are palpably untenable. Those beliefs do not correspond at all to the realities of American and English law.

Have conventionalists badly stumbled in the way that Dworkin suggests? Or are his criticisms trained instead on a caricature of the doctrines that are actually advanced by jurisprudential positivists? We should opt for an affirmative answer to the latter question; here and often elsewhere, Dworkin has not sufficiently endeavored to present an accurate and constructive account of positivism. His toppling of straw men does not tell us much about the genuine merits of the positivist stance.

Any sensible conventionalist will happily acknowledge the salience of self-reflective deliberation and contestation in the American and English legal systems (and in other relevantly similar legal systems). The state of affairs in those legal systems is very much in keeping with the conventionalist model, since the role of the deliberation and contestation is carved out by conventions. When lawyers and judges make arguments in which they call for the transformation of various substantive or methodological norms, they do so because their fellow officials expect or at least permit such arguments—and because the arguments are very likely to be pondered, even if they do not ultimately prevail. Officials' attitudes and beliefs form a matrix of interconnected expectations, within which the officials can count on one another to anticipate (tolerantly, if not receptively) that some arguments in favor of altering the law may well be advanced. Were there no such matrix, the propounding of those arguments by any official would be pointless and perhaps counterproductive; but, given that the set of interlocked expectations does in fact exist, the reasoned appeals for change do indeed have a point. Legal conventions provide the opportunities for disputation concerning possible modifications to the conventions themselves. They render legitimate the questioning of their own bearings, and provide fora where such questioning can be carried on.

In short, we should eschew Dworkin's assumption that conventions are inevitably static and that adjustments to them must occur through external interventions rather than through opportunities generated within the conventions themselves. We can thereby reject his claim that conventionalists are unable to account for the patterns of evolution in the American and English legal systems. Conventional practices that serve recurrently as platforms for the initiation of changes to themselves are indeed thoroughly conventional, just as much as conventional practices that are not similarly dynamic. In connection with this matter, as in connection with other matters, Dworkin has erred by presuming that legal positivism insists on one particular mode of adjudication. In fact, the positivist conception of law is fully consistent with a mode of adjudication that leaves room for arguments about the advisability of various departures from the status quo. Such a style of adjudication involves nothing that cannot be accommodated within a conventionalist model; after all, the space for challenges to

the regnant conventions is cleared and maintained by the conventions themselves.

Before leaving the current section of this chapter, we should note three points.
First, nothing said here is at odds with anything in the preceding section.
Although the American and English legal systems are relatively dynamic, and
although Dworkin is correct in thinking that any adequate theory of law must be
able to account for the internal adaptability of those legal regimes, the dynamism
occurs within an overall context of routineness and settledness. Dworkin makes
clear that the processes of change on which he focuses are highly gradual, extending over several decades. He further observes quite aptly that a fluid and
contested state of affairs in any particular area of the law is accompanied by
stability in numerous other areas. '[T]he level of agreement . . . is high enough at
any given time to allow debate over fundamental practices like legislation and
precedent to proceed in the way I described . . . contesting discrete paradigms one
by one, like the reconstruction of Neurath's boat one plank at a time at sea' (LE,
139). My defense of conventionalism has endeavored to show that the dynamic,
self-reflective aspects of American and English legal institutions can be readily
explained along conventionalist lines; there has been no suggestion whatsoever
that the dynamic self-reflectiveness is a chaotic flux that excludes or greatly
impairs the general settledness of legal norms.

Second, contrary to what Dworkin implies, a legal positivist does not perforce
have to accept that the workings of any legal system are fundamentally conventional. Though all or most legal positivists are indeed (wisely) conventionalists,
there is a bit of room for a positivist to take the view that the functioning of each
legal system is based on a coincidence of officials' independent convictions. What
the positivist then has to argue—in order to remain a legal positivist—is that the
convictions need not be moral in tenor. In a wicked legal system, the convictions
can be purely prudential. Each official might seek to give effect to certain
precepts because he feels that acting on those precepts is in his interest (and in his
evil regime's interest) irrespective of whether his fellow officials are largely in
accord with him. So long as the officials' independent prudential calculations
converge to yield a substantial degree of regularity and co-ordination, a functional
legal system can ensue. To be sure, any such model of law would be extremely
far-fetched; but it would not be flatly unintelligible or self-contradictory.

Third, the present section of this chapter has sought to demonstrate that the
view of Anglo-American law as a set of conventions can withstand Dworkin's
criticisms. To establish as much is not *per se* to establish that Dworkin's own view
of Anglo-American law as a confluence of independent moral convictions is
incorrect or inferior. A rejection of his view—even a partial rejection thereof—
must rest on further arguments. (For the sake of concision, my discussion here
will mention only American law; but every facet of this terse discussion will
apply equally to English law.)

Now, any proponent of conventionalism should allow that the institutions of

American law are very likely perceived by most American judges as morally worthy on the whole. Because of this perception on the part of American judges, most of them are naturally inclined to regard the general aspects of their work as morally worthy. For example, having an independent conviction in the moral correctness of the principle of legislative supremacy, a judge will feel morally obligated to give effect to legislative enactments irrespective of whether his fellow judges do the same. In broad outlines, then, Dworkin's model of consensus-based-on-independent-convictions enjoys credibility as an explication of the workings of American law. It is a plausible alternative to the conventionalist model, at an abstract level.

As soon as we move down into the details of American legal institutions, however, the Dworkinian approach becomes strained. Though it is not utterly inconceivable that American judges harbor independent moral convictions about each of the various complex layers and ramifications in their Rule of Recognition, the likelihood of such a state of affairs is vanishingly small. Dworkin himself is not unaware of this point, as he acknowledges the limits of his model:

This argument does not prove that absolutely nothing is settled among American or British lawyers as a matter of genuine convention. Perhaps no political argument could persuade American judges to reject the proposition that Congress must be elected in the manner prescribed by the Constitution, as amended from time to time in accordance with its own amending provisions. Perhaps all judges do accept the authority of the Constitution as a matter of convention rather than as the upshot of sound political theory. (LE, 138)

Nevertheless, he goes on to state that 'nothing *need* be settled as a matter of convention in order for a legal system not only to exist but to flourish' (LE, 138, emphasis in original). On the one hand, strictly speaking, his statement is true; the idea of a legal regime based entirely on officials' independent moral convictions is not starkly unintelligible or self-contradictory. Yet, on the other hand, such an idea is extravagantly outlandish. No one can credibly maintain that American judges accept all elements of the criteria in their Rule of Recognition on the grounds of convention-independent moral principles.

At most, then, the Dworkinian model is only a partial alternative to the conventionalist model as an interpretation of the American legal system. A view of that system as a set of conventions can claim credibility at an abstract level and great cogency at a somewhat more detailed level. By contrast, Dworkin's approach can claim credibility at the abstract level but virtually no plausibility whatsoever at the somewhat more detailed level. Thus, even if we concede *arguendo* that Dworkin's protestantism is superior to conventionalism as an account of the general contours of American legal officials' endeavors, we have every reason to think that conventionalism will be needed in order to account for much of the texture of those endeavors. Even more plainly will conventionalism be pertinent if we are seeking to understand regimes of law that are far less morally benign than the American regime.

## F. Morality and Truth

According to Dworkin at many junctures in his major jurisprudential writings, the theory espoused by positivists has committed them to denying that any legal system's Rule of Recognition can ever include substantive moral tests among its criteria. Because his assertions and arguments along these lines have frequently been assailed,[13] no full-scale exploration of them here is warranted. However, a brief treatment is in order. Let us initially observe *en passant* that most legal positivists firmly reject Dworkin's characterization of their position. Apart from Joseph Raz and his followers,[14] few present-day legal positivists endorse the thesis that moral principles can never serve as legal touchstones for determining the existence and content of valid legal norms. As far as most positivists are concerned, the question of the status of moral principles as criteria for the ascertainment of legal norms is an empirical question about each particular system of law.

The principal task of the current section of this chapter is to rectify an unduly sweeping concession made by Hart in his posthumously published riposte to Dworkin on the topic. Throughout the Postscript to the second edition of *The Concept of Law*, Hart resisted Dworkin's efforts to classify him as a 'plain-fact positivist'; he squarely avouched that moral principles as well as social facts can amount to sources of law ('Postscript', 247–8, 250–4, 265–6). Whether such principles do indeed amount to such sources in any particular regime is an empirical matter, rather than something to be settled by verbal stipulation. By taking this view—by accepting that the criteria for legal validity can encompass moral requirements—Hart embraced a stance which he labeled as 'soft positivism'.

Hart thus made clear that jurisprudential positivism's treatment of the adjudicative role of moral principles is chiefly a doctrine concerning what does not have to be, as opposed to a doctrine concerning what has to be. Specifically, soft positivists subscribe to both of the following two theses: (1) no legal system *has* to include moral principles among its criteria for ascertaining the law; and (2) any legal system *can* include moral principles among those criteria. Dworkin has persistently declared that positivists are logically committed to rejecting the latter of these theses, but his unflinching insistence on this point is dubious in light of Hart's robust proclamations to the contrary. Or so we could straightaway conclude, if Hart in his Postscript had not made an unwise concession to the Dworkinian position. Before a verdict against Dworkin can be entered, that concession must be withdrawn.

To understand Hart's concession and to grasp its unwisdom, we must take a

---

[13] For the most sustained challenge to Dworkin on this issue, see W. J. Waluchow, *Inclusive Legal Positivism* (Oxford: Clarendon Press, 1994), chs VI and VII.

[14] For a recent statement from this school, see Eleni Mitrophanous, 'Soft Positivism', 17 *Oxford Journal of Legal Studies* 621 (1997).

glance at the claim by Dworkin to which Hart was responding. In *Taking Rights Seriously*, but not in *Law's Empire*, Dworkin contends that the doctrine of soft positivism commits its proponents to the idea of 'an objective realm of moral facts' (TRS, 349; 'Reply', 250). His argument runs as follows. Soft positivists maintain that moral requirements can be among the official standards for identifying norms as legal norms. Thus, for example, if the workings of a particular legal system *L* are subject to a constitutional provision which invalidates any legislative enactments that impose cruel punishments, then the legal validity of any punitive enactment in *L* will hinge on a moral test relating to cruelty. However, if propositions about the legal validity of punitive enactments in *L* can be true—in much the same way that other propositions of law in *L* can be true—then there must be some set of objective facts to which those propositions can correspond. And since those propositions are partly moral in tenor, some of the relevant facts must be moral facts. Hence, by allowing that moral precepts can figure as authoritative criteria in a legal system's Rule of Recognition, the soft positivists have logically committed themselves to a realist metaphysics of morals (i.e., a doctrine affirming that moral values are belief-independent). Such a logical commitment is troubling for the soft positivists in two respects. First, it loads them with what some of them would perceive as murky ontological baggage. Second, theses concerning the metaphysically objective status of morality may well turn out to be false or unintelligible; if so, then the tenets of soft positivism entail the conclusion that a myriad of pertinent legal propositions in some societies such as the United States are false or are neither true nor false. Vast areas of law in those societies will be spheres of judicial discretion.

Having become uneasy by 1984 with this sort of metaphysical conjuring ('Reply', 300 n. 12), Dworkin omits this line of argument altogether in *Law's Empire*. In his recent work, as we shall presently observe, his conception of moral truth prevents or defuses such a line of argument. None the less, Hart apparently felt rather disconcerted by Dworkin's raising of the specter of moral realism. Hart seems to have endorsed the view that, unless a realm of metaphysically independent moral facts exists, the incorporation of moral criteria into a Rule of Recognition will mean that any norms validated by reference to those criteria are not pre-existing laws: '[I]f there are no [objective moral] facts, a judge, told to apply a moral test, can only treat this as a call for the exercise by him of a law-making discretion in accordance with his best understanding of morality and its requirements and subject to whatever constraints on this are imposed by the legal system' (Hart, 'Postscript', 253). Accurately but somewhat lamely, Hart remarked that the upshot of debates over the ontological status of morality will not make any practical difference for judges. Irrespective of whether moral propositions have any ultimate grounding, each judge will labor under a duty to deliberate carefully when applying any moral criterion that plays a part in determining the validity and substance of legal norms. Having discounted the practical significance of the question of moral ontology, Hart then offered a major theoretical concession:

Of course, if the question of the objective standing of moral judgments is left open by legal theory, as I claim it should be, then soft positivism cannot be simply characterized as the theory that moral principles or values may be among the criteria of legal validity, since if it is an open question whether moral principles and values have objective standing, it must also be an open question whether 'soft positivist' provisions purporting to include conformity with them among the tests for existing law can have that effect or instead, can only constitute directions to courts to *make* law in accordance with morality. ('Postscript', 254, emphasis in original)

Given that Hart was almost certainly using the phrase 'objective standing' to mean far more than 'determinate correctness', this passage effectively marks a wholesale capitulation in the face of Dworkin's original attack on soft positivism.

For two main reasons, Hart was unwise in surrendering. First, Dworkin's more recent conception of moral truth disallows his own original challenge to the soft-positivist model. Furthermore, his challenge can be deflected even in some contexts where his revised conception of moral truth might be deemed partly inapplicable. Let us consider each of these points in turn.

In *Law's Empire*, Dworkin draws an important distinction between internal and external skepticism (LE, 76–86). As applied to morality, internal skepticism focuses on the correctness or incorrectness of various answers to moral problems, and addresses the question whether any answer to each problem is (uniquely) correct. By contrast, external skepticism focuses not on the correctness or incorrectness of answers to moral problems, but on the ultimate metaphysical posture of those answers. Dworkin neither opposes nor endorses external skepticism in *Law's Empire*; instead, he puts it aside as having no bearing on his interpretive approach to jurisprudence. He is interested solely in the questions tackled by internal skepticism. That is, he seeks to evaluate moral theories and outlooks in order to come up with the right answers to legal and moral problems. Given his purposes and concerns, a rejection of external skepticism would be as misguided as an espousal of it. Instead, it is best dismissed as irrelevant. Striving to apprehend moral truths, Dworkin has no reason to engage in metaphysical speculations—since, even if the speculations are intelligible, they are wholly external to the inquiries wherein moral truth is pursued.

In a generally valuable recent article, 'Objectivity and Truth: You'd Better Believe It',[15] Dworkin has extended and reinforced the stance taken in *Law's*

---

[15] The article is marred by only a few inadvisable passages, of which the longest is a two-page critique of Richard Rorty ('Objectivity', 95–6). Therein, Dworkin misrepresents Rorty's epistemological relativism as the ontological doctrine of Berkeleian idealism. Rorty does his best to dodge and dismiss the metaphysical questions to which Berkeley supplied idealist answers.

Of course, some positivists may not wish to join Rorty and the later Dworkin in dodging metaphysical questions about objectivity. Those positivists can instead seek to defuse the early Dworkin's stance by engaging in philosophical inquiries that unpack the concept of objectivity into a number of conceptions, some of which will not involve any moral-realist baggage for a theorist who embraces them. For an approach along these lines, see Jules Coleman and Brian Leiter, 'Determinacy, Objectivity, and Authority', in Andrei Marmor (ed.), *Law and Interpretation* (Oxford: Clarendon Press, 1995), 203, 241–78.

*Empire*. More strongly than ever, he emphasizes that questions about the objectivity and truth and universality of moral propositions are themselves moral rather than metaphysical. He now does reject external skepticism—not because he views it as wrong, but because he views it (and also any metaphysical stance opposed to it) as unintelligible. If claims about the timelessness and objectivity of moral truths are to make any sense at all, they have to be understood as moral rather than metaphysical claims; accordingly, any skeptical stance which doubts those claims must likewise be understood as a moral stance, if it is to be intelligible at all. Both the affirmations of the objectivity of moral truth and the challenges to any of those affirmations are internal to the deliberations wherein such truth is pursued. To grasp the correct answers to the moral questions about objectivity or to any other moral questions, we have to determine which moral principles and arguments are best (morally best, of course). Having determined as much, we shall not have left anything undone. There is no further set of meaningful inquiries about a correspondence between the best moral principles and some metaphysical realm.

Despite the laconicism of this account of Dworkin's thoughtfully developed views about moral truth—an account that reports some of his conclusions without rehearsing the forceful arguments which support them—the implications for his critique of soft positivism should be clear. No longer can Dworkin consistently allege that the soft positivists are committed to a moral-realist doctrine simply by dint of their acknowledging the pre-existence of many legal norms that have been identified partly through moral tests. Soft positivists need only accept that many moral propositions are true; an acceptance of such a claim does not commit them to an ontologically realist account of morality. Instead, they will be committed merely to the view that moral argumentation on any particular issue (within some range of issues) can in principle yield a verdict that is superior to every other verdict on the issue in question. Such a view is a moral thesis rather than a metaphysical tenet. It does not burden the soft positivists with what many of them would see as unwanted ontological lumber.

Thus, when gauged from the perspective of Dworkin's writings in the 1980s and 1990s, his attempt in *Taking Rights Seriously* to establish an integral connection between soft positivism and moral realism has turned out to be unsustainable. Moral objectivity is a moral matter, to be postulated and verified (or doubted) through moral discourse; it is not something that can be intelligibly verified or disproved through purely metaphysical speculation. If the soft positivists wish to maintain that a moral test invoked in some particular legal system can yield objectively true answers in various circumstances, they need not be setting forth a realist ontological hypothesis. Instead, as Dworkin himself now emphasizes, the claim about objectivity and truth should be regarded as nothing more than an emphatic moral assertion. Hence, when the soft positivist declares that legal propositions can be true even if the propositions are about norms that owe their jural validity partly to moral tests, he or she is not necessarily taking on any realist ontological commitments.

To be sure, Dworkin's current conception of morality is still objectivist—in that it reconstrues, rather than denies, the objectivity of moral truths. Moreover, his conception is not uncontroversial. Does either of these facts undercut my arguments here? That is, does either of them preclude my defense of soft positivism against Dworkin's original strictures?

Although a soft positivist who avoids moral realism by adopting Dworkin's recent account of moral truths is indeed thereby committed to the notion that such truths are objective (in the sense described by my last few paragraphs), the operative conception of objectivity here does not run afoul of the challenge mounted in *Taking Rights Seriously*. When posing that challenge, Dworkin maintains:

The . . . claim I took positivism to make is . . . connected with a more general theoretical position that would have to be modified if this claim were abandoned. This . . . claim is most clearly put in the following way. We may suppose propositions of law to be true or false, accurate or inaccurate, without thereby accepting any ontology beyond an empiricist's ontology. The truth of a proposition of law, when it is true, consists in ordinary historical facts about individual or social behaviour including, perhaps, facts about beliefs and attitudes, but in nothing metaphysically more suspicious.   (TRS, 348)

Dworkin goes on, of course, to contend that soft positivism must abandon the claim delineated in this passage. However, precisely what his current conception of morality enables soft positivists to do is to avoid committing themselves to 'any ontology beyond an empiricist's ontology'. They can presume that numerous legal propositions based partly on moral judgments are true or false, accurate or inaccurate, without having to accept the existence of any entities that would be viewed by empiricists as 'metaphysically . . . suspicious'. In other words, the conception of moral objectivity currently advanced by Dworkin is not the conception of objectivity from which Hart and other legal positivists have sought to keep their jurisprudential analyses disjoinable. Insofar as Dworkin has shown that moral propositions can be definitively correct (or incorrect) without being grounded in a realist ontology, he has shown that soft positivists are not logically committed to such an ontology and that they are therefore not vulnerable to his original critique.

Dworkin's own recent account of moral truth, however, is controversial—perhaps no less so than moral realism itself. Does his original critique succeed, then, in establishing that soft positivists must abandon 'Hart's ambition (and . . . the ambition of positivists generally) to make the objective standing of propositions of law independent of any controversial theory either of meta-ethics or of moral ontology' (TRS, 349)? A negative answer is clearly warranted here, for the point of my discussion is not to conclude that soft positivists have to endorse Dworkin's non-realist stance; my point, rather, is to indicate that they do not have to endorse a moral-realist position. So long as they accept that many moral propositions are objectively correct and that many other such propositions are objectively incorrect, they do not have to align themselves clearly with either Dworkin's stance or moral realism. Soft positivism is independent of either of those controversial theories because it is consistent with each of them.[16]

By taking aboard Dworkin's recent reflections on moral truth, then, we can eschew the undue concession made by Hart in his defense of soft positivism. Let us now suppose that a soft positivist does not fully subscribe to Dworkin's optimism about the existence of a single right answer to virtually every legal problem. What are the implications for the matter which we have just been considering?

Although any sensible soft positivist will undoubtedly believe that there are uniquely correct answers to quite a few moral questions (such as the question whether genocide is wrong), he or she might well believe that there are no uniquely correct answers to much trickier moral questions. Such a belief is moral rather than metaphysical, but is no less firm for that; quite the contrary. Of course, if the soft positivist becomes a judicial official, then he or she will have to take stands on tricky moral questions insofar as the taking of such stands is necessary for carrying out the judicial task of ascertaining the law. The pressures of an institutional role that centrally involves decision-making will impel the soft-positivist judge to opt for an answer—and therefore to leave aside other plausible answers—to each knotty moral question $Q$ which he or she must address. However, the judge's fulfillment of his or her institutional responsibilities does not perforce betoken a belief that $Q$ itself is answerable in a uniquely correct way. Furthermore, even if every judge takes the view that $Q$ is indeed so answerable, a theorist removed from the pressures of judicial institutions may well take a contrary view.

Suppose that a soft positivist does in fact think that there are no uniquely correct responses to a number of difficult moral questions which American judges must answer in the course of their law-ascertaining duties.[17] Is he or she thus committed to the view that, when legal norms are validated partly on the basis of the judges' answers to those difficult questions, the norms have had no legal status prior to the validative decisions? In other words, must the soft positivist accept that such norms cannot rightly be deemed pre-existent laws which the judges discover rather than introduce? If so, then Dworkin's critique of soft positivism appears to be pertinent within the limited range of cases involving norms of the sort just described. Apparently, only a soft positivist as robustly confident as Dworkin about the existence of uniquely correct answers to vexed moral questions will be able to evade the aforementioned critique entirely.

From the perspective of the soft positivist, one way of reacting to the new lease

---

[16] It is likewise consistent with other doctrines such as Simon Blackburn's quasi-realism. For a vigorous and occasionally acrimonious Internet exchange between Blackburn and Dworkin on the nature of moral truth, see http://www.brown.edu/Departments/Philosophy/bears/symp-dworkin.html.

[17] For the sake of concision, I refer here only to American judges. My discussion applies, however, to any legal system wherein moral principles figure among the criteria for ascertaining the law.

of life for Dworkin's critique is to shrug with indifference. After all, the critique now holds up only in regard to norms whose legal status has been determined partly on the basis of moral tests that do not yield uniquely correct outcomes. Many soft positivists will be happy to admit that judges who decide cases by reference to such norms are extending the law rather than exclusively finding it. So long as the soft positivist believes that most moral questions which American judges must address are questions with uniquely correct solutions, he or she need not worry about the occurrence of peripheral cases where no such solutions exist. (Of course, if a soft positivist foolishly believes that all or most of the moral questions which American judges must address are questions *without* uniquely correct solutions, then he or she will be vulnerable to a revised version of Dworkin's original strictures.) Dworkin's critique, in its new and reduced guise, reinstates the core/penumbra distinction that has always been to the liking of positivists. The critique now merely shows that most legal norms validated partly through moral tests are pre-existent laws, and that a small proportion of legal norms validated partly through moral tests are not pre-existent laws. Soft positivists may well retort: 'So what?!'

Another reply available to the positivists goes still further. Even in the relatively small proportion of cases where the ascertainment of the law proceeds via moral questions for which there are not usually any uniquely correct solutions, there can be such solutions in the specific institutional contexts. Suppose that the American legal system requires judges to ask a certain moral question $Q$ when determining whether legislative enactments are valid laws. Suppose further that a soft-positivist theorist has concluded that there is no uniquely correct answer to $Q$ when it is asked about enactments of a certain type $E$. None the less, the theorist is not automatically committed to the conclusion that $E$-enactments in the United States are never valid laws until they are implicitly or expressly declared to be such by the courts. Let us presume that American legislative and judicial officials are unanimous or virtually unanimous in thinking that $Q$ should be answered affirmatively when posed in connection with $E$-enactments. Any maverick officials opting to answer negatively will incur reprimands from their colleagues and superiors, who will reverse the mavericks' decisions and deem them to be plainly in error. Legislative officials pass $E$-enactments with the expectation that $Q$ will be answered affirmatively in regard to those enactments; judicial officials are aware of the expectations of the legislators, and fully share the legislators' view about the appropriate answer to $Q$. In these circumstances, the understandings and expectations of the officials confer a context-specific determinacy on $Q$ as applied to $E$-enactments. Within the American legal system as described here, the uniquely correct assessment of $Q$'s bearing on any such enactments is that the test laid down by $Q$ has been passed. Hence, within that system, an $E$-enactment can rightly be designated as a law whose validity antedates any implementation of the enactment by a court—even though that validity hinges on a moral question to which there would not usually be a uniquely correct answer (in connection with an $E$-enactment).

Dworkin himself adverts to a situation that is strikingly similar to the one just sketched: 'A positivist may hold a theory of statutory interpretation such that, if a statute provides that a contract is invalid when it is unconscionable, and the vast majority of [officials think] that a particular sort of contract is unjust, then that sort of contract is, as a matter of law, invalid' (TRS, 348). However, Dworkin presumes that the sort of theory which he mentions is different from soft positivism in claiming only 'that *beliefs* about justice may be part of the truth conditions of propositions of law' (TRS, 348, emphasis in original). He elaborates: 'This theory makes beliefs about moral facts, not moral facts themselves, decisive for propositions of law. But for a [soft] positivist the legal validity of a contract might depend, not on whether a contract is believed to be unjust, but whether it is unjust. That theory [i.e., soft positivism] . . . makes a moral fact itself part of the truth conditions of a proposition of law' (TRS, 348).

For two reasons, these observations by Dworkin do not cast doubt on the pertinence of my scenario involving *E*-enactments. First, that scenario has been presented here because it deals with a moral test for which (*ex hypothesi*) there is not usually a uniquely correct determination. In such circumstances, there is no moral truth—no morally best answer—that could serve as part of the truth conditions for certain propositions of law. If there are any truth conditions, they must lie elsewhere; my scenario has suggested where they might reside, as has Dworkin's terse account of the beliefs surrounding a contracts statute. Were we instead pondering the implications of a moral test under which there is a uniquely correct determination in each case, the alternative truth conditions would be superfluous. No account of the officials' beliefs would be needed. But in situations where morality itself does not provide truth conditions, and where soft positivism along the lines recounted by Dworkin is therefore not an option, some alternative truth conditions are indeed necessary (unless we are willing to grant—not unreasonably—that the legal propositions asserted in such situations are neither true nor false). In sum, my scenario involving *E*-enactments is focused only on circumstances to which Dworkin's own description of soft positivism is inapplicable. If my scenario proposes an abandonment of soft positivism, it does so only for settings where the retention of soft positivism is infeasible.

Let us turn to a second and even more important reason for thinking that the pertinence of my scenario is not diminished at all by Dworkin's distinction between moral principles and beliefs about moral principles. His observations tend to run together the perspective of the theorist and the perspective of the participant. If a theorist knows that there usually are no uniquely correct verdicts concerning *Q*'s bearing on *E*-enactments, then she knows that morality itself does not furnish any of the truth conditions for propositions about *E*-enactments within the American legal system. She knows that those conditions must instead consist partly in the unanimous or nearly unanimous beliefs of the American officials—when there is indeed unanimity, and when there consequently are indeed truth conditions for the aforementioned propositions. By contrast, the officials who participate in running the American legal system do not answer $Q$ by reference to their fellow officials' beliefs. They aptly regard $Q$ as a moral criterion, in the application of which they have to make moral judgments; they do not view it as a sociological or psychological criterion, in the application of which they have to make empirical judgments.

Of course, a legal system could include within its Rule of Recognition a sociological or psychological criterion. Officials in some system might take the view that the operative touchstone for legal validity is not the morally correct answer to $Q$, but the beliefs of one another about the morally correct answer to $Q$. In other words, instead of asking what the correct answer to $Q$ is, each official would seek to determine which answer to $Q$ is perceived as correct by all or most of his fellow officials. But such an odd arrangement, though quite conceivable, is not the state of affairs to which the soft positivists call attention. They are not advancing a thesis about officials' reliance on sociological or psychological criteria; rather, they are advancing a thesis about officials' reliance on moral criteria. Soft positivists concern themselves with legal systems wherein the officials inquire not about their fellow officials' beliefs, but about the correct answer to $Q$ (or to any other moral question that affects legal validity).

Hence, although Dworkin's remarks on the unjust-contracts statute appropriately imply that my scenario involving $E$-enactments has seized upon American officials' virtually unanimous beliefs as some of the truth conditions for propositions about the $E$-enactments, his remarks are misleading if they suggest that the American officials themselves take a similar view of the matter. When considering the implications of $Q$ for $E$-enactments, each official presumes that the truth of her determination stems from the nature of the test imposed by $Q$; she does not presume that the truth of her determination derives from the substance of the beliefs held by other officials. Each official is focused only on the contents of her own beliefs about $E$-enactments and $Q$—which happen also to be the contents of almost every other official's beliefs about $E$-enactments and $Q$, *ex hypothesi*. Each official, in other words, is engaged in exactly the sort of moral decision-making that has been singled out by the soft positivists as one aspect of the process of ascertaining the law in certain jural regimes. No official bases her decisions on sociological or psychological judgments about the attitudes of her fellow officials. For the task of pondering $Q$'s bearing on $E$-enactments, moral judgments (as opposed to sociological/psychological surveys) are what is involved.

Dworkin himself, when delineating the tenets of positivism, distinguishes between the semantics and the truth conditions of legal propositions (TRS, 348). His distinction reinforces my present point. From the perspective of the officials in the American legal system, there is no disjuncture between the semantics and the truth conditions of their statements about the implications of $Q$ for the validity of $E$-enactments. As far as the officials can tell, those statements are about the implications of a moral requirement, and the truth conditions consist (partly) in

the nature of that requirement. However, from the perspective of the soft-positivist observer—who knows that there is not generally a uniquely correct answer
to $Q$ when it is asked about $E$-enactments—the semantics and the truth conditions
of the officials' statements diverge. Their statements are indeed about the implications of a moral requirement, whereas the truth conditions of the statements do
not lie in the nature of that requirement at all. Rather, from the knowledgeable
perspective of the soft-positivist observer, the truth conditions can be seen to
consist (partly) in the officials' *beliefs* about the nature of the moral requirement.

Thus, Dworkin's comments on the unjust-contracts statute do no harm whatsoever to my account of the American officials' applications of $Q$ to $E$-enact-
ments. When soft positivists maintain that moral principles can serve as criteria
for officials' identification of legal norms, they have not debarred themselves (in
appropriate circumstances) from characterizing officials' beliefs as part of the
truth conditions for propositions about the validity and content of those legal
norms. Though the soft positivists' classification of some moral principles as law-
ascertaining criteria in some legal systems is typically a doctrine concerning truth
conditions set by the principles themselves, it is sometimes a doctrine concerning
truth conditions set by officials' beliefs about the principles. Invariably, however,
it is a doctrine concerning the moral tenor of the judgments and statements that
are made by officials as they invoke the moral principles for the purpose of deciding what the law is.

## II. THE MORAL OF THE STORY FOR POSITIVISM

No one familiar with Dworkin's work can fail to be aware of his view that
jurisprudence and law are both fundamentally enterprises of moral justification.
In the second half of this chapter, we explore the arguments and assumptions that
underlie his stance. As was indicated at this chapter's outset, Dworkin has built
his stance on the basis of several conflations; he tends to run together various
aspects of law and legal theory that are quite plainly separable. Already we have
noted his tendency to swing back and forth between referring to law and referring to the law—that is, between referring to an abstract phenomenon and referring to a particular instance of that phenomenon (chiefly the American instance).
His conflation of law and the law is clearly of considerable importance for my
present topic. After all, notwithstanding the many ways in which the American
legal system falls short of perfection, it is morally benevolent on the whole. As
a consequence, a large number of statements about its moral posture will not be
safely generalizable to legal regimes that are far less benign. (Conversely, of
course, a large number of statements about the moral posture of a flagitious legal
system would not be safely generalizable to regimes that are far less malign.)
Dworkin's sanguine view of law as a domain for the working out of moral principles is undoubtedly due in part to his American background and especially to

his preoccupation with American constitutional law. We should never entirely
lose sight of the fact that some of his most dubious jurisprudential positions are
less dubious when construed as theoretical encapsulations of the fundaments of
American law.

None the less, Dworkin throughout his writings has advanced an array of arguments and contentions at a jurisprudential level of abstraction. Some of his lines
of reasoning in support of his positions are broadly conceptual and have been
construed as such. We certainly do not do him any injustice when we perceive his
efforts as those of a philosopher and when we gauge their success accordingly. In
any event, a defense of legal positivism against Dworkin's onslaughts is bound to
take up philosophical issues. Positivist theses are philosophical theses pertaining
to the general concept of law, abstracted from the peculiarities of the law in any
particular society. Therefore, anyone undertaking a confrontation with Dworkin
in defense of those theses can hardly be satisfied to inquire merely whether *Law's
Empire* illuminatingly captures some features of American constitutional law.

In short, although Dworkin's frequent conflation of law and the law will
indeed loom as a major target of my rejoinders, it should not blind us to the fact
that his writings are very much about law as well as about the law. Precisely
because of the jurisprudential sweep of many of his arguments, his handling of
certain jurisprudential distinctions—mentioned near the beginning of this chapter—is especially problematic. My ripostes to Dworkin on the issue of law's
moral significance begin by examining his treatment of two of those distinctions:
theory versus practice, and observer versus participant.

## A. A Matter of Perspective

One of Dworkin's central tenets is that jurisprudence and adjudication (and
indeed other activities within a legal system) are not separate endeavors. On each
occasion when a judge reaches a decision, she has to construct the same basic
kind of legal theory that is constructed by a jurisprudential scholar. When a
judge's theory is not expressly elaborated but is only implicit—as it very often
is—it lurks beneath the surface as the formative underpinning of her analyses and
conclusions. Or so Dworkin declares: '[A]ny judge's opinion is itself a piece of
legal philosophy, even when the philosophy is hidden and the visible argument is
dominated by citation[s] and lists of facts. Jurisprudence is the general part of
adjudication, silent prologue to any decision at law' (LE, 90). For Dworkin, the
gap between theory and practice largely disappears. Anyone engaged in the practical task of adjudication has to engage as well in the theoretical task of subsuming the law within a jurisprudential model, albeit probably a model that is not
explicitly fleshed out. Such a model is composed of moral principles that serve to
justify the law by presenting it in its best light.

If the officials who run a legal system must adopt the perspective of the
jurisprudential scholar in the course of their work, then so too the jurisprudential

scholar must adopt the perspective of the officials. We encounter this claim very early in *Law's Empire*, where Dworkin responds to some imagined critics who might fault him for not taking a social-scientific approach to the study of law (LE, 11–15). These critics would urge that the truly important questions about any legal system pertain to its causal relationships with its economic, social, political, and cultural surroundings. According to these critics, a causal-explanatory approach to their discipline can avoid the aridity and naïveté of Dworkin's interpretive method, which debilitatingly makes jurisprudential scholars 'like anthropologists sucked into the theological disputes of some ancient and primitive culture' (LE, 13).

Dworkin replies forthrightly to these hypothetical opponents and their view that a satisfactory account of law must stem from an external perspective concerned with charting and explaining the interaction between law and other phenomena. Though he acknowledges that there is a legitimate role to be played by the external perspective in legal scholarship, he declares that the insights of such a perspective are dependent on the internal focus of his own interpretive method. Unless sociologists and historians adopt the internal viewpoint of the participants in a legal system, their understanding of the institutions which they seek to explain will be meager—too meager to enable them to come up with any adequate explanations. As Dworkin submits:

[T]he historian [or sociologist] cannot understand law as an argumentative social practice, even enough to reject it as deceptive, until he has a participant's understanding, until he has his own sense of what counts as a good or bad argument within that practice. We need a social theory of law, but it must be jurisprudential just for that reason. Theories that ignore the structure of legal argument for supposedly larger questions of history and society are therefore perverse. They ignore questions about the internal character of legal argument, so their explanations are impoverished and defective, like innumerate histories of mathematics. (LE, 14)

Having argued that any theory which proceeds purely from the external perspective of an observer is unacceptably superficial, Dworkin firmly declares his intention to proceed differently: 'This book takes up the internal, participants' point of view; it tries to grasp the argumentative character of our legal practice by joining that practice and struggling with the issues of soundness and truth participants face' (LE, 14).

Now, one need not be enamored of socio-legal studies to feel uneasy about Dworkin's treatment of the theory/practice and external/internal distinctions. Before we move on to investigate the shortcomings of his arguments, however, we should briefly consider why his treatment of the foregoing distinctions is relevant to the second half of my current chapter (which focuses on the moral significance of law). The upshot of Dworkin's discussions is the primacy of the participant's viewpoint for the study of law. Both because jurisprudential theorizing is an endeavor that underlies the decisions of judges (perhaps sometimes *malgré eux*), and because jurisprudential theorists must embrace the judge's internal perspective if they want to produce satisfactory accounts of law, the judicial participant's point of view is the indispensable fundament or lodestar of legal thought. Anyone hoping to provide an adequate exposition of law must join in the same basic patterns of reasoning—judicial reasoning—that are being expounded.

On the one hand, to be sure, most of the rest of this chapter will maintain that Dworkin's pronouncements about the inherently moral tenor of law are unsustainable even if the judicial participant's perspective is taken as our point of reference. Yet, on the other hand, Dworkin's arguments in favor of the primacy of the participant's perspective do render more understandable his depiction of jurisprudence and law as enterprises of moral justification. After all, as should be evident from some of my previous chapters, the participant's perspective has often struck theorists as a fruitful site on which to center their claims about the intrinsically moral nature of law. Although each theory advancing such claims has proved to be untenable, the untenability has not been immediately obvious; only after close analysis have the claims lost their initial plausibility. Hence, if Dworkin were correct in thinking that legal philosophers have to place themselves in the position of judges when they present their theses, his characterization of jurisprudence as an exercise in moral justification would be more credible than it is. Contrariwise, by impugning his arguments which purport to establish the primacy of the participant's perspective, this section of my chapter will attempt to show that his portrayal of jurisprudence is even more doubtful than his portrayal of law.[18]

The principal weakness in Dworkin's prioritization of the participant's viewpoint is his reliance on a stark external/internal dichotomy. To be sure, if the available theoretical stances were limited to the social scientist's causal-explanatory approach and the Dworkinian judge's interpretive approach, then we would have quite good grounds for favoring the latter over the former; unless the former were exceedingly superficial, it would be parasitic upon some version of the latter. In fact, however, a legal positivist need not and should not choose either of those perspectives. At least two other points of view are far more promising for the positivist conception of law.

---

[18]   For some previous criticism, see Michael Bayles, above, n. 6, at 380; Hart, 'Comment', 36–7; Hart, 'Postscript', 242–4; Andrei Marmor, above, n. 3, at ch. 3; W. J. Waluchow, above, n. 13, at 27–9. My delineation of perspectives in this section of my chapter is obviously indebted to Hart, *Concept*, 55–6, 86–8; H. L. A. Hart, 'Introduction', in *Essays in Jurisprudence and Philosophy* (Oxford: Clarendon Press, 1983), 1, 14–15; Neil MacCormick, *Legal Reasoning and Legal Theory* (Oxford: Clarendon Press, 1978), 275–92; Joseph Raz, *Practical Reason and Norms* (Princeton: Princeton University Press, 1990), 175–7; Joseph Raz, above, n. 6, at ch. 8. Also illuminating is Meir Dan-Cohen, 'Interpreting Official Speech', in Andrei Marmor (ed.), *Law and Interpretation* (Oxford: Clarendon Press, 1995), 433, which I came upon after I had written this chapter.

There are some points of resemblance between my analysis in this section and the analysis in Stephen Perry, 'Interpretation and Methodology in Legal Theory', in Marmor (ed.), *Law and Interpretation*, 97. However, the differences between my approach and Perry's approach (which is largely pro-Dworkinian and strongly anti-Hartian) are considerably more numerous and significant than the similarities. For a critique of Perry, see the final section of Ch. 8 below.

We should therefore take account of four perspectives: the extreme external, the moderate external, the simulative, and the internal. The extreme external theorist perceives legal institutions as sets of regularities in the observable behavior of people. Such a theorist makes no effort to see people's actions in the ways that they are seen by the people themselves. Instead, he charts the regularities in their conduct—the regularities formed by people's compliance with legal norms, and the regularities formed by officials' handling of malefactors—in much the same manner as a meteorologist might trace the patterns of cloud-formation or atmospheric pressure. Confining himself to the surface of people's behavior, the extreme external observer uses concepts such as 'cause', 'effect', 'regularity', 'pattern', 'predictability', and 'probability' as the dominant categories for his account of legal institutions. Though he need not actually deny that people harbor attitudes and beliefs, he takes no notice of those phenomena except insofar as they gain expression in observable instances of conduct (such as reprimands or commendations).

A moderate external theorist certainly does not ignore the features of law that are the preoccupation of the extreme external theorist, but he focuses centrally as well on people's attitudes and beliefs. In particular, he attributes normative attitudes and beliefs to the people whose behavior indicates that they accept certain rules and standards as binding. He takes account of the ways in which people view their own actions and institutions, and he incorporates their perceptions into his overall exposition of law. Although he sees law as a domain of regularities and patterns, he also sees it as a domain in which concepts such as 'justifiability', 'acceptance', 'commitment', and 'allegiance' are pertinent. While he himself might not feel a commitment to any system of legal norms which he explicates— at least insofar as he occupies a genuinely external perspective—he highlights the attitude of commitment felt by officials and usually by many citizens. (Though not of direct relevance to my discussion in the present section of this chapter, an important caveat should be entered straightaway. The attitudes or outlooks ascribed by a moderate external theorist to the participants in a legal system are not necessarily moral. As should be plain from my previous chapters, each official's acceptance and commitment and allegiance can be based on prudential considerations through and through.)

Someone who occupies the simulative perspective does not merely attribute normative beliefs to officials and some citizens, but actually gives expression to those beliefs. He speaks or writes from a certain point of view without being committed to it. To some degree, the word 'recitative' would be a good designation for this perspective, since the person engaged in simulation is quite closely akin to a theatrical actor. If an actor plays Iago in a production of *Othello*, he will recite Iago's lines and generally do his best to convey Iago's thoughts and emotions—his point of view—to the audience. Even a superb performance of the role, however, does not count at all as an endorsement of Iago's villainy. When a good actor strives to fathom Iago's outlook and thereby manages to deliver a splendid performance, he none the less may disapprove strongly (and probably does disapprove strongly) of the misdeeds which he himself is feigning to carry out.

Yet, in one important respect, the analogy between the theatrical performer's recitation and the simulative theorist's discourse breaks down. Though some productions of plays require or permit the improvisation of numerous lines, most do not; they involve the recitation of lines that have been written beforehand. In a typical production of *Othello*, the man who plays Iago will recite some or all of the lines for that character which were written by Shakespeare, and will add few or none himself. By contrast, the theorist who adopts the simulative perspective will frequently elaborate the implications of the set of beliefs which he is expressing. He may well draw inferences or develop lines of argument or undertake extensions that have not thitherto occurred to anyone. Even when his discourse is a straightforward recapitulation of thoughts and sentiments that have previously been articulated by other people, he typically does not simply repeat lines verbatim that have already been written. In sum, a simulative utterance is both illuminatingly similar to recitation and importantly different from it. Each of those two modes of communication consists in giving voice to a point of view that is not one's own, but—even if we allow for the creativity and ingenuity that are involved in a deft theatrical performance—the simulative perspective leaves much more latitude for innovation than does the recitation of lines.

Crucially different from the three main perspectives just recounted is the internal viewpoint, the viewpoint of the committed participant. Someone occupying the internal perspective is seeking to sustain the workings of an institution, for moral reasons or for prudential reasons.[19] Such a person exhibits the critical reflective attitude described by Hart (and mentioned briefly earlier in this chapter). That is, she takes a censorious attitude toward violations of the institution's norms—including her own violations—and she cites the norms in justification of her criticism. She demands conformity with the norms as such, and she acknowledges the warrantedness of any pertinent demands and criticisms that are directed at her by her fellows. Even if some of the norms strike her as regrettable in themselves, she endorses the character of the institution as a whole, and she therefore adopts the critical reflective attitude toward most of its norms (perhaps toward all or virtually all of them, with varying degrees of intensity). The posture of endorsement is what distinguishes this perspective from the other perspectives; to embrace the internal point of view is to forsake disengagement.

Dworkin is correct in thinking that a jurisprudential theory advanced from the extreme external viewpoint is bound to be inadequate *sans plus*. Any such theory

---

[19] As is briefly observed in Ch. 3 n. 35 above, there can exist legal systems in which every official (as well as every citizen) is motivated only by fear. In these possible but exceedingly improbable circumstances, the distinction between the internal perspective and the simulative perspective has become blurred altogether. In the more likely event that *some* officials are motivated only by fear, the internal/simulative distinction has become blurred in relation to them.

omits too much. He therefore concludes that jurisprudential scholars must take up the internal perspective alongside judges and other officials; they must aim for nothing less than full-scale justifications of the legal systems whose basic features they expound. We are now in a position to resist this conclusion. An eschewal of the extreme external standpoint does not entail an endorsement of law or of any specific legal regime, since it can lead to the moderate external perspective or to the simulative perspective as easily as to the internal perspective of the engaged participant. The simulative viewpoint is perhaps especially suitable for doctrinal synopses, where the law on a given topic or set of topics in a particular jurisdiction is frequently recounted as if from the perspective of the officials who shape the law. In jurisprudence, by contrast, the moderate external perspective is probably most suitable and most commonly taken up. (For example, at least since Hart's *The Concept of Law*, few if any legal positivists neglect to ascribe normative attitudes and beliefs to the officials who operate legal systems.) Either the moderate external perspective or the simulative perspective is apt for the sort of project which Dworkin so often appears to have in mind—a theoretical explication of the basic principles and processes at work in the American legal system. Such a project can surely be undertaken by someone who is not necessarily seeking to justify the details or the overall tenor of American law.

Given that the moderate external vantage point and the simulative vantage point are apposite and readily available for legal and jurisprudential scholarship, some of the chief elements of Dworkin's own jurisprudential approach are called into question. In the first place, of course, we should reject his insistence that any adequate account of law (or the law) has to be justificatory in character. A jurisprudential theory delivered from the moderate external perspective is descriptive rather than prescriptive, notwithstanding that it attributes prescriptive attitudes and beliefs to people. Likewise, a doctrinal compendium delivered from the simulative perspective is not perforce justificatory at all, any more than an arresting performance of the role of Iago is perforce a justification of his deeds.

A closely related aspect of Dworkin's interpretive approach that has been placed in doubt is his insistence on the constructiveness or supportiveness of the jurisprudential theorist's stance. At a number of junctures in *Law's Empire*, Dworkin avails himself of the fact that full-fledged participants in a legal system are very likely to do what they can to develop their system in favorable directions. He declares, for example, that '[j]udges normally recognize a duty to continue rather than discard the practice they have joined. So they develop, in response to their own convictions and instincts, working theories about the best interpretation of their responsibilities under that practice' (LE, 87). Hence, if the jurisprudential analyst could not put forth a satisfactory theory without embracing the participant's internal perspective, then the relationship between jurisprudence and law would indeed be constructive almost invariably. In fact, however, no embrace of the internal perspective is necessary. Because of the availability of the moderate external viewpoint and the simulative viewpoint, the jurisprudential theorist and the doctrinal synopsist have ample leeway to decline to portray law (or the law) in an especially appealing light. Not tied to the internal perspective, and therefore disengaged from the institutional and personal grounds for the overwhelmingly constructive orientation of that perspective, the legal scholar may elect to high-light the unattractive features of the law while playing down its more appealing features. An unflattering or even harshly critical approach is always a live option for such a scholar. To be sure, a negative approach is no more preordained than a favorable approach; the jurisprudential or doctrinal writer may exhibit the same degree of constructiveness as a typical official. None the less, the latitude for fiercely destructive criticism is undoubtedly much greater for the writer, whose own fortunes are not directly linked to the health of the institutions which he may choose to assail.

To close this section, let us consider two ways in which the defenders of Dworkin would probably respond to the arguments herein. They might first contend that the simulative and moderate external perspectives cannot genuinely be set in contrast with the internal perspective. In *Law's Empire*, after all, Dworkin squarely submits that an interpreter of a self-reflective social practice must join the practice which she presumes to expound. She joins it by dint of having to come up with an understanding of its overall character—an under-standing that will be in competition with the various understandings formed by the sundry participants in the practice. As Dworkin states, the interpreter must '*join* the practice he proposes to understand; his conclusions are then not neutral reports . . . but claims . . . *competitive* with [the claims advanced by participants]' (LE, 64, emphases in original). Thus—the defenders of Dworkin will argue—someone who occupies the moderate external viewpoint or the simulative view-point for the exposition of law will not be able to stay aloof from the debates and deliberations that occur among officials. She will have to enter those debates and deliberations, by plumping for some positions and disfavoring any contrary stances.[20] Her presentation of the views of officials, whether through attribution or through simulation, is not an isolated venture. For such a presentation, the legal scholar must engage in the same sorts of reflections and ponder the same sorts of considerations that preoccupy officials. She has to arrive at her own verdict on the significance of a legal regime (or of law in general), for only thus will she have managed to plumb the nature of the regime (or of law) in a manner that enables her to comprehend the perspective of a participant. When a moderate external theorist ascribes certain attitudes and beliefs to officials, she is not reporting a set of data gleaned from a poll. Rather, she is attributing to the officials some outlooks that make sense in the light of her own understanding of their regime's general workings—an understanding which she gains only by applying herself to

---

[20] Of course, Dworkin does not preposterously maintain that jurisprudential scholars render or seek to render adjudicative decisions by virtue of devising their theories. Though the Dworkinian theorist undoubtedly hopes to influence the practice of adjudication, she can hardly fail to realize that she is not directly engaged in that practice herself.

the same task of constructive interpretation which the officials have carried out. Much the same can be said, *mutatis mutandis*, about the simulative theorist.

If the supporters of Dworkin were to offer this reply, they would be missing the point of my critique. Nothing in my description of the moderate external perspective or the simulative perspective is at odds with the suggestion that an exposition of a self-reflective social practice has to offer an interpretation which competes with the interpretations devised by the participants in the practice. (Though I shall here concentrate on the moderate external perspective, my remarks will apply quite straightforwardly to the simulative perspective as well.) Suppose that a moderate external theorist $X$ wishes to provide an account of a highly self-reflective legal system. Although $X$ will obviously pay attention to the officials' conceptions of the overall workings of their system, he need not and should not view his task as a matter of simply reporting those conceptions. In the first place, as Dworkin himself emphasizes (LE, 63–4), the participants' conceptions within a highly self-reflective social practice will diverge on a number of points, at least in matters of detail. Thus, a mere rehearsal of those conceptions would not yield a fully uniform account that could be associated with the internal perspective of the participant. In addition, and more important, precisely because $X$ does not feel obliged to endorse the viewpoint which he seeks to fathom, he may well think that the officials' own conceptions of their legal regime are unduly favorable. He may wish to highlight certain aspects of their outlooks—certain prejudices, for example—which the officials themselves barely apprehend.

$X$ ascribes attitudes and beliefs to officials that make sense of their statements and activities within their legal system. In that respect, he is attempting to understand them on their own terms. However, because of the variations in detail among the officials' own perceptions of the workings of their system, and because $X$ in any event is not necessarily endeavoring to highlight the same facets of those perceptions that would be highlighted by the officials themselves, his understanding of them on their own terms is competitive rather than coincident with their self-understandings. To an extent, then, $X$ has joined the interpretive process in which the officials engage; like them in their highly self-reflective regime of law, he aims to grasp the overall tenor and principles of the regime. He thereby will have grasped the officials' point of view. But he does so not in order to embrace the set of beliefs which he has recounted, but in order to impute that set of beliefs to the officials who run the system. Although his approach is hermeneutical or partly hermeneutical, his ends are descriptive and analytical. In other words, although he explores how the operations of the legal system are seen from the perspective of the officials therein, he carries out such an exploration solely because he strives for a rich and accurate comprehension of the system. He may not like the official beliefs and attitudes which his exploration discloses, and he certainly does not have to uphold them as his own.

The Dworkinian reply sketched three paragraphs ago has overlooked the capacity of a moderate external theory for innovation and elaboration. Like the simulative theorist, who does not merely recite lines that have already been written, the moderate external theorist undertakes a project that requires considerable creativity as well as analytical sharpness and empirical meticulousness. Trying to put together a sophisticated picture of other people's perceptions of their situation is a task that involves the drawing of inferences and the application of categories that are frequently much more developed and subtle than those which figure in the perceptions themselves. Such a task of understanding, especially in regard to a highly self-reflective social practice, involves apprehending the overall tenor of the enterprise in which the participants are engaged. Only then is the theorist in a position to say which sorts of outlooks must be harbored by the participants if their enterprise is to make sense. Moreover, exactly because the moderate external theorist is not bound to countenance those outlooks, he may be inclined to unfold their implications in ways that depart notably from the self-understanding of any actual participant. His posture of ascribing rather than endorsing (or rather than automatically endorsing) leaves him with greater interpretive flexibility than would be true of someone who sets out with the objective of justification.

In sum, given the only sense in which the moderate external theorist joins the debates and deliberations of participants, the Dworkinian riposte goes no way toward effacing the distinction between attribution and advocacy. An account of a legal regime from a moderate external perspective does compete with the accounts to which the regime's officials subscribe, but the rivalry does not bespeak (or does not necessarily bespeak) a common quest for the most favorable portrayal of the regime. Instead, the rivalry can bespeak quite different pursuits. The fact that a theorist strives to fathom the perceptions and attitudes of officials—by reference to what he apprehends as the general principles of their regime—does not oblige him in any way to identify himself with those perceptions and attitudes.

Let us consider, then, a second response that might be anticipated from the defenders of Dworkin—a response focused specifically on my remarks about the dispensability of constructiveness in interpretation. When discussing literary and artistic interpretation in the second chapter of *Law's Empire*, Dworkin considers the possibility that explications of certain texts might be hostile rather than supportive. He writes:

I do not mean that every kind of activity we call interpretation aims to make the best of what it interprets—a 'scientific' interpretation of the Holocaust would not try to show Hitler's motives in the most attractive light, nor would someone trying to show the sexist effects of a comic strip strain to find a nonsexist reading—but only that this is so in the normal or paradigmatic cases of creative interpretation. Someone might set out to discredit a writer, of course, by trying to show the latter's work in the worst not the best light, and he will naturally present his case as an interpretation, as a claim about what that writer's work 'really is.' If he really does believe that no more favorable interpretation fits equally well, then his argument falls under my description. But suppose he does not, and is suppressing a more attractive reading that is also eligible given the text. In that case his strategy is parasitic on the normal description, because he will succeed only if his audience is unaware of his true aims; only if they believe he has tried to produce the best interpretation that fits. (LE, 421–2 n. 12)

Dworkin makes two overlapping points in this passage. He contends that constructive interpretations as opposed to censorious interpretations are normal or paradigmatic, and he further contends that someone advancing a censorious interpretation must conceal the availability of any interpretations that are more favorable. We have to consider whether these two claims by Dworkin tell against my arguments concerning interpretive constructiveness. Let us begin with the latter of the two claims.

When Dworkin maintains that someone presenting a jaundiced reading of a text must suppress any readings that cast the text in a more attractive light, he conflates the question of attractiveness and the question of truth or accuracy. After all, his assertion would be persuasive if it pertained to someone who submits an interpretation which is inaccurate and which is known by her to be inaccurate. She will not succeed in winning adherents to her reading of the text unless she covers up the distortions or misrepresentations which she has perpetrated; and, because she is aware of those distortions or misrepresentations, she will very likely engage in just such dissimulation. By contrast, someone trying to highlight the unattractive features of a text will not perforce be deceitful at all. Such an interpreter may readily acknowledge that some more laudatory readings of the text are possible. Indeed, she may wish to emphasize the fact that those other readings are available, in order to underline the importance of her own interpretation as a caution against one's being seduced into an unreservedly favorable assessment of the text that is under consideration. (For example, while granting that John Locke's labor theory of property can aptly be seen as an expression of Locke's belief in the dignity of the individual, a critic may choose to highlight the less appealing features of the theory—such as the strong parallels between it and the seventeenth-century arguments in favor of the expropriation of the American Indians.[21] Far from weakening the critic's case, her acknowledgment of the possibility of some strongly admiring appraisals of Locke's theory helps to indicate why the theory is to be taken seriously and therefore why its shortcomings are a cause for genuine concern.) At any rate, so long as a negative interpretation is neither guilty of fabrications nor ludicrously tendentious and lop-sided, the person putting it forward has nothing whatsoever to fear from the plausibility of other interpretations that are more supportive.

To be sure, if a reading of a text were incorrect simply by virtue of being less laudatory than other plausible readings, then the person seeking to discredit a writer's work (while more kindly interpretations are quite conceivable) would

---

[21] Cf. Matthew H. Kramer, *John Locke and the Origins of Private Property: Philosophical Explorations of Individualism, Community, and Equality* (Cambridge: Cambridge University Press, 1997), 9.

*ipso facto* be guilty of falsehood. Consequently, if aware of the possibility of kindlier assessments, the hostile interpreter would have to conceal her knowledge of them. None the less, we have no reason to acquiesce in this conflation of attractiveness and truth, unless we take as axiomatically correct the theory of constructive interpretation which Dworkin offers—the theory under which an interpreter must strive to construe the object of her interpretation in the most favorable way that satisfies the criterion of fit. (According to Dworkin's jurisprudential theory, the most laudatory reading that fits the relevant legal materials well is uniquely correct; ergo, all other readings are wrong.) Yet that theory is precisely what is in question here. My discussion in this section has offered reasons for thinking that Dworkin's model of persistently constructive interpretation will often be inapplicable to legal scholarship that is written from a moderate external perspective or a simulative perspective. Defenders of Dworkin cannot effectively respond to my discussion by taking for granted the impregnability of his stance. However, unless they do take the unqualified soundness of his theory for granted, they cannot sustain his remark about the hostile interpreter's need to suppress the availability of more commendatory readings. We can see now that the substance of that remark amounts merely to a reaffirmation of Dworkin's constructive approach, rather than to a buttress or basis for it. The remark obscures the distinction between unfavorableness and untrueness—a distinction that will normally be respected by anyone who is not thoroughly enamored of Dworkin's interpretive method.

Is Dworkin's comment about the normal or paradigmatic status of constructive interpretation any more damaging to my arguments than his comment about the suppression of alternative readings? A negative answer to this question is clearly warranted, because of the differences between the internal perspective of legal officials and the moderate external perspective of many legal theorists. (Again, purely for the sake of concision, I concentrate here on the moderate external viewpoint and do not explicitly treat of the simulative viewpoint.) As has already been noted, officials participate directly in a legal system to which their fortunes are therefore tied. Most of them on most occasions will have ample reasons to make their system as healthy as possible by understanding and developing it in ways that will strengthen it. In their official interpretations of legal materials, then, a constructive attitude—an attitude favorably disposed toward the materials—is indeed normal or paradigmatic. We encounter a very different situation, however, when we turn our attention to jurisprudential theorists who write from the moderate external perspective. Because they are not directly implicated in the institutions which they analyze, they do not face the same reasons for constructiveness which the officials face. As has been observed more than once in this section, a moderate external theorist has much more leeway for the adoption of a harshly negative posture or an iconoclastic posture than does a typical official. Likewise, the moderate external theorist has far more leeway for the adoption of a noncommittal stance attuned exclusively to analytical considerations. Hence, in regard to legal theorists as opposed to legal officials, Dworkin's description of constructive interpretation as 'normal or paradigmatic' is overconfident. The pressures of direct involvement that cause the constructive attitude in legal interpretation to be normal among officials are typically missing—or are typically far less prominent—among legal theorists, whose 'involvement' is at a remove.

## B. A Superfluous Supplement

My discussions in the remainder of this chapter do not further impugn Dworkin's claims about the need for jurisprudential theorists to embrace the constructive attitudes of officials. Instead, the focus shifts to the internal perspective of the officials themselves. Henceforth, that is, this chapter concentrates on the position of people who generally feel a commitment to their regime of law and who wish to ensure the vibrancy of its workings. We have to inquire into the nature and implications of that commitment. Specifically, we have to inquire whether Dworkin is correct in presuming that the officials' orientation must be a moral orientation based on moral ideals.

For an opening challenge to the Dworkinian conception of the moral significance of the officials' role, legal positivists can fasten on one principal way in which Dworkin explains the relationship between the two dimensions or criteria of legal interpretation. At numerous junctures in *Taking Rights Seriously* and *Law's Empire*, Dworkin suggests that the criterion of moral attractiveness is needed as a supplement to the criterion of fit.[22] Because more than one interpretation in each difficult case before a court will fit the relevant legal materials quite well, judges have to rely on some standard that will select among the competing interpretations which have satisfied the requirement of fit. For that supplementary purpose, the judges have recourse to the criterion of moral appealingness. As Dworkin writes: 'No [judicial] theory can count as an adequate justification of institutional history unless it provides a good fit with that history; it must not expose more than a low threshold number of decisions,

---

[22] Among the relevant passages are the following: TRS, 66–8, 103, 106–7, 340–2; 'Reply', 254; LE, 231, 233, 255–6, 259; 'Theory', 14. For some of the secondary works that have touched on this aspect of Dworkin's thought, see Larry Alexander, 'Striking Back at the Empire: A Brief Survey of Problems in Dworkin's Theory of Law', 6 *Law and Philosophy* 419, 427–31 (1987); Larry Alexander and Ken Kress, 'Against Legal Principles', in Andrei Marmor (ed.), *Law and Interpretation* (Oxford: Clarendon Press, 1995), 279, 284–5, 287–8; Trevor Allan, 'Justice and Fairness in Law's Empire', 52 *Cambridge Law Journal* 64, 68, 75–6, 84–5 (1993); John Finnis, above, n. 2, at 373–4; David Lyons, 'Moral Aspects of Legal Theory', in *Moral Aspects of Legal Theory* (Cambridge: Cambridge University Press, 1993), 64, 94–5; Gerald Postema, above, n. 6, at 293–5. I shall not here explore a difficulty that has been pointed out by Joseph Raz among many other commentators: 'Fit is a threshold test [in Dworkinian adjudication,] and we are given no guidance at all on what counts as meeting the test' (Raz, 'Dworkin: A New Link in the Chain', 74 *California Law Review* 1103, 1118 n. 38 [1986]). For an especially astute investigation of some further difficulties relating to Dworkin's criterion of fit, see Nigel Simmonds, 'Imperial Visions and Mundane Practices', 46 *Cambridge Law Journal* 465, 477–80 (1987).

particularly recent decisions, as mistakes; but if two or more theories each provide an adequate fit, on that test, then the theory among these that is morally the strongest provides the best justification, even though it exposes more decisions as mistakes than another' (TRS, 340). As he elsewhere states: 'Very often—perhaps even typically—the data will under-determine the [correct interpretation of legal materials]. In that event normal interpretation aims to make, of the material being interpreted, the best it can be' ('Theory', 14).

Now, given Dworkin's portrayal of the criterion of moral attractiveness as a supplement which compensates for the fact that results are underdetermined by the criterion of fit, a legal positivist can reply quite straightforwardly. Both in the untold multitude of ordinary situations where people's interaction does not generate lawsuits, and in the numerous easy cases that do come before trial courts (perhaps only to be settled), the supplementary criterion of moral appealingness is wholly superfluous. In such circumstances, the touchstone of fit is sufficient on its own to determine results. Dworkin's supplementary criterion is needed only in the small proportion of lawsuits that are difficult cases; it is not needed in easy cases, and it is manifestly not needed in the vast array of situations where the bearings of the operative legal norms are too clear-cut to become objects of contention at all. Hence, if we take on board Dworkin's own account of the role of his moral criterion for adjudication, we should conclude that that criterion is triggered only in hard cases and that it is simply beside the point in all other circumstances. In other words, Dworkin's account suggests that judicial and executive officials seldom have to make moral judgments when giving effect to the law. A jurisprudential theory that proclaims the fundamentally moral character of legal decision-making has turned out to shunt morality to the margins of such decision-making. To be sure, as will become evident later in this chapter, legal positivists should not accept even that hard cases must be decided on the basis of moral principles. All the same, merely by showing that any necessary place for those principles is confined to such cases, critics of Dworkin can effect a devastating curtailment of his anti-positivist ambitions.

Within Dworkin's writings there are two chief lines of reasoning which his defenders would invoke as responses to the argument outlined in my last paragraph. First, at a couple of junctures in *Law's Empire*, Dworkin has squarely affirmed that judges (and other officials) rely on moral principles in easy cases as much as in hard cases. Second, both in his earlier work and in his more recent work, he has submitted that the criterion of fit is itself a moral criterion; hence, even if fit were the only operative dimension of legal decision-making in easy cases, it would still necessarily imbue that decision-making with moral significance. Let us probe each of these Dworkinian ripostes.

1. Twice in *Law's Empire*, Dworkin directly confronts the claim that his moralized account of adjudication is applicable only to hard cases. In the first of these passages, he seeks to counter an imaginary opponent (whom he designates as a 'minor critic'). Dworkin ascribes to the opponent an argument roughly resembling mine, with a focus on the perfect Dworkinian judge Hercules:

Now this critic trims his sails. 'In any case Hercules has too much theory for easy cases. Good judges just know that the plain meaning of a plain statute, or a crisp rule always applied and never doubted in precedent, is law, and that is all there is to it. It would be preposterous, not just time-consuming, to subject these undoubted truths to interpretive tests on each occasion. So law as integrity, with its elaborate and top-heavy structure, is at best a conception for hard cases alone. Something much more like [legal positivism] is a better interpretation of what judges do in the easy ones.' (LE, 265–6)

Dworkin retorts quite brusquely:

Law as integrity explains and justifies easy cases as well as hard ones; it also shows why they are easy. It is obvious that the speed limit in California is 55 because it is obvious that any competent interpretation of California traffic law must yield that conclusion. So easy cases are, for law as integrity, only special cases of hard ones, and the critic's complaint is then only what Hercules himself would be happy to concede: that we need not ask questions when we already know the answer. (LE, 266)

When Dworkin addresses a partly similar objection later in *Law's Empire*, he delivers a closely similar reply:

Hercules does not need one method for hard cases and another for easy ones. His method is equally at work in easy cases, but since the answers to the questions it puts are then obvious, or at least seem to be so, we are not aware that any theory is at work at all. We think the question whether someone may legally drive faster than the stipulated speed limit is an easy one because we assume at once that no account of the legal record that denied that paradigm would be competent. (LE, 354, footnote omitted)

When construed as anticipatory responses to my argument about the superfluousness of the supplementary criterion of moral attractiveness, these passages by Dworkin constitute an *ignoratio elenchi*. My argument has not been designed to show that he is unable to accommodate easy cases within his theory; nor has it been designed to show that his mode of adjudication is somehow ruled out by the occurrence of such cases. As he rightly indicates, his theory can account for easy cases very smoothly. What my argument is meant to establish, however, is the redundancy or superfluousness of his elaborate theoretical apparatus in the disposition of easy cases. Though his two-dimensional interpretive model is plainly *compatible* with the occurrence of straightforward cases, it is wholly *unnecessary* for understanding or resolving such cases. Given his own conception of the criterion of moral appealingness as a touchstone that is activated only when the criterion of fit cannot by itself determine a uniquely plausible outcome, we can infer that the former criterion is dispensable in the large majority of situations where legal norms are applied. In easy cases and in the myriad circumstances where no legal disputes arise at all, the law's bearing on a particular set of facts can be determined without recourse to the standard of moral attractiveness. In such situations, that standard is surplus baggage; a one-dimensional model of legal decision-making is sufficient.

What should be emphasized once again is that my discussion in this section has not suggested that Dworkin's two-dimensional interpretive apparatus is strictly belied by the existence of easy cases. His apparatus can account satisfactorily for the straightforwardness of such cases, and is entirely consistent with the occurrence of them. None the less, his explanation of such cases can readily be eschewed in favor of a simpler explanation, a one-dimensional explanation, that accounts just as well for the data. The familiar analytical guideline known as 'Occam's Razor' militates in favor of choosing the latter explanation over the former.

2. Even if we heed Occam's Razor and opt for the sparer of two equally good accounts of routine cases, we then have to ask whether that sparer account— which gives pride of place to the criterion of fit, in most circumstances—is suitable for legal positivism. That is, we have to ask whether the account manages to avoid posing any necessary connections between legality and morality. Such a question must indeed be confronted here, for Dworkin has maintained that the adjudicative criterion of fit is profoundly moral in its basis and implications. In *Taking Rights Seriously*, for example, he submits that '[t]he gravitational force of a precedent may be explained by appeal . . . to the fairness of treating like cases alike. . . . Hercules will conclude that this doctrine of fairness offers the only adequate account of the full practice of precedent' (TRS, 113). In *Law's Empire*, the specific value on which Dworkin focuses has changed, but his analysis is virtually the same. He contends that a judge's insistence on the requirement of fit 'express[es] his commitment to integrity: he believes that an interpretation that falls below his threshold of fit shows the record of the community in an irredeemably bad light, because proposing that interpretation suggests that the community has characteristically dishonored its own principles' (LE, 257). Since the value of integrity is itself an aspect or offshoot of the cardinal values of equality and community, the moralized conception of fit in Dworkin's later work is basically at one with the conception in his earlier work. Dworkin also makes clear that the reason for judges' general adherence to the terms of legislative enactments—even legislative enactments that are substantively ill-advised—is a moral reason: 'Legislative supremacy, which obliges Hercules to give effect to statutes . . . is a matter of fairness because it protects the power of the majority to make the law it wants' (LE, 405). If Dworkin could somehow sustain these quoted comments as general jurisprudential theses rather than only as observations concerning the American legal system (and other liberal-democratic legal systems), he would have landed a telling blow against legal positivism. After all, if his comments were indeed generalizable, then easy cases as much as hard cases would perforce be decided on the basis of fundamentally moral considerations in every legal system.

As should be apparent from some of my earlier chapters, however, Dworkin's view of fit as a morally pregnant criterion is untenable when applied to many heinous regimes of law. Though of course the requirement of fit is an expression of moral ideals in liberal-democratic legal systems, it plays a very different role and stems from very different motives in many monstrous regimes. Wicked rulers who feel no essential concern for the interests of their citizens will nevertheless typically have strong reasons for abiding by the criterion of fit with considerable regularity. As has been argued in earlier chapters, a substantial degree of compliance by evil rulers with the requirement of fit is conducive to their interests partly because it helps to create incentives for people to act in accordance with the rulers' evil mandates. When people know that they will probably be punished for defying those mandates and will very likely be safe from punishment if they heed the mandates, they have solid reasons for obedience (reasons that obtain regardless of the fact that they might be outweighed by prudential or moral reasons against obedience). Furthermore, as is discussed in my third chapter, the wicked officials are able to co-ordinate their nefarious designs much more effectively if they keep their actions largely in conformity with the terms of the various legal norms which they have laid down. Far from serving invariably as an acknowledgment of the dignity and equality of individuals, the requirement of fit can amount to a key vehicle for the adept perpetration of evils.

Thus, insofar as Dworkin presumes that his characterization of the touchstone of fit is a general jurisprudential thesis—rather than an explication of the underlying moral principles of liberal-democratic regimes—his stance is unsupportable. Legal positivists have nothing to fear from his drawing of connections between the dimension of fit and deep moral values. Positivists do not deny that that dimension is morally significant within liberal-democratic systems of law; they only deny that the moral significance must be present in all systems of law.

## C. Discourse on Method

Dworkin relies in a slightly different way on the moral status of the criterion of fit when he attacks legal positivists for resorting to wooden stipulations. This attack occurs in the course of several exchanges between Hart and Dworkin concerning the moral force of legal rights under wicked regimes.[23] During the first couple of rounds of those exchanges—rounds that will not be charted in detail here—Hart made several points which are sound in themselves (and which indeed bear a resemblance to some strands of the analysis in the opening half of my second chapter), but which misrepresent Dworkin's position on the matter under debate. At least since 1984, Dworkin's replies to the inadvertent misrepresentations have rendered his position clear.

Dworkin distinguishes between three broad classes of legal norms (or three broad types of situations within certain legal systems). First are morally benign

---

[23] The relevant texts by Hart are *Essays on Bentham* (Oxford: Clarendon Press, 1982), 150–3; 'Comment', 40–2; 'Postscript', 271–2. The relevant texts by Dworkin are 'Reply', 256–60; LE, 104–8; 'Theory', 18–19. For some secondary works that bear on the present topic, see Larry Alexander, above, n. 22, at 427–31; Michael Bayles, above, n. 6, at 375–80; David Lyons, above, n. 22, at 75–6; Philip Soper, above, n. 1, at 1181–3; W. J. Waluchow, above, n. 13, at 45–6, 58–64.

norms, under which the moral force of legal rights derives from two chief sources: the substantive principles which inform the norms and which therefore underlie the rights, and the legitimate expectations that have been formed by citizens on the basis of the norms. Second are evil norms, under which the weak moral force of legal rights derives only from the expectations that have been formed by citizens on the basis of the norms. If the expectations are not entirely illegitimate, then they have some moral weight—even if the weight is mightily overridden by countervailing substantive considerations. Third are thoroughly flagitious norms, under which any expectations of enforcement are wholly illegitimate. There are no prima-facie moral reasons whatsoever in favor of satisfying the requirements imposed by such norms.

As described so far, Dworkin's position on this matter contains nothing with which the legal positivist would disagree. However, Dworkin pits himself against positivism when he expands on the norms that fall into his third class; he makes clear that he does not regard them as legal norms at all. Because truly heinous enactments (and judicial decisions) do not bestow even the weakest prima-facie moral rights on anyone, Dworkin urges us to conclude that they do not bestow any legal rights, either. As he explains, with reference to a Nazi statute that provides for the confiscation of property from Jews and the conferral of the property upon Aryans:

> [T]he question whether a particular [political] history gives rise to even a minimal moral right that the dictates of those in power be enforced is, obviously, a moral question. . . . My point is . . . that the question of whether a statute gives rise to legal rights is just that moral question, so that a judge who denies that the confiscatory statute provides even a weak reason for deciding for the aryan plaintiff has no reason to say that the statute creates any legal rights at all. We need the idea of a legal right, which someone might have in virtue of a bad law, in order to express the conflict between two grounds of political rights that might sometimes conflict: in order to express the idea that the community's political history often provides an independent ground for a moral argument that may compete with, though it may fall before, other moral arguments that are disconnected from that history. But the concept of legal right can serve that useful purpose only if we do not use it when we mean to *deny* that this independent ground is in fact available, when we mean to assert that the case presents no moral conflict at all.   ('Reply', 259, emphasis in original)

Having staked out this natural-law position, Dworkin then trains his ire on legal positivism:

> If we want to define the terms of our jurisprudence so as to illuminate the structure of complex political decisions, we must be careful not to break the connection between legal and moral rights entirely. But suppose Hart were to . . . insist that the aryan plaintiff just *does* have a legal right, in the nature of the case, even though that right presents no moral reason at all for deciding in his favor. We are suddenly in the peculiar world of legal essentialism. Why does the plaintiff just, in the nature of the case, have a legal right? It cannot be in virtue of the linguistic rules governing the phrase 'legal right.' The concept of a legal

right is a contested concept, and therefore is not governed by necessary and sufficient conditions laid down in linguistic rules. What other reason might legal philosophy provide? I can think of none. A theory of legal right makes sense only as a theory of when there is at least some minimal ground, in political history, for a political decision honoring the supposed right.    ('Reply', 259–60, emphasis in original)

To the charge of legal essentialism, a retort of '*tu quoque*' seems appropriate. If legal positivists are trying to stipulate the meanings of terms such as 'law' and 'legal right', then so is Dworkin; he is insisting that those terms be construed along natural-law lines, whereas the positivists maintain that the terms need not and should not be construed in that fashion. Likewise, if legal positivists are arguing about 'the nature of the case', then so is Dworkin. Either his allegations about essentialism are false, or they apply as much to him as to any positivists.

In fact, of course, the debate between Dworkin and legal positivists is far more than a quarrel over stipulated uses of words or an arid conflict about 'the nature of the case'. Dworkin is arguing on moral grounds for his moralized conception of law and legal rights, whereas I have argued throughout this book on analytical grounds for a positivist conception of law. My positivist orientation is methodological as well as substantive. To be sure, a reliance on analytical grounds must involve judgments about the importance or unimportance of various aspects of the phenomena that are being pondered. Much the same is true of any theory about anything. But judgments of importance are not perforce moral judgments; the considerations that have guided my focus throughout this book are nonmoral considerations.[24]

Legal positivists should respond to Dworkin in two principal ways. First, we can query why he is not content to use overtly moral language to articulate and explore the moral issues that preoccupy him. Given a clash or potential clash between prima-facie moral rights that are grounded in expectations and prima-facie moral rights that are independent of expectations, and given the possibility of circumstances in which the prevailing legal norms are too wicked to generate any prima-facie moral rights based on expectations, the moral values at stake in any of these situations can be contemplated most directly and minutely if they are expressed squarely as moral values. To be sure, someone who wishes to consider and weigh those values can draw on legal language in the process. Such language may be indispensable, to a certain extent. However, Dworkin's recommendation for the use of that language is unhelpful, as it does nothing to sharpen or clarify the moral issues that are to be deliberated. Instead of wondering whether or not the designation of 'legal rights' should be withheld from certain positions of advantage that are conferred by an authoritative system of evil norms, someone appraising the moral status of those positions is best advised to focus directly on the relevant moral questions: questions about the norms' substance, and questions about the expectations that have been engendered by the particular norms and by the overall system of norms. At best, the withholding of the label of 'legal rights'

[24] In this respect, though not in certain other respects, I agree with Joseph Raz, *Ethics in the Public Domain* (Oxford: Clarendon Press, 1994), 219–21.

is a superfluous dressing up of assessments that have already been reached on more perspicuous grounds. At worst, it is a misleading distraction from the fine-grained moral problems to which the aforementioned assessments should be attuned.

A second and more important response to Dworkin lies in a defense of the present book's analytical focus. Instead of distinguishing between the legal and the non-legal on the basis of moral considerations, the present book has located the hallmarks of legality in the features that have been discussed at length within my chapters on Fuller and Raz: normativity, generality, regularity, durability, and comprehensiveness. A regime and its norms can partake of those features while being too flagitious to generate even the weakest prima-facie moral reasons in favor of the enforcement of the norms (or, therefore, even the weakest prima-facie moral rights for the people who stand to benefit from that enforcement). Hence, the legal/non-legal distinction operative throughout this volume is not endowed with moral significance. It is, however, undoubtedly endowed with analytical significance. That is, it stems from judgments about the relative importance of various aspects of human life and social institutions. In this connection, let us consider two points.

In the first place, the qualities singled out here (and in my previous chapters) as distinctively legal are acknowledged as such by any plausible theory of law. No such theory can credibly maintain, for example, that a system of governance involving hardly any general norms or hardly any regularity in the effectuation of the norms is a legal system. Of course, not every legal dictate or every set of official actions will exhibit any of the features that are characteristic of law; but a regime almost wholly lacking in one or more of those features would not be a legal regime at all. (Fuller was quite correct to insist as much about his principles of legality.) To be sure, theorists like Dworkin want to employ a moral touchstone for deciding whether the particular protections conferred by a system of norms are legal rights. None the less, for such theorists, the moral dimension supplements rather than displaces the fundamental features of law that have just been mentioned. No one can plausibly deny the indispensable role of those features in any legal regime.

Apart from being seen by everyone as necessary for the existence of a legal system, the qualities highlighted here as distinctive of law are extremely serviceable for the attainment of benevolent rulers' objectives and wicked rulers' objectives alike. As my third chapter has sought to explain, the officials who govern a society have solid reasons for exercising their sway through a regime of laws, irrespective of the moral worthiness or unworthiness of the officials' ends. Virtuous rulers are well advised to opt for a legal regime partly because the characteristics of that sort of regime are promotive of values such as procedural due process, and partly because the co-ordinational efficiency of such a regime facilitates the achievement of the rulers' worthy substantive aims. Malignly self-serving rulers are likewise well advised to opt for a legal regime, partly on the ground that the characteristics of such a regime are promotive of people's incentives for compliance with the rulers' mandates, and partly on the ground that the co-ordinational efficiency of a legal regime facilitates the achievement of the rulers' evil aims. Precisely because the basic features of law can further the ends of nefarious rulers as well as of benign rulers, the institutions comprising those features can fruitfully be studied together as an important and distinctive form of governance—notwithstanding that the moral merits of those institutions will vary markedly. Not only can the fundamental features of law be singled out, but their conduciveness to the objectives of wicked governors and benevolent governors alike can be expounded. To avoid neglecting the latter point, which cuts directly across any division between good and evil, my theoretical focus throughout this book does not take any such division as determinative of the standing of a regime as a legal regime. The evaluative judgment of importance that informs my focus is analytical rather than moral, in that it is based on a desire to trace the full implications of a mode of governance whose attributes are specifiable without recourse to moral assessments.

Before leaving this section, we should note that Dworkin himself adopts a somewhat more flexible and nuanced stance in *Law's Empire* than in his earlier work. In his discussion of heinous legal systems (LE, 101–8), he takes due account of the quite evident fact that 'law' in ordinary discourse—at least within the Western liberal democracies—is used sometimes as a morally neutral term and at other times as a term fraught with moral significance. He recommends an adaptable and relaxed attitude toward this equivocality of meaning, with close attention to the contexts in which 'law' and cognate terms are wielded. For example, with reference specifically to statements about the Nazis' legal system, Dworkin writes:

> We need not deny that the Nazi system was an example of law, no matter which interpretation we favor of our own law, because there is an available sense in which it plainly was law. But we have no difficulty in understanding someone who does say that Nazi law was not really law, or was law in a degenerate sense, or was less than fully law. For he is not then using 'law' in that sense; he is not making that sort of preinterpretive judgment but a skeptical interpretive judgment that Nazi law lacked features crucial to flourishing legal systems whose rules and procedures do justify coercion. His judgment is now a special kind of political judgment for which his language, if the context makes this clear, is entirely appropriate. (LE, 103–4)

Contrary to what Dworkin suggests throughout his discussion, his call for context-sensitive flexibility can readily be accepted by legal positivists.[25] None of

---

[25] I of course acknowledge that some highly sophisticated legal positivists have resisted Dworkin's stance. See e.g. W. J. Waluchow, above, n. 13, at 58–64. Cf. Steven Burton, above, n. 2, at 125–7. Indeed, what prompted Dworkin to issue his call for flexibility was Hart's adducing of moral reasons in favor of the legal-positivist use of 'law' (in *Concept*, 203–7). I regard Hart's position—which has been followed and amplified by Neil MacCormick in his 'A Moralistic Case for A-Moralistic Law', 20 *Valparaiso Law Review* 1 (1985)—as inconclusive and ill-advised. For an excellent corrective, see Philip Soper, 'Choosing a Legal Theory on Moral Grounds', in Jules Coleman and Ellen Frankel Paul (eds), *Philosophy and Law* (Oxford: Blackwell, 1987), 31. For a rather strident (but not inapposite) reply to Hart from a natural-law perspective, see Deryck Beyleveld and Roger Brownsword, 'The Practical Difference Between Natural-Law Theory and Legal Positivism', 5 *Oxford Journal of Legal Studies* 1 (1985).

the analyses in this book has purported to lay down guidelines for univocal patterns of usage in everyday political disputation. Such guidelines would be clumsy, undesirable, and futile. Legal positivism is not a semantic theory that tries to set rigid rules for the correct employment of legal-conceptual terms, without regard to differing contexts and pragmatic needs.

All the same, one especially interesting context for the legal positivist is that of jurisprudential argumentation about the relationship between law and morality. In respect to this context, the positivist can rightly submit that the scope of reference for the word 'law' and its cognates should be expansive and morally neutral rather than cabined and morally pregnant. Within this context, each of those two patterns of usage—the broad and morally neutral, or the narrower and morally significant—is arrantly question-begging unless it is supported by independent considerations. Dworkin (in his earlier work) opts for the latter pattern of usage, on moral grounds. As has been argued tersely above, his classification of heinous regimes of authoritative norms as non-legal is at best superfluous and at worst confusing and distracting. Still, my response to his position has *not* been to suggest that the positivists' classification of such regimes as legal is somehow to be preferred on moral grounds. My response instead has been to adduce analytical considerations in favor of the positivist pattern of usage; the version of legal positivism defended in this book is methodological as well as substantive. As has been maintained—both here and in some of my previous chapters—a morally neutral use of 'law' and cognate terms, with a consequent grouping together of benevolent legal regimes and monstrous legal regimes, can reveal important aspects of law's workings that would otherwise tend to be obscured. (Recall, for example, how some of Fuller's defenders have overlooked the fact that scrupulous rule-of-law observances can be highly serviceable for unscrupulously evil purposes.) Hence, while allowing that the word 'law' and related words can be used honorifically in a variety of contexts with perfect correctness, my discussion here suggests that the legal-positivist use of those words should be preferred in the context of jurisprudential inquiries concerning the connections between law and morality. Moreover, my discussion has arrived at this verdict for analytical or theoretical reasons, not for moral reasons.

## D.  Unsupported Hopes

We shall henceforth assume that legal decision-makers must indeed typically draw upon some criterion or set of criteria to supplement the criterion of fit. Why, we may ask, must the supplementary standard be a moral standard? Dworkin tells us that judges will endeavor to make of their legal system the best it can be, and he takes for granted that 'best' means 'morally best'. Indeed, because he so thoroughly takes this point for granted, he hardly ever seeks to substantiate it. We must now consider just how vulnerable he has left himself.

Before turning to the extremely limited set of passages in which Dworkin tries to support his view of judicial decision-making as a practice of moral justification, we should note how the arguments in my earlier chapters militate against his chances of success. Those chapters have sustainedly contended that, while officials in a monstrous legal regime will have ample reasons for abiding by rule-of-law principles quite strictly, their conformity to those principles can occur on the basis of purely prudential considerations. When the officials need to supplement the criterion of fit in the course of their decision-making, they will probably consult their own well-being rather than the requirements of morality. Striving to make of the monstrous regime the best it can be, each official might well define 'best' not as 'morally worthiest' but as 'maximally promotive of my interests as someone who benefits immensely from the regime's dominance'.

Until now, however, most of this book has portrayed the officials of a vile regime as if they were always closely in accordance with one another. Let us very briefly think about some ways in which the possible divisions among the branches of an evil government might affect the prudential calculations of judges. Heretofore, those calculations have largely been portrayed as pitting the interests of the wicked officials *en masse* against the interests of citizens. Suppose, however, that judicial officials are concerned not only to maximize and entrench their exploitation of citizens, but also to outmaneuver the officials who operate the executive and legislative branches of government.

If the outmaneuvering consists in fending off the wrath of the mightier rival branches, then the judges will be attentive not only to securing their regime's dominance over citizens but also to avoiding decisions that are likely to irritate the officials in the other branches. The prudential calculations of the judges have a dual focus: they seek to sustain and fortify their position of superiority *vis-à-vis* citizens, and they seek to shield themselves in their position of inferiority *vis-à-vis* their fellow officials. Having to supplement the criterion of fit with a criterion of attractiveness (prudential attractiveness) when giving effect to their regime's laws, the judges adopt a supplementary criterion that guards their own flanks while maximizing their regime's exploitation of the populace. (Of course, a substantial degree of judicial deference toward the other branches is common even in benevolent systems of governance. Although such deference in those circumstances may stem from moral convictions relating to the proper role of democratically elected legislatures, it can likewise stem from considerations that are principally or exclusively prudential.)

By contrast, if the judiciary's outmaneuvering of the executive and legislative branches consists in galvanizing the officials of those branches to develop increasingly effective means of realizing their wicked objectives, the judges will not shrink from taking the lead and stepping on toes in regard to numerous issues. In doing so, they not only strengthen their regime's grip over the citizenry but also strengthen their own position within the regime. Their boldness enables them to set their stamp conspicuously on the shape of the overall scheme of governance. Hence, when faced with the need to supplement the criterion of fit, the judges will embrace a criterion or a set of criteria that will further the repressive interests of their overall regime and their own interests as they jockey for power within the regime (against the other branches).

In any event, whether the evil judges work closely in harmony with their fellow officials as a bloc, or whether there is considerable jockeying for power between the judges and the other branches, the key point here is that the unavoidability of judicial reliance on standards besides the criterion of fit is not at all a guarantee that the supplementary standards will be moral in character. Wicked judges in monstrous legal regimes will be apt to guide their decisions by reference to purely prudential principles. So my earlier chapters have argued at length. Thus, when confronted with a jurisprudential theory which suggests that judges will perforce draw on moral principles (perhaps unsavory moral principles) to arrive at their determinations, we should adopt an exceedingly wary attitude. We should expect at the very least to see an impressive array of arguments adduced in confirmation, or ostensible confirmation, of the theory's claim. In fact, however, Dworkin makes hardly any efforts to offer arguments that might form a basis for his view of legal decision-making as inevitably a species of moral decision-making; most of the time, he appears to presume that his view is too plainly correct to be in need of support. Having already looked at one of his few attempts to lay a foundation for his moralized approach to law—the argument against Hart on the matter of legal rights—we should now probe his few other attempts.

1. In *Taking Rights Seriously*, Dworkin squarely addresses himself to our present topic (in response to an objection raised by David Richards). Endeavoring to parry the claim that not all adjudicative principles are moral principles, he first quite properly observes that his model of law does not presuppose that the principles actually invoked by judges will be *sound* moral principles; he has always allowed that the moral precepts which inform any particular adjudicative determinations may be far from ideal. Having appositely reiterated this point about the potential distastefulness of adjudicative principles, Dworkin then emphasizes that all such principles—whether benign or not—are indeed moral (i.e., nonprudential) in character. He writes:

[L]egal principles are always moral principles in form (whether they are sound or unsound, compelling or despicable as moral judgments) rather than, for example, prudential judgments or historical generalizations. . . . The word 'moral' may cause trouble here, as it often does, but I . . . mean that the principles that figure in legal arguments make claims about the rights and duties of citizens and other legal people, rather than stating, for example, prudential judgments or historical generalizations. As I have just said, I suppose that the process of 'drawing' principles from institutional history is the process of judging justifications of that history, where justification is distinguished from explanation. Even if it is right that all the decisions reached in contract law in Wisconsin for a period of years were such as to benefit the local Republican party, that fact, however important it might be to the historian or sociologist or critic, might not be thought to provide a justification (even a bad justification) for these decisions, and therefore would not require judges to decide future cases under the alleged principle that what is good for Republicans is good for justice. (TRS, 343)

In this long passage, Dworkin advances two main theses which supposedly establish that all adjudicative principles are moral principles. First, he declares that all adjudicative principles assign rights and duties to people instead of encapsulating prudential judgments. Second, he affirms that the process of distilling adjudicative principles from legal materials is a process of justification that is to be distinguished from explanation. Let us crisply examine each of these points in turn.

The first of these contentions by Dworkin is somewhat reminiscent of Raz's view of officials' obligation-asserting statements. Unless Dworkin is assuming that the rights and duties to which he refers are perforce seen by judges as *moral* rights and duties, his conclusion does not follow from his premises; and, of course, if he is indeed simply assuming that those rights and duties are perforce seen by judges as moral rights and duties, then he is quite heavy-handedly begging the question. Legal duties are requirements imposed by legal norms (including legal principles, of course), and legal rights are protections—protections against interference or uncooperativeness—conferred by legal norms.[26] Judges can give effect to those legal positions without intending or professing in any way to rely on moral considerations as the bases for their decisions. A requirement imposed by a legal mandate is no less a legal duty for being the product of officials' starkly prudential calculations. Likewise, a protection conferred by a legal norm is no less a legal right for being the product of such calculations.

As my third chapter has explained in some detail, the moral or prudential tenor of legal principles and other legal norms cannot be gauged without reference to the officials' motives for the adoption and implementation of the norms. That is, the moral or prudential character of any legal precepts and decisions will hinge on the reasons that underlie them. If officials adhere to certain legal principles for purely prudential reasons, then those principles are themselves purely prudential—even if the legal entitlements conferred and legal duties imposed by the principles would otherwise be straightforwardly moral.

Notwithstanding that a person's decision to stop smoking will probably yield some morally salutary consequences, the decision itself may have derived exclusively from prudential concerns. If so, the decision is prudential through and through, as is any statement by the person which expresses the decision. Much the same is true of the legal norms which bestow legal rights and create legal duties. So long as the reasons which underlie those norms are thoroughly prudential—that is, so long as the norms and the rights and duties engendered by them are established solely because they further the interests of officials, without

[26] For a book-length elaboration of this one-sentence analysis of rights and duties, see Matthew H. Kramer, 'Rights Without Trimmings', in Matthew H. Kramer, N. E. Simmonds, and Hillel Steiner, *A Debate Over Rights: Philosophical Enquiries* (Oxford: Clarendon Press, 1998), 7.

regard to any moral considerations (and without regard even to the consideration of *appearing* to be morally virtuous)—the norms are thoroughly prudential as well. Hence, Dworkin errs when he suggests that the fact that legal principles 'make claims about the rights and duties of citizens and other legal people' is somehow enough to rule out the possibility that those principles are 'stating . . . prudential judgments'. In monstrous regimes, there is no incompatibility whatsoever between those two aspects of legal principles.

The second main thesis in the long quotation from Dworkin above, the thesis about justification as opposed to explanation, can be handled more pithily. Plainly, there is an important distinction between justification and explanation; but there is also a crucial difference between moral justification and prudential justification. Whereas a moral justification of a decision by an official will be directed at least as much toward citizens as toward other officials, a prudential justification is directed exclusively or almost exclusively toward one's fellow officials. Judicial officials in a wicked legal system may well engage only in the latter sort of justification (implicitly or explicitly) when they render their decisions. As they arrive at those decisions, they invoke principles and guidelines that best serve their own interests by serving the interests of their nefarious regime. With or without any explicit reference to the import of those principles and guidelines, the officials' reliance on them serves to justify (to their fellow officials) any decisions that are reached. Whether the justification is spelled out expressly or is evident without any need for elaboration, it amounts to a prudential assurance concerning the sustainment and reinforcement of the wicked scheme of governance from which all the officials benefit. For example, when an evil official in a heinous legal system adheres to the Fullerian principle of congruence between legal-norms-as-formulated and legal-norms-as-implemented, the justification implicit in his adherence is that the congruence helps to foster the incentives that will secure people's compliance with the legal system's oppressive mandates. Insofar as the officials of such a system select legal principles by implicitly or explicitly selecting among justifications of their enterprise, they are engaging in a task that involves the outright consulting of their own interests. In other words, any tacit or overt justifications favored by these officials are strictly prudential, and are directed by the officials to one another rather than to the downtrodden people whom they rule.

My remarks earlier in this section about possible divisions among the branches of an evil government will apply to the scenario that has just been sketched. Suppose that the judges in a monstrous regime feel that their institutional strength is clearly inferior to that of the other branches. In that event, their choices of principles (and concomitant justifications) will be determined not only by their desire to solidify the dominance of their regime over the citizenry, but also by their desire to avoid encroachments on the other branches' traditional functions. Each of these foci is prudential. The solidification of the regime's dominance advances the judges' interests as well as those of the other officials; and the avoidance of encroachments is obviously in the judges' interests, as a means of averting the wrath of stronger colleagues/rivals. The justifications that are implicit or explicit in the judges' choices of principles will be directed in part to all officials (including the judges themselves) and in part specifically to the stronger colleagues/rivals.

Suppose, conversely, that the judges feel that their institutional strength enables them to call the tune (to some extent) for the officials in the other branches of government. In that event, they will be inclined to select principles which not only will reinforce their regime's evil grip but which also will sustain or extend the judges' own influence *vis-à-vis* the officials in other branches. By selecting the prudentially correct principles, the judges further their own interests in the vibrancy of their overall regime and also their interests in maintaining their position of special influence within that regime. The justifications tacitly or expressly involved in the judges' choices of principles will be directed in part to all officials and in part specifically to the judges themselves.

Before moving on to plumb Dworkin's other attempts to support his moralized account of legal decision-making, we should note two important points. First, my claim here is not that the judges in *every* wicked legal system will draw on purely prudential precepts for the reaching of their decisions. In some heinous legal systems, as Dworkin quite rightly suggests, the judges rely on shockingly misguided moral principles rather than on thoroughly prudential principles. The wickedness of the judges' decisions and outlooks is then due not to their arrant preoccupation with their own interests, but to their grotesquely misconceived notions of how they should be advancing other people's interests. Nothing said herein is meant to deny that the evil of a nefarious legal system can be due to its officials' pursuit of hideously incorrect moral ideals rather than to their pursuit of purely prudential objectives. My claim is simply that many atrocious legal systems—whether actual or easily imagined—are indeed atrocious precisely because their officials act not out of misguided moral concern but out of devotion to their own interests.

Second, although there is only a very low probability that every official throughout the whole array of a wicked legal system's workings does not take account of any moral considerations whatsoever (even woefully ill-advised moral considerations), there is a very high probability that purely prudential motives will figure quite prominently in the operations of such a system. Rebarbatively evil officials may not always tailor the bases for their decisions essentially to their own interests—without even a pretense of moral rectitude—but they probably often do so and almost certainly sometimes do so. The fact that they sometimes do so is sufficient to belie Dworkin's contention that legal principles are perforce moral principles. Although many legal principles in an atrocious regime of law may be adopted for moral reasons (thoroughly inapposite moral reasons), some of the legal principles in such a regime will almost certainly be embraced on starkly prudential grounds. *Pace* Dworkin, legal principles of the latter sort are the expressions of prudential judgments.

2. Dworkin's second chief attempt to substantiate his claims about the ineluctably moral character of legal decision-making is virtually identical to part of his first attempt, and thus it can be treated here very quickly. Dworkin writes: 'An explanation does not provide a justification of a series of political decisions if it presents, as justificatory principles, propositions that offend our ideas of what even a bad moral principle must be like. This explains why the explanation of a series of statutes, that they were enacted in order to win the next election, does not provide a justification of those statutes' ('Reply', 299 n. 4). Now, one should of course readily agree (again) that there is an important difference between explanation and justification. One should also readily grant that every legal decision involves a tacit or explicit justification—a justification for choosing one position in preference to another. But, as has been argued above, the justification can be prudential rather than moral. That is, it can be some tacit or explicit assurance by an official to himself and his fellow officials, affirming that his decision serves his and their interests in sustaining the operations and promoting the objectives of their wicked regime. Hence, although an explanation is never in itself a justification, the motivating reason ferreted out by an explanation can figure in an implicit or overt justification, regardless of whether the reason is prudential or moral. An underlying prudential reason can figure in a prudential justification.

Quite tentatively, Dworkin goes on to suggest that flagrantly discriminatory principles might not be classifiable as moral principles at all. If so, 'then we should reject, on this ground alone, the idea that a discriminatory principle might figure in the best justification of Nazi law' ('Reply', 299 n. 4). Here Dworkin again takes for granted that the relevant justification is moral in character, and that the 'best' justification is the one which is morally most worthy. His assumptions will be sound when applied to benevolent regimes where officials are morally conscientious, and even when applied to wicked regimes insofar as the officials therein rely on moral principles (perhaps unsavory moral principles) for their decision-making. However, given that he is supposed to be expounding and embracing the perspective of participants, his assumptions fail when applied to evil regimes in which the officials base their decisions on purely prudential considerations. For each of them, 'best' does not mean 'morally most worthy'; rather, as was stated earlier, it means 'maximally promotive of my interests as someone who benefits from the dominance of my regime'. Likewise, if we accept *arguendo* Dworkin's suggestion about seemingly moral principles that are too monstrous to be properly classifiable as moral, we must conclude that his assumptions about justification fail when applied to regimes in which the officials have recourse to truly monstrous principles for their decision-making.

In short, these laconic remarks by Dworkin go no way toward buttressing his view that legal principles and legal decision-making are perforce moral in tenor. On the contrary, his remarks presuppose that view. As a consequence, he again leaves himself unable to accommodate many heinous legal systems within his theory of law. Such a blind spot should be troubling for anyone who expects from a jurisprudential theory the kind of analytical clarification that was discussed in my preceding section—analytical clarification that requires the highlighting of similarities between wicked legal systems and benign legal systems.

3. We can detect one further line of reasoning put forward by Dworkin in support of his moralized account of law and adjudication. He writes as follows:

Law is a political concept not just because it is contested but because of the way it is contested. It takes its sense from its use: from the contexts of debates about what the law is, and from what turns on which view is accepted. And all this is deeply, densely political. So until someone suggests a different point to our legal practices—a point that makes such practice innocent of political theory—we would do well to look for the deep sources of important theories of law in some assumptions of political morality. ('Reply', 256)

Although Dworkin is here talking principally about jurisprudence rather than about the workings of legal systems, the final sentence in the passage mentions those workings explicitly. Besides, as someone who views jurisprudence as the general part of adjudication, Dworkin must see the gist of his comments here as fully applicable to judicial decision-making. Thus, in all pertinent respects, his stance is the same as in *Law's Empire*, where he asserts that 'in hard cases judges must make controversial judgments of political morality whichever conception of law they hold' (LE, 163).

What, then, is the line of reasoning discernible in Dworkin's remarks? Behind his insistence that the operations of legal systems are not innocent of political theory, and behind his assertion that judges must always make controversial judgments of political morality in hard cases, there seems to lie the following train of thought. When legal officials (especially judges) arrive at their decisions and carry out their authoritative functions, they are making choices that impinge directly and often heavily on people's lives. Human beings' interests are always at stake, and their vital interests are frequently at stake, when legal determinations are made. Those determinations deal sometimes with life-or-death matters and typically with important matters. A judge or any other official in his authoritative capacity cannot but affect people's lives significantly. When he acts in one way as opposed to an alternative way, he favors some people's interests over those of other people; and when he declines to act, he likewise favors some people's interests over those of other people. Thus, however he elects to formulate or implement legal norms, he will be making morally significant choices (even if they are the wrong choices). In sum, judges must inevitably engage in moral decision-making. So Dworkin appears to have reasoned.

One should certainly accept the premises of the argument that has just been sketched, and one should even accept the conclusion if one construes it in a way that makes it follow from the premises. So construed, however, the conclusion yields no support for Dworkin's account of legal decision-making as a practice of moral justification. The snag here is similar to one of the snags that were highlighted in my chapter on Michael Detmold, who stumbles by conflating a broader sense and a narrower sense of the term 'moral'. If the more expansive sense is assigned to that term in my foregoing paragraph's conclusion—the conclusion that 'judges must inevitably engage in moral decision-making'—then the argument outlined in the paragraph is valid, but is wholly unsuitable for Dworkin's purposes. By contrast, if the term 'moral' carries its narrower sense in my foregoing paragraph's conclusion, then the argument of the paragraph is invalid.

Let us briefly recall the two relevant senses of 'moral', which were delineated along with two other main senses of the term in my first chapter. On the one hand, a decision can be designated as a moral decision if it has a nontrivial impact on the interests of some person or set of persons other than the decision-maker. In this broad sense, the designation 'moral decision' does not distinguish at all between choices made essentially out of concern for one's own interests and choices made essentially out of concern for others' interests. By contrast, exactly such a distinction is at work when 'moral' is defined more narrowly in opposition to 'prudential'. Only choices made out of nonderivative concern for others' interests are moral decisions in this second sense. (Of course, even when moral decisions are contrasted with prudential decisions in this way, the former can be badly misguided to the point of being wicked. Nonprudential efforts to promote others' interests are not necessarily morally worthy, by any means. If one wished to take 'moral' to mean 'morally worthy' or 'morally acceptable', one would need to insert a worthy/unworthy distinction or an acceptable/unacceptable distinction into the narrower sense of 'moral', in order to demarcate a third meaning of the term that was limned in Chapter 1. However, my response to Dworkin at this stage does not need to invoke that additional meaning.)

The premises of the argument that was outlined three paragraphs ago—henceforth labeled as argument *A*—have claimed in effect that legal decision-making is moral decision-making, *in the broad sense of 'moral'*. Such a claim is fully warranted; as has been remarked in my chapter on Detmold, anybody who is not very foolish or ignorant should know that authoritative determinations by legal officials produce significant impacts on other people's interests. Every legal decision or virtually every legal decision is moral in this expansive sense, and thus each such decision along with any person responsible for each decision will be open to moral assessment.

Now, given that the premises of argument *A* are plainly true, the conclusion of that argument will likewise be true (as well as valid) if the word 'moral' therein carries its broad sense. After all, if 'moral' is so defined, the conclusion amounts to a mere recapitulation of the premises. Yet, if 'moral' is indeed so defined, the conclusion will not avail Dworkin at all—since it is perfectly consistent with an acknowledgment that judges in monstrous regimes are likely to focus on starkly prudential considerations as the bases for some or all of their rulings. That is, the conclusion of argument *A* is wholly consistent with a forthright denial of Dworkin's prime assumption: his assumption that legal decision-making is perforce an enterprise of nonprudential deliberation and nonprudential justification.

If Dworkin tries to square the upshot of argument *A* with his jurisprudential credo by presuming that the term 'moral' in the conclusion carries its narrower sense, then he will have rendered the argument invalid. The conclusion in argument *A* follows from the premises only when the instance of 'moral' in that conclusion has been defined expansively rather than narrowly—i.e., only when it has been defined to encompass purely prudential decisions rather than to exclude them. In sum, Dworkin has to choose between a valid argument that belies his position and an invalid argument that contains the verdict which he desires. His attempts to ground and buttress that verdict have left it entirely unsupported.

### III. A SUMMATION

This chapter has studied the two chief prongs of Dworkin's attacks against legal positivism. His challenge to the positivist account of the Rule of Recognition has turned out to be useful in pointing the way toward some beneficial clarifications and refinements, but has certainly not turned out to be devastating. My rejoinders to Dworkin on this matter have been fourfold. First, he does not establish that judges disagree with one another at a criterial level in easy cases; second, even if criterial disagreements are indeed present (at least subterraneously) in all cases, they will be quite sharply limited by the need for regularity at the level of outcomes in a functional legal system; third, Dworkin errs in thinking that legal conventions must be static, and he further errs in thinking that the adjudicative practices of American law can plausibly be portrayed as based solely on convictions and not on conventions; finally, with his latest reflections on the metaphysics of morals, he helps to reveal the resilience of a doctrine (viz., soft or inclusive positivism) which he seeks to confute.

Though Dworkin's broadsides against the notion of the Rule of Recognition do not bring down their target, they do helpfully expose some shortcomings therein—shortcomings which are fairly important but which, happily, are plainly remediable. Dworkin's anti-positivist approach to the relationship between law and morality is less successful; indeed, it unintentionally underscores the contingency and variability of that relationship. My ripostes to his position have proceeded along three main paths. First, Dworkin fails to demonstrate that jurisprudential theorizing must embrace the perspective of the officials who operate a legal system. Second, even if we grant *arguendo* his claim about the proper perspective for jurisprudence, we have plenty of room to doubt that the officials in most cases must rely on the criterion of attractiveness to supplement the criterion of fit for their decision-making. Third, even if we grant *arguendo* the claim about a supplementary criterion, we have no reason to think that that criterion must be moral rather than prudential.

In short, legal positivism in both its 'positive' guise and its 'negative' guise can withstand Dworkin's powerful onslaughts. At a jurisprudential level, moreover, his interpretive and moralized approach to law is too provincial. At the jurisprudential level, in the interest of rigor and comprehensiveness, we are best advised to seek a model of law without trimmings.

PART II

*Positivism Extended*

# 7

## *Disclaimers and Reassertions*

Throughout the five chapters that make up Part I, this book has endeavored to vindicate legal positivism by fending off a number of theories that impugn the separability of law and morality. Although some additional critiques will turn up in my final three chapters, they will not be nearly as sustained as those which have already been presented; moreover, as the Introduction to this book has made clear, the critiques in the concluding chapters are subordinate to some general observations and analyses. Those observations and analyses will aim both to clarify and to reinforce the claims of legal positivism. Of course, the pursuit of clarification is itself a crucial means of reinforcement, since the robustness of positivist contentions cannot become fully apparent until some common misunderstandings of them have been dispelled.

In the first main portion of this chapter, we shall take account of several theses that are *not* entailed by positivist affirmations of the separability of law and morality. Each of those theses has attracted some attention in one or more of the preceding chapters, or will attract some attention in one of my subsequent chapters; hence, none of them will be discussed at great length here. Though perhaps the expositions of them in the present chapter are largely elaborations of certain points made in other parts of this book, these expositions do bring together and amplify some dispersed reflections on the nature of legal positivism's tenets. By specifying methodically some untenable views that have often been mistakenly attributed to positivists, my discussions should help to clarify the views which a positivist actually espouses.

In the second chief portion of this chapter, we move into new territory. After having duly pondered some propositions that are *not* entailed by an insistence on the disjoinability of morality and law, we shall see once again how far-reaching that insistence is. Challenging an unwarranted concession that has been made by some legal positivists, my discussion will maintain that there are no necessary connections between the content of legal norms in any society $S$ and the content of the conventional morality in $S$. (Exactly what is meant here by 'conventional morality' will become clear at the appropriate juncture.) Although a considerable degree of convergence between the mandates of $S$'s law and the precepts of $S$'s conventional morality is hardly unusual, it need not obtain. In the end, such convergence is a contingent matter. By underlining the contingency of that state of affairs, this chapter will reassert the claims of legal positivism—after it has dissociated those claims from some much more dubious propositions.

Some of the opponents of legal positivism have harbored few misconceptions about the doctrine which they are oppugning, and have therefore engaged in illuminating debates. All too often, however, attacks against positivism abound with outright misconceptions. Strongly advisable, then, is an overview of some law–morality connections which are readily acknowledged by all or virtually all legal positivists but which are sometimes perceived by critics as telling against positivism.

## A. Contingency Embraced

No jurisprudential positivist would deny that the contents and effects of legal norms can be morally worthy. Indeed, every positivist would be inclined to emphasize the possibility and the frequency of contingent connections between law and morality. As has been stated more than once in this book, separability does not amount to inevitable separateness. Only if positivists were fools, would they fail to recognize that numerous legal systems and myriad legal norms are worthy of praise on moral grounds (perhaps not unalloyed praise, but praise all the same). In fact, all legal positivists do recognize this point very happily. Though they gainsay the idea of necessary connections between law and morality, they likewise firmly gainsay the idea of a necessary lack of connections.

In particular, legal positivists gladly accept that the array of procedures constituting the rule of law can be a morally precious expression of highly laudable values. In liberal democracies, the institutions which give effect to the rule of law do indeed embody respect for values such as fairness, individual autonomy, due process, freedom, and formal equality. Imperfect though liberal-democratic regimes may be in many respects, their virtues are typically estimable; and those virtues are both manifested and promoted by the quite steadfast adherence of such regimes to the rule of law. At least to some extent, the officials in those regimes abide by the requirements of the rule of law for reasons essentially pertaining to the well-being and fundamental dignity of the people whom they rule.

Nothing in the foregoing paragraph is inconsistent in any way with jurisprudential positivism. What would be inconsistent therewith, of course, is an assertion that the morally salutary import of law in liberal-democratic societies must be characteristic of law in all other societies as well. However, such an assertion is not supported at all, much less entailed, by anything in the foregoing paragraph. The absence of support or entailment is gratifying, since any universalizing assertion along the lines just mentioned has been thoroughly refuted by my lengthy analysis of the rule of law in Chapter 3 (and also in some of the other chapters). As has been argued there, the rule of law can be invaluably serviceable for the realization of tyrannical objectives. Executive and judicial officials intent exclusively on pursuing their own interests in preserving and solidifying their positions of dominance will have strong reasons for abiding by rule-of-law requirements to a significant degree. Yet, plainly, their fulfillment of such requirements does not bespeak any moral compunctions and does not partake of any moral worthiness. They adopt their patterns of conduct solely in order to further their selfish and nefarious ends, and not in order to comply with moral obligations which they owe to citizens. Their reasons for action—their reasons for embracing the rule of law—are wicked and purely prudential. For them, the rule of law is nothing more (and nothing less) than an efficient means toward the sustainment and extension of their powerfully repressive reign. Their situation reveals, then, that the rule of law is not an inherently moral ideal.

In sum, while unhesitatingly granting that the rule of law can serve to express and realize moral aspirations of the most elevated sort, legal positivists insist that that benevolent function is a contingent rather than necessary feature of rule-of-law observances. The moral significance or status of the rule of law varies from regime to regime; notwithstanding its morally lofty role in liberal-democratic societies, it can operate in certain other societies as an essential vehicle for the consolidation of despotism and the effectuation of iniquitous designs by self-devoted officials. Still, one's insistence on this point is fully compatible with one's recognizing that the rule of law can embody and foster truly admirable values. Indeed, an insistence on the point about the highly variable moral status of rule-of-law principles is *dependent* on a recognition of the potential worthiness of those principles in appropriate settings.

Thus, when legal positivists affirm the separability of law and morality, they are perfectly well aware that those two phenomena partially coincide within many societies. Though necessary connections between those phenomena are denied, contingent connections are very willingly acknowledged. Hence, when critics of positivism write about 'the positivist thesis on the gulf between law and morality',[1] their comments are at best misleading and are at worst distortively hyperbolic.

## B. Moral Values in the Ascertainment of the Law

As has been noted in Chapters 5 and 6, Joseph Raz and his followers contend that moral values cannot serve as criteria for ascertaining the existence or content of legal norms. Although Raz of course accepts that moral values figure prominently in legal reasoning—because legal reasoning is not confined to the identification of existing laws—he submits that they cannot play any role either in the task of finding out whether certain legal norms exist or in the task of discerning what the contents of those norms are. In this respect, then, Razian positivists believe in a

---

[1] George Fletcher, *Basic Concepts of Legal Thought* (New York and Oxford: Oxford University Press, 1996), 139.

strict separation between determining what the law is and determining what the law morally ought to be. Those two aspects of the overall enterprise of legal reasoning are not only separable; they are ineluctably distinct.

As has also been noted in Chapters 5 and 6, however, most jurisprudential positivists disagree with Raz and his followers on this count. For most positivists, the question whether moral principles qualify as criteria for ascertaining the existence and contents of legal norms is an empirical question—an empirical question that may well be answered differently from one legal regime to the next. In some regimes, the process of law-ascertainment will be a straightforward matter of inquiring into the terms of the norms and decisions that have been laid down by authoritative sources such as legislative enactments and judicial rulings. In those regimes, any official who needs to identify the prevailing laws does not have to make moral judgments concerning what the laws ought to be. In other legal systems, by contrast, the identification of the prevailing laws (the identification of their existence, their content, or both their existence and their content) will involve the application of moral tests. In such legal systems, the officials have to make moral judgments in order to determine what the prevailing law is on any specific topic or set of topics.

In the eyes of most legal positivists, the pertinence or irrelevance of moral tests during the ascertainment of legal norms is a product of officials' behavior within each particular legal system. Neither the applicability nor the inapplicability of such tests is conceptually preordained, and therefore neither the applicability nor the inapplicability is conceptually disallowed. Everything hinges on the mutable normative preconceptions that underlie the official actions which collectively make up the practice of law-ascertainment in each regime. Of course, when highly abstract moral tests do obtain in any scheme of governance that is aptly classifiable as a legal system, they must obtain in combination with other law-ascertaining touchstones. In their sweeping indefiniteness, they cannot by themselves be exhaustive.[2] If officials in their concrete decisions are always directly invoking vague moral principles without any reference to legislative enactments or previous official decisions, then they are not operating a system of law at all. Any genuine legal regime will involve the regulation of conduct through norms that are more determinate than abstract moral ideals, regardless of whether those legal norms have been explicitly enacted by lawmaking bodies or are merely

---

[2] Whether or not the abstract moral tests are ontically indefinite, they certainly are epistemically indefinite. That is, whether or not those tests in principle yield uniquely correct answers to the questions which they address, they will often fail to engender widespread agreement about the correctness of various answers. Disaccordance on many points will be inevitable or virtually inevitable. That disharmony of opinions is not troublesome when the abstract moral tests play only a confined role in the ascertainment of legal norms; but, when those tests are the be-all and end-all of the process of ascertainment, their epistemic indefiniteness becomes disruptively prominent. In a system of governance where those abstract tests are exhaustive of officials' law-ascertaining criteria, the lack of uniformity in the application of the tests will produce a degree of irregularity that is inconsistent with the existence of a genuine legal system.

inferred by officials (and citizens) from past official decisions. Even in a primitive society where the distinction between legal judgments and moral judgments is largely effaced, some of the norms that bear directly on people's conduct are more textured and determinate than grand moral principles—at least if the society's arrangements for the regulation of conduct and the resolution of disputes are rightly classifiable as legal arrangements (primitive legal arrangements).

None the less, although any mode of governance-through-law must involve norms that are more concrete than are rarefied mottoes, the ascertainment of the content and existence of those norms can proceed partly on the basis of moral criteria. Nothing in the very nature of legality will have ruled out the possibility that the tests for legal validity in some particular regime include moral precepts. At any rate, such is the view of most legal positivists (including me).

Among the manifold legal positivists who favor that view, there are some differences of opinion concerning when a moral touchstone becomes a criterion for identifying what the law is. Some positivists hold that a moral principle is a law-ascertaining standard only if it is expressly presented as such in a constitutional provision or a statute or a judicial doctrine or some other explicit source of law. Other positivists allow that a moral principle is a law-ascertaining standard not only in the circumstances just mentioned but also when a regime's officials regularly rely on the principle implicitly—with no basis in an explicit source—as they pin down the existence and content of legal norms.[3]

In any event, no matter which side one chooses in this intra-positivist dispute, the crucial point is that most jurisprudential positivists acknowledge the possible role of moral values as authoritative tests or standards for determining the validity and substance of legal norms. Those values not only amount to prescripts for deciding what the law ought to be, but also can amount to guidelines for apprehending what the law is. They might not function as such guidelines in any particular legal system, but they plainly can do so. Thus argue most legal positivists. Their flexible view of this matter—a view that takes the law-identifying role of moral principles to be possible but not inevitable—is very much in keeping with the general flexibility of the 'negative' side of positivist theorizing. (Moreover, as has been seen in Chapter 6, that flexible view does not entail any particular doctrines in the metaphysics of morals.) Consequently, when some jurisprudential theorists attribute to positivists the thesis 'that it is *always* just a question of fact what the law is',[4] they are not adequately taking account of the stances which most positivists have in fact adopted.

---

[3] For some further reflections on this debate, see Jules Coleman, 'Authority and Reason', in Robert George (ed.), *The Autonomy of Law* (Oxford: Clarendon Press, 1996), 287. See especially ibid., at 315 n. 5. Like Coleman, I subscribe to the second of the two positions which I have outlined in the text.

[4] Ronald Dworkin, *Taking Rights Seriously* (Cambridge, Mass.: Harvard University Press, 1978), 342 (emphasis added).

## C. On the Moral Assessment of Law

In Chapters 1, 5, and 6, we have looked at a distinction between the moral and the nonmoral—a distinction between one's decisions that affect others' interests in significant ways and one's decisions that do not affect others' interests in ways that are more than trivial. When morality is defined via this dichotomy, we can readily assent to the proposition that all determinations by legal officials are moral decisions. As officials arrive at judgments about various entitlements and obligations, they obviously are taking stands that importantly bear on the well-being of the individuals or corporations whose legal positions are under consideration. Hence, insofar as we take 'moral' to mean 'nontrivially affecting others' interests', we should certainly accept that legal officials' judgments are perforce moral judgments. No jurisprudential positivist would plump for any other view.

Because the decisions of legal officials and the workings of a legal system are inevitably moral in the sense just defined, those decisions and workings are open to moral assessment. Somebody who morally evaluates them is engaged in a fully apposite enterprise, even if his or her specific evaluations are misguided; we can perfectly intelligibly deem legal rulings and legal norms to be unjust or benign, irrespective of whether our specific characterizations are accurate. By contrast, moral appraisals would not be pertinent at all if brought to bear on a person's decision to select one set of rules rather than another for a game of solitaire. In regard to such a decision, neither moral censure nor moral acclamation would be germane. Anybody who might invoke moral touchstones to gauge the merits of such a decision would be committing a category mistake. Very different from that situation is the situation of someone who invokes moral standards to gauge the merits of a legal system. Far from being beside the point or out of place, those standards are entirely suitable for the task. Of course, other sorts of standards can be marshaled for other sorts of assessments of a legal system's workings. All the same, moral touchstones are clearly appropriate as the bases for moral assessments—which themselves are clearly appropriate with reference to institutions that profoundly shape and direct people's lives. Every legal positivist would grant as much.

Let us note another reason for holding that the officials who operate legal systems can rightly be held morally responsible for what they decide and do. So far, this section has concentrated on the fact that the determinations and actions of those officials impinge significantly on the well-being of other people. In this respect, their determinations typically differ from (say) the choice made by someone who elects between tackling a crossword puzzle and putting together a jigsaw puzzle as a way of passing some spare time. Yet, although the actual presence or intended presence or reasonably foreseeable possibility of nontrivial impacts on others' interests from some course of conduct is necessary for the pertinence of moral assessments, it is not sufficient. After all, countless natural events dramatically affect the well-being of people without subjecting the causes of those events to any apposite moral evaluation.

Suppose that an asteroid hurtles into the earth and wipes out a large proportion of the human species (along with other species) in the aftermath of the collision. The effect on people's interests will be far-reaching indeed, but the asteroid cannot rightly be deemed immoral or wicked. What is missing from its plunge into the earth, quite plainly, is the consciousness of a rational agent who decides to act in one way as opposed to another. Moral responsibility does not attach to the asteroid, because its collision does not stem from anyone's intentionality or negligence. The workings of a legal system, obviously, are quite different. Legal norms are established and applied by mature human beings who can aptly be held accountable for their deeds. Not only do those norms and their applications heavily affect people's interests—often people's vital interests—but, what is more, they derive from the choices of human adults. Thus, in regard to such norms and their applications, moral approbation or disapprobation has a suitable object. No jurisprudential positivist who is minimally sensible would ever suggest otherwise. Hence, when we encounter allegations that legal positivists perceive law as 'simply a datum of nature' and that they approach law 'like the scientist who discovers a uniformity of inanimate nature',[5] we can easily see that we are confronting outright calumnies. (Of course, nothing in this paragraph is meant to imply that the intentions of legal officials always match the consequences of their actions; the occurrence of unintended consequences is no less likely during the creation and administration of legal norms than within any other area of life. Still, even when the consequences of legal norms or rulings are not anticipated, they are the products of human acts and decisions. Because of their status as such, they are susceptible to moral assessment and are thus unlike the damage caused by an asteroid. The lack of intendedness will almost certainly soften the moral appraisals that are reached, but will not render all such appraisals simply beside the point.)

Before leaving this topic, we should consider one further complication. In regard to many products of human design that can importantly affect people's interests, moral evaluations are not pertinent. Consider, for example, an ordinary kitchen knife. Such an item can serve people's interests as a handy culinary utensil, but can also harm people's interests severely as an instrument for murder. None the less, an assessment of an ordinary kitchen knife as either morally commendable or morally iniquitous would be ridiculously out of place. In connection with a weapon designed specifically for assaults, to be sure, a negative moral assessment would be perfectly comprehensible—even to someone who does not endorse the assessment. Such an evaluation of a kitchen knife, however, would not simply be wrong; it would be bizarre. Much the same can be said about moral judgments brought to bear on any number of other manmade products, ranging from table lamps to umbrellas. What should we make of this fact? Why

---

[5] Lon Fuller, *The Morality of Law* (New Haven: Yale University Press, 1969) (rev. edn.), 148, 151.

should we assume that legal norms and legal systems as manmade things are indeed susceptible to moral evaluations?

Four overlapping observations are appropriate in reply to these questions. The first of these observations should begin by acknowledging that not every legal norm on its own is a suitable object of moral judgments. As has been noted fleetingly in Chapter 2, many of the fine-grained technical requirements in areas such as commercial law and electoral law do not lend themselves to being gauged morally, at least when they are considered on their own rather than as components of an overall scheme of jural regulation. In relation to many of those requirements by themselves, neither moral plaudits nor moral plaints would be apposite. In this respect, then, some legal norms resemble the various other things (such as ordinary kitchen knives and table lamps and armchairs) to which the application of moral judgments is out of place. Nevertheless, other legal norms are pertinently open to moral evaluation—perhaps because of their obvious moral commendableness or deplorableness, or perhaps simply because they deal with matters that are of evident moral significance. Likewise, a legal system as a whole is undoubtedly open to moral evaluation, since it inevitably deals with matters that are of deep moral significance (such as the preservation of peace and security). Whether it handles those matters effectively or poorly, the fact that it must address them is sufficient to render a legal system susceptible to appraisal on moral grounds. Moreover, any such system is bound to include a host of norms whose moral goodness or badness subjects the overall system to apposite moral scrutiny.

Second, to a considerably greater extent than ordinary umbrellas or armchairs, some legal norms are directly expressive of moral choices. Because many such norms regulate important aspects of human interaction, they unavoidably reflect moral judgments about the ways in which those dimensions of human intercourse ought to be arranged. (N.B. Recall that, in this section, the word 'moral' is being contrasted solely with 'nonmoral' rather than with 'prudential' or 'ignoble'.) A legal regime as a whole or the large bodies of norms within such a regime will be even more plainly expressive of moral choices than are most individual norms. After all, an overarching legal regime or a set of legal doctrines must inevitably reflect certain judgments about the ways in which human beings should interact with one another throughout countless areas of their lives. Those judgments are moral judgments, in the sense defined by this section.

Third, because a legal system uses actual or potential coercion to require certain actions and forbid certain actions while permitting or authorizing still other actions, the touchstones especially appropriate for evaluating its workings are bound to be moral touchstones. Not only does a legal system lay down determinations on innumerable issues that affect people's basic interests, but its own operations (involving actual or potential punishments) affect those interests directly as well. That is, a legal regime produces major impacts on people's vital concerns not only in its legislative/adjudicative role as a setter of standards, but also in its executive role as an implementer of those standards. An institution that intervenes so strikingly into people's lives is a fitting object of moral assessments.

Fourth is a point that amounts largely to an offshoot of the three preceding considerations (particularly the first two). What makes an ordinary kitchen knife or table lamp insusceptible to moral evaluations is that any morally significant uses of such an item are attributable primarily or exclusively to the person who engages in the uses, rather than to the central purpose of the item itself. Although an artefact such as an ordinary umbrella can of course be put to uses that are notably malevolent or notably benevolent, the connections between the notably malevolent uses and the central purpose of the umbrella are not much closer or more tenuous than the connections between that purpose and the notably benevolent uses. As a result, the moral credit or discredit attaches entirely to the user rather than to what is used. By contrast, when the connections between an item's central purpose and a malevolent use of the item are especially close—as is true of assault weapons, in the eyes of some people—the item itself can quite intelligibly be judged negatively on moral grounds. Equally, a favorable moral assessment of something is intelligible if there are especially close connections between the thing's central purpose and a benevolent use of the thing (as might be true of many vaccines, for example). While the murderous use of an assault weapon by a thug or the solicitous use of a vaccine by a doctor will of course warrant the passing of a moral judgment on the thug or the doctor and also on the act of murder or inoculation, it can furthermore lead to the passing of an intelligible moral judgment on the assault weapon or the vaccine itself.

Numerous legal norms are much more like assault weapons or vaccines than like armchairs or table lamps. That is, the connections between some legal norms and certain benevolent uses thereof are clear-cut and are far more easily anticipated than are connections with various evil uses to which the norms might be put; similarly, the connections between some other legal norms and certain evil uses thereof are clear-cut and are far more easily anticipated than are connections with various benevolent uses to which those norms might be put. Moral appraisals of such norms themselves—as well as of the decisions that are generated by them—will manifestly be intelligible and, if accurate, will be suitable in every respect. Much the same can be said about moral appraisals of the legal systems which contain many such norms. (Quite obvious is the relevance here of my earlier point about the relatively precise expressiveness of legal norms. Exactly because legal norms tend to be so effective as vehicles for the articulation of stances on morally significant questions, the links between them and their applications are frequently tight.)

As this section of my current chapter has sought to emphasize, then, jurisprudential positivists should happily acknowledge—and do happily acknowledge— that legal norms and legal systems can generally be subjected to moral assessments quite appropriately. Whereas moral categories are not pertinent for the evaluation of sunsets or ordinary pencils or ordinary crossword puzzles, they are indeed typically pertinent for the evaluation of legal norms and legal regimes. A diehard jurisprudential positivist (such as the author of this book) has no reason whatsoever to suggest that moral categories are somehow out of place. No tenable insistence on the separability of law and morality is in any way tantamount to a denial of the fact that the norms and workings of legal regimes are apt objects of moral scrutiny.

## D. Law's General Role

In Chapter 9 we shall explore at some length the implications of law's general role or function in human society. Hence, a laconic treatment of that role will here suffice. Both in laying down authoritative standards for conduct, and in averting or settling disputes by giving effect to those standards, law plays an indispensable role in bringing about the orderliness that is a *sine qua non* of any viable human society. In any social structure that exists over the long term or even over the medium term, there must be considerable regularity, security, and co-ordination. In any social structure larger than a few families, moreover, those desiderata (regularity, security, and co-ordination) cannot obtain in the absence of law. Though the workings of a legal regime are not *exclusively* responsible for the preservation of social order and co-ordination, they are indeed *crucially* so. Especially on the scale of a nation or a large city, but even on the scale of a small town, the standard-setting and dispute-resolving functions of law are unforgoable. No human society could abide without the presence of those functions, for their absence would in effect preclude the basic orderliness that enables a society to abide. In other words, the existence of law is a necessary condition for the existence of any sustainable scheme of multi-faceted human intercourse on a large scale or even on quite a modest scale. And since human beings cannot live in proximity to one another in fairly large numbers without the existence of some societal arrangements—at least if their lives are to be minimally satisfactory and secure—the existence of law is a necessary condition for the ability of people to live in the presence of one another. Although Thomas Hobbes was wrong in thinking that the only realistic alternative to lawlessness is a despotic sovereign, he was entirely correct in thinking that people under conditions of lawlessness will lead lives that are solitary, poor, nasty, brutish, and short.

Few if any legal positivists would disagree with the line of argument in my last paragraph. There is certainly not the slightest reason for them to disagree. Indeed, all or nearly all of them would concur heartily with what has been said. For example, as will be recounted in Chapter 9, H. L. A. Hart developed an elaborate and sophisticated version of the argument above. Yet the whole-hearted approval of that line of argument by jurisprudential positivists may seem baffling to some critics of positivism. After all, the argument's conclusion is that the existence of law is a necessary condition for the ability of people to live in the presence of one another and thus to enjoy the myriad benefits of civilization.

Surely, the opponents of positivism might respond, this general role of law in human society forms an ineluctable connection between law and morality—an ineluctable connection not only between law and morality-as-contrasted-with-nonmoral-factors, but also between law and morality-as-contrasted-with-unworthiness. The latter conjunction, between law and moral worthiness, would appear to undermine positivist claims about the thoroughgoing separability of legal obligatoriness and moral obligatoriness. Law, by dint of its very nature as law in human society, fulfills a morally commendable function.

To this hypothetical line of reasoning that might be propounded by positivism's detractors, Chapter 9 will offer a full reply. My present discussion will confine itself to a few quick observations. Let us begin by noting a markedly inadequate reply to the anti-positivist line of reasoning—a reply that will not be submitted or endorsed herein, in light of its inadequacies.

A rather wooden defense of positivist claims about the lack of necessary ties between law and morality might seize upon the conception of necessity that is operative in the antepenultimate paragraph above. The thesis put forward by the aforementioned paragraph is that, given some basic facts about human beings and the world that surrounds them, the chances of their being able to live alongside one another in fairly large numbers without the existence of law are overwhelmingly slim. For all practical purposes, indeed, the chances are nil. In this important sense, the existence of law is a necessary condition for the ability of people to interact sustainedly with one another and thus to live securely and satisfactorily. Now, plainly, the physical and psychological characteristics of human beings and the physical characteristics of their world are not *logically* necessary features of their condition. As a matter of logical possibility, human beings and their physical environment could be utterly different from what they are. Moreover, even when the basic traits of people and the basic qualities of their planet are taken as given, the existence of law cannot rightly be deemed *logically* necessary for the ability of people to live alongside one another in large numbers with a reasonable degree of security and co-ordination. The argument in my antepenultimate paragraph is concerned with overwhelmingly high probabilities rather than with strict logical necessity. Perhaps a heavy-handed defender of positivism would be inclined to dwell on this point about logical necessity, in the hope of salvaging positivism's insistence on the absence of necessary connections between morality and law. Such a defender would maintain that the conception of necessity operative in the theses of legal positivism is purely logical necessity. That is, positivists would be portrayed as attacking only the notion of logically necessary links between legal norms and moral precepts; they would be portrayed as countenancing the notion of links that are 'necessary' in some weaker sense of the term.

Any defense of legal positivism along these lines should clearly be abjured. On the one hand, to be sure, positivists must indeed deny that there are conceptual/logical links between law and morality. Any proof of such links would be in direct contradiction with the central claims of legal positivism.

Consequently, most of my previous chapters have fought long battles against theories that appear to tie law and morality together conceptually. On the other hand, although the undoing of putative logical connections between legal norms and moral values is indeed essential for a defense of positivism, it is not sufficient. Positivists must likewise assail the line of reasoning that was attributed to critics of positivism (hypothetically) three paragraphs ago.

According to the line of reasoning just mentioned, the role of law as an indispensable condition for any extensive and non-ephemeral human intercourse is itself a necessary point of intersection between legality and morality. We are told that that fundamental role of law endows every legal system $S$ with some degree of moral worthiness simply by dint of $S$'s status as a legal system. In other words, we are told that a certain degree of moral worthiness is a necessary aspect of every viable legal regime. Here the word 'necessary' means 'inevitable except in utterly fanciful circumstances which (though logically possible) have never occurred and will never occur'. Now, if jurisprudential positivists were to condone the idea of a necessary law–morality nexus along these lines, they would be retreating markedly from their firm insistence on the separability of morality and law. At least in regard to the present point of contention, that insistence would be reduced to a claim about the nature of law in a logically possible world that never will exist and never has existed. Such a feeble claim would scarcely be worth defending. If jurisprudential positivism is to be a truly interesting doctrine in dealing with the present point of contention, it must set itself against any necessary law–morality conjunction of the sort defined above. Positivists must resist any move from a premise about law's indispensable orderliness-sustaining role to a conclusion about each legal system's inherent moral commendability. My ninth chapter impugns exactly that move.

Although the arguments of Chapter 9 obviously cannot be fully recounted here, we should anticipatorily glance at one key point that is of particular relevance to this portion of my current chapter. When seeking to gauge the moral worthiness or unworthiness of a legal regime, an observer should recognize that his evaluation must rest on an implicit or explicit comparison.[6] Some baseline for the comparison is presupposed or expressly specified, and the legal regime under examination is then favorably or unfavorably contrasted therewith. When the orderliness-sustaining role of law is invoked in justification of the thesis that every viable legal regime partakes of some degree of moral worthiness, the baseline for the requisite comparison with each legal regime is a situation of lawlessness. Each such regime fares well in a comparison with the horrors of chaotic anarchy, despite sundry shortcomings that may mar any particular regime in other respects. Each legal system is therefore perceived as morally commendable to some extent (perhaps only to a very limited extent, in certain cases) simply by

---

[6]  This point is aptly emphasized in Kent Greenawalt, *Conflicts of Law and Morality* (New York and Oxford: Oxford University Press, 1989), 192–4.

virtue of being characterized as a system of law—i.e., simply by virtue of being characterized as an alternative to lawlessness.

What my ninth chapter will challenge, among other things, is the notion that the appropriate baseline-for-comparison in one's evaluation of a legal system is a situation of anarchy. While circumstances of lawlessness are appalling, and while the existence of law is thus essential for the avoidance of morally catastrophic states of affairs, each legal regime should be assessed not primarily in contrast with lawlessness but primarily in contrast with other possible legal regimes (which amount to other alternatives to lawlessness). Although the full set of arguments behind my stance here will not emerge until Chapter 9, a somewhat crude example will at present furnish a sketchy prefiguration of one of those arguments.

Consider a situation in which a bully $B$ kicks his victims fiercely but stops short of slaying them. If in our evaluation of his conduct we take as our baseline-for-comparison a situation in which the bullying results in outright murder, then we shall conclude that $B$'s conduct partakes of some degree of moral worthiness notwithstanding its overall wrongness. Contrariwise, if in our evaluation of his conduct we take as our baseline-for-comparison a situation in which no bullying occurs, then we shall conclude that his conduct is unequivocally immoral—even though it is less egregiously immoral than is bullying that culminates in the slaying of its victims. Let us now modify the example to increase the resemblance between the situation portrayed therein and the functioning of a wicked legal system. Suppose that $B$ and his henchmen run a protection racket, under which they treat their victims very roughly and extort crushingly heavy 'fees' in return for providing two 'services': their forbearance from murdering their victims, and their fending off of other thugs who would mistreat the victims even more appallingly. (Manifestly, they fend off the other thugs not out of any altruistic impulses, but out of a desire to preserve their own posture of lucrative dominance. Because their own takings will decline if other gangsters muscle in on their territory, they have a strong stake in keeping the others out. Their abstention from murdering their victims is likewise a product of icy self-interest. The victims will cease to be profitable sources of 'fees' if they are dead.) If in our evaluation of the protection racket we take as our baseline-for-comparison a situation in which the victims are brutally murdered, then we shall conclude that the actions of $B$ and his cronies partake of moral worthiness to some extent despite the overall wrongness of those actions. Conversely, if in our evaluation we take as our baseline-for-comparison a situation in which the ordinary people are left largely or wholly untroubled by gangsters, then we shall conclude that $B$ and his henchmen are engaging in conduct that is unalloyedly immoral—even though their racket is less rebarbative than the murderous depredations that might be inflicted by other thugs.

What is the appropriate baseline, then? As will be seen in Chapter 9, an answer to this question depends chiefly on two factors: the basic moral entitlements of people, and the attainability of various states of affairs. Let us presume that both a state of affairs devoid of protection rackets and a state of affairs abounding with misconduct even worse than protection rackets are reasonably attainable. Under any moral code acceptable within the Western liberal-democratic tradition, each person has a straightforward moral right to the realization of the former state of affairs. Hence, the appropriate baseline-for-comparison in an evaluation of *B*'s misdeeds is the state of affairs largely or wholly devoid of racketeering. His misdeeds should thus be branded as unequivocally immoral. Let us now presume, however, that the only alternative to *B*'s racketeering is an even worse state of affairs. In other words, any really serious efforts to bring about a preferable state of affairs (a society largely or wholly devoid of racketeering, for example) would involve unacceptably high moral costs such as rampant strife and slaughter. Though each person in these circumstances will still of course have a straightforward moral right against being subjected to the mistreatment and demands of racketeers, the moral right to the realization of a society devoid of racketeering and similar evils is suspended[7]—because, *ex hypothesi*, any earnest attempts to gain the fulfillment of such a right would involve unacceptably high moral costs. In these circumstances, the appropriate baseline-for-comparison in an evaluation of *B*'s misdeeds is a situation marked by oppressive evils that are even worse than those misdeeds. Hence, although *B*'s racketeering should certainly still be classified as wrong (because it violates the right of each person against being subjected to extortion), it partakes of some degree of moral commendability as the best of a set of bad options. The foremost practical consequence of such commendability is that each person *in these circumstances* has a prima-facie obligation to acquiesce in the racketeering despite its wrongness. Each ordinary person owes that obligation not to *B* and his cronies, who plainly have no entitlement to compliance with their dictates; rather, the obligation is owed by each ordinary person to every other ordinary person.

In some respects, as will become apparent in Chapter 9, this brief discussion of racketeering has greatly oversimplified the issues that must be pondered in one's assessment of a legal system. For example, it has directed attention to a very small set of alternatives—(1) no racketeering, (2) racketeering, (3) murderous rampages worse than racketeering—and has therefore neglected to indicate that the alternatives to be considered during an appraisal of a legal system are typically numerous. Moreover, my discussion has concentrated on general schemes of social intercourse rather than on particular instances of the patterns of behavior that make up those schemes. It has therefore failed to indicate that the task of figuring out the consequences of a legal regime's moral tenor is usually a task

---

[7] I am inclined to say that the right temporarily becomes a nominal right (i.e., a right for which there is no power-of-exercise). However, because the distinction between genuine entitlements and nominal entitlements is less straightforwardly applicable in morality than in law—as I have acknowledged in my 'Rights Without Trimmings', in Matthew Kramer, Nigel Simmonds, and Hillel Steiner, *A Debate Over Rights* (Oxford: Clarendon Press, 1998), 7, 8–9—I have opted here to say that the moral right itself is suspended.

focused on specific norms and on specific sorts of occasions for conformity with norms.

Nevertheless, though misleading in the ways just noted (and in some other ways), the discussion here enables us to apprehend why jurisprudential positivists can accept both of the following two theses:

A. The existence of a legal system in any society is indispensable for the securing of basic orderliness and co-ordination, which are desiderata of overriding moral importance.

B. It is not the case that a legal system necessarily partakes of some degree of moral worthiness just by dint of its nature as a legal system which secures basic orderliness and co-ordination.

The first of these theses does not entail the negation of the second, even if we temporarily leave aside the fact that some legal systems may be worse for some innocent people than a situation of lawlessness would be. (My whole discussion in this section has left aside that fact.) Only if the sole alternative to each particular legal system were the horrors of chaotic anarchy or of an even worse legal system, would the first of these theses clash with the second. Only then would the pertinent baseline-for-comparison in an assessment of every legal system be a state of affairs marked by those horrors. In fact, however, we have absolutely no reason for thinking that a situation of arrant lawlessness is invariably or typically the sole alternative to the continuation of the present legal system in each society. Nor do we have the slightest reason for thinking that all morally preferable alternatives to any wicked legal system will never be reasonably attainable. Morally superior legal systems will often be realizable. Consequently, we have not the slightest reason for thinking that every monstrous legal regime is to some extent morally worthy by virtue of its sheer status as an orderliness-securing alternative to anarchic turmoil.

In sum, because the two theses above are fully compatible, no jurisprudential positivist needs to deny the first of them. Few if any jurisprudential positivists do deny it. An insistence on the separability of law and morality is perfectly consistent with a recognition that the existence of law is a necessary condition for the fulfillment of a morally vital function that makes human society possible.

## II. LEGAL NORMS AND CONVENTIONAL MORALITY

So far, this chapter has recounted a number of connections between law and morality that can be acknowledged with equanimity by legal positivists. Those connections do not undermine in any way the positivist claim that the domain of morality and the domain of law are always separable. The first half of this chapter has not marked a retreat from legal positivism at all; it has sought to clarify positivist theses rather than to dilute them. In order to underscore the uncompromisingness of the positivist stance which this book defends, the remainder of this chapter is devoted to casting doubt on the ineluctability of a law-morality nexus that has sometimes been perceived as an inevitable feature of every possible legal system.

This discussion should begin by distinguishing tersely between critical morality and conventional morality. Such a distinction, of ancient lineage, has been drawn in more recent times by H. L. A. Hart and others.[8] *Conventional* moral values and principles are those values and principles which prevail in some particular society as the widely accepted touchstones for determining what is right and what is wrong. By contrast, the validity of *critical* moral values and principles transcends the acceptance or non-acceptance of them in any particular society; their force as standards for judging the merits of conventional moral codes is dependent only on their own correctness and not on their having been embraced by most people in this or that community.

Every jurisprudential positivist would deny that legal norms necessarily coincide with critical moral precepts. A wide-ranging correspondence between the norms of a legal regime and the precepts of critical morality is a purely contingent matter rather than something preordained by the nature of law. (My ninth chapter—and, indirectly, this chapter—will go further by arguing that any concrete correspondence at all between those norms and those precepts is a contingent matter.) Some supporters of positivism have suggested, however, that the links between legal norms and *conventional* morality are not purely contingent.[9] Within each society, the law is the jural codification or embodiment of the regnant moral ethos. Because legal norms and the decisions reached by reference to them are fundamentally judgments about what is appropriate and what is inappropriate behavior, they cannot but be shaped by the dominant values that undergird such judgments in a particular society.

This position seems to be adopted by Jules Coleman, for example. Though he does not state the position forthrightly, he appears to opt for it—or something approximating it—in a combination of two passages from one of his well-known essays. In the first of those passages he writes as follows:

> It is tempting to confuse the separability thesis [i.e., the thesis that law and morality are always separable] with the very different claim that the law of a community is one thing and its morality another. This last claim is seriously ambiguous. In one sense, the claim that the law of a community is one thing and its morality another may amount to the very

[8]  See H. L. A. Hart, *Law, Liberty, and Morality* (Oxford: Oxford University Press, 1963), 17–20.
[9]  One opponent of jurisprudential positivism has submitted that an insistence on the necessity of links between law and conventional morality is fully compatible with positivism: 'For given its conventionalism about the morals to which law relates, such a view is really a kind of legal positivism: what is legally required does not depend on what is morally right, but only upon a certain kind of social fact, namely, whether a group of people have the requisite moral beliefs. . . . [A positivist who takes this view] is as much a natural lawyer's opponent as is the more traditional kind who seeks to keep even shared moral beliefs out of his theory of law' (Michael Moore, 'Law as a Functional Kind', in Robert George (ed.), *Natural Law Theory* [Oxford: Clarendon Press, 1992], 188, 192).

strong assertion that there exists no convergence between the norms that constitute a community's law and those that constitute its morality. Put this way, the thesis is an empirical one whose inadequacies are demonstrated by the shared legal and moral prohibitions against murder, theft, battery and the like.[10]

Before looking at the second (and more directly relevant) passage from Coleman's essay, we should note two problematic features of the extract above. First, it handles a familiar and piquant slogan of legal positivism in a very odd manner. Writers who wield that slogan to encapsulate the theses of positivism have certainly not purported to be making an *empirical* claim either about some particular community or about all communities. (Even less has anyone brandishing that slogan endeavored to maintain that legal norms and moral precepts *cannot* converge.) Instead, the slogan has amounted to a catchy summation of the so-called separability thesis.

Another problematic feature of the extract above is that its conclusion is broad enough to apply to critical morality as much as to conventional morality. Any plausible set of critical moral precepts will include the prohibitions which Coleman mentions. We therefore have to ask whether Coleman feels that the critical/conventional distinction is of importance for legal positivism. His answer comes in an endnote, where he addresses the question 'whether the separability thesis [i]s a claim about the relationship between law and critical morality or between law and conventional morality. My understanding of the separability thesis is as a denial of a constitutive relationship between law and critical morality' ('Positivism', 343 n. 3). Although this rendering of the separability thesis does not logically commit Coleman to the notion of a constitutive relationship between law and conventional morality, it does strongly suggest such a relationship—especially in light of the first passage quoted above.

A variant of the same basic position has been put forward by Richard Tur, who espouses a doctrine which he designates as 'normative positivism'. He declares that the formal normativity of law is filled with the substance of 'the values, beliefs, intuitions, ideals, interests and emotions of whosoever has the lawmaking function in hand'.[11] He asserts that any legal system, 'replete with content flowing from the "millenary labour" of many heads, hearts and hands, constantly in flux, but also sufficiently determinate to guide conduct, may be regarded as a socially valid positive system of morality. If so, "normative positivism" legitimates the view that law is *necessarily* in the business of upholding moral values'

---

[10] Jules Coleman, 'Negative and Positive Positivism', in *Markets, Morals and the Law* (Cambridge: Cambridge University Press, 1988) ['Positivism'], 3, 5–6.

[11] Richard Tur, 'Criminal Law and Legal Theory', in William Twining (ed.), *Legal Theory and Common Law* (Oxford: Basil Blackwell, 1986) ['Theory'], 195, 208. For a view largely similar to Tur's, see Jules Coleman, 'On the Relationship Between Law and Morality', 2 *Ratio Juris* 66, 72 (1989): 'The rule of recognition is authoritative because it is a social rule. . . . Law is ultimately a matter of social convention; and the duties of conventional morality need not coincide with what morality requires.'

('Theory', 208, emphasis in original, footnote omitted). Tur summarizes his doctrine in a manner that highlights its place within my current discussion: 'Normative positivism asserts what legal positivists deny, namely that there is a *necessary* connection between law and positive morality. At the same time . . . normative positivism radically separates itself from any suggestion that there is a necessary connection between law and any critical morality' ('Theory', 209, emphasis in original).

Before we probe the putative necessity of the connection between law and conventional morality, we should glance at two differences between Tur's and Coleman's respective remarks—apart from the fact that Coleman displays far more circumspection than does Tur. First, whereas Coleman does not specify whether the principal adherents of the formative conventional moral precepts are officials or are citizens or are both officials and citizens, Tur clearly focuses on officials as the principal adherents (while of course not ruling out the possibility that the officials' morality will be shared by citizens). Second, unlike Coleman, Tur perpetrates an error that has been one of the prime targets in several of my earlier chapters. That is, he presumes that the critical reflective attitude of officials—their posture of engagement or allegiance—is necessarily moral rather than prudential. Because that mistake has been repeatedly exposed as such in this book, and because it will be countered still further in my next chapter, my present discussion can forbear from dwelling upon it.

Even if we assume that officials' actual or professed reasons for action in their authoritative capacities must be moral rather than prudential, we should decline to accept that there is any necessary connection between law and conventional morality. We should briefly consider two broad scenarios wherein that connection breaks down.

1. In the first of these scenarios, the connection between the norms of a society's legal regime and the precepts of the society's conventional morality has dissolved because the moral values of the officials in the regime differ strikingly from the moral values of the community at large. In this scenario, then, the conventional morality which fails to gain expression in the law is that of the citizens as opposed to that of the officials. (Hence, Tur's doctrine of normative positivism will not be fully parried until my second scenario.) Quite readily imaginable is a situation in which the moral values embraced by the officials of a legal system are either much more enlightened or much more benighted than the moral values of the citizens whose behavior is regulated by the system. For present purposes, let us suppose that the officials are much more benighted than the citizens. They run a harshly repressive regime and refuse to permit many forms of behavior which the citizens would tolerate or countenance. At the same time, they adopt or condone myriad noxious forms of behavior which the citizens detest. In these circumstances, where the officials' evil values are thoroughly reflected in the norms of their society's law, those norms differ markedly in substance from the precepts of the conventional moral code to which the citizens

*Disclaimers and Reassertions* 213

remain attached. A society's conventional morality residing in the outlooks of its citizens has become disconnected from the objectives and priorities that suffuse the society's legal framework.

A defender of the idea of necessary connections between law and conventional morality might deliver a rejoinder roughly along the lines of the chief point in the first extract from Jules Coleman's work. That is, while allowing that the correspondence between law and conventional morality can be highly imperfect, such a person might want to maintain that there are irreducible areas of convergence between them. After all, as has already been acknowledged in this chapter, some basic prohibitions—chiefly including those mentioned by Coleman—must figure among the norms in any viable legal regime. Accordingly, such prohibitions must figure among the norms of the legal regime sketched in my last paragraph; and because *ex hypothesi* those norms thoroughly reflect the values of the regime's officials, their values must encompass the aforementioned prohibitions. If the officials endorse those prohibitions, however, then surely the citizens (who are much more enlightened than the officials, *ex hypothesi*) endorse them as well. Besides, any tenable scheme of conventional morality must incorporate those prohibitions. Thus, in regard to a number of fundamental mandates, there are inevitable convergences between the norms of any society's legal framework and the conventional moral principles of the society's citizenry.

This riposte to my argument will withstand scrutiny only if the basic proscriptions that figure in every sustainable legal regime are described at quite a high level of abstraction. As soon as we move down to the level of concreteness at which the norms of a regime are apt to be formulated, there is ample room for significant divergences between the basic proscriptions contained in those norms and the basic proscriptions favored by the citizenry. In a society of the type outlined two paragraphs ago, the officials and the citizens agree that murders and thefts and assaults should be prohibited, but they harbor very different conceptions of those wrongs. For example, let us suppose, the society's legal norms forbid most intentional slayings committed against officials (by other officials or by citizens) and also forbid many intentional slayings committed against some citizens, while allowing most intentional slayings that are committed against people who belong to groups despised by the officials. Most citizens, by contrast, are aghast at the legal permissibility of those slayings. Let us suppose further that the officials and their legal norms countenance most physical attacks and acts of plunder against the members of the despised groups, and that they also countenance some physical attacks and acts of robbery against other citizens in some circumstances—even though most citizens would regard those attacks and robberies as entirely illegitimate. Let us suppose as well that the prohibitions on various types of thefts are operative in a context where many aspects of the prevailing scheme of property are viewed by most citizens as largely or wholly illegitimate (presumably because far too much wealth ends up in the hands of the officials and their major supporters). In all of these ways, and in other ways that can easily be imagined, the substance of the basic prohibitions in a society's law can differ greatly from the substance of the basic prohibitions that are seen by most citizens as appropriate. Agreement at an abstract level on the need for certain fundamental proscriptions can be accompanied by far-reaching disagreement at the more concrete level where the proscriptions are spelled out. What might seem to be inevitable areas of convergence between legal mandates and the conventional morality of citizens can turn out to be areas of profound disaccordance between them.

2. Let us now concentrate on a situation where the conventional morality that prevails among citizens in some society is shared by the legal officials therein. Will the law in that society inevitably reflect the values of the shared conventional morality, at least to a very large extent if not in every detail? To see that the answer to this question is 'no', we should ponder a scenario involving people (citizens and officials alike) who believe in the existence of a malevolent god. Admittedly, the vividness of the scenario may bring with it some degree of fancifulness; however, the general point of the example could be made just as pertinently by reference to a credible situation where legal officials adopt numerous hateful laws with an eye toward appeasing a formidable and malevolent nation that might otherwise invade the officials' land.

In a society *S*, most citizens and most legal officials alike harbor enlightened moral views. Yet, despite the benignity of the conventional morality in *S*, the legal norms are largely horrific. People in *S* believe that any changes to their atrocious legal framework (which has undergone hardly any modifications for centuries) will provoke the wrath of a malignant deity *D* who takes pleasure in beholding the suffering that is caused by his odious array of norms. The people believe that *D* will afflict them with catastrophes or even destroy them altogether if they rebel against him by introducing laws that will come closer to reflecting their own benevolent values. Hence, dearly though they would like to give expression to their conventional morality in the form of a much more enlightened legal regime, they blench at the prospect of confronting *D*'s wrath. In order to shield their society from quick destruction or devastating calamities, they unhappily retain a host of legal norms which they regard as deeply evil. Their conventional morality does not significantly inform the legal framework of their society.

Someone might retort to this example by invoking again the basic prohibitions that must be included in the legal regime of any viable society. Here the suggestion would be that there are irreducible areas of convergence between the horrible legal system and the admirable conventional morality in *S*—areas of convergence focused on the basic prohibitions, of course. Naturally, the enlightened conventional morality of the people in *S* will encompass those prohibitions; similarly, given that the legal framework retained out of fear of *D* is consistent with the continuation of *S* as a society, the aforementioned prohibitions must be comprehended within it. Hence, there might appear to be solid grounds for the proposition that law and conventional morality necessarily converge in significant ways.

Plainly, any such retort to my argument can be countered in much the same manner as the parallel retort to my earlier argument. At quite a high level of abstraction, the conventional morality and the legal framework in *S* can be said to overlap with regard to certain fundamental proscriptions. However, at the more concrete levels where legal norms are formulated and implemented, the areas of congruence between the conventional morality and the law turn out to be areas of wide-ranging divergences. In the present example, of course, the divergences stem not from the legal officials' wickedness but from their fear of *D*. Let us suppose that the matrix of legal norms retained on the basis of that fear is similar to the matrix of such norms in my earlier example involving benighted officials. That is, the legal protections against murder and assault and theft do not extend at all to some people, and they do not extend to anyone in several sorts of circumstances where every decent person would think that they should apply. Moreover, those protections reach to many sorts of situations where they disallow perfectly legitimate activities (activities which are viewed as perfectly legitimate by most people in *S*). Furthermore, the prohibitions on theft uphold a distribution of wealth that is correctly perceived by most of *S*'s officials and citizens as gravely inequitable. In all of these ways, the basic proscriptions in the law of *S* are strikingly at odds with the basic proscriptions favored in the conventional morality of *S*'s people. Because of the widely shared fear of *D*, the widely shared conventional morality has no significant influence on the content of the law.

Once again, then, a society's legal norms and its conventional morality have proved to be separable. There is no necessary correspondence between them, just as there is no necessary correspondence between legal norms and critical moral precepts. Although substantial convergences between the values immanent in a society's law and the values upheld in the society's conventional morality are undoubtedly probable in most contexts, they are never automatic or preordained. Those convergences are contingent, just like all other connections between morality and law. In short, my present discussion has resolutely reaffirmed a central theme of this book. By so doing, I have sought to make clear that the first several sections of this chapter are clarifications or amplifications of that theme rather than retrenchments of it. Far from offering laurel branches to the opponents of jurisprudential-positivist theses, this chapter has endeavored to forestall any misrepresentation of those theses and has thereby endeavored to indicate why opposition to them is misguided.

# 8

## *Elements of a Conceptual Framework*

At various junctures in this book, a number of major jural concepts have undergone explications that have laid emphasis on the separability of law and morality. My present chapter assembles and extends some of those explications. No theory of law can stand if it cannot take proper account of the key concepts that structure our thought and discourse about legal institutions. Hence, no positivist theory of law can stand if it cannot elaborate those concepts in ways that reveal their detachability from moral concepts. Many portions of this book have sought to highlight that detachability; the current chapter recapitulates and expands some of those efforts methodically.

This chapter begins by briefly rehearsing my analyses of the concepts of formal justice, authority, normativity, and obligation. It thereby brings together many of the foremost elements in the conceptual matrix that must underlie any positivist account of law. Thenceforward, my focus in this chapter will lie sustainedly on the concept of allegiance or committedness. That is, my chief concern in the closing sections of the chapter will be to expound the general attitude of acceptance and supportiveness displayed by officials (and some other people) toward the functioning of their legal regime.

People who run a legal system typically exhibit a commitment to its overall continuation and to all or most of its specific workings; unless they exhibit such an attitude of allegiance, indeed, their legal system cannot long endure as such. What the present chapter will argue, in line with what this book has argued at several points already, is that the requisite attitude of committedness among officials need not be moral rather than prudential. My discussion herein will build on my earlier analyses as it examines the arguments of four theorists—Deryck Beyleveld and Roger Brownsword, John Finnis, and Stephen Perry—who have maintained that the allegiance of officials (and of other participants in the operations of legal systems) is perforce a fundamentally moral posture. As will be seen, those theorists have disregarded or markedly underestimated the potency of prudential reasons-for-action. Consequently, their arguments do not throw any genuine doubt whatsoever on the credibility of a positivist approach to the concept and phenomenon of official allegiance.

### I. SOME THUMBNAIL EXPLICATIONS

Among the jural concepts that may seem most troublesome for legal positivists are those of formal justice, authority, normativity, and obligation. In regard to each of these concepts, the difficulty for a positivist explication is to steer a course between the Scylla of natural law and the Charybdis of the Austinian gunman-writ-large. On the one hand, that is, the analysis of each concept must avoid any suggestion that the processes or outcomes of legal decision-making are necessarily morally worthy or are necessarily based on nonprudential considerations; to endorse any such suggestion would be to abandon legal positivism. On the other hand, the analysis must give attention to the crucial features of law that are omitted from any simple gunman model. Several of my earlier chapters have endeavored to satisfy these requirements when explicating the concepts listed above. By presenting together the relevant lines of analysis from those chapters (in a very short compass), my current discussion can draw attention to the broad affinities—and the mutual reinforcement—of the conceptual elements in a positivist theory of law.

## A. Formal Justice

As Chapter 2 has contended, David Lyons goes astray in thinking that not all deviations from the terms of applicable legal norms by law-administering officials are formal injustices. We have seen that formal justice consists in a meticulous adherence to the terms of applicable legal norms by anyone who invokes those norms in order to pass judgment on someone else (or, indeed, on himself). Formal *in*justice arises exactly insofar as officials or other people depart from the terms of applicable legal norms when they gauge the status of anyone's behavior. In this respect, the concept of formal justice is inseparable from the concept of law-administration; the attainment of formal justice is nothing more and nothing less than the unfailing implementation of legal norms in accordance with their terms.

Now, the inseparability of the concept of formal justice and the concept of law would be exceedingly problematic for legal positivism if formal justice were an intrinsically moral value. Precisely because Lyons perceives formal justice as such a value, he (as a legal positivist) denies any necessary connection between it and the strict administration of legal norms.[1] Given the actuality of a necessary connection of that sort, and given the inherent moral significance of formal justice, legal questions and moral questions could never be fully segregated; jurisprudential positivism's insistence to the contrary would be untenable. Lyons is correct in suggesting as much, but he is quite wrong in thinking that formal justice is indeed perforce a moral value. As my second chapter has argued, there are circumstances in which the pursuit of formal justice is neither prima facie obligatory nor even prima facie permissible. Though the concept of formal justice

---

[1] From an opposite perspective, John Finnis (among many other theorists) has likewise characterized formal justice as an intrinsically moral value. See John Finnis, *Natural Law and Natural Rights* (Oxford: Clarendon Press, 1980) [NLNR], 358–9.

is inseparable from the concept of law, it is fully separable from any moral ideals such as substantive justice. Its inseparability from the concept of law is therefore not damaging at all to positivist claims about the thorough disjoinability of law and morality.

Throughout Chapter 2, morality is understood primarily in contrast with unworthiness. That is, the positivist approach of that chapter to the status of formal justice is an effort to demonstrate that such justice does not necessarily partake of moral worthiness to any degree. (My approach in that chapter is also of course an effort to demonstrate that formal justice consists in the strict implementation of applicable legal norms.) Situations can arise in which the officials of a legal regime have no prima-facie moral obligation nor even any prima-facie moral liberty to arrive at formally just decisions. In such circumstances, those decisions would have no claim to moral correctness.

My third chapter also gives attention to the worthiness/unworthiness distinction—by considering the potential iniquity of formal justice—but it focuses more lengthily on the distinction between morality and prudence. It ventures to show that formal justice (as well as certain other formal aspects of law) is not necessarily moral, in that the pursuit and sustainment of such justice by officials can very credibly derive from their purely prudential concerns. Officials who care only about maximizing the formidableness and efficacy of their tyrannical regime will often have strong reasons for abiding quite closely by the terms of the various laws which they have laid down. Frequently, they can do most to serve their own distasteful interests by generally complying with the requirements of formal justice.

In short, while recognizing an inherent link between the concept of formal justice and the concept of law, this book recognizes no such link between the first of these concepts and any moral posture. When formal justice is portrayed by opponents of positivism (or even by positivists) as inevitably partaking of moral worthiness to some degree, we can point to the circumstances in which the attainment of such justice is neither prima facie morally obligatory nor prima facie morally legitimate. When conformity to the requirements of formal justice is portrayed by opponents of positivism as inevitably grounded in nonprudential considerations, we can highlight the circumstances in which the attainment of such justice is pursued by officials solely because of its tendency to enhance their despotic grip on power and to further the accomplishment of their evil aims. On the one hand, as my seventh chapter has emphasized with reference to the rule of law generally, the realization of formal justice in appropriate settings can be expressive and promotive of lofty moral aspirations. In liberal-democratic societies, the reluctance of judicial and executive officials to deviate from the terms of applicable legal norms is frequently a matter of moral compunctions; for example, the officials accept the principle of legislative supremacy on democratic grounds, and they also wish to protect legitimate expectations (which can of course be engendered by judicial and executive rulings as well as by legislative enactments). On the other hand, not all societies and legal systems are liberal-democratic. When the officials who rule over a society are overridingly preoccupied with the interests of their wicked regime, they may well abide by the terms of their flagitious legal norms quite sedulously—because such a tack creates the right incentives for citizens to obey the norms, and because it improves the co-ordination and thus the efficacy of the regime's programs. Far from being a product or expression of moral compunctions, formal justice in such circumstances is a vehicle for wickedness and selfishness. As a condition adaptable to any number of substantive ends, it does not occupy an intrinsic moral status.

## B. Legal Authority

My principal discussion of legal authority occurs in Chapter 4. Perhaps to a greater extent than the matters probed in any of my other conceptual explications, the present topic requires some difficult maneuvering between an excessively austere conception and an unduly moralized conception of law. On the one hand, legal authority cannot amount to the mere ability to compel someone to do something which he or she would not otherwise be inclined to do; if legal authority were so reducible, then every gunman would be exercising such authority when relieving his victims of their wallets. On the other hand, a jurisprudential positivist should not accept that legal authority *must* involve moral bindingness, moral legitimacy, a claim to moral bindingness, or a claim to moral legitimacy.

Though these constraints that have to be respected by a successful positivist account of legal authority are in tension, they can both be satisfied through a focus on the normative systematicity of law. As my fourth chapter has argued—in much greater depth than is possible here—legal authority consists in three broad entitlements, with many different instantiations: a *power* and a *liberty* to alter, create, eliminate, or implement the enactments and rulings that confer the various entitlements (rights, liberties, powers, and immunities) in a legal system; and a *right* to the obedience of the people who are subject to the sway of the system. Each instance of these entitlements is a normative position or status, and is therefore a consequence of some prevailing norms. Each derives either from the bedrock normative principles that underlie all official acts and decisions within a particular legal regime, or from some norms that are themselves ultimately derivative of those bedrock principles (perhaps through several intermediate layers of norms). Legal authority, then, depends on the workings of a systematic matrix of norms, including of course the fundamental norms which undergird all others within the matrix.

How does this highly compressed account of legal authority steer a path between Austinianism and natural-law theory? Although a full answer to this question lies in Chapter 4, and although some aspects of the answer will be treated in the next section of the present chapter (which discusses normativity and obligation), a few points should be touched upon here. Let us begin by acknowledging again that the Austinian gunman-writ-large model of legal systems does include a number of crucial features of law (generality, durability, and so forth) which are missing from the simple situation of an ordinary highwayman and his victims. However, Austin neglected the crucial role of prescriptive discourse among officials; furthermore, in defining 'obligation' solely by reference to the likelihood of one's undergoing punishment for violating a mandate, he scanted the formal nature of legal norms; moreover, he largely disregarded the existence and effects of norms other than obligation-imposing mandates. In these respects, his conception of the workings of a legal system was impoverished. Hence, given that legal authority is perforce rooted in those workings—in other words, given that such authority is as much a product of those workings as a precondition for them—Austin's account of legal authority or sovereignty was gravely inadequate. The account defended in this book has sought to distance itself from the short-comings in his account.

Neither when morality is defined in opposition to unworthiness nor when morality is defined in opposition to prudence, can the workings of legal systems (*qua* workings of legal systems, rather than *qua* workings of benevolent legal systems) ever correctly be regarded as intrinsically moral. Hence, legal authority, which is both the consequence and the animating force of those workings, is like-wise not intrinsically moral. Of course, the contents of the norms of any particu-lar legal system may be admirably benevolent; likewise, the decisions and actions of the officials in any particular legal system may be based essentially on concern for citizens' interests, rather than essentially on concern for the officials' own self-ish interests. If both of these possible sets of circumstances are actualized in some legal regime, then the workings of the regime and the authority exercised therein are unalloyedly moral in tenor—both because of their worthiness and because of the moral orientation of their motivational underpinnings. Legal authority can undoubtedly be commendable and can undoubtedly be exercised by officials on the basis of nonprudential considerations. However, the clear possibility of such a situation is not at all tantamount to the necessity thereof. Far from being invari-ably moral in either way just described, legal authority can be thoroughly iniqui-tous and can be exercised by officials on the basis of thoroughly prudential considerations.[2]

Whether wicked or benign, legal authority exists and operates as legal author-ity when the sundry instances of the three broad entitlements mentioned above—the power and liberty to change or establish or effectuate norms, and the right to citizens' compliance with the resultant norms—typically yield the results that constitute a functional legal system. In other words, the following two conditions are jointly sufficient and individually necessary for the existence and operation of legal authority. First, insofar as a legal system endows officials with powers and

---

[2]  Whether the general orderliness-sustaining role of law in human society makes any difference here is a question broached in Ch. 7 and explored at length in Ch. 9.

liberties to shape and administer the system's norms (including the norms which confer those powers and liberties, of course), the norm-shaping or norm-administering implications of officials' exercises of those powers and liberties must be recognized and given effect by their fellow officials on most or all relevant occasions. Second, the legal right of a regime to compliance by citizens with its mandates and the legal right of each official to compliance by citizens with his directives must be typically, though not perforce invariably, heeded (however grudging or fearful the compliance might be). No further conditions are necessary; moral worthiness, moral compunctions, claims to moral worthiness, and claims to moral compunctions are all unnecessary for the functioning of legal authority.

## C. Normativity and Obligation

In the foregoing accounts of authority and formal justice, and in most other portions of this book (especially Chapters 3 and 4), the concept of normativity has figured saliently. Two distinctions are of particular importance here: moral normativity versus prudential normativity, and prescriptive norms versus imperative norms. Let us consider the first of these distinctions in regard to the interaction of officials with one another, and the second distinction chiefly in regard to the interaction of officials with citizens.

The distinction between morality and prudence need not here be expounded yet again, but we should recall its precise applicability in the context of exhortations or instructions by officials to one another. Let us concentrate on second-person exhortations and instructions. (Everything said here will apply *mutatis mutandis* to first-person statements and third-person statements as well, though the latter are somewhat more complicated than second-person statements.) In connection with any second-person exhortation or instruction between officials, two main sets of interests are involved: those of the addressor(s) and those of the addressee(s). If the addressor's reasons for articulating an exhortation or instruction are thoroughly prudential, and if the exhortation/instruction implicitly or explicitly presents reasons for the addressee's compliance that are essentially promotive of the addressee's interests, then the exhortation or instruction itself is unequivocally prudential. Contrariwise, if the addressor's reasons for articulating an exhortation or instruction are strictly moral, and if the exhortation/instruction implicitly or explicitly presents reasons for the addressee's compliance that are independent of the addressee's interests, then the exhortation or instruction itself is unequivocally moral in tenor. Intermediate situations are also possible, of course. What is of central importance here is that all or many of the statements among officials in a wicked legal system can be unequivocally prudential in the sense defined above. As my third chapter has endeavored to show (not least in its Postscript), the interaction of evil officials can be largely or wholly focused on their shared interest in sustaining the dominance of their repressive regime, which bestows positions of power and privilege on them. In the second half of the current chapter, we shall investigate this point further in the face of several anti-positivist challenges to it.

Chapter 4 has explored the distinction between prescriptive norms and imperative norms in detail. Obligation-imposing norms, which are general directives that establish standards requiring certain acts or omissions by the people to whom the norms are addressed, fall into two broad classes. On the one hand, such norms may be prescriptions which direct how people *ought* to behave. As prescriptions, the obligation-imposing norms express or presuppose reasons for the addressees to behave in the required fashion. In the context of a legal system, where obligation-imposing legal norms are invoked as justifications for the penalizing of violations of those norms, the expressed or presupposed reasons-for-action must be punishment-independent. Furthermore, because the obligation-imposing norms of any legal system frequently require deeds or omissions from each person that are against his or her interests, the reasons-for-action that are expressed or presupposed by legal norms must frequently be nonprudential. Those reasons, in other words, must frequently be moral reasons (if we define 'moral' in opposition to 'prudential' rather than in opposition to 'evil'). Hence, if all legal norms had to be prescriptions or had to present themselves as prescriptions, then they would frequently have to be moral norms or would have to present themselves as such.

Moreover, even though the reasons-for-action expressed or presupposed by legal prescriptions might sometimes be thoroughly prudential, there would continue to exist a significant connection between law and morality. When officials formulate and implement legal norms that require acts or omissions which are presumed to further nonderivatively the interests of each person from whom the acts or omissions are required, the officials are evincing moral concern for each addressee of the norms. They are like a mother who forbids a child to touch a hot object and who will slap the child's hand in the event of disobedience, as a means of bringing the child to recognize his or her own best interests. In short, a model of legal norms as invariably prescriptive would portray legal officials as always either laying down moral norms or exhibiting moral concern (albeit moral concern that might be badly misguided).

However, as Chapter 4 has argued, not all legal norms are prescriptions. Some norms in tyrannical legal regimes are imperatives, which do not express or presuppose any punishment-independent reasons for the addressees to conform their behavior to the requirements of the norms. Imperatives decree what people *must* do (or must forbear from doing), rather than what they *ought* to do (or ought to forbear from doing). Imperatives do not set forth moral requirements at all, and they do not set forth requirements that are designed to benefit their addressees as opposed to their addressors; without any moral warrant, they demand acts or abstentions that essentially serve only the interests of the officials who impose the demands. The intrinsic force of imperatives as mandates derives exclusively from the punishments that back them up. Furthermore, the officials who invoke the imperatives in justification of punishments do not need to characterize them as anything other than what they are. Even if officials eschew any pointlessly unconvincing mendacity and thus decline to commend their imperative norms as morally worthy, and even if they are not so frank as to acknowledge openly the norms' moral deplorableness, they can simply refrain from saying anything about the norms' moral status at all. They can establish laws devoid of moral concern and moral worthiness, and they can contemptuously abstain from attributing any proper concern or worthiness to those laws. In sum, once we grasp that not all legal norms are prescriptions and that some legal norms in wicked regimes are sheer imperatives, we can perceive that officials are not always either laying down moral requirements or exhibiting moral concern.

Legal obligations are the requirements imposed by any legal norms that render certain courses of conduct mandatory. Those obligations differ sharply from the orders of a highwayman or of an ordinary group of gangsters, since they are established (directly or indirectly) by general and durable mandates which belong to a comprehensive array of norms that regulate the multifarious aspects of social and economic and political life—in a particular land—with a substantial degree of regularity in their implementation.[3] However, *pace* Austin, one's legal obligations also differ from the likelihood of one's being punished for acting or failing to act in certain ways. A legal obligation is specified by a norm or set of norms, and is describable as a legal obligation by dint of the place of the norm (or set of norms) in a functional legal system. Although most norms in a legal regime have to be given effect most of the time if the regime is to exist as an operative system of law, there will be some legal norms in almost any society that are largely or wholly unimplemented. Within an overall context of the regular enforcement of other legal norms, those unimplemented mandates can rightly be said to impose obligations (albeit largely or entirely uneffectuated obligations). No theory that defines 'legal obligation' by reference to the probability of being punished can acknowledge this straightforward point about unimplemented laws.

Most important for a jurisprudential-positivist theory is that legal obligations are wholly separable from moral obligations. This separability pertains most obviously to the substantive tenor of those respective obligations. Because legal obligations are established by legal norms whereas moral obligations are established by moral norms, and because legal mandates can thoroughly diverge from moral precepts, there is no necessary coincidence of content between the two sorts of obligations. The requirements imposed by legal norms can be devoid of moral worthiness. As my seventh chapter has argued (and as will be argued

[3] As I remark in Ch. 4, the regulatory control effected by legal norms certainly does not have to involve any heavy-handed monitoring or highly detailed instructions. A free-market framework, consisting principally in the development of general private-law norms, is as much a scheme of legal regulation as is a stiflingly intrusive regime of socialist law. See Matthew H. Kramer, *In the Realm of Legal and Moral Philosophy* (Basingstoke: Macmillan Press, 1999), ch. 7.

further in my next chapter), this point about potential dissimilarities of content applies even to the basic prohibitions that must form part of any viable legal system. Although the legal obligations erected by those prohibitions do tally with fundamental moral precepts when described at a high level of abstraction, they can prove to be grossly immoral at the more concrete levels where the prohibitions are actually formulated and effectuated as laws.

Just as legal obligations can be utterly unworthy, they can likewise derive from the purely prudential objectives of the officials who lay them down. If officials adopt and enforce certain obligation-imposing norms because they perceive those norms as serviceable for their selfishly power-hungry ends, then the obligations established by the norms are mere instruments for the officials' own aggrandizement; they are not legal positions created out of any sense of concern for others' interests. Because legal norms can be sheer imperatives, the obligations imposed by them can be completely unattuned to the interests of citizens.

Moreover, as my present discussion has remarked (in line with a point developed more fully in Chapter 4), the officials in a wicked regime of numerous stark imperatives may well opt not to pretend that their mandates and the legal obligations established by the mandates are based on solicitude for citizens' interests. Choosing not to engage in laughably unpersuasive protestations of concern for citizens' interests, while also choosing not to acknowledge openly the wicked selfishness of their legal norms and of the legal obligations created thereunder, the officials can simply ignore all questions about the moral status of those norms and obligations. A brusquely dismissive attitude toward all such questions, in lieu of mendacious self-exoneration or frank self-condemnation, is a far-from-outlandish posture that might be adopted by the issuers and enforcers of imperatives. Not only can legal obligations lack any moral force, and not only can they derive from the purely self-interested aims of the officials who impose them, but, in addition, their nature as evil means for the officials' power-hungry ends need not be concealed or misrepresented by the obligation-asserting statements which the officials make.

## II. THE INTERNAL PERSPECTIVE OF ALLEGIANCE

My discussion of normativity leads quite smoothly into the second half of this chapter, where we explore further the stance of committedness or allegiance (the 'internal perspective') that is adopted by anyone who seeks to uphold certain norms or practices. Of particular relevance here, of course, are the officials of any legal system. Although some or all ordinary citizens may evince a sense of allegiance toward the scheme of laws under which they live, the officials are the people with the most obvious and direct stake in the effective implementation of that scheme. All or most of them must take a generally supportive attitude toward all or most of the institutions and norms that make up their legal regime, if a functional regime is to exist.

As has been maintained in many parts of this book, the discourses among officials and the authoritative statements made by officials to citizens can be pervasively informed by the officials' selfish and immoral ends. The normativity of the internal perspective of officials can be a thoroughly prudential normativity. None the less, as we have seen, many opponents of jurisprudential positivism claim that the internal perspective is an intrinsically moral (i.e., nonprudential) posture. Several of my earlier chapters have lengthily probed some arguments which purport to demonstrate such a claim; in the rest of this chapter, we shall investigate a few more such arguments.

## A. Beyleveld and Brownsword

In an effort to disclose deep tensions or contradictions within H. L. A. Hart's positivist theory of law, Deryck Beyleveld and Roger Brownsword profess to show that Hart's theory at once acknowledges and gainsays the morally pregnant character of the internal perspective of legal officials.[4] They contend that Hart had to embrace two inconsistent theses. In order to distance his theory from the one-sidedly predictive orientation of the Legal Realists' model of law, he had to give due prominence to the typically justificatory tenor of officials' authoritative pronouncements. According to Beyleveld and Brownsword, then, Hart had to espouse a 'legitimation thesis, which means that the social function of appealing to legally valid rules and the like must be viewed as the function of giving a special kind of reason and justification for action, namely that the demands of such rules are morally legitimate' ('Positivism', 504). We are told, in other words, that Hart had to concede that officials' statements of the law in the course of legal decision-making are inherently moral judgments. Hart supposedly had to avouch that any such statements, which invoke legal norms as justifications for concrete decisions, maintain (explicitly or implicitly) that those norms and their applications are morally appropriate and obligatory. 'The legitimation thesis . . . entails that moral reason is necessarily implicated in judgments of legal validity, and that the legal enterprise must be viewed as a moral enterprise' ('Positivism', 504). Yet, in order to present a positivist account of law, Hart also had to endorse a 'separation thesis, which entails . . . a conception of law in which moral reason does not necessarily impinge upon judgments of legal validity' ('Positivism', 504). Hence, according to Brownsword and Beyleveld, Hart glaringly contradicted himself. In an attempt to put forward a jurisprudential-positivist theory that would overcome Legal Realism's blindness to the justificatory role of officials' pronouncements, he was impelled to deny *and* affirm that officials inevitably make moral judgments and exhibit moral commitments whenever they apply legal norms.

Let us glance at the chief line of reasoning with which Beyleveld and

---

[4]   Deryck Beyleveld and Roger Brownsword, 'Normative Positivism: The Mirage of the Middle-Way', 9 *Oxford Journal of Legal Studies* 463–73, 488–512 (1989) ['Positivism'].

Brownsword prosecute their attack against Hart. After drawing a distinction
between following a norm and merely acting in accordance therewith, they draw
a further distinction between two ways in which a norm can be followed. On the
one hand, somebody might *simply* follow a norm; on the other hand, somebody
might embrace the norm as an apposite standard of conduct. To some extent, this
distinction is closely similar to Hart's own distinction between obedience and
acceptance. That is, simply following a norm consists in obeying it without adopting any critical reflective attitude toward it. A simple follower of a norm obeys it
because its requirements happen to coincide with his interests on a certain occasion or because he will probably suffer punishment if he is disobedient. He does
not feel or display any sense of commitment to the norm. He does not look
askance at anyone else's transgressions of it (so long as those violations do not
affect his own interests), and he himself will violate the norm as often as expedi-
ency warrants. 'Compliance with the rule will always be an open question, in the
sense that the agent will comply only so long as it is convenient' ('Positivism',
491). By contrast, somebody who upholds a norm as an appropriate standard of
conduct does indeed take a critical reflective attitude toward it. She displays a
commitment to the norm by criticizing any nontrivial breaches of it, by usually
doing her best to abstain from such breaches herself, and by acknowledging the
pertinence of criticisms that are directed at her when she does deviate from the
norm's demands.

As described so far, Beyleveld's and Brownsword's distinction between
simply following norms and embracing them as standards of conduct is identical
to Hart's obedience/acceptance distinction. We should now take account of a
crucial difference, however. Whereas Hart submitted that an official's acceptance
of a norm (and thus her adoption of a critical reflective attitude toward it) could
be based on purely prudential considerations as plausibly as on moral considerations, Beyleveld and Brownsword insist that treating a norm as a standard of
conduct must involve a moral commitment to it. Their entire critique of Hart's
positivism, indeed, rests on this point. After all, their basic line of argument is as
follows:

(1) On the whole, the officials in a functional legal regime must treat its norms
    as binding standards of conduct. They cannot simply follow (i.e., merely
    obey) those norms.
(2) Upholding a norm as a binding standard of conduct entails an endorse-
    ment of it on moral grounds.
(3) Ergo, contrary to what Hart presumed, the characteristic perspective of
    officials—the internal perspective—is an inherently moral posture.
    Anyone who takes up that perspective in regard to a certain set of norms
    has thereby taken up a nonprudential commitment to those norms.

The first premise of Beyleveld's and Brownsword's argument would of course be
fully acceptable to Hart and to just about any legal positivist. As Hart rightly

contended, all or most officials have to adopt a critical reflective attitude toward most of the norms in their legal system on most relevant occasions, if their system is to be sustainable. However, Hart would clearly not subscribe to the conclusion of Beyleveld's and Brownsword's argument; nor should any jurisprudential positivist. Now, since the conclusion validly follows from the two premises, and since the first premise is unproblematic, the dubious step in the argument is obviously the second premise.

The claim in that second premise was explicitly rejected by Hart and has been repeatedly rebutted in my previous chapters. Hence, Beyleveld and Brownsword have to shoulder a heavy burden of proof. They have to establish that a norm which is treated as a binding standard of conduct must ipso facto be treated as *morally* binding; and, in order to establish that point, they have to overcome or evade the major lines of reasoning that can be posed against it. Let us see how well they fare.

Beyleveld and Brownsword endeavor to clinch their case by dwelling on the counter-inclinational force of legal obligations. They sound this theme prominently when they first explain what is involved in upholding a norm as a standard of conduct:

Agents may *simply* 'follow' a rule, or they may treat a rule as a 'standard of conduct'. In the former case, the rule is not treated as categorically binding; in the latter case, it is. By treating a rule as 'categorically binding', we mean treating a rule as having conatively independent force (ie as having binding force notwithstanding the circumstance that the agent has particular occurrent wants and desires to act contrary to what the rule prescribes) and as being overriding (ie as automatically taking precedence where its requirements conflict with other reasons for action). ('Positivism', 490–1, emphasis in original)

A norm treated as a standard of conduct is a second-order reason 'to refrain from acting for reasons generated by the agent's contrary particular occurrent wants and desires' ('Positivism', 491).

Beyleveld and Brownsword advert again and again to the counter-inclinational role of obligations, in the subsequent elaboration of their critique. They declare, for example, that legal obligations are like moral obligations in 'overrid[ing] self-interest', and that legal standards of conduct 'must be seen as overriding an agent's self-interest' ('Positivism', 492, 497). They likewise contend that, when legal norms are treated as binding standards of conduct, those norms' 'claims . . . take priority as against an agent's self-interest' ('Positivism', 499). By contrast, when people do not treat norms as binding standards of conduct, 'the reason for compliance may be non-moral, eg simply self-interest (for such agents, legal reason may simply be prudential reason)' ('Positivism', 497, parenthetical words in original). The importance of the counter-inclinational force of legal obligations is also apparent in the following passage, where Beyleveld and Brownsword differentiate between officials who accept legal norms as standards of conduct and officials who might take a different view:

For those officials who regard the rules of [a legal] system as standards of conduct, the reason [for compliance with the rules] would be that the institutional framework for governance within the polity (the positive constitution) should be supported as right and correct. For such officials, in other words, the official ... rules would be seen as obligatory. By contrast, officials who did not regard the rules of the system as standards of conduct, would defend the application of the secondary rules as a requirement for anyone wishing to participate in the [system]. Such a requirement, however, would be optional/definitional rather than obligatory.   ('Positivism', 499)

Beyleveld's and Brownsword's case thus hinges on the claim that the general capacity of legal obligations to override each person's self-interest (insofar as there are any clashes between the self-interest and the obligations) is sufficient to warrant an inference that anyone who upholds those obligations as such is perforce embracing them on moral grounds. That inference is the second premise in Beyleveld's and Brownsword's basic line of argument, which was delineated above. In seeking to counter their claim, my present discussion will certainly not dispute the fact that norms accepted as binding standards of conduct are necessarily thereby accepted as standards that should trump short-term expedience or desires. Even less will my discussion dispute the fact that, when people do not accept norms as binding standards of conduct, they will not regard general compliance with those norms as morally obligatory. What *will* be contested here is the assumption that the counter-inclinational role of legal obligations must be grounded in morality rather than in prudence.

As has been argued in Chapter 3 and more briefly in some of my other chapters (including this chapter), wicked legal officials who are motivated only by self-interest will often have strong reasons to abide scrupulously by the norms of their system. Close adherence to those norms will tend to promote suitable incentives for citizens' obedience and will likewise tend to enhance the efficient coordination of the officials' evil operations. In such circumstances, the demands which officials make on one another and on citizens will clearly display a firm acceptance of the prevailing legal norms but will derive from purely prudential concerns. How is such a situation reconcilable with the counter-inclinational force of legal norms? Plainly, the answer to this question lies in a quite familiar distinction between long-run interests and short-run interests.

The posture of commitment or allegiance which is characteristic of the internal perspective of officials can be based entirely on self-interested considerations; but those considerations pertain to the officials' long-run interests, which will override their short-run interests or desires insofar as there arise any clashes between the long run and the short run. Although one's acceptance of the counter-inclinational sway of legal requirements can of course stem from their perceived moral worthiness, it can equally well stem from their perceived ability to advance one's long-run interests. We need not look outside the realm of prudence to find a potential source of curbs on short-run inclinations. When Beyleveld and Brownsword warrantedly proclaim that one's endorsement of legal norms as standards of conduct must involve one's readiness to forgo norm-transgressing actions that are grounded in one's 'particular occurrent wants and desires' ('Positivism', 491), they are not saying anything that supports their moralized conception of the internal perspective of officials. They are unwittingly leaving wide open the possibility that, in some societies, the officials' endorsement of legal norms as standards of conduct will derive from arrant self-interest—arrant self-interest with a long-run orientation.

Let us ponder again the example of the cartel that was discussed in the closing pages of Chapter 3. Each member of the cartel accepts its rules and thus abstains from indulging his desire to reap short-run gains by lowering his price (or by otherwise engaging in actions that could undermine the cartel members' agreement). However, no member of the cartel accepts its rules on moral grounds. None of them feels any sense of moral responsibility toward consumers—who pay extortionate prices—or even toward one another. Each member views the others solely as people with whom he must collaborate in order to realize his own selfish ends most effectively. And since that very objective (of maximally realizing one's own selfish ends) is accurately perceived as necessitating quite a strict adherence by every member to the terms of the cartel's agreement, the need for that strict adherence overrides any contrary short-run goals or impulses that would otherwise lead members astray. The counter-inclinational force of the cartel's rules is a product of out-and-out prudence.

Of course, if there were no means for disciplining refractory members of the cartel who deviate from the terms of its arrangements, then those arrangements would very likely be unstable. Even if each member recognized the need for virtually unswerving compliance with the aforementioned terms in order to maximize his own long-term prosperity, the lure of short-run windfalls might prove too enticing for some members if they were not liable to incur any retaliatory or rectificatory measures. An awareness of this situation among the members would breed a sense of insecurity and would therefore increase the likelihood of defections. Hence, a reasonably stable cartel will include provisions for dealing with violations. Accordingly, another crucial prudential consideration that motivates each member to abide by the cartel's rules is the prospect of chastisement in the event of noncompliance.

In the cartel hypothesized (credibly) here, the members are driven entirely by self-interest; it should thus go without saying that the admonitions and complaints directed against members who commit infractions will not be moral in tenor at all. The violators will be upbraided for acting stupidly—i.e., for acting against their own long-run interests—rather than for acting unfairly. Moreover, although the condemnations will focus on the interests of the addressees, they will not be expressive of any moral concern on the part of the addressors. Instead, the addressors simply opt to frame their reprimands in ways that will most effectively serve their own selfish interests. Accusations of unfairness would accomplish nothing, whereas allegations of foolish short-sightedness may well avert or eliminate breaches of the cartel's rules and may thereby help to secure the continuation of the cartel, which greatly benefits all the members.

Let us return to pondering an iniquitous legal regime in which the officials are wholly preoccupied with entrenching their privileged positions and pursuing their evil designs. Though there are some differences between the legal regime and a cartel, the similarities between them are far more prominent and arresting. Just as the cartel cannot endure unless its members adhere quite persistently to the terms of their agreement, so the legal regime cannot function as such unless its officials adhere quite persistently to the terms of its norms. As has already been mentioned in this discussion, the officials' regular effectuation of those norms will tend to create strong incentives for citizens' conformity therewith; people will be apt to conform if they know that obedience will spare them from the harsh punishments that will usually be inflicted on them if they are disobedient. Equally, the regular effectuation of the laws by the officials will manifestly be of assistance in co-ordinating the sundry tasks and roles which the officials have to perform. If they are erratic in their implementation of the law, then they will almost inevitably work against one another in a variety of ways. Their ability to realize their evil objectives will consequently be impaired. In light of these factors—which have been contemplated at length in some of my earlier chapters—the purely self-interested officials of a wicked legal regime have ample prudential reasons for subordinating their short-run desires and impulses to the need for their consistent administration of the law. The counter-inclinational force of their matrix of legal norms is rooted in unalloyed self-devotion, focused on the long run.

To a large extent, then, the power-hungry officials of a repressive legal system abide by the system's norms because they are happy to go along with institutions that endow them with highly advantageous positions, and because they are aware that their abiding by the norms is important for the effective functioning of those nefarious institutions. Nevertheless, perhaps to an even greater degree than in connection with the members of a cartel, the prudential calculations of the selfish officials must usually be inflected by the likelihood that punitive measures will be taken against judges or administrators who fail to carry out properly their adjudicative or executive tasks. Since the people who operate a legal system are typically far more numerous than the members of a workable cartel, the damagingness of any single official's deviations from his system's norms will typically be less than the damagingness of any single member's deviations from his cartel's rules. Thus, the punishment-unrelated reasons for adherence to the legal system's norms may seem less weighty or pressing to some of its officials than the corresponding reasons for compliance with the cartel's arrangements may seem to each of the cartel's members. As a result, the role of sanctions for mavericks might have to loom larger in the legal system than in the cartel. Even though most of the self-devoted officials will probably be motivated chiefly by the factors mentioned at the beginning of this paragraph, most of them may also need to be spurred by the knowledge that significant departures from the terms of their system's norms will usually subject them to chastisement from their fellow officials. (Any denunciation will be thoroughly prudential; it will be impelled by the selfish interests of the denouncers and will address itself to the selfish interests of the denounced.) In other words, while all or most of the officials will probably adopt the critical reflective attitude toward the norms of their regime primarily because they feel an unforced commitment to the institutions that generate their privileges, they will also doubtless wish to avoid the consequences of failing to adopt such an attitude.[5] At any rate, both the stimulus of fear and the objective of shoring up the source of one's own power are straightforwardly prudential factors. Once again we find that the counter-inclinational force of legal norms can ensue from the self-seeking of the officials who uphold those norms.

Let us conclude this discussion of Beyleveld and Brownsword by returning to the thesis which they advance in the last of the long passages quoted above. Therein they draw a distinction between the obligatoriness of norms that are treated as standards of conduct and the optionality of norms that are simply followed: 'For those officials who regard the rules of the[ir] system as standards of conduct . . . the . . . rules would be seen as obligatory. By contrast, officials who did not regard the rules of the system as standards of conduct, would defend the application of the . . . rules as a requirement for anyone wishing to participate in the practice. Such a requirement, however, would be optional/definitional rather than obligatory' ('Positivism', 499). Three points should be made about this extract.

First, especially in light of some sentences that precede those which have just been quoted, Beyleveld and Brownsword appear to be committing here the same error which they commit elsewhere in their essay. They write: 'The essential difference between those officials who regard a regime of primary and secondary rules as standards of conduct and those who do not . . . is that the former regard themselves as participating in, and upholding, a practice, *the claims of which take priority as against an agent's self-interest*, whereas the latter see themselves as simply acting in line with the ground rules which define their practice' ('Positivism', 499, emphasis added). The implication here seems to be that, when norms are endorsed only on prudential grounds and not on moral grounds, they cannot have any counter-inclinational force. Enough has been said in my present discussion to indicate that such a suggestion is a *non sequitur*. By distinguishing long-run interests from short-run interests, we can discern the potential for the systematic overriding of the latter by the former. Officials can accept the counter-inclinational sway of law without feeling or displaying any moral commitments.

Second is a closely related point. Suppose that Beyleveld and Brownsword are not maintaining in these passages that norms endorsed for exclusively prudential

---

[5] In an extreme situation, as I observe in Ch. 3 n. 35, this secondary motivational factor can be the sole such factor for every official. However, as I also observe in that footnote, a situation wherein all officials are motivated exclusively by fear would be exceedingly unstable.

reasons must be devoid of counter-inclinational force. Suppose that they instead are contending merely that norms endorsed for such reasons do not generally override the *long-run* interests that have motivated the endorsements. Though such a contention is sound in itself, it lacks any pertinence or tellingness in the present context. It does no more than establish that, when a legal system and its norms are embraced by officials on purely prudential grounds, the system serves the long-run interests of the officials or at least is perceived by them as serving those interests. If Beyleveld and Brownsword are espousing such a position, then they are championing the jurisprudential-positivist view that has been defended by my current discussion. If they presume to have gone further by implying that officials' selfish long-run interests cannot be the bases of a legal system, then they are flatly begging the question in lieu of offering arguments. As my discussion here and my discussions in earlier chapters have shown, a legal regime operated by officials purely out of concern for their own aggrandizement can credibly include all the essential features of law, such as generality, normativity, regularity, comprehensiveness, and a counter-inclinational force that trumps the short-run interests of officials as well as those of citizens. Unless Beyleveld and Brownsword can somehow offer an additional *argument* in favor of denying that such a regime is a regime of law, they will have offered nothing but dogmatic and sterile assertions. (Some methodological remarks, along the lines of those in the second half of Chapter 6, would clearly be germane here. However, because my next section's response to John Finnis's work will include a number of such remarks, a charge of dogmatism against Beyleveld and Brownsword will suffice for the moment.)

A third dubious aspect of the two passages most recently quoted above—albeit a shortcoming that does not amount to an outright error—is their emphasis on the optionality of the self-devoted officials' acceptance of the prevailing legal norms. Beyleveld and Brownsword almost seem to envisage the selfish officials' acceptance as if it resembled a decision to play a game of checkers or a decision to tackle a crossword puzzle. (Each of those decisions would typically involve an acceptance of the applicable rules.) On the one hand, to be sure, even the officials' adherence to the norms of their wicked legal system is indeed optional in the sense that the requisiteness of their adherence hinges on their objectives. In Kantian terminology, the requisiteness of the officials' upholding of legal norms is hypothetical or instrumental rather than categorical. That is, it obtains only insofar as the officials desire certain ends; by contrast, moral obligatoriness obtains irrespective of what anybody's aims might be. Yet, on the other hand, the ends pursued by the evilly self-seeking officials are viewed by them as enormously important. The officials set great store by their positions of power, and would certainly not relinquish their privileges lightly. Their commitment to the vibrancy of their legal system is thus far more profound than the commitment of an ordinary player of checkers or an ordinary solver of crossword puzzles to the rules for either of those pastimes. (The officials' commitment is more like that of a high-earning professional player of some game, especially if he or she benefits immensely from the game's current rules.) Moreover, as has been observed herein, each self-devoted official's adoption of a critical reflective attitude toward the norms of his wicked legal regime may also be partly due to his desire to avoid the indignation of his fellow officials. Doubtless some of the officials, perhaps many of them, choose to uphold those norms exclusively because they wish to reinforce the system which endows them with prized prerogatives; but every official's choice is made in conditions where any significant failure to uphold the norms would trigger untoward consequences. Hence, a description of the officials' conduct as 'optional' is rather misleading, at least inasmuch as it purports to capture their own perception of their situation.

Before we move on, one quick caveat should be entered—a caveat which, *mutatis mutandis*, has also occasionally been entered at some other junctures in this book. Nothing in my present discussion is meant to suggest that all members of cartels or all officials in wicked legal regimes are motivated solely by prudential considerations. Though such a motivational pattern is probably far from uncommon in cartels and iniquitous legal institutions, it is very likely not characteristic of some of the people in most such settings. My arguments herein have not endeavored to show what the psyches of wicked officials must be like; I have instead endeavored to show that, even if the officials are indeed driven wholly by self-concern, they will have strong reasons to opt for a scheme of governance which partakes of all the essential features of law that were mentioned two paragraphs ago. Not only is such a scheme of governance compatible with the arrant pursuit of selfish interests by officials, but it can actually be highly serviceable for that pursuit. Beyleveld and Brownsword are mistaken in thinking that the pervasiveness of self-seeking among officials is inevitably at odds with the counter-inclinational sway of law or with any of law's other indispensable features.

## B. John Finnis and the Focal Case

John Finnis, the foremost natural-law theorist of the twentieth century, has received attention (albeit somewhat fleeting attention) several times in this book. My current section will focus on some of his methodological pronouncements, for they closely relate to his conception of the internal perspective of officials. Although many strands of his overall natural-law theory are not inconsistent with legal positivism,[6] the basic method that informs his analysis of the workings of legal systems is indeed irreconcilable with some of the conclusions reached in my earlier chapters. My short discussion here will probe Finnis's methodological tenets only insofar as they bear on his understanding of the attitudes and alle-

---

[6] I take exception to several of those strands, however, on other grounds. For some of my doubts, see the first two principal essays in Matthew H. Kramer, above, n. 3.

giances of legal officials; but a full-scale critique of his work could extend my remarks to some of his other analyses as well.

In the first chapter of his deservedly famous book *Natural Law and Natural Rights*,[7] Finnis observes that any theory of legal institutions (or other institutions) must proceed on the basis of certain assumptions about the relative importance of the various facets of those institutions. If a theory were to highlight everything, then it would highlight nothing—since it would give no greater prominence to anything than to anything else. Thus, if a 'theory is to be more than a vast rubbish heap of miscellaneous facts described in a multitude of incommensurable terminologies' (Finnis, NLNR, 17), it must impose order on its field of study by treating some things as more important than others. A fundamental methodological concern at the outset of any investigation of legal institutions, then, lies in determining which characteristics of those institutions are most important. That methodological concern immediately raises the following question: 'From what viewpoint, and relative to what concerns, are *importance* and *significance* to be assessed?' (NLNR, 9, emphases in original.)

In response to the foregoing question, Finnis first maintains that we need to ascertain the 'focal meaning' of the concept of law. The social arrangements which instantiate that concept in its focal meaning are the 'central cases' of legal institutions. Those arrangements are the most fully developed and most readily identifiable instances of the concept which they embody. They are central rather than peripheral cases of legal institutions, in that the classification of them as exactly such institutions is wholly unproblematic; the features which they include are all the essential features specified by the concept of law in its focal meaning. Those features are the truly important aspects of legal institutions. Hence, by singling out the arrangements which partake of those features, we single out the quintessential or paradigmatic examples of the rule of law—the examples in contrast with which the less straightforward instances of legal institutions can be seen as lacking in key respects. By distinguishing between the central embodiments and the peripheral embodiments of the rule of law, 'one can differentiate the mature from the undeveloped in human affairs, the sophisticated from the primitive, the flourishing from the corrupt, the fine specimen from the deviant case, the "straightforwardly", "simply speaking" (*simpliciter*), and "without qualification" from the "in a sense", "in a manner of speaking", and "in a way" (*secundum quid*)' (NLNR, 10–11).

Having drawn this distinction between central cases and marginal cases, Finnis

---

[7] Finnis, NLNR, 9–18. The other main piece of writing by Finnis which I have in mind here is his 'Comment', in Ruth Gavison (ed.), *Issues in Contemporary Legal Philosophy* (Oxford: Clarendon Press, 1987) ['Comment'], 62, 66–9. For an endorsement of Finnis's approach, see Stephen Perry, 'Interpretation and Methodology in Legal Theory', in Andrei Marmor (ed.), *Law and Interpretation* (Oxford: Clarendon Press, 1995) ['Interpretation'], 97, 124–5 n. 63. For a more skeptical assessment, see Michael Moore, 'Law as a Functional Kind', in Robert George (ed.), *Natural Law Theory* (Oxford: Clarendon Press, 1992), 188, 225–6.

then has to pin down the distinctive features of the central cases of legal institutions. '[B]y what criteria is one meaning to be accounted focal and another secondary, one state of affairs central and another borderline?' (NLNR, 11.) This question, of course, is really just a reformulation of the question concerning how importance is to be assessed. In accordance with modern positivist jurisprudence, Finnis submits that theorists' judgments about importance should take account of the vantage points of the participants in legal institutions. Stated in the terminology of my sixth chapter, his view is that jurisprudential theorizing should eschew the extreme external standpoint and should adopt the moderate external standpoint or the simulative standpoint. Legal theorists need to recognize the internal perspective of the participant even though they do not actually adopt it. Their judgments about importance—about centrality and peripherality—can then be based on a rich awareness of the workings of legal institutions. In short, the legal philosopher needs to 'assess importance or significance in similarities and differences within his subject-matter by asking what would be considered important or significant in that field by those whose concerns, decisions, and activities create or constitute the subject-matter' (NLNR, 12).

Finnis heartily agrees with modern positivists that the internal perspective of the participant must be taken into account by any satisfactory jurisprudential theory, but he insists that the positivists have not gone far enough. Having endeavored to explicate the internal perspective in order to apprehend the operations and fundaments of the central cases of legal institutions, they have not turned the central-case method upon the internal perspective itself. In positivist jurisprudence—as should be abundantly clear from my earlier discussions—the internal perspective of legal officials is not necessarily a moral perspective. The normativity of that perspective, and thus the nature of officials' allegiance to their regime, can be prudential through and through. Finnis contends that, by lumping together an internal perspective based on self-devotion and an internal perspective based on moral concern, the positivists have failed to separate the peripheral from the central. What should be acknowledged, he maintains, is that the central case of the internal perspective is unalloyedly moral (both in being nonprudential and in being correctly attuned to moral requirements). Any prudential variant of that perspective is deviant and derivative. As he explains:

[The official] who is moved by 'calculations of long-term interest' (sc. self-interest) waters down any concern he may have for the function of law as an answer to real social problems; like Raz's anarchistic judge, he dilutes his allegiance to law and his pursuit of legal methods of thought with doses of that very self-interest which it is an elementary function of law (on everybody's view) to subordinate to social needs. . . . [T]hese considerations and attitudes, then, are manifestly deviant, diluted or watered-down instances of the practical viewpoint that brings law into being as a significantly differentiated type of social order and maintains it as such. Indeed, they are parasitic upon that viewpoint.  (NLNR, 14)

We shall presently examine some additional layers of Finnis's reasoning, but we should straightaway notice two errors in the extract above that are very closely related to each other (indeed, virtually identical to each other). First, the argument in the extract rests on an erroneous assumption which Finnis later states explicitly and which we explored in Chapter 3: his assumption that wicked rulers motivated by self-interest will have no reason to adhere quite scrupulously to the rule of law. Second, like Beyleveld and Brownsword, Finnis presumes that officials' acceptance of counter-inclinational legal requirements must be based on moral considerations rather than on prudential factors. The underlying misstep here is his failure to distinguish between long-run and short-run selfishness. Power-hungry officials wishing to pursue their heinous designs with great effectiveness will have substantial reasons for subordinating their short-run impulses to the requirements of the rule of law. They thereby enable themselves to generate strong incentives for citizens to comply with their mandates, and they shrewdly facilitate the co-ordination of their own evil efforts. (As has already been mentioned in the course of this chapter, the ways in which wicked officials can benefit from persistently sustaining the rule of law have been expounded at much greater length in my third chapter's critique of Lon Fuller.)

Thus, whereas Finnis in the extract above declares that officials' preoccupation with their own interests 'dilutes [their] allegiance to law and [their] pursuit of legal methods of thought', an abandonment of his erroneous assumptions enables us to see that a preoccupation with selfish interests can *solidify* officials' allegiance to law and their pursuit of legal modes of thought. Insofar as wickedly selfish officials grasp the advantages of a legal regime for the effective accomplishment of their iniquitous aims, their allegiance to the rule of law—their critical reflective attitude, grounded thoroughly in their self-devoted lust for power—will be firm. Whereas the passage quoted above supposes that moral concern is intrinsic to 'the practical [i.e., normative] viewpoint that brings law into being as a significantly differentiated type of social order and maintains it as such', an abandonment of Finnis's erroneous assumptions enables us to see that the normativity of the standpoint (of officials) which upholds legal institutions can just as plausibly be prudential as moral. In sum, once we recognize that officials who care only about their own evil interests will often have powerful reasons for adhering quite steadily to the rule of law, we should reject Finnis's claim that legal regimes based on officials' prudential calculations are peripheral or watered-down or parasitic instances of legal institutions. After all, as Finnis himself emphasizes (NLNR, 10; 'Comment', 67–8), the distinction between central and peripheral is not a matter of statistical frequency. Rather, the distinction is between the fully developed or flourishing and the shallow or derivative. Yet, since the long-run selfish interests of evil officials can be a solid basis for the existence and continuation of a vibrant legal regime (albeit an oppressive regime), a situation in which those interests perform such a role is a central case of legal institutions. To classify a regime of that sort as peripheral is to mistake its wickedness for precariousness.

Within Finnis's discussion, there are two lines of thought that could serve as replies to the critique that has just been presented here—a substantive reply and a methodological reply, which we shall consider in turn. The substantive reply can be glimpsed in the long extract above, where Finnis asserts that an official 'who is moved by "calculations of long-term interest" (sc. self-interest) waters down any concern he may have for the function of law as an answer to real social problems'. This potential rejoinder is even more clearly stated in the following passage:

[T]he theorist cannot identify the central case of that practical viewpoint which he uses to identify the central case of his subject-matter, unless he decides what the requirements of practical reasonableness really are, in relation to this whole aspect of human affairs and concerns. In relation to law, the most important things for the theorist to know and describe are the things which, in the judgment of the theorist, make it important from a *practical* viewpoint to have law—the things which it is, therefore, important in practice to 'see to' when ordering human affairs. (NLNR, 16, emphasis in original)

According to this line of thought, any delineation of the central case of legal institutions must derive in part from 'assessments of human good and of its practical requirements' (NLNR, 17). One's specification of that central case must draw on one's knowledge of the basic function of law; for the attainment of such knowledge, one's making of judgments about human good and about its practical requirements is indispensable.

Any substantive rejoinder along these lines would be manifestly question-begging. If we assume that the sole function or the chief function of law is to provide human beings with security and autonomy and social co-ordination, then a normative outlook primarily oriented toward the achievement of those desiderata will indeed be the central case of the internal perspective of legal officials. Regimes wherein the officials share such an outlook would then be the central cases of legal institutions; other regimes would be peripheral, to varying extents. However, the very point at issue here is whether the aforementioned function of law is indeed invariably the principal function of full-fledged legal systems. To be sure, no one should doubt that benevolent legal regimes are characterized by the primacy of such a function. But in certain other full-fledged legal systems, the paramount function resides in the sustainment of the officials' oppressive dominance and the pursuit of their sundry flagitious objectives. Though virtually every such regime will probably provide most people with greater security than would exist in conditions of anarchic chaos, the provision of the security is derivative of the regime's primary purpose and is therefore carried on only inasmuch as it serves that purpose. Both in fact and in the eyes of the wicked officials who run such a regime, its overriding function is to reinforce their potent sway. The internal perspective of the officials is oriented toward the accomplishment of that function and is thus entirely prudential in its tenor. Yet, in connection with that very function, there will be strong reasons for those officials to endow their regime with the essential characteristics of law—the characteristics singled out earlier in the present chapter and more lengthily in some previous chapters—to just as great an extent as would be undertaken by the officials in a benevolent legal system. When the evil officials act on those reasons, their regime in all its monstrousness is a straightforward instance (a central case) of legal governance.

Since the nature of the principal purpose of any full-fledged legal regime is precisely the point of contention here, a substantive reply by Finnis which invokes that purpose is bound to beg the question. Consequently, let us turn to the other main rejoinder that is discernible in his account of officials' internal viewpoints. That other potential response consists in a methodological claim about the superior explanatory and analytical strength of a theory that highlights the perspectives of officials whose attitudes toward the enterprise of legal governance are fundamentally nonprudential and morally worthy. Finnis seeks to underline this claim with a rhetorical question: 'What reason could the descriptive theorist have for rejecting the conceptual choices and discriminations of these persons, when he is selecting the concepts with which he will construct his description of the central case and then of all the other instances of law as a specific social institution?' (NLNR, 15). In a footnote to *Natural Law and Natural Rights*, Finnis states his methodological position directly: 'Behind Aristotle's cardinal principle of method in the study of human affairs—viz. that concepts are to be selected and employed substantially as they are used in practice by the *spoudaios* (the mature man of practical reasonableness)—lies Plato's argument that the lover of wisdom can understand the concerns of men of other character, while the converse does not hold; in other words, the concerns and understanding of the mature and reasonable man provide a better *empirical* basis for the reflective account of human affairs' (NLNR, 15, emphasis in original, citations omitted). A similar statement occurs in a more recent essay:

[T]he mature person of practical reasonableness [who 'considers that morality, and a rationally imperative impartiality of concern for others, require him to co-operate in establishing and/or maintaining legal order'] can understand and appreciate the concerns and the reasons for action of the merely self-interested, the mere conformist, the mere careerist, *but the converse does not hold*. So, adoption of this person's practical concerns as the criterion for discerning what features really do 'cluster together' as a coherent, meaningful, and important social institution will make possible not only the most intelligible account of legal reasons for action (including reasons for having law and the rule of law at all) but also the best *empirical* account of this aspect of human affairs. ('Comment', 69, emphases in original)

Here we return to the methodological questions that were pondered in my sixth chapter—though, in contrast with Dworkin and in accordance with my own approach, Finnis gives his methodological stance an analytical/explanatory focus rather than a political/moral focus. In keeping with the biblical observation that 'no good tree bears bad fruit' (Luke 6: 43), we should contemplate the results of

Finnis's method in order to gauge the soundness of his claims about the method's special incisiveness. On this point, despite the elegance and sophistication of his overall theory, his claims can be found wanting. Let us recall my third chapter's discussion of his remarks on the rule of law (remarks made in some later portions of *Natural Law and Natural Rights*). As was seen there, Finnis completely overlooks the fact that the officials in monstrously oppressive regimes will typically have weighty prudential reasons for adhering quite firmly to the rule of law—and that they will have such reasons even if they make little or no effort to pretend that their adherence is motivated by moral compunctions. Though Finnis in the last extract above suggests that his method enables him to 'understand and appreciate the concerns and the reasons for action of the merely self-interested', his unduly moralized conception of law in fact renders him inattentive to exactly those concerns and reasons. Officials bent on furthering their own interests by enhancing the vitality and toughness of their wicked regime will not act upon moral reasons when complying with rule-of-law requirements, of course, but they will have their own reasons for such compliance. Those reasons become obscured within Finnis's analyses.

My own theoretical approach, by contrast, is alert to the reasons-for-action of morally solicitous officials and evilly selfish officials alike. If any regime governs in accordance with rule-of-law requirements to a significant extent, then my approach classifies it as a central case of legal institutions. Precisely because the reasons for a regime's fulfillment of those requirements are left open, we are encouraged to contemplate the wide variety of factors that can constitute such reasons. Throughout, this book has acknowledged and indeed emphasized that adherence to the rule of law can derive from moral considerations and can amount to a morally elevated state of affairs. Law's essential features connect importantly with the exercise of human agency; hence, those features can readily be embraced and sustained on the basis of officials' morally worthy concerns, which will almost inevitably include a concern to show respect for the agency of individuals. None the less, because the exploitation of that agency is a crucial element of most evil rulers' designs, the essential features of law can also be embraced and sustained on the basis of officials' ignoble and ruthlessly selfish aims. To remain attentive to this possibility, we should adopt a methodological posture that promotes reflection on it.

## C. Stephen Perry and Moral Reasons

In an essay that endeavors to outline the proper techniques and objectives of jurisprudence, Stephen Perry submits that the internal perspective of legal officials is fundamentally moral (i.e., nonprudential) in its orientation. He likewise submits that any adequate jurisprudential theories must establish their claims through moral argumentation. Not surprisingly, Hart is the chief target of Perry's strictures, whereas Dworkin is invoked as Perry's major intellectual forebear.[8] (My responses to Perry here will frequently refer to the four perspectives—extreme external, moderate external, simulative, and internal—that were delineated in my sixth chapter.)

Perry begins by recounting Hart's approach to jurisprudential theorizing. He correctly observes that Hart rejected any jurisprudential theories that proceed from the extreme external perspective. Although such a perspective might be serviceable for certain social-scientific theories, it is unacceptable for a philosophical analysis that attempts to explicate the basic concepts of legal thought and discourse. Hart aptly insisted that any such analysis must take account of the internal viewpoints of the participants in legal institutions. Taking account of those viewpoints does not entail adopting them, of course, but it does involve our recognizing how the participants perceive their own activities and commitments. Although the participants' perceptions are by no means the exclusive objects of attention for a jurisprudential theory, they are crucial elements that cannot be omitted—if we wish to avoid conceptual explications that are flatly one-sided, misleading, shallow, and impoverished.

As my sixth chapter and my present chapter have emphasized, and as Hart repeatedly maintained, the distinctive characteristic of the participants' internal perspective is the critical reflective attitude of committedness or allegiance. The presence of that attitude is a point of distinction not only between the internal vantage and the extreme external vantage, but also between the internal vantage and either the moderate external or simulative vantage. For example (in connection specifically with law), the distinction between justifying legal outcomes and predicting legal outcomes is a salient aspect of the distinction between the internal viewpoint and either of the external viewpoints. Hence, given that any adequate jurisprudential analysis must apprehend and expound the internal perspective, it must obviously expound the critical reflective attitude.

Perry offers an unexceptionable summary of Hart's conception of the internal perspective and the critical reflective attitude ('Interpretation', 102–3), but his own understanding of the internal viewpoint is very different. He stipulates that the internal perspective of a participant in a legal regime is occupied by anyone who regards the regime as a source of reasons-for-action. Though Perry quite often appears to think that his conception of the internal perspective is Hart's own conception which Hart did not properly unfold, it is in fact markedly different. Whereas Hart held that the internal viewpoint of legal officials consists in their acceptance of certain norms (i.e., the various criteria in the Rule of Recognition),

---

[8] Perry, 'Interpretation'. Perry also draws heavily on Joseph Raz's writings, but his construal of those writings is in some respects tendentious. Perry suggests that Raz discusses law from the internal perspective (à la Dworkin) or from the simulative perspective. In fact, Raz generally discusses law from the moderate external perspective, just as Hart did. What distinguishes Raz from Hart is not their theoretical standpoints, but the contention by Raz that certain morally pregnant claims are intrinsic to the internal perspective of officials.

Since I shall be unremittingly critical of Perry's essay, I should note that it is an intelligent and stimulating piece. I should mention also that I have admired some of his other work.

Perry holds that the internal viewpoint should be understood much more broadly. As has just been stated, he construes that viewpoint expansively to encompass any belief by anyone that the law gives him or her reasons-for-action. As a result, Perry contends that the Holmesian bad man—the man who seeks to know the law solely because he wants to avoid punishments—is a participant in a legal system. Presumably, then, Perry is willing to maintain that a young lady is a participant in the periodic rampages of a mob because she rightly feels that they give her a strong reason to hide herself carefully in her home. Likewise, apparently, my mother was a participant in the various conflicts in the Balkans during the early 1990s because she regarded them as giving her strong reasons to stay far away from that part of the world. Exactly why we should be expected to opt for this curious and gravely misleading manner of speaking is quite unclear.

Perry attempts to bolster his indictment of Hart by highlighting what he sees as a troublesome equivocation in Hart's conception of the extreme external perspective. Perry points out that Hart wrote about the extreme external perspective sometimes as a theoretical stance and at other times as a practical stance ('Interpretation', 109–10). On some occasions in *The Concept of Law*, the external viewpoint is presented as a posture occupied by theorists who contemplate the behavioral regularities that make up a legal system. On other occasions it is presented as the posture of Holmesian bad men who look upon a legal system as a source of punishment-centered reasons-for-action. Perry seizes upon this alleged equivocation in order to accuse Hart of running together an external standpoint and an internal standpoint: 'Given that the rationale for taking account of the internal point of view in theorizing about social practices like law is precisely to elucidate the reason-giving character of those practices, one would have thought that the [bad men's] perspective should, rather than being conflated with the extreme external point of view, be treated as a second kind of *internal* point of view' ('Interpretation', 110, emphasis in original). Several comments are warranted here.

First, and least important, is an observation that may tell not only against Perry but also slightly against Hart. Holmesian bad men need not occupy the extreme external perspective; they can even more appositely occupy the moderate external perspective. Their predictions about the infliction of punishment and their consequent avoidance of sundry modes of behavior do not have to be associated with a thoroughgoing disregard of the agency of legal officials. Although the Holmesian bad men merely obey the law and do not accept it, they can recognize that the acceptance shown by officials is based on certain normative beliefs. Indeed, by taking up the moderate external perspective—by duly noticing that a legal regime is operated by human beings rather than by inanimate forces—the bad men (and their lawyers) will undoubtedly improve their ability to arrive at accurate predictions.

Second, as should be plain from the quotation in the penultimate paragraph above, Perry's argument here depends entirely on his rejection of the Hartian conception of the internal perspective and on his substitution of his own conception. The Hartian distinction between the internal and the external is a distinction between the presence and the absence of the critical reflective attitude. Holmesian bad men are clearly situated on the external side of such a dichotomy; the fact that they regard the law as a source of reasons for action is immaterial, since their adjusting of their behavior in line with those punishment-centered reasons is not accompanied at all by the critical reflective attitude. If we stay with Hart's understanding of the internal viewpoint instead of shifting to Perry's, and if we therefore engage with Hart instead of talking past him, then we shall have no grounds for thinking that Holmesian bad men look at the law from an internal point of view.

Third, there is no equivocation whatsoever in Hart's approach to the extreme external perspective. Sometimes that perspective is theoretical, and at other times it is practical. So what? Suppose that Jane initially observes the motions of the clouds each day because she is fascinated by them and wants to understand their varying patterns. Suppose that she then observes the motions of dark clouds because she wants to engage in her daily walk at a time when she can avoid their potentially rainy presence. She now regards the clouds as a source of reasons for action; has she thereby shifted from the extreme external viewpoint to the internal viewpoint, and has she thus become a participant in the clouds' swirling or in their emitting of rain? If Perry replies affirmatively to this question, then his line of analysis is exceedingly strange indeed. If he replies negatively, then he will have implicitly acknowledged that an extreme external observer of a legal system does not become a participant therein simply because she notes the regularities of its workings in order to ascertain the modes of behavior from which she should refrain (in the interest of avoiding untoward reactions, which anyone other than an extreme external observer would classify as punishments).

Of course, in some extravagantly broad sense a Holmesian bad man can be said to 'participate' in an overall scheme of legal regulation by dint of viewing it as a set of punishment-centered reasons-for-action. In an equally broad sense, Jane can be said to 'participate' in the overall climatic condition created by dark clouds. What is unclear, however, is why anyone would feel that the enterprise of jurisprudential analysis can be advanced by this lumping together of Holmesian bad men and committed officials under a single expansive rubric of 'participants' (even if we then distinguish between alienated and socialized participants [Perry, 'Interpretation', 109–10]). Among the disquieting consequences of this conceptual and linguistic stretching is that it will lead us to classify many dogs as participants in legal regimes. After all, through primitive reasoning, dogs are perfectly capable of adjusting their behavior in response to their observations of the activities of officials who enforce ordinances dealing with stray canines. Hart surely cannot be faulted for having eschewed a conception of the internal perspective that places vagrant dogs and Holmesian bad men in the same category as committed officials.

A fourth comment is very closely related to the second and the third. Hart maintained that the earmark of the extreme external perspective is a complete indifference to the reason-guidedness of the behavior of the participants in an institution. That is, the extreme externality of an observer of a legal system hinges on her inattentiveness to officials' reason-guided outlooks—and not on the practical reason-guidedness or absence of practical reason-guidedness in her own outlook. Thus, although someone occupying the internal viewpoint has to be practically oriented, someone occupying the extreme external viewpoint can be either practically oriented or purely theoretically oriented. Perry's approach to the distinction between the internal and the extreme external is strikingly different. Instead of focusing on the observer's alertness or unalertness to the reason-guided outlooks of officials, Perry focuses on the practical reason-guidedness or absence of practical reason-guidedness in the observer's own outlook. For Perry, in other words, the determinative factor that separates the internal from the extreme external is a factor that does not play any such role within Hart's analysis. Hence, when Perry accuses Hart of ambiguity and confusion, he is shadow-boxing. His own conception of the internal perspective, which serves as the fundament for his accusations, has blurred the distinctions which Hart highlighted and has underscored distinctions which Hart de-emphasized. Although Perry is of course at liberty to draw his own distinctions, he ought not to assume that Hart was groping for them as well.

Fifth, Perry's portrayal of a competition between Hart's theory of law and Holmes's theory of law is highly misleading at best. Hart's jurisprudential model does not pretermit or sweep aside the perspective of the Holmesian bad man; Hart fully recognized the likelihood that some citizens will merely obey the law rather than accept it, and he left open the possibility that all non-officials in any particular society will merely obey the law. Hart's theory thus comprehends Holmes's theory but also goes far beyond it by devoting sustained attention to the internal perspective of officials, which Holmes obscured. Hart adopted his emphasis on officials' justificatory discourse as a supplement, rather than as an alternative, to Holmes's emphasis on the predictive discourse of many ordinary citizens and their lawyers. (Perry is not unaware of this point, but he allows it to disappear as he pits Hart against Holmes in a straightforward conflict.)

Let us now move on by supposing that there is indeed a stark Hart/Holmes competition of the sort which Perry recounts. In a section of *The Concept of Law* directed primarily against Hans Kelsen but also against Holmes, Hart declared that the chief function of law is to guide and control citizens' behavior by laying down standards of conduct. Perry seizes upon Hart's declaration and submits that it 'is most plausibly interpreted as referring to the *moral value*, or *point*, of the institution of law' ('Interpretation', 114, emphases in original). He continues:

Hart appears to be saying that when law is understood in accordance with his analysis, then it has moral value, or at least potential moral value, because it is capable of guiding conduct in a way that is socially beneficial. This idea is to some extent fleshed out by

Hart's thesis of the minimum content of natural law. . . . Although Hart's original theoretical ambitions were apparently limited to pure social description on the one hand and
explanation of normativity on the other, one of the principal arguments he makes in favour
of his own theory of law over a rival theory seems to be *moral* in character: it is grounded
in a certain understanding of the moral point or value of the institution of law.
('Interpretation', 114, emphasis in original)

Although Perry here maintains that Hart 'appears' and 'seems' to be making a
moral claim, he provides no evidence for such an attribution—an attribution that
saddles Hart with a position patently contrary to his position in his exchanges
with Lon Fuller. (Perry's reference to the doctrine of the minimum content of
natural law is his sole attempt to substantiate his interpretation. Because that
doctrine has been broached in my seventh chapter and will be investigated at
greater length in my final chapter, it will not be discussed directly here.) In fact,
Hart undoubtedly felt that the moral status of the guiding-and-controlling functions of law is dependent on the substantive tenor of the norms in any particular
legal regime. When the Nazis directed Jews and others to the gas chambers, the
chief function of their behests was to guide and control people's behavior (in
ways that facilitated a program of extermination); to say as much, however, is
not to affirm that that function was morally worthy. Likewise, when a
monstrously oppressive regime lays down various legal norms proscribing
numerous ordinary activities, the chief function of those mandates—and of their
strict implementation—is to guide and control people's behavior. Again,
however, the oppressive guidance and control do not deserve any moral
commendation simply by virtue of amounting to guidance and control. In other
words, we cannot know the moral status of the function of steering people to do
φ, until we know what is designated by 'φ'. In the abstract, the functions of guidance and control are morally neutral.

    Perry cannot successfully avail himself here of his suggestion (in the extract
above) that law with its guiding-and-controlling function has 'at least potential
moral value, because it is capable of guiding conduct in a way that is socially
beneficial'. Such an assertion is reminiscent of Fuller's claim that law partakes of
intrinsic moral worthiness because the existence of law is necessary for the existence of good law. Like Fuller's claim, Perry's assertion is otiose because it can
easily be offset or complemented by a diametrically opposed thesis: viz., the
thesis that law with its guiding-and-controlling function is at least potentially
*im*moral because it is capable of guiding conduct in a way that is iniquitous. (As
some of my earlier discussions have contended, the distinctive functions of law
can play an indispensable role in yielding the incentives and co-ordination that
are needed for the pursuit of wicked objectives on a large scale over a long period
of time.) Just as the thesis about law's potential immorality does not establish that
law's guiding-and-controlling function is inherently immoral, so Perry's assertion
about law's potential moral value does not go any way toward establishing the
inherent moral worthiness of the aforementioned function. That function in the

abstract is morally open-ended. Hence, Perry cannot salvage his claim that Hart's abstract ascription of such a function to law must be a moral ascription.

Nor can Perry successfully resort here to his view that Hart's imputation of a guiding-and-controlling function to law is inconsistent with the Hartian notion that all or most citizens in a given society might follow the law only out of obedience rather than out of acceptance. Perry presents his view as follows:

Nor could [Hart] simply mean that guidance of conduct is one of the *effects* of law, since the law's influence on bad men is also one of its functions in this sense. . . . Of course, if [Hart's ascription of the guiding-and-controlling function to law] is to be an argument against Holmes's 'bad man' theory, Hart cannot suppose that most ordinary citizens take the [punishment-focused] perspective, as his own theory seems in fact to allow. Interestingly, Hart thus seems to be attributing a value to law that emphasizes the role of the internal point of view (as he understands it) not just for judges, but for ordinary citizens as well. (Perry, 'Interpretation', 114, emphasis in original.)

Perry might try to join the claim in this extract to the further premise that citizens who comply with wicked legal norms under an oppressive regime are merely obeying the law rather than accepting it. By combining those two theses, he could submit that monstrous legal norms do not perform the guiding-and-controlling function which Hart attributed to law; that function, Perry could contend, is performed only by morally acceptable legal norms. Hence, he would conclude, the function which Hart attributed to law is indeed a morally pregnant function.

There are two major weaknesses in the argument described by my last paragraph. First and perhaps slightly less important is the probable falsehood of the premise that people who comply with wicked legal norms are always or almost always merely obeying the law rather than accepting it. For example—as will be familiar to anyone acquainted with the history of the American South or with the history of anti-Semitic laws in Europe—people in favored groups who are required or authorized to discriminate harshly against people in disfavored groups may often take advantage eagerly of their privileged legal status.

An even more important shortcoming in the hypothesized argument is that the quoted claim by Perry therein is based on a wrenching of Hart's remarks out of their context. Although Hart did have Holmes's theory in mind when he attributed a guiding-and-controlling function to law, his primary target was Kelsen's thesis that legal norms are addressed to officials (for the application of sanctions) rather than to citizens. Hart wished to emphasize that the primary role of law is to induce citizens to behave in specified ways, and that legal provisions for the imposition of sanctions come into play only when the law's primary role has foundered. He wrote specifically as follows, in words which Perry quotes: 'The principal functions of the law as a means of social control are not to be seen in private litigation or prosecutions, which represent vital but still ancillary provisions for the failures of the system. It is to be seen in the diverse ways in which the law is used to control, to guide, and to plan life out of court.'[9] In these sentences, Hart was not distinguishing between the influence of the law on people who merely obey and the influence of the law on people who accept legal norms. Rather, he was distinguishing between the law's *infliction of penalties for viola-tions* of legal norms and the law's *steering of people toward compliance* with those norms (whether the compliance takes the form of acceptance or of mere obedience). That is, he was not differentiating between the two main types of conformity with legal norms—obedience and acceptance—but was instead differ-entiating between situations of nonconformity and situations of conformity. Thus, the guiding-and-controlling function which Hart ascribed to law is a function applicable to grudgingly obedient people as much as to keenly law-upholding people. Citizens inclined to do no more than obey are still in need of guidance concerning the patterns of behavior that constitute punishment-averting obedi-ence. They receive the requisite guidance from the law in its primary function, quite as much as do their fellow citizens who fully accept the law's mandates.

Let us move on, once again. At several junctures, Perry states that officials' acceptance of the law is portrayed by Hart as 'an essentially unreflective phenom-enon' ('Interpretation', 116). What Perry means is that, according to Hart, the legal officials never ponder the general purpose or point of law: 'Reflection about the point or value of law is . . . not, according to Hart, itself an aspect of the social prac-tice' ('Interpretation', 116). Perry does not provide any citations or quotations to substantiate his allegation that Hart viewed officials' allegiance as 'essentially unre-flective', and his repeated statements of the allegation do not in themselves render it true. Although Hart quite rightly maintained that officials' acceptance of legal norms *can* be unreflective, he never suggested that their acceptance *must* be unre-flective or even that it typically *is* unreflective. When listing some possible motiva-tions for officials' allegiance, he mentioned 'calculations of long-term interest' and 'disinterested interest in others', before also mentioning 'an unreflecting inherited or traditional attitude' and 'the mere wish to do as others do' (*Concept*, 198). Now, although the last two of these possible motivations are largely or wholly unreflec-tive, the first two certainly need not be so; indeed, they are typically reflective.

More seriously objectionable than Perry's unfair reading of Hart is his belief that any reflection by officials on the significance of law must be moral reflection on a moral significance. That underlying belief is apparent in the sentence with which Perry expounds his claim about Hart's view of law as essentially unreflec-tive: 'Hart does not assume that judges and other persons who adopt the internal point of view within law have any views at all on the moral value of law as an institution, let alone a shared, canonical view of some kind' ('Interpretation',

---

⁹ H. L. A. Hart, *The Concept of Law* (Oxford: Clarendon Press, 1961) [*Concept*], 39. Although I am of the view that Hart slightly oversimplified Kelsen's position, there is no need for me to pursue that matter here. I have discussed some different aspects of the Hart–Kelsen exchanges in my *Legal Theory, Political Theory, and Deconstruction: Against Rhadamanthus* (Bloomington: Indiana University Press, 1991), 137–9.

116). Perry's assumption concerning the moral tenor of officials' reflections on the purpose of law is also present, albeit slightly obliquely, in the following passage: 'Hart does not think that there is a coherent participants' viewpoint. Acceptance of a social rule is just a brute social fact that is not necessarily or even typically accompanied by a belief in the moral justifiability of the rule. The social practice of law does not, according to Hart, extend to reflection about the nature and justification of law' ('Interpretation', 121–2). Perry's clearest statement of his position occurs in a footnote: 'So far as the study of social practices is concerned, a theorist who takes up the reflective point of view is inquiring into the moral justifiability of the practice; it is hard to see what this could mean, other than putting the practice in its morally best light' ('Interpretation', 131–2 n. 85).

Both in light of certain arguments made already within this chapter and in light of many of the arguments made within my previous chapters, the untenability of Perry's stance should be plain. Officials who reflect on the purpose of their legal regime can indeed be engaging in moral reflection on a moral purpose, but they can equally well be engaging in prudential reflection on the purpose of maximizing their overall power and privileges—if their legal institutions are fundamentally devoted to that purpose. Although the officials who eagerly run a monstrous legal regime might be acting on the basis of misguided moral beliefs, they are just as likely to be acting on the basis of sheer self-interest. They reflect on the ways in which their regime endows them with numerous advantages and in which it serves to accomplish their various wicked designs (such as the utter subordination of despised groups of people); on the basis of their reflections, they formulate and implement legal norms that are calculated to serve their own interests by reinforcing the strength of their regime. In these circumstances, which are always possible though admittedly far from inevitable, the highly reflective nature of the officials' activities does not consist in moral deliberations at all. (Of course, Perry's assumption about the inevitably moral tenor of officials' reflections will be belied even by legal institutions in which some instances of those reflections are indeed moral while other such instances are purely prudential.)

A number of other dubious contentions in Perry's essay could be challenged here,[10] but my discussion will close by examining his dismissal of Hart's account of the provenance of legal obligations. Although Perry satisfactorily summarizes that account ('Interpretation', 102–8), he goes on to complain that it does not withstand scrutiny.[11] To assess his complaint, we should first recall

[10] For instance, Perry declares that Jules Coleman's espousal of soft positivism—a doctrine that was discussed in Ch. 6 above—is indicative of the fact that 'Coleman implicitly accepts that the point of law extends beyond the provision of source-based guidance to include principled adjudication' (Perry, 'Interpretation', 130). Now, Hart firmly embraced soft positivism; yet, as Perry would certainly agree, Hart did not regard principled adjudication as a necessary aspect (rather than a contingent aspect) of law. Why, then, should we assume that the acceptance of soft positivism by Coleman enables us to infer that he sees principled adjudication as an essential element of law?

[11] For an important part of my response to Perry on this point, see the Excursus at the end of this chapter (pp. 251–3).

Hart's argument that legal obligations are requirements imposed by legal norms, which in turn gain their force through the adherence of officials to certain fundamental law-ascertaining criteria. The people who devise and implement legal standards of conduct have adopted the internal perspective of committedness toward the underlying norms that authorize and require their official activities; those underlying norms amount to the Rule of Recognition that prevails in a particular regime. Those norms and their authorizations and requirements are not necessarily moral, either in the sense of being morally worthy or in the sense of being embraced by officials on nonprudential grounds. Hence, legal obligations—the requirements imposed by legal mandates, which are generally recognized and effectuated by legal officials—do not necessarily coincide with moral obligations at all. Their bindingness is not perforce moral bindingness. None the less, they exist as obligations because they are constraints ordained by standards of conduct that are generally operative within the prevailing system of governance.

Perry states the following objection to Hart's account of legal normativity and obligations:

> [A] binding obligation does not necessarily come into being merely because (a majority of) a group of persons adopt the internal attitude, in Hart's sense, towards a rule. Put even more simply, believing does not make it so. Thus, the internal point of view is not a factor in explaining how and whether law really gives people reasons for action; its role could only be to help us understand how they *perceive* law to create reasons for action. ('Interpretation', 122, emphasis in original)

To this passage is attached the following footnote: 'This is true not only of Hart's social rules, but also of Holmes's [punishment-centered] reasons; the existence and character of a [punishment-centered] reason depend on the objective probability of both the occurrence of a sanction and of its severity, and people might radically mis-estimate these probabilities' ('Interpretation', 122 n. 60).

Let us first ponder Perry's footnote and then investigate the argument in the passage from his text. In the final clause of the footnote, Perry has plainly shifted his focus from the beliefs and attitudes of legal officials to the beliefs and attitudes of ordinary citizens. The Hartian argument about legal normativity and obligations is focused on the attitudes and allegiances of officials; both the binding force of the Rule of Recognition for each official and the binding force of other legal mandates for citizens (and officials) are ultimately products of the adherence by officials to the criteria that make up the Rule of Recognition. Yet Perry's remark about radically mis-estimated probabilities clearly pertains to ordinary citizens rather than to officials. After all, if the officials were in radical disagreement with one another about the circumstances in which they should inflict punishments, then their so-called regime would not be a functionally cohesive scheme of governance at all. (This point has been emphasized in my sixth chapter's discussion of the need for considerable agreement among officials on the 'bottom line' within any sustainable legal system.) Once we realize that Perry's analysis should be concentrating here on the beliefs of officials, and once we further realize that the functionality of a legal regime depends on a substantial degree of convergence among officials in regard to the appropriate occasions for the imposition of penalties, we can see that Perry is wrong about the determinative power of the relevant beliefs or attitudes. Officials' committed attitudes toward their regime and toward specific norms within their regime do create punishment-centered reasons for citizens' compliance with those norms— because the shared attitudes of the officials will lead them to inflict punishments if citizens fail to comply. *Pace* Perry, believing (on the part of the officials, who have the means to give effect to their beliefs) does make it so.

Although Perry does not shift his focus from officials to citizens in the main extract quoted above, he goes astray in a different way. His argument there is wholly unsupportable unless its references to binding obligations and to reasons-for-action are confined to *morally* binding obligations and *moral* reasons-for-action. (Indeed, as we shall see, his pronouncements are too broad even after being so qualified.) However, if Perry is making claims about moral obligations and moral reasons-for-action, then he is talking past Hart rather than landing any genuine blows. In developing an account of officials' allegiance to the Rule of Recognition, Hart sought to explain legal normativity and legal obligations— which he aptly perceived as distinguishable from moral normativity and moral obligations. Let us explore each of these points.

If Perry is indeed restricting his remarks to obligations that are morally binding, then the first sentence of the main extract above is perfectly warranted. We should certainly agree that the mere fact of officials' adopting the internal perspective in regard to some particular norms does not *necessarily* give rise to any moral obligations. Indeed, even if the reasons for the officials' adoption of the internal perspective are nonprudential, their stance does not necessarily engender or involve any real moral obligations. Legal officials can be firmly convinced of the moral correctness and obligatoriness of their regime's activities, while being profoundly mistaken. Officials who formulate and administer genocidal laws are not under any moral obligation to do so, however deeply they all may feel that their acceptance of those laws is morally required and legitimate.

Yet, even if we continue to assume that Perry's references to obligations and reasons encompass only moral obligations and moral reasons, the remaining two sentences of the extract above are too sweeping. Although the adoption of the internal perspective does not *necessarily* create moral obligations, it *can* create them. Believing can make it so. If the criteria in a legal system's Rule of Recognition are morally legitimate, and if the norms accepted as legally valid on the basis of those criteria are likewise morally legitimate, then the overall process of devising and effectuating those norms will tend to foster many legitimate expectations among officials and citizens. The people who operate the system will have prima-facie moral duties to shape their policies of law-administration in accordance with those expectations. Thus, their adoption of the internal perspective in regard to their Rule of Recognition (and in regard to the norms legally validated by reference to their Rule of Recognition) does give rise to moral reasons-for-action.

As construed heretofore, Perry's argument contains some assertions that are too broad. All the same, the chief problem with the argument so construed is its wholesale lack of pertinence as a riposte to Hart. As has already been noted, Hart explicated the internal perspective of legal officials in order to account for legal normativity and legal obligations, which are not perforce moral normativity and moral obligations. Hence, if Perry's argument is to stand any chance of serving as an apposite rejoinder to Hart, it has to be focused on legal normativity and legal obligations. When so focused, however, it does not survive close inspection at all.

If legal officials are running a viable regime, and if they therefore agree substantially on the foremost criteria in the Rule of Recognition and on the 'bottom line' in most situations, then their shared beliefs and attitudes do create legal obligations for each of themselves and for citizens. If any official departs significantly from what his fellow officials regard as a plausible understanding of the Rule of Recognition, then he will typically be subject to criticism and perhaps to punishment. Likewise, if any official or citizen violates a norm that is accepted by officials as legally valid on the basis of the Rule of Recognition, then he or she will typically be liable to undergo penalties (which might or might not be severe). Thus, the officials' adoption of the internal perspective toward the Rule of Recognition and toward legally valid norms does perforce involve and engender a host of binding obligations—legal obligations, which are not necessarily moral obligations. To say that the officials collectively accept the cardinal criteria in the Rule of Recognition is to say that they have placed each of themselves under legal obligations to abide by those criteria.

Contrary to what is declared by the final sentence in the extract from Perry's text, the adoption of the internal perspective by legal officials toward their Rule of Recognition does give reasons-for-action to each of them. What cannot be determined *in abstracto*, of course, is the nature of those reasons-for-action; of decisive importance here is the substantive tenor of any particular regime. As has already been mentioned, a regime with a morally legitimate Rule of Recognition—that is, with a moral legitimacy that comprises both the Rule of Recognition's criteria and the norms that are validated as laws thereunder—will tend to generate legitimate expectations about officials' adherence thereto. Officials will collectively have placed themselves under prima-facie moral duties to avoid the thwarting of those expectations.[12] Their adoption of the internal perspective toward their Rule of Recognition has thus given rise to moral reasons-for-action.

---

[12] As will become clear in my next chapter, I am slightly oversimplifying matters here. However, the minor oversimplification is utterly immaterial in the present context.

In a regime with law-ascertaining criteria or substantive norms that are strongly illegitimate, the officials may often be morally obligated to depart (benignly) from those criteria. None the less, the collective acceptance of the criteria by the officials will have given each of them some other reasons for adherence thereto—prudential reasons, of course. In the first place, a general adherence to the wicked Rule of Recognition may well serve each official's interests by strengthening the iniquitous scheme of governance wherein each official occupies a privileged and powerful position. Moreover, even when the interests of some particular official might be served by significant departures from the Rule of Recognition, the attitudes of his fellow officials will give him prudential reasons for abstaining from such departures; unless he does indeed abstain, he will face the prospect of reproaches and disciplinary measures at the hands of his fellows. Their adoption of the internal perspective in regard to the Rule of Recognition creates punishment-centered reasons for him to fall into line, even if it creates no moral reasons and no other prudential reasons.[13]

In sum, Perry's argument against Hart's account of legal normativity is no more cogent or successful than his other anti-positivist claims about the internal perspective of legal officials. In endeavoring to fathom that perspective, we need not and should not abandon a positivist model of law. Hart's account, both in its methodological austerity and in its substantive positivism, is fundamentally sound.

### AN EXCURSUS ON PERRY AND NORMATIVITY

Perry's attack against Hart's account of the origins of legal normativity is heavily influenced by Joseph Raz, *Practical Reason and Norms* (Princeton: Princeton University Press, 1990), 50–8, which in turn is heavily influenced by G. J. Warnock, *The Object of Morality* (London: Methuen, 1971), chs. 4–5. Raz's important critique of Hart's conception of social norms has been widely endorsed. See e.g. Scott Shapiro, 'The Difference That Rules Make', in Brian Bix (ed.), *Analyzing Law* (Oxford: Clarendon Press, 1998), 33–5. We should here consider Raz's central claim—his claim that Hart's account of the provenance of normativity in social practices is unable to distinguish between social norms and widely recognized reasons.

In the example propounded by Warnock and Raz, which will here be slightly modified along American lines, the outfielders on a baseball team shift their positions toward the right (as viewed from home plate) whenever a left-handed person comes to bat. If an outfielder forgets to undertake such a shift, he will be criticized by his fellows—especially

---

[13] My argument here is of course applicable to circumstances in which the punishment-unrelated interests of more than one official would be served by significant departures from the Rule of Recognition. In fact, my argument will fully apply even to a situation of perfect tyranny, in which *every* official's only reason for adhering to the Rule of Recognition lies in a desire to avoid punishment at the hands of the other officials. Punishment-centered reasons are indeed reasons; hence, the situation of perfect tyranny is no counterexample to my claim that the officials' adoption of the internal perspective creates the reasons-for-action that permeate the normative workings of a legal system.

if a batted ball has gone uncaught as a result—and he will doubtless acknowledge the justi-fiability of the criticisms. He and his fellows will seek to avoid any similar lapses in the future. Hence, all the elements of the Hartian critical reflective attitude are present. None the less, the adoption of that attitude in regard to the outfielder's blunder does not uphold or bespeak a rule requiring the rightward shift of location. There is no such rule, or so we are asked to presume. Consequently, because the critical reflective attitude can be present when no rules are operative, it cannot in itself be the hallmark of social rules. Some other factor must account for the difference between situations with rules and situations without them.

Let us accept *arguendo* the dubious proposition that no rule requiring rightward adjust-ments is operative in the scenario just sketched. (Obviously, no rule with that content appears in the formal code of rules and regulations for the game. Whether such a rule exists informally is quite another matter.) While granting as much, we should stoutly resist the further thesis that no relevant *norm* is at work in the aforementioned scenario. As has often been noted in other contexts, Hart's terminology and some of his analyses in *The Concept of Law* can easily lead readers to infer that his focus lay entirely on rules as opposed to vaguer standards and principles. We should refrain from drawing any such inference and should grasp that Hart was presenting an analysis of social norms generally—social norms of countless different degrees of specificity or abstraction. In the example of the outfield-ers, the key prevailing norm *N* is a broad precept requiring every baseball player to take all appropriately performable steps (within the rules of the game) to help his team to outdo the opposing team. Every player accepts *N*, as do all or most of the devotees of each team. The acceptance of *N* is the ultimate grounding for the criticisms directed against the blun-dering outfielder.

Of course, some or all of the players might not consciously think of themselves as following a norm of the sort just described. *N* might be a taken-for-granted fundament of their activities and discourses, rather than a standard which they explicitly heed and invoke. My analysis of the normative aspects of those activities and discourses does not necessarily reflect perfectly the self-perceptions of the people who participate therein. Though their general attitudes are the object of my attention, those attitudes can be best fleshed out and elucidated when they are apprehended through categories that reveal the attitudes' presuppositions—presuppositions that might not be expressly acknowledged on a day-to-day basis by some or all of the people who harbor those attitudes. My analysis seeks to clarify the players' statements and behavior by disclosing the grounds thereof; accordingly, it might not be an entirely straightforward report of the ways in which the players describe their own enterprise.

But, some readers might ask, does not *N* fail to make any difference in the practical reasoning of the players? Without *N*, after all, will not there still be ample reasons for each outfielder to shift to the right when a left-handed batter comes to the plate? And therefore will not the condemnation of the absent-minded outfielder be aimed at his having neglected to act upon those reasons, rather than at his breach of some underlying norm? Ergo, should not we conclude that *N* is wholly superfluous?

These questions present no genuine difficulties at all for my analysis. Let us begin with the third question. The criticism of the outfielder may well concentrate on the stupidity of his particular lapse rather than on his having breached *N*; but that possibility is no more troubling than the fact that condemnations of a person's belch at the dinner table may concentrate on the disgustingness of his particular lapse rather than on his having infringed a norm against belching. An eructation-proscribing norm is a familiar element in many codes of etiquette, and its existence in any given setting is scarcely belied by the fact that it does not get expressly invoked. Much the same can be said about $N$ in the normative structure of a baseball game. It obtains as a norm in the game's structure because the players and spectators *rely* on it, irrespective of whether they explicitly *refer* to it.

Let us now address the other questions in the penultimate paragraph above. Each of them suggests that my adducing of $N$ is a superfluous layer in an explication of the baseball players' conduct. Those questions go astray by overlooking the fact that the existence of $N$ makes the difference between the mere *advisability* of the outfielders' rightward shift and the *mandatoriness* thereof. To ponder this point, we should embrace *arguendo* the Warnockian/Razian conception of mandatory norms as exclusionary reasons; we may assume, in other words, that each such norm is a second-order reason for excluding certain considerations as permissible bases for one's actions within the domain covered by the norm. In exactly this sense, the rightward shift of the outfielders—as an appropriately performable step that will help their team to defeat the opposing side—is mandatory. Though some factors militating against such a shift can doubtless be taken into account legitimately, other factors are excluded by $N$. For example, if an outfielder is offered a bribe (by an opposing player or a gambler) to refrain from moving to the right when a left-handed person is at bat, $N$ excludes the bribe as a legitimate ground of action. If an outfielder accepts the pay-off and abstains from the rightward adjustment, he might be acting on the balance of the first-order reasons-for-action, but he is flouting the second-order exclusionary force of $N$. Indeed, he will equally have disregarded $N$'s exclusionary force if he refuses the bribe solely because the value of it is outweighed by other first-order considerations. (Of course, the chief message of this scenario does not depend on the presence of a monetary bribe. Equally pertinent would be a scenario involving an outfielder who wants to win the favor of a beautiful woman or to avenge an insult leveled at him by a team mate, for example.)

In sum, the existence of $N$ does indeed make a difference in the practical reasoning of the baseball players. Because they adhere to $N$—whether or not they often advert to it explicitly—they are unentitled to regard certain factors as permissible reasons-for-action. Though an outfielder will plainly have some leeway in deciding whether a rightward shift is a suitable response to the left-handedness of a particular batter, his leeway does not encompass the array of considerations that are excluded by $N$. All such considerations are excluded not because of the first-order reasons in favor of the move toward the right, but because of the underlying norm that disallows the offsetting of those reasons by any reasons that detract from a player's appropriately diligent striving for the victory of his team.

# 9

## Law and Order: Some Implications

This final chapter ponders some of the implications of a basic function performed by law in human society.[1] As has been discussed in Chapter 7, the existence of law—the existence of authoritative norms for the general regulation of conduct, with some adequate means for giving effect to those norms—is indispensable for the preservation of order and the achievement of co-ordination in any society. It is therefore indispensable for satisfactory intercourse among people who live in proximity with one another. Without the orderliness-securing and co-ordination-promoting effects of law, the attainment of various desiderata for human beings would remain impossible or would be severely impaired. In short, the existence of law within any community is a necessary condition for the rewardingness of individual lives and the fruitfulness of social/economic/political relations therein.

To explore the jurisprudential implications of this crucial function of law, we shall take as our point of departure the famous discussion by H. L. A. Hart on the kernel of truth in natural-law theory. Hart in the course of his discussion focused on the essential orderliness-preserving role of law, and he briefly but illuminatingly considered the bearing of that role on the debate between natural-law theorists and legal positivists. My present chapter builds on his discussion in order to investigate a question that is as prominent within political philosophy as within jurisprudence: the question whether there obtains a prima-facie moral obligation to obey every legal mandate by dint of its sheer status as such a mandate. (Henceforth, that comprehensively applicable and universally borne obligation will be designated as the 'obligation-to-obey'. Any individual instance or offshoot thereof will be designated as an 'obligation of obedience'.) In political philosophy, this question belongs to a wider set of issues relating to the topics of political obligation and political legitimacy. Hart's exposition of the defensible element in natural-law theory, indeed, draws heavily on some of the classic accounts of

---

[1] I should here issue a caveat. Whenever I mention legal norms in this chapter, I am referring primarily or exclusively to norms that impose legal duties. I am largely putting aside legal norms that establish liberties, powers, or immunities. Given the topic of this chapter, the restrictedness of my focus is appropriate and virtually inevitable. Nevertheless, as is indicated in Ch. 4, I have no intention whatsoever to discount the importance of legal norms that yield results other than the imposition of duties; my inattentiveness to such norms herein, necessitated by my current topic, certainly does not bespeak any such intention.

One further terminological observation is advisable at the outset. I use the term 'obey' to mean 'act in accordance with' or 'abstain from violating'. I do not attach any stronger sense to the term. (Much the same can be said, of course, about my use of the term 'obedience'.) By defining 'obey' expansively, this chapter takes a generous approach to the arguments which it opposes, since it presents the claims of those arguments in their most plausible or least implausible forms.

political obligation and legitimacy put forward by writers such as Thomas Hobbes, John Locke, and David Hume. Although Hart's own discussion does not broach the obligation-to-obey specifically, it is especially germane here because of its jurisprudential sophistication. It helps to bring out the jurisprudential importance of the disputes concerning the obligation-to-obey.

Throughout this chapter, my inquiry into the obligation-to-obey is part of my overall defense of legal positivism. That is, my approach to that obligation concentrates on the nature of law more than on some of the issues that would be contemplated at length by many political philosophers and political theorists. Although the analyses herein will have to include some moral/political judgments—because this chapter is seeking in part to determine whether a certain moral obligation exists—those judgments are at an extremely high level of abstraction that keeps them consistent with a wide array of contemporary political stances. (In this respect, as well as in other respects to be mentioned shortly, this chapter resembles Chapter 2.) Given that my primary concerns are jurisprudential rather than political, the abstractness of my moral/political assumptions is perfectly warranted. For the same reason, a number of political questions will not be tackled at all here. For example, this chapter does not attempt to indicate when people's disobedience will be mandatory rather than merely permissible. Likewise, my arguments say nothing at all about the forms which anybody's posture of disobedience should take.

In focusing on the obligation-to-obey, this chapter does not squarely address other possible moral consequences that might be thought to follow from the orderliness-sustaining and co-ordination-arranging functions of law. For instance, we shall not directly probe the claim that officials' formulating or implementing of legal norms always enjoys a prima-facie moral legitimacy; such a claim would contend that (prima facie) the formulating or implementing does not violate anyone's moral rights and that it is therefore an activity which (prima facie) the officials are always morally at liberty to undertake. Also left unexamined is the thesis that officials who implement legal norms always have prima-facie rights against interference with their labors. Such a thesis would amount to the claim that each citizen always bears a prima-facie duty to abstain from interfering with officials' law-administering endeavors.

The theses about a prima-facie duty of noninterference and about a prima-facie moral legitimacy, along with other theses containing alternative moral conclusions that might appear to follow from law's general role in human society, will be largely or wholly uninvestigated here for three reasons. First, some such theses—for example, the claim about the prima-facie moral legitimacy of officials' law-implementing activities—have received attention in Chapter 2 or in some of my other chapters. Second, most of the theses about the moral consequences of law's security-providing and co-ordination-enabling role have not been presented as unfailingly applicable; that is, their inapplicability to some situations that are partly or wholly within the sway of legal norms has been

acknowledged. For instance, theorists who argue for a prima-facie duty of noninterference have conceded that such a duty does not obtain in connection with the
implementation of wicked laws by wicked regimes.[2] (Even Hobbes, who was
hardly in favor of political and social instability, accepted that some actions of
outright interference with the implementation of legal norms can be morally
permissible and indeed morally obligatory—even if the actions of implementation are also morally permissible.[3]) A third reason for confining the scope of this
chapter to the obligation-to-obey is that several of the arguments herein against
the existence of such an obligation could be marshaled, *mutatis mutandis*,
against various other claims that might be made about the moral significance of
law's basic function. Though the details of the arguments would have to be
modified, some of my general lines of analysis could quite readily be adapted
and broadened.

As has been stated in this book's Introduction, the current chapter's treatment
of the obligation-to-obey is in many respects a complement to my second chapter's analysis of formal justice. Whereas the focus in my discussion of formal
justice lies on the situation of officials who are charged with the task of giving
effect to legal norms, the focus here will lie on the situation of citizens who are
subject to the governance of those norms. In Chapter 2, the central theme is that
legal officials sometimes have neither a prima-facie moral duty nor a prima-facie
moral liberty to implement the law strictly in accordance with its relevant terms.
Before we can say whether the pursuit of formal justice in any particular situation
is prima facie obligatory or even prima facie permissible, we have to know the
substance of the legal norms that are involved. The mere status of those norms as
legal norms is in itself plainly not sufficient to warrant the strict application or
enforcement of their requirements. In the present chapter, a fundamentally similar conclusion will be reached in relation to the obligation-to-obey for citizens.
Just as the legal-positivist insistence on the separability of law and morality is not
threatened at all by the conceptual link between formal justice and law-administration, so too it remains unthreatened by the fact that the existence of law is a
necessary condition for the security and co-ordination that underlie any tolerably
decent societal arrangements. Before we can say whether the sustainment of
public orderliness and co-ordination through the existence of a legal regime is
sufficient to engender any particular obligations of obedience for each citizen, we
have to know two things: the specific substance of the norms in the regime, and
the degree to which improvements are reasonably attainable. Strictly speaking,
then, there is no obligation-to-obey. In other words, there is never a prima-facie
moral obligation to obey legal norms simply by virtue of their status as legal

[2]   See e.g. William Edmundson, 'Legitimate Authority without Political Obligation', 17 *Law and
Philosophy* 43 (1998); A. John Simmons, 'Voluntarism and Political Associations', 67 *Virginia Law
Review* 19, 24–6 (1981).
[3]   Thomas Hobbes, *Leviathan* (Cambridge: Cambridge University Press, 1991) (Richard Tuck
ed.), 93–4, 98, 150–1.

norms (rather than by virtue of their substance as benevolent legal norms or by virtue of their prevailing as legal norms in regard to which no preferable alternatives are reasonably attainable). In sum, even when we fully take into account the basic function of law in human society, we should conclude that law *qua* law does not carry any intrinsic moral import. Its sheer existence as such does not give rise to any degree of moral obligatoriness.

This chapter will proceed as follows. Because my analyses herein will concentrate on the functional significance of law, we shall first look quickly at some general arguments propounded by Michael Moore who characterizes law as a 'functional kind'.[4] Moore, who has produced a substantial body of work on natural law (much of which deals with meta-ethical problems that are not at issue in this book), ascribes inherent moral significance to law on the basis of its distinctive function. An examination of his arguments, with their functionalist focus, can thus serve as a valuable prolegomenon to this chapter's inquiry into the jurisprudential implications of the key function of law. A recountal of Hart's discussion of that function will begin the second and much longer half of this chapter. My analyses will then expand his discussion by pondering whether Hart laid out a foundation for the obligation-to-obey. Though the issues to be probed are complicated and ramified, legal positivism's stance on the relationship between law and morality will emerge safely intact.

I. PRELIMINARY REFLECTIONS ON THE NATURE OF FUNCTIONS

Moore maintains that the essence of law resides less in any of its structural features than in the end which it advances. To apprehend the distinctive nature of law, we should ask not about the formal or procedural aspects of legal systems but about the function which a legal system characteristically fulfills. When we ascertain the useful purpose which is served by law and which cannot be similarly served by any other institution, we shall have ascertained what law is—by recognizing it as the institution which serves that purpose. Its hallmark lies in what it does.

Many of the specific lines of argument put forward by Moore do not stand in need of scrutiny here. For example, when he presumes that the satisfaction of Lon Fuller's eight principles of legality will inevitably promote moral ideals such as liberty and autonomy (Moore, 'Law', 222), he is committing errors that have been amply criticized in my third chapter. Far less objectionable is his contention that institutions which comply with Fuller's principles will tend to foster social co-ordination; but that contention can likewise be put aside here, since its significance will be explored throughout the second half of this chapter. What deserves

---

[4] Michael Moore, 'Law as a Functional Kind', in Robert George (ed.), *Natural Law Theory* (Oxford: Clarendon Press, 1992) ['Law'], 188.

attention straightaway is the bedrock assumption that informs Moore's whole approach to functionalist jurisprudence—his assumption that the function performed by law must be benign.

Moore embeds his jurisprudential position in a broader theory about the attribution of functions to institutions and processes and objects. Having introduced his theory with a discussion of the function of the heart's beating—the function of circulating the blood which in turn promotes the health of the body[5]—he contends that two basic judgments or sets of judgments are involved in the identification of that function. In the first place, we need to engage in causal investigations to recognize that certain states of affairs are effects (immediate effects or intermediate effects) of the heart's beating. In the second place, we need to single out the relevant effects by reference to the overall goal of the system, the bodily system, in which the heart's beating occurs. This second step obviously necessitates the specification of the system's goal. Endeavoring to explain how that specification is to be accomplished, Moore submits: 'There are two leading possibilities for how we discover the overall goals of some system: we either find that the system naturally tends to maintain itself in some state of equilibrium despite widely disequilibrating conditions; or we discover that of all the human goods there are some but not others that either are or can be served by the system in question. The first is a value-free enterprise while the second is value-laden' ('Law', 210–11). Moore declares that, of these two ways of discovering a system's goal, the second is much more common than the first. 'Most of the time, [the first way of discovering a system's goal] is not how we assign functions. Most of the time we are evaluating something as good when we say what it is good for (i.e. what its function is). In such cases we consult our list of all the good things there are and ask, which of these, if any, does/can this system promote?' ('Law', 211.) Thus, for instance, when we impute to the heart the function of circulating the blood, we are implicitly relying on two unproblematic theses. We take as given the causal thesis that the circulation of the blood tends to sustain the health of the body, and we likewise take as given the evaluative thesis that physical health is a good. Because the circulation of blood is not in itself a good—that is, because it counts at most as only an instrumental good—our classification of it as the function of the heart's beating must presuppose a link between the circulation and an intrinsic good. That presupposition of a link comprises the causal and evaluative theses that have just been mentioned.

Moore believes that the example of the heart's beating is illustrative of the general character of functional ascriptions. His view is that, whenever we sincerely maintain that the function of $X$ is to bring about a state of affairs $Y$, we tacitly or expressly presume that $Y$ is either good in itself or promotive of something good in itself. He repeatedly states this view in connection with law. For

---

[5] This aspect of the heart's functioning is also mentioned in H. L. A. Hart, *The Concept of Law* (Oxford: Clarendon Press, 1961) [*Concept*], 186–7.

instance, he asserts that the task of singling out the goal (and hence the function) of law 'requires nothing less than a full theory of the good and the right. One has to know, that is, what is objectively good and one has to know the permissible means of reaching it through action. Then one can decide which of [the suggested goals of law] are goods and thus which could be what a legal system is good for' ('Law', 215). Moore states his position in a similar vein when he criticizes Fuller for having deemed the goal or purpose of law to be the subjection of human conduct to the governance of rules. 'As many of Fuller's contemporary critics have pointed out, there is nothing intrinsically good about that goal. By itself, guiding persons by rules cannot be the goal of law because, by itself, guiding persons by rules is not a good' ('Law', 216, citation omitted). To the same effect, and even more pointed, is the following statement: '[I]f law is a functional kind then necessarily law serves some good and thus, necessarily, law is in that way related to morality' ('Law', 221). Moore proceeds along exactly the same lines when he writes that 'functional jurisprudence seeks some distinctive end that law serves. The very idea that law is a functional kind depends on there being some . . . good that law can uniquely serve' ('Law', 223). Many other passages from his essay could be pertinently quoted here.

All of Moore's claims about functional jurisprudence are ultimately based on his general conception of functional attributions—his thesis that every such attribution must pertain either to a self-equilibrating system (and its components) or to a system that promotes some distinctive good. Moore presumes that these two types of functional attributions are exhaustive, and he of course presumes that law is a system of the second type. As a diehard natural-law theorist, he likewise presumes that any genuine legal regime will perform the function of law without being marred by any serious injustice. Unfortunately for Moore's project, none of these assumptions is tenable.

Without perforce accepting that the structural features of law are subordinate to its function, we may agree that a distinctive function of law can be specified. However, that function is the Fullerian function of subjecting the whole range of human conduct to the governance of a matrix of norms. Such a function, as Moore himself readily acknowledges in his criticism of Fuller, is by no means inherently benevolent. 'If such an instrumental good were the only thing law was good for, then like a knife or a steam-engine such an instrument can equally well be used for good or for evil' ('Law', 222). As has already been noted, Moore is wrong in thinking that the satisfaction of Fuller's eight procedural preconditions for the existence of law will inevitably tend to further the ideals of liberty and autonomy. He is equally wrong in thinking that the tendency of law to promote social co-ordination has any straightforward moral significance. (Not only will the lack of any straightforward moral significance become apparent in the second half of this chapter, but it should also be plain from some of the discussions in my earlier chapters—such as Chapter 8's critique of John Finnis, which observes that the co-ordination-enhancing and security-providing effects of law can be wholly derivative of its role as a vehicle for wicked oppression.) We are left, then, with a functional essence of law that is morally neutral.

Under Moore's approach to jurisprudence, the reply to what has just been said is that the ascription of a morally neutral function to law does not really amount to the ascription of a function at all. Under his approach, as has been emphasized here, the imputation of a function to law must tacitly or expressly affirm that legal institutions distinctively serve to realize some desideratum. We now ought to probe and question his underlying premise, however. Why must every functional attribution pertain either to a self-equilibrating system or to a system that promotes some intrinsic good? Why cannot a functional attribution pertain to an institution that serves the evil purposes of the people who run it? Moore presumes that no such attribution is acceptable, but he does not provide any backing for his position. He apparently believes that his stance on this matter is too plainly correct to be in need of support. Even when he responds to a different charge of begging the question ('Law', 219–21), he takes for granted that any genuine recognition of the function of law must consist in a discovery of the distinctive *good* which law brings about. To be sure, he does not presuppose that law has a functional essence—and therefore he is not vulnerable to the charge of begging the question on that point—but he does presuppose that, if law has a functional essence, its function (and the goal which that function serves) must be benign. Both the question that is not begged and the question that is indeed begged are evident in the following sentences:

The theory that law is a kind and that its nature is given by such and such a goal is just that, a theory, falsifiable as is the atomic theory of gold. It is not a foundational assumption about law's nature that begs the question, 'Is law related to morality?' True, *if law is a functional kind then necessarily law serves some good and thus, necessarily, law is in that way related to morality*. But this [i.e., the status of law as a functional kind] is a discovery, not a posit, of functionalist jurisprudence.   ('Law,' 221, emphasis added)

Moore does not take as given that the institution of law is a functional kind, but he does take as given that the status of law as a functional kind (if in fact it is a functional kind) must consist in law's furtherance of a benevolent purpose. Without any buttressing arguments, that is, he disallows functional ascriptions that would point to evil purposes or morally neutral purposes for which the operations of law are highly serviceable.

Moore's wholly unsupported assumption about the nature of functional attributions is extremely dubious. My rejoinder can perhaps best proceed by presenting one or two scenarios that will lead into some more general reflections. Suppose that a historian *H* is conducting a technical study of the gas chambers and other mechanisms with which the Nazis exterminated their victims during the Second World War. *H* carefully examines the machines which the Nazis used, but he is puzzled about a particular part of the apparatus on some of the gas chambers. Though he can tell that the part was not merely ornamentative, he is not sure how it contributed to the gas chambers' murderous operations. Turning to an expert who is with him, he asks: 'What was the function of this component of the machinery?' Suppose now that *H* extends his study to encompass not only the technological dimension of the Holocaust, but also the bureaucratic workings of the Nazi regime. He studies the various offices and office-holders in the administrative ranks of the Gestapo, and he becomes puzzled about the exact responsibilities and prerogatives of one particular office. Turning to a knowledgeable colleague, he inquires: 'What was the function of this man in the running of the Gestapo?' Far from being scandalous or unacceptable, these inquiries by *H* are perfectly comprehensible and indeed routine. Unless Moore is engaged in some strangely arid and question-begging terminological regimentation, he cannot deny that *H*'s inquiries are about functions and that the answers to those inquiries are functional attributions.

What *H*'s inquiries and the answers to those inquiries bring out is that a functional attribution need not rest on an ascription of goodness to the institution or mechanism wherein the specified function is performed. A functional attribution requires only an ascription of some goal (or some intended result) to the relevant institution or mechanism; the benignity or malignity of that goal is a separate matter which is not settled or determined by the goal's sheer status as a goal. When *H* and his interlocutors discuss the function of the component of the gas chamber and the function of the administrative official in the Gestapo, they manifestly do not believe that those functions or the overall workings of the gas chambers and the Gestapo were benign. Their references to functions stem not from any ghastly beliefs of that sort, but from their awareness that the mechanisms or institutions under discussion were employed (with greater or lesser effectiveness) to achieve certain purposes. Those mechanisms or institutions were the vehicles for the pursuit of certain projects—certain flagitious projects—by the people who made use of them. In speaking about the functions of those mechanisms and institutions, and about the functions of the components of those mechanisms and institutions, *H* and his colleagues focus not on intrinsic goodness but on serviceability for a purpose. They grasp that, in regard to human affairs, the performance of a function consists in the execution of actions or processes that contribute to the realization of an intended result. Whether the intended result is morally commendable or deplorable or neutral, the furtherance of it in the way just mentioned is the carrying out of a function. (Of course, the contribution of a function to the occurrence of an intended result can sometimes proceed in ways that are unsought and even unperceived by the people who are directly affected. Nothing said here is meant to suggest that every function must involve the conscious adaptation of means to ends.)

In connection with law, then, the Fullerian function described earlier is indeed a function. The enterprise of subjecting the full range of human conduct to the governance of a matrix of norms is undertaken in order to advance certain purposes or ends. In benevolent and malevolent regimes alike, that enterprise will be seen as crucial in securing the basic orderliness and co-ordination of a society. However, the more specific objectives of those regimes will diverge markedly— as will the substantive bearings of their norms, of course. In a benevolent (liberal-democratic) regime, officials' performance of the Fullerian function is aimed at enhancing the liberty, autonomy, security, and integrity of individuals. Both the substance and the implementation of such a regime's legal norms will be shaped by a concern for those values. By contrast, in a monstrously illiberal regime of power-lusting officials devoted to their own interests, the carrying out of the Fullerian function is aimed at advancing those selfish interests (in ways recounted by my earlier chapters); the securing of orderliness and co-ordination is entirely derivative of that aim. Accordingly, the Fullerian function does not partake of any inherent moral significance. It can serve deplorable ends as efficaciously as worthy ends. Nevertheless, it is plainly a function, for it does indeed play a central part—a prominent and indispensable part—in bringing about those ends.

In short, Moore cannot warrantedly maintain that the very notion or state of functionality is value-laden (and that it is therefore tilted in favor of natural-law theory and against legal positivism). To be sure, the ascription of a function is indissociable from the tacit or explicit ascription of some goal or objective; thus, in regard to human institutions, it is indissociable from the ascription of an intended outcome or result. All the same, there is no reason whatsoever for thinking that that outcome or result must be morally worthy. Many of the objectives which people pursue are decidedly unworthy. Consequently, many a functional attribution—such as each of those uttered by *H* and his colleagues—does not or should not rest on a supposition that the institution which performs or comprises the attributed function is promotive of human good.

## II. LAW, ORDER, AND OBLIGATION

Having seen that the separability of law and morality is not belied by the mere fact that law has a distinctive function, we should now look more closely at that function. Though its sheer nature as a function does not endow it with moral worthiness at all, its substance might do so. That substance must hence come under scrutiny, as we contemplate whether the orderliness-providing and co-ordi-nation-enabling role of law imposes on each citizen in any legal regime a prima-facie moral obligation to obey every one of the regime's legal mandates.

## A. Hart on the Minimum Content of Natural Law

In a justly renowned discussion, H. L. A. Hart explored the character and some of the jurisprudential implications of law's essential role in any viable human society (*Concept*, 187–98). Like the corresponding discussion in my seventh chapter, Hart's analysis will set the stage for our broader examination of the extent to which the norms of a legal regime possess obligatory force simply by dint of being legal norms. Hart observed that certain elementary facts of the human condition combine to necessitate the existence of law in any community beyond the size of a few families. If a society of even a moderate size is to stand any chance of enduring, then it must be held together in part by a scheme of legal governance. The five basic aspects of human beings and their environments which Hart highlighted are as follows: (1) the vulnerability of each human being to harms that might be inflicted by other human beings; (2) the approximate equality of people, in that the physical and mental disparities among them are generally not overwhelming; (3) the mixture of selfishness and solicitude in the make-up of virtually every human being; (4) the scarcity of valuable resources, and the fact that most such resources must be subjected to considerable labor before they become capable of satisfying human wants directly; and (5) the limit-edness of people's understanding and strength of will, which leads some people to favor their short-term interests at the expense of their long-term interests. Given these characteristics of human beings and their world—characteristics which overlap to some degree—the regulatory sway of legal norms is essential for the sustainability of any community beyond the tiniest size. (As should be clear from my seventh chapter, terms such as 'essential' do not here mean 'logically necessary'. Unlike the notion of a round square [for example], the notion of the long-term existence of a fairly large human community without legal norms is not a logical contradiction. None the less, the possibility of such a state of affairs is no more than the barest of logical possibilities. It is so formidably unlikely that we can very safely disregard any chance of its actualization.)

Not only do Hart's five central features of the human condition render the existence of law indispensable, but they also ensure that the legal mandates in any lasting society will include certain fundamental prohibitions. As Hart observed (and as my seventh chapter has likewise noted), legal norms forbidding murder, assault, vandalism, serious fraud, and other grave misdeeds are unforgoable in setting the terms for durable human interaction. If such norms were absent or wholly unenforced, the security that distinguishes civilization from the frenzy of chaotic anarchy would *ipso facto* be absent. Every viable scheme of governance must encompass those basic proscriptions, if it is to encompass anything at all. Yet, since the substance of those proscriptions is at one with the substance of key moral precepts, Hart's five facts of the human condition necessitate a convergence between the demands of law and the demands of morality. The area of that inevitable convergence is what Hart labeled as the 'minimum content of natural law'.

Despite that label, Hart immediately raised one important point that goes some way toward revealing the severe limits on his concession to the natural-law camp. After highlighting the unavoidability of the basic legal prohibitions within any feasible social arrangements, and after noting the affinities between those prohibitions and the interdictions that are central to morality, he remarked: 'The protections and benefits provided by the system of mutual forbearances which underlies both law and morals may, in different societies, be extended to very different ranges of persons' (*Concept*, 195). Although the minimum of security essential for the sustainment of a society must be extended to quite a number of people, it need not be extended to everyone. A community can endure as such even if some people who reside within it are denied the basic protections that are enjoyed by other people, who belong to relatively privileged groups. '[I]t is plain that neither the law nor the accepted morality of societies need extend their minimal protections and benefits to all within their scope, and often they have not done so. In slave-owning societies the sense that the slaves are human beings, not mere objects to be used, may be lost by the dominant group' (*Concept*, 196). As Hart elaborated: 'These painful facts of human history are enough to show that, though a society to be viable must offer *some* of its members a system of mutual forbearances, it need not, unfortunately, offer them to all' (*Concept*, 196). People excluded from the protective ambit of the elementary legal prohibitions may very likely be worse off than they would be in a situation of lawlessness. As far as they are concerned, the coercive force of a scheme of legal governance is marshaled to 'subdue and maintain, in a position of permanent inferiority, a subject group whose size, relatively to the master group, may be large or small, depending on the means of coercion, solidarity, and discipline available to the latter, and the helplessness or inability to organize of the former. For those thus oppressed there may be nothing in the system to command their loyalty but only things to fear. They are its victims, not its beneficiaries' (*Concept*, 197). When pondering the plight of such people, who are less secure within a prevailing scheme of law than they would be in the absence of law altogether, we should perhaps recall a comment made by John Locke. Replying to the proponents of absolute monarchy such as Robert Filmer, who decried all challenges to the legitimacy of any monarch's brutal oppression, Locke famously declared: 'As if when Men quitting the State of Nature entered into Society, they agreed that all of them but one, should be under the restraint of Laws, but that he should still retain all the Liberty of the State of Nature, increased with Power, and made licentious by Impunity. This is to think that Men are so foolish that they take care to avoid what Mischiefs may be done them by *Pole-Cats*, or *Foxes*, but are content, nay think it Safety, to be devoured by *Lions*.'[6]

When mulling over the jurisprudential implications of law's security-engendering and co-ordination-facilitating role, we shall plainly have to take account of Hart's point about conceivable states of affairs where only quite limited numbers of people benefit from the fundamental prohibitions in the legal structures that hold sway over them. Before moving to a general exploration of the moral consequences of law's bedrock functions, we should note three other points (each of

---

[6] John Locke, 'The Second Treatise of Government', in *Two Treatises of Government* (Cambridge: Cambridge University Press, 1988) (Peter Laslett ed.), § 93 (emphasis in original).

which has been developed in my seventh chapter). First, although the elementary mandates of morality and the elementary mandates of law inevitably coincide or overlap at an abstract level, they can significantly diverge at a more concrete level—even in a society where everyone is covered by the protections of those legal mandates. So long as the fundamental prohibitions in a legal regime confer enough security on enough people to avert a slide into chaos, they can keep a society intact while failing to shield people from numerous harms that are forbidden under any tenable moral code. Merely from the fact that legal norms bestow protection on individuals sufficiently to prevent a social structure from falling apart, we cannot infer that they provide the degree of protection that would be minimally required by valid moral precepts. Even in a viable community where everyone enjoys the same level of security as everyone else, that level can fall far short of what it morally ought to be.

Second, the provision of substantial security through basic proscriptive mandates in a system of legal governance is consistent with monstrous oppression. Perhaps the engendering of the security is itself a source of such oppression, as people are protected from one another via the imposition of extremely harsh penalties for minor breaches (as well as major breaches) of laws against theft, vandalism, assault, and the like. Or perhaps the security enjoyed by each person is accompanied by stiflingly severe restrictions on the permissibility of any actions that might threaten the dominance of the prevailing regime. In such circumstances, each person can live in safety *vis-à-vis* his fellows and *vis-à-vis* the regnant government—so long as he never utters any open criticisms of the government, never signs any petitions or engages in any protests, never uses a photocopier, and so forth. That is, even in a society where each citizen is protected on the same terms as every other citizen by fundamental legal curbs, those curbs can be situated in an overall matrix of norms that is suffocatingly harsh and confining.

Moreover, as should be evident from several of my earlier chapters, the fundamental legal curbs themselves can be introduced and maintained by officials for purely prudential reasons. So long as citizens are suitably submissive and productive, they will usually be far more valuable for evil officials' exploitative purposes when alive than when dead. Hence, officials who are thoroughly self-devoted and power-hungry will have ample reasons for establishing legal prohibitions that protect citizens from one another. Similarly, in order to foster incentives for compliance with their wicked behests, the officials will have strong reasons for extending to each compliant person a much greater degree of security against the officials' own coercive measures than is extended to any recalcitrant person. In sum, the inclusion of elementary protections (for all or many citizens) among a society's legal norms is not perforce an indication of any moral concern on the part of the society's legal/governmental officials. Those officials might be motivated purely by the sorts of prudential considerations that impel a heartless owner of livestock to attend to the security of the animals in his herd.

## B. Orderliness and Obligation

In the rest of this chapter, we shall investigate how far the legal-positivist stance on the separability of law and morality is threatened by the indispensable role of law in enabling the security and co-ordination that are prerequisite to societal cohesion. More specifically, this portion of my chapter will seek to ascertain whether the aforementioned role of law imposes on each person in any viable legal regime a prima-facie moral duty to act in accordance with every one of the regime's directives. (As has been stated, that comprehensively applicable and universally borne moral duty—a prima-facie moral duty—will here be designated as the 'obligation-to-obey'.) Some theorists have contended that just such a prima-facie obligation is engendered by law's central function.[7] Naturally, the position adopted here is very different. If every legal requirement carried some modicum of prima-facie moral obligatoriness simply by dint of amounting to a legal requirement, then a powerful intrinsic connection would exist between law and morality. The fact of legal requisiteness would always be accompanied by the value of prima-facie moral bindingness. No jurisprudential positivist should concede the existence of such a connection.

This discussion will begin with an effort to clarify what is meant by the phrase 'prima-facie obligation'. Although most people who write on the present topic

---

[7] See e.g. William Boardman, 'Coordination and the Moral Obligation to Obey the Law', 97 *Ethics* 546 (1987); Neil MacCormick, 'Legal Obligation and the Imperative Fallacy', in A. W. B. Simpson (ed.), *Oxford Essays in Jurisprudence (Second Series)* (Oxford: Clarendon Press, 1973), 100, 128–9; Neil MacCormick, 'Natural Law and the Separation of Law and Morals', in Robert George (ed.), *Natural Law Theory* (Oxford: Clarendon Press, 1992), 105, 117. Cf. Monroe Beardsley, 'Equality and Obedience to Law', in Sidney Hook (ed.), *Law and Philosophy* (New York: New York University Press, 1964), 35, 41–2.

The literature on the topic of this chapter is formidably large. For two very good (and extremely pithy) introductory treatments, see J. W. Harris, *Legal Philosophies* (London: Butterworths, 1997), ch. 16; Jonathan Wolff, *An Introduction to Political Philosophy* (Oxford: Oxford University Press, 1996), ch. 2. More advanced are several highly sophisticated and thought-provoking studies: Chaim Gans, *Philosophical Anarchism and Political Disobedience* (Cambridge: Cambridge University Press, 1992); Leslie Green, *The Authority of the State* (Oxford: Clarendon Press, 1988); Kent Greenawalt, *Conflicts of Law and Morality* (New York: Oxford University Press, 1989), chs. 4–9; John Horton, *Political Obligation* (London: Macmillan, 1992); Heidi Hurd, 'Challenging Authority', 100 *Yale Law Journal* 1611 (1991); George Klosko, *The Principle of Fairness and Political Obligation* (Lanham: Rowman & Littlefield, 1992); Joseph Raz, *The Authority of Law* (Oxford: Clarendon Press, 1979) [*Authority*], chs. 12–13; Joseph Raz, *Ethics in the Public Domain* (Oxford: Clarendon Press, 1994), chs. 14–15; A. John Simmons, *Moral Principles and Political Obligations* (Princeton: Princeton University Press, 1979); Philip Soper, *A Theory of Law* (Cambridge, Mass.: Harvard University Press, 1984); Philip Soper, 'The Obligation to Obey the Law', in Ruth Gavison (ed.), *Issues in Contemporary Legal Philosophy* (Oxford: Clarendon Press, 1987), 127. Stimulating collections of essays are in Sidney Hook (ed.), *Law and Philosophy* (New York: New York University Press, 1964) [*Law*], pt. I; in the February 1981 (vol. 67) issue of the *Virginia Law Review*; and in Paul Harris (ed.), *On Political Obligation* (London: Routledge, 1990) [*Political Obligation*]. I disagree with all of these works on certain important points, and I disagree with some of them on myriad points. None the less, each of them is rigorous and admirable. Anyone writing about the obligation-to-obey can benefit immensely from a wide examination of the relevant literature.

have used that phrase in much the same way as it will be used in this chapter, some writers have attached other meanings to it. Distinct sets of issues have become conflated as a result. Some brief preliminary labors of terminological and conceptual clarification will therefore be salutary here.

After disentangling a few important matters that have occasionally been run together, this chapter inquires whether the existence of any sustainable regime of legal norms is characterized by the obligation-to-obey. We shall examine two broad types of law-violations that do not run afoul of such an obligation (even on a prima-facie level): utterly harmless violations of benign laws and many wicked-ness-defying violations. Instances of these types of disobedience are morally legitimate, and—especially in regard to the second type—can even be morally obligatory. Law's function as the cardinal means of security and co-ordination in human society does not by itself suffice to confer even the slightest measure of prima-facie moral obligatoriness on certain legal directives. Not only do the formal features of law bear no intrinsic moral significance, but, in addition, the necessary substantive features of law (the features that make up the 'minimum content of natural law') are devoid of any inevitable moral implications.

## 1. Defining One's Terms

The obligation under scrutiny in this chapter, the obligation-to-obey, is a prima-facie moral duty to comply with the requirements of every directive laid down by any particular scheme of legal governance. What is a 'prima-facie' duty? In line with most of the writings on this topic, and in line with the previous chapters of this book, my present chapter will take 'prima-facie' to mean 'overridable' or 'defeasible'. That is, a duty with only a prima-facie status rather than an invariably conclusive status does not *per se* finally establish what anyone morally ought to do. Such a duty is subject to being outweighed by other moral considerations that are more pressing or more substantial. It is not absolute. Of course, a full process of deliberation about a specific set of circumstances may eventuate in the verdict that a person should act in conformity with this or that prima-facie obligation. Obviously, it is not inevitable that any particular prima-facie moral obligation will indeed be overridden in a given context by a more powerful moral obligation; on countless occasions, no overriding factors will be present. None the less, if the outweighing of a prima-facie duty is not inevitable, it is always possible. The designation of 'prima-facie' indicates precisely this state of defeasibility, a state of potential subordination to some competing obligation that takes priority. In sum, 'prima-facie' here means 'determinative of what to do, unless overtopped by a more important demand or set of demands'. (Plainly, an over-topped moral duty continues to exist and to have force. Because it remains a moral reason for action, any failure to abide by it—however strongly salutary, on the whole—is an occasion for regret and perhaps for censure or other penalties.)

We are well advised to note that the putative obligation-to-obey has only a prima-facie status. After all, if the obligation under perusal here were deemed by this chapter to be invariably conclusive, then we would be looking at an obligation that has never (or virtually never) been portrayed by anyone as attaching perforce to every legal norm. No sensible theorist presumes that all legal mandates impose conclusive moral obligations purely by virtue of being legal mandates. Everyone who is not ludicrously authoritarian recognizes that there can arise circumstances wherein some actions that work against the fulfillment of legal directives are what morally ought to be done, all things considered. Hence, if this chapter were concentrating on claims about an absolute obligation-to-obey, it would be indulging in pointless shadow-boxing. No one advances such claims, and thus the refutation of them would serve no purpose. If jurisprudential positivism is to be defended in this chapter against real opponents rather than against straw men, then the focus here must lie on arguments about a *prima-facie* obligation-to-obey. We should not waste time on fanciful arguments about some categorical obligation.

Now, although the definition of 'prima-facie' set forth above is in keeping with the use of that adjective by many moral and political philosophers, a few writers have adopted a different pattern of usage (either in combination with the more common pattern or in lieu of it).[8] Instead of employing 'prima-facie' to indicate something about the force of a specified obligation, these writers employ it chiefly or exclusively to make an evidentiary point about the way in which an obligation should be upheld or rejected. They submit that, in regard to any prima-facie duty, the burden of proof lies on people who deny the actuality of the duty rather than on people who affirm it. A presumption obtains in favor of the duty's existence; if that presumption is to be overcome, then the person *P* who gainsays the existence of the duty must adduce sufficient grounds for thinking that his stance is correct. Whereas the contrary stance (a belief in the duty's existence) will prevail by default if neither *P* nor anyone else adequately makes a case against it, the confutation of the duty by *P* will founder unless he can offer enough reasons to support his position.

Under the view preferred here, the matter of burden-of-proof should be clearly separated from the matter of overridability. We should distinguish among the following questions that can be asked in connection with the topic of this chapter:

(1) If there are any content-independent moral obligations to obey the demands of legal norms, are those obligations absolute or defeasible?

---

[8]  See e.g. William Boardman, above, n. 7, at 555–6; Tony Honoré, 'Must We Obey? Necessity as a Ground of Obligation', 67 *Virginia Law Review* 39, 48 (1981). For some salutary correctives, see Richard Brandt, 'Utility and the Obligation to Obey the Law', in Hook, *Law*, above, n. 7, at 43, 46; David Lyons, 'Need, Necessity, and Political Obligation', 67 *Virginia Law Review* 63, 66–8 (1981). Of course, although the prevailing pattern of usage is convenient and largely defensible, it is not entirely beyond reproach; for some perceptive but overstated doubts about its appropriateness, see A. John Simmons, above, n. 7, at 24–8.

(2) Is there an overridable moral obligation to obey every directive in any viable legal regime?
(3) Where lies the burden of proof for answering question 2?
(4) If the answer to question 2 is negative, then where lies the burden of proof for deciding whether there is an overridable moral obligation to obey any particular law or set of laws?
(5) Irrespective of whether the answer to question 2 is negative or affirmative, where lies the burden of proof for deciding whether there is a conclusive obligation to obey any particular law or set of laws?

Restated within the pattern of terminology favored here, the first of these inquiries asks whether any content-independent obligations of obedience are prima-facie or invariably conclusive. As has been emphasized, the claims about the obligation-to-obey which this chapter seeks to rebut are claims about a prima-facie obligation; preposterous claims about an absolute obligation-to-obey would be ridiculous straw men, rather than theses that have actually been propounded by any serious analyst. Hence, the answer to the first inquiry above is that, if any content-independent obligations of obedience exist at all, they are prima-facie (i.e., overridable). Precisely because of this answer to the first question, the fifth question will go unaddressed here. My concern is to investigate whether a premise recounting the basic functions of law—in combination with a premise recounting the elementary demands of fairness or equitability—can warrant a conclusion about a prima-facie moral obligation to obey every legal mandate. The focus here is only on the existence or inexistence of that prima-facie obligation. Quite beyond the scope of this chapter is any specification of the circumstances in which a prima-facie duty of obedience is dispositive or becomes dispositive. Consequently, questions about the burden of proof in relation to the specifying of those circumstances are beside the point.

Much more germane, of course, is the second of the inquiries above. As has already been made clear, this chapter's answer to that inquiry is negative. As will be argued in detail, there is no prima-facie moral obligation to comply with all the directives of any legal regime. At any rate, no successful case for the existence of such an obligation can be founded on law's security-providing and co-ordination-facilitating role. Though that role is indispensable for the sustainability of a legal regime and is thus indispensable for the enjoyment of the sundry benefits which the sustainment of such a regime can yield, it does not generate any across-the-board duty of obedience. The sheer status of a norm as a legal norm—the sheer fact that it belongs to an institution of a general type which makes civilization possible—does not carry any automatic moral consequences, be they overridable or otherwise.

The third question above is ambiguous; or, rather, an attempt to answer it can reveal an ambiguity in the second question. Faced with a query about the burden of proof for showing that the obligation-to-obey does or does not exist, we need to know whether the query is being posed about discussions concerning every conceivable legal system or about discussions concerning only some particular legal regime. If the second question and thus the third question pertain to discussions concerning all conceivable legal systems, then the answer to the third question undoubtedly is that the relevant burden of proof lies on people arguing for the existence of the obligation-to-obey. Quite outlandish is the claim that, in regard to *every* legal system, each citizen bears a prima-facie moral duty to comply with every one of the system's mandates. Such a claim can hardly prevail by default, and must therefore be buttressed by supporting arguments. Accordingly, the proponents of such a claim have indeed furnished arguments to substantiate their position. The most plausible such argument—combining a principle of fairness and an emphasis on law's essential functions—is the target of this chapter. Hence, this chapter's defensive or reactive posture reflects the appropriate assignment of the burden of proof; only because some theorists have mounted arguments to vindicate their view that the obligation-to-obey exists within every viable legal system, does the confutation of that view become a pertinent and vital task.

If instead the second and third inquiries above pertain to discussions which are each focused only on this or that particular legal regime, then—as will be contended later in this chapter—the answer to the third inquiry will hinge on the justness of the regime. If the regime is benevolently liberal-democratic, then the burden of proof in answering question 2 lies on anyone who wishes to deny that there is a prima-facie moral obligation to comply with each of the regime's mandatory norms. If the legal regime is fundamentally evil, by contrast, the burden of proof lies on anyone who wishes to affirm the existence of such an obligation. In application to any particular regime, then, the third of the questions above is a moral question to which a suitable response must take account of the regime's substantive bearings. Much the same can be said about question 4. When a decision has to be made whether a specific legal norm imposes at least a prima-facie moral obligation of obedience, the allocation of the burden of proof will depend on the benignity or malevolence of the legal system to which the norm belongs. More will be said on this matter later in this chapter. (Note, incidentally, that questions 3 and 4 relate only to the burden of proof. One's answers to them do not predetermine one's response to question 2 or to the inquiry described in question 4. This chapter will maintain that the proper answer to question 2 is negative, even when that question is asked only about a benignly liberal-democratic regime; yet this chapter will also maintain that, when question 2 is indeed asked about a liberal-democratic regime, the burden of proof in answering should lie on the challenger rather than on the supporter. A similar situation obtains in regard to question 4. Although there will be an initial presumption that any particular legal norm within a benevolent regime engenders a prima-facie obligation of obedience, that presumption can be overcome whenever noncompliance will predictably be free of any harmful effects on legitimate interests. While serving as an advantage for the supporters of a legal norm over the assailants thereof, the presumption in favor of the prima-facie obligation of obedience certainly does not rule out successful challenges.)

Having clarified at some length the meaning of 'prima-facie', and having sought to differentiate the issue of overridability from the issue of the burden of proof, this chapter should now also clarify what is meant here by 'obligation' or 'duty'. Let us begin indirectly by examining a dichotomy that will make no appearance or virtually no appearance in my subsequent arguments. A moral obligation or duty is a moral reason-for-action, distinguishable from any moral reasons-for-action that involve mere commendability rather than requisiteness. When someone can perform a supererogatory deed which would be morally commendable but which (as a supererogatory deed) is not morally required, he can be said to have a moral reason-for-action. Nevertheless, he does not have an obligation to undertake the deed. A moral duty exists only when some act or forbearance is indeed morally required rather than simply morally praiseworthy. A state of moral requirement obtains when a failure to act or to forbear from acting in some specified manner is morally wrong and is therefore deserving of ethical censure or other penalties. By contrast, some act or forbearance is supererogatory when a failure to engage in it warrants the withholding of special praise or admiration but not the leveling of condemnation. A failure of this milder sort indicates not that a person is guilty of some moral fault, but instead that he is only modestly endowed with some virtue. Though he has declined to do more than was owed by him to others, he has not omitted to do what was owed (unless he has breached a moral obligation in addition to shrinking from a supererogatory deed).

Without a doubt, the distinction between obligatory deeds and supererogatory deeds—in Lon Fuller's terms, the distinction between the morality of duty and the morality of aspiration—is far from clear-cut in practice. In any event, none of the arguments in the subsequent portions of this chapter will invoke that distinction or rely on it, since the position taken herein is that there are often neither obligatory reasons nor credible supererogatory reasons for compliance with particular legal norms. All the same, even though the distinction between those two types of moral reasons does not have any real bearing on my subsequent lines of argument, the drawing of it here calls attention to the fact that a moral obligation is always a moral reason-for-action. Hence, in situations where there are no moral reasons for behaving in a specified way, there is *a fortiori* no obligation to behave thus. What, then, is a moral reason-for-action? Such a reason is a factor or consideration that will be possessed of affirmative weight in an appropriate balancing of factors or considerations to determine the morally correct course of conduct in a given set of circumstances. In short, a genuine moral reason-for-action resides in the demands of a sound moral precept or in the aspirational pull of a sound ethical ideal.

This straightforward point about moral obligations as moral reasons-for-action is occasionally somewhat obscured in the literature on the obligation-to-obey. For example, Kent Greenawalt, whose explorations of the obligation-to-obey are formidably impressive, has written as follows:

> Let us initially grant the (implausible) assumption that in every case of disobedience of law an official will or might suffer disappointment. We would now have *a reason* for obeying the law in every instance. . . . [But] having *a reason* to obey is not always enough to create a prima-facie obligation. Although every murder may help alleviate the overpopulation problem, we do not have a prima-facie obligation to commit murder, nor do we have such an obligation to give robbers money though our submission will please them. To generalize, we do not have a prima-facie obligation to do things that are independently wrong or are wrongly demanded of us.[9]

Though a victim of the robbers may have a prudential reason to please them by giving them his money (in order to save his life), and though a murderer might be said to have a tenuous prudential reason for alleviating the overpopulation problem through his brutal methods, those reasons—which are centered on the victim's and murderer's own interests—obviously do not amount to prima-facie moral obligations. Does either the robbers' victim or the murderer have a moral reason for behaving as he does? Only such a reason can amount to a moral obligation. A genuine moral reason, as has been stated above, resides either in the requirements of a sound moral mandate or in the beckoning of a sound ethical ideal. Do the actions of the robbers' victim or the murderer fall within the scope of any such mandate or any such ideal?

Before attending to Greenawalt's own terse remarks on his examples, we should passingly contemplate a possibility that is overlooked in those remarks. Suppose that the robbers' victim wants to stay alive not solely out of concern for himself but also out of concern for his dependents and for the community which he serves in various capacities. In that event, he is indeed acting upon moral reasons when he seeks to please the robbers by handing over his money. At least with regard to the dependents and perhaps also with regard to the community, he probably has a moral obligation to take all sensible steps that will help to ensure his survival. That obligation is owed to the dependents (and perhaps also to the community) rather than to the robbers, of course; but it is indeed a moral obligation, which may well be fulfilled by his submission to the robbers.

Leaving aside the point outlined in the last paragraph, we should turn our attention back to Greenawalt's fleeting comments. Greenawalt believes that, because citizens' violations of flagitious legal norms cause officials to suffer disappointment (*ex hypothesi*), citizens have a reason to obey those norms. He likewise accepts that the alleviating of the overpopulation problem is a reason for the commission of murder and that the eliciting of pleasure in robbers is a reason for

---

[9] Kent Greenawalt, 'Comment', in Ruth Gavison, *Issues in Contemporary Legal Philosophy* (Oxford: Clarendon Press, 1987), 156, 165 (emphases in original). For a largely similar passage, see Kent Greenawalt, above, n. 7, at 102.

a victim to surrender money to them. Now, as was noted above, prudential reasons-for-action are irrelevant here; hence, Greenawalt must be presuming that the three reasons just mentioned are moral reasons. (Admittedly, his stance on this point is slightly murky. Immediately after the passage quoted above, he focuses specifically on moral reasons-for-action. That seeming shift of focus might be taken as an indication that the three reasons mentioned in the extract above are not perceived by him as moral. However, given that prudential reasons would be irrelevant, and given that the nonprudential objectives of alleviating the overpopulation problem and preventing the frustration of other people's hopes would be morally worthy objectives under ordinary circumstances, we can pertinently infer that Greenawalt sees his three reasons as moral reasons.) To be sure, Greenawalt insists that those three putative moral reasons do not constitute prima-facie obligations. None the less, he thinks or appears to think that there are indeed some genuine moral reasons for the murderer to perpetrate a slaying and for the citizens to abide by nefarious laws and for the robbers' victim to relinquish the money.[10]

We should reject Greenawalt's way of characterizing the situations in his briefly sketched examples. Instead of involving moral reasons-for-action that do not ground or constitute prima-facie obligations, those situations do not involve any genuine moral reasons—i.e., any morally worthy reasons—at all. Let us concentrate here on the examples of the obedient citizens and the robbers' victim, which bear directly on the topic of this chapter. On moral grounds (rather than on strictly analytical grounds), we should reject the thesis that the opportunity to avert disappointment for officials is a moral reason-for-action when the officials are running a heinous regime; and we should take much the same view about the opportunity to please the robbers. This point becomes forcefully apparent when we contemplate an example even more vivid than those which Greenawalt discusses. Think of a Nazi concentration camp or death camp where the guards repeatedly stomp on the head of each baby to whom any Jewish woman in the camp has given birth. Some or all of the guards undoubtedly derive keen sadistic and racist pleasure from crushing the soft skulls of the babies. Does the opportunity to provide the guards with this pleasure constitute a moral reason for a Jewish mother to decline

---

[10] Of course, the victim of robbers might somehow think that the opportunity to please them is indeed a moral reason for action. He might even act in accordance with that perceived reason. If so, then we can say that he has acted for a moral (i.e., nonprudential) reason, albeit a woefully misguided moral reason. We are then using the phrase 'moral reason' to mean 'nonprudential consideration that has been given weight by someone in determining what he should do'. Such a definition is appropriate when one's sole or chief objective is to explain why somebody has behaved in a certain fashion. In the present chapter, however, the focus is moral rather than explanatory. We are concerned not with perceived moral reasons but with genuine moral reasons—that is, not with the nonprudential considerations to which people *do* give weight but with the nonprudential considerations to which they *should* give weight. My references to moral reasons thus construe 'moral' in opposition to 'unworthy' and not merely in opposition to 'prudential'. From the perspective of this chapter, then, the opportunity to please the robbers is not a genuine moral reason at all, in any ordinary circumstances. (*Mutatis mutandis*, everything in this note is just as straightforwardly applicable to Greenawalt's other scenarios as to the situation of the robbers' victim.)

to conceal her newborn child? An extreme version of utilitarianism, which refuses to draw any distinctions whatsoever between legitimate and illegitimate pleasures, would answer this question affirmatively. Such an answer is not flatly unintelligible, to be sure, but it is grossly iniquitous (even though the proponents of the extreme utilitarian stance would of course hasten to maintain that the moral reason described in the question is greatly outweighed by the moral reasons in favor of concealing the child). Precisely because the affirmative answer flows from an extreme utilitarian doctrine, we are very well advised to forswear that doctrine. When a Jewish mother's concealment of her baby prevents the German guards from experiencing the sadistic glee which they would have undergone if they had felt the baby's brains splattering under their boots, that aspect of her conduct is a point in its favor rather than something that counts against it. Since the guards' pleasure is rebarbatively illegitimate, we should see that the thwarting of it is morally superior to the indulgence of it—even if we temporarily exclude the suffering of the baby and the mother from a direct place in our moral calculations.

What has been said here about the foiling of the German guards' evil mirth is likewise applicable, albeit perhaps less dramatically, to the disappointment of wicked officials over citizens' disobedience and to the displeasure of robbers at the unsubmissiveness of a victim. Given that the demands of wicked officials for citizens' compliance with appalling laws are utterly illegitimate, the officials' disappointment at the flouting of those demands is salutary rather than undesirable—even if our moral calculations leave out all the other effects of the disobedience. In the absence of very unusual circumstances, much the same can be said about the frustration of the robbers' hopes for their victim's ready capitulation to their snarling dictates. Those hopes are thoroughly illegitimate, and thus the dashing of them is not something that detracts from the moral status of a victim's resistance. Hence, at least until Greenawalt's scenarios relating to the officials' disappointment and the robbers' unhappiness are significantly embellished, there are no moral reasons for submission (to heinous laws or to the robbers' orders) in either of them. Submission is not required by any sound moral precept and is not rendered especially laudable or virtuous by any sound moral ideal, in the absence of factors like those discussed three paragraphs ago. Consequently, in the absence of those factors, there are no moral reasons for the submission. Compliance with wicked laws may not even be morally permissible; compliance with robbers' behests is doubtless morally permissible but is neither morally mandatory nor especially praiseworthy. In short, Greenawalt errs when he suggests that his situations involve moral reasons without prima-facie obligations. It is indeed true that no prima-facie obligations are operative therein, but it is also true that no genuine moral reasons at all are present.

## 2. Out of Harm's Way

Efforts to demonstrate the existence of the obligation-to-obey—that is, efforts to demonstrate the existence of a prima-facie moral obligation to obey every authorized mandate in any viable legal regime—have run aground on two broad types of disobedience that cannot be deprived of legitimacy by those efforts. We shall later take up the issues surrounding noncompliance with repulsive legal norms; for the present, we shall investigate instead the issues surrounding harmless violations of good laws. Occasions for thoroughly harmless disobedience can and do arise within benevolent legal regimes, albeit less frequently than within legal systems that are much more oppressive. Throughout this discussion of harmless infractions, then, we can confine our attention to societies with benignly liberal-democratic schemes of governance. Even in each of those societies, where everyone benefits from the scheme of governance and where no monstrous laws obtain, there are numerous settings in which the nonfulfillment of legal requirements is completely innocuous and therefore unalloyedly legitimate.

This discussion, like the whole of this chapter, is seeking to counter one notably influential line of argument that might appear to establish the existence of the obligation-to-obey. As has already been observed, that line of argument consists of two cardinal premises: a premise recounting the benefits bestowed by law in enabling the continuation and flourishing of human society, and a premise asserting a principle of fairness that requires an equal sharing of burdens where no relevant differences among people exist. Now, given that the present discussion deals only with benign legal systems and has thus abstracted itself from the difficulties posed by evil regimes, the first of the foregoing two premises implies that acts which endanger the effective functioning of law are prima facie wrong. It implies, in other words, that each person has a prima-facie duty to abstain from engaging in such acts. The second premise helps to determine which acts of lawbreaking should count as unacceptable. We should ponder the drift of that second premise, before we proceed any further.[11]

### (a) *Fairness as the Sharing of Burdens*

Under the terms of the second premise in the argument for the obligation-to-obey, the consequences of each violation of the law are not to be judged in isolation; rather, each such violation should be regarded as a course of conduct in which everyone might engage, and its consequences should be judged accordingly. That is, when trying to ascertain whether a particular breach of a legal norm is likely to impair significantly the effective functioning of law, we have to ask not only about the consequences of that lone breach but also about the consequences of the commission of comparable breaches by all the people whose conduct is subject

---

[11] Virtually all of the sources that are cited in n. 7 above discuss the principle of fairness, many of them at length. For a piquant but sometimes error-marred early discussion, see C. D. Broad, 'On the Function of False Hypotheses in Ethics', 26 *International Journal of Ethics* 377, 387–92 (1916). For the two laconic essays that have inspired much of the recent literature on the principle of fairness, see H. L. A. Hart, 'Are There Any Natural Rights?', 64 *Philosophical Review* 175, 185 (1955); and John Rawls, 'Legal Obligation and the Duty of Fair Play', in Hook, *Law*, above, n. 7, at 3.

to the sway of the norm. 'What if everyone behaved in this way' is the relevant inquiry when we gauge the acceptability of an act of law-breaking. An inquiry of that sort is appropriate because it reflects the basic equality of the individuals who live under the governance of a legal regime. It ensures that everyone alike is morally required to bear the burden of complying with legal directives—directives which cumulatively provide enormous benefits (security and co-ordination) for everyone.

The fulfillment of legal mandates is often burdensome for the people to whom the mandates are addressed, but is also essential for the viability of any legal system. Unless there is a high degree of conformity with those mandates, a legal regime cannot function as such. However, a high degree of conformity need not amount to a complete absence of violations; indeed, it can sometimes fall quite far short of perfect conformity, so long as the violations do not become so numerous and conspicuous that they lead to a major breakdown of public order. In regard to legal requirements, then, there are many opportunities for free-riding by people who are clever enough to avoid being penalized for their deviations from those requirements. Such people will be able to enjoy the benefits of law—the orderliness and co-ordination which law promotes—without bearing their full shares of the burden of upholding legal norms through compliance therewith. In relation to any legal norms with which some people must conform if a legal system is to be sustainable, the free-riders will be taking advantage of the compliers' law-abidingness. Hence, if we were to contend that the free-riding is morally legitimate because it does not imperil the continuation of a legal regime, we would in effect be maintaining that the exploitation of some people by others is morally legitimate. That is, we would be allowing that a situation of equally shared benefits and unequally shared burdens is permissible simply because some people are inclined to break the law and are sufficiently shrewd to escape punishment. Since neither an inclination to violate legal norms nor a punishment-eluding shrewdness is in itself a morally exonerative factor, the differences among people in those respects do not warrant the disparities among them in their taking up of the burden of law-abidingness. Given that that burden has to be borne by some people if a minimally decent life is to be secured for everyone, and given that there are no morally significant differences among sane adults in their general capacities for bearing that burden, it should be borne by everyone of adequate mental competence.

Myriad scenarios can be constructed in which the principle of fairness is highly appealing to one's moral sense. We should briefly consider one such scenario before we explore some of the complications and presuppositions of that principle. Suppose that, in a town with no municipal garbage-collection service, nearly all of the families in a neighborhood agree to split the cost of hiring a private firm to pick up the garbage once a week from their street. From only one family does there come a staunch refusal to cooperate in paying for the service. Yet, despite having declined to bear any part of the expense of the garbage collection, the head of that family puts out several garbage bags each week for removal. Let us suppose that those bags do not add to the cost borne by the other families in the neighborhood; the trash-removal company charges one fee for the whole street, irrespective of the number of bags that are put out by the various households. None the less, in these circumstances, the co-operative families will be on a very solid footing if they complain about the unfairness of the maverick family's behavior.

Note that the unfairness does not consist in the sheer fact that the uncompliant family have refused to pay a share of the total fee and have thus declined to lighten the per-household cost for everyone else on the street. Although such a refusal might well be deemed unneighborly or unobliging, it would not be open to attack as unfair if it were not combined with the family's taking advantage of the very scheme to which the refusal of assistance pertains. Conversely, the sheer fact that the head of the uncooperative family puts the trash bags out each week is not in itself detrimental at all to any of the other families, since it does not increase the cost of the trash-collection arrangement. It is the unobliging family's failure to pay, rather than their availing themselves of the rubbish-removal service, which makes the price of that service higher for each of the cooperative families than it otherwise would be. In sum, neither the maverick family's unwillingness to make any payment nor their use of the rubbish-removal scheme is on its own an instance of unfairness; but those two things together are indeed such an instance. The unfairness consists precisely in the conjunction of an equal sharing of benefits and a markedly unequal sharing of burdens.

In one respect, the foregoing scenario may suggest that the scope of the principle of fairness is more straitened than it in fact is. In that scenario, the head of the uncooperative family chooses to take advantage of the garbage-collection service by putting the bags out for removal. He could have abstained from making use of the service—in which case his overall conduct would not have been unfair. In many other ordinary situations, however, the option of abstaining from the enjoyment of various benefits will not be present. Suppose, for example, that the families of the neighborhood had arranged for a street-cleaning service rather than for a trash-collection scheme. Situations of this sort have been highlighted in a famous discussion by Robert Nozick,[12] who has led some commentators to think that the principle of fairness applies only when the option of forgoing a certain benefit is realistically available. The reasoning is that, unless the aforementioned option can indeed be chosen, there will be a danger of obligating people to meet the costs of 'benefits' which they would prefer to do without; to safeguard their autonomy, the reach of the principle of fairness must be cabined. Now, if that principle were indeed so limited, its implications would not have much bearing on the general topic of this chapter. After all, the foremost desiderata brought about by law (viz.,

---

[12] Robert Nozick, *Anarchy, State, and Utopia* (New York: Basic Books, 1974), 90–5. My own discussion of this matter is quite close to that in Chaim Gans, above, n. 7, at 57–66.

societal orderliness and co-ordination) are presented to each person irrespective of his or her choice in the matter. Why should anyone be morally required to shoulder the burden of sustaining a state of affairs which confronts him or her as a *fait accompli*?

Fortunately for the champions of the principle of fairness, Nozick's position does little or no damage to that principle in the present context. All of his examples of unwanted benefits—i.e., involuntarily received benefits that are valued less than whatever must be given up in return for them—involve goods (such as clean streets and public entertainment) which people might reasonably opt to eschew. Someone could get along perfectly well without those goods. Consequently, we cannot safely presume that every individual will perceive or should perceive those goods as worth the costs of helping to give rise to them. Thus, any fairness-oriented demands for individuals willy-nilly to bear those costs can be highly inimical to the ideal of autonomy; such demands can seriously encroach on the domain of individual self-determination. No comparable worry arises in connection with the chief desiderata engendered by the workings of a legal system. The basic orderliness and co-ordination which hold together a society are preconditions for the tolerably decent interaction of large numbers of people over long periods of time. No minimally sensible person could wish to live alongside numerous other people in the absence of those conditions *tout court* (even though the concrete forms which the conditions should take are matters of intense controversy). Hence, the fact that law's fundamental benefits cannot realistically be forgone is of little significance. Nobody would want to forgo those benefits altogether, in any event. Accordingly, nobody's autonomy is jeopardized by having to accept them. (Of course, nothing in this paragraph should be taken to imply that the security and co-ordination provided by law will automatically confer moral obligatoriness or even moral legitimacy on any particular legal regime or legal norms. As is emphasized by my current chapter and by the discussion of this topic in my seventh chapter, the moral indispensability of law-in-the-abstract will hardly serve to guarantee the moral obligatoriness or legitimacy of any specific set of legal norms.)

We should note another important respect in which the principle of fairness is more far-reaching than it may at first appear. That principle can be operative under evil legal regimes as well as under benevolent regimes. Though its applicability is more obvious and more common under benign schemes of legal governance, it extends also to many situations where the institutions and programs of legal governance are much more malevolent. Chapter 7's scenario of the establishment of a protection racket illustrates this point. In the circumstances described there, each victim of the racket has a moral duty to submit to it in order to ward off even worse modes of mistreatment. That duty is owed by each victim not to any of the racketeers—who certainly have no moral right to the submission of the people whom they exploit—but to each of the other victims. Each person is obligated, under the unhappy circumstances, to bear his share of the burden of preserving a dismal state of affairs that benefits people by averting the calamitous consequences which would ensue from the termination of that state of affairs. The principle of fairness is pertinent because the miserable circumstances of the protection racket's victims involve the following elements: a benefit shared equally by all the people (i.e., the meager benefit of avoiding even worse oppression by other thugs), a burden that must be borne by a substantial number of the people if the benefit is to be attained, and the roughly equal ability of each person to bear the share of the burden which the racketeers have assigned to him or her via their behests. Given these facets of the situation, the principle of fairness obligates everyone to comply with the racketeers' dictates. The wickedness of those dictates is not determinative, in the specific circumstances outlined. Recall, once again, that the obligation of fair play is owed by each victim to every other victim and not to any of the racketeers.

As we have seen, then, the principle of fairness ranges more widely than has sometimes been presumed. Nevertheless, it is scarcely free of difficulties. Although its applicability will be granted *arguendo* throughout my analyses in the subsequent portions of this chapter, we should here glance at a few of its problematic aspects.[13] First, as should be plain from the exposition so far, an invocation of the principle of fairness in regard to the obligation-to-obey presupposes that the burden of fulfilling that obligation is roughly the same for everyone. If that burden is in fact much greater for some people than for others, then a pattern of invariable conformity by everyone with legal norms will not amount to an equal sharing of burdens in return for law's benefits. Consequently, the principle of fairness in such circumstances will not call for a pattern of invariable law-abidingness.

Now, throughout my current investigation of harmless disobedience, we are assuming away the problems posed by wicked legal systems. Hence, we need not concern ourselves here with some of the most distasteful ways in which the posture of constant law-abidingness can be disparately burdensome for various people. One of the virtues of a benevolent legal regime is that it does not (deliberately) impose any undeserved legal restrictions or exactions on some groups of people that are far more onerous than the corresponding legal requirements imposed on other groups. None the less, even though we have temporarily put aside the problem of invidious discrimination under evil systems of law, we have no solid reason for thinking that everyone can discharge the obligation-to-obey with roughly the same degree of ease or difficulty as everyone else. In the benevolent legal system of England, for example, people are held to an ordinary standard of reasonable care when they engage in sundry modes of conduct. For dim-witted people, such a standard is extremely burdensome in many settings and is sometimes altogether beyond their capabilities; none the less, in most

---

[13] For a particularly deft examination of some of these problems—and also a fine examination of the principle of fair play under conditions of injustice—see Kent Greenawalt, above, n. 7, at ch. 7.

circumstances, they are legally obligated to live up to that standard. In that respect, the burden of complying with the obligation-to-obey is much more oner-ous for unintelligent people than for intelligent people. Moreover, it is highly likely that there are many other inequalities among people's capacities for shoul-dering the burden of fulfilling the obligation-to-obey, and that those inequalities do not simply offset one another. In sum, we can confidently surmise that that burden lies much more heavily on some types of people than on others, even in societies with liberal-democratic schemes of governance.

Less worrisome, though not entirely unproblematic, is the fact that the bene-fits of law's existence are also unevenly shared. A person of enormous wealth will stand to gain more from the security-providing function of law than will someone with a modest income. All the same, this difficulty is perhaps less damaging to the principle of fairness than is the problem of unequally shared burdens. After all, even if some people fare considerably better than others in their possessions or attainments, the desiderata of orderliness and co-ordination which law engen-ders are immensely valuable to everyone—at least in societies with no ruthlessly downtrodden members. The difference between the well-being of an affluent landowner and the well-being of a laborer $L$ in a securely and benignly law-governed society is typically much less gaping than the difference between the well-being of $L$ in such a society and the well-being of $L$ in conditions of anar-chic chaos. Thus, although the principle of fairness does not emerge wholly unscathed from the problem of disparately accrued benefits, it may be less gravely weakened by that problem than by people's uneven sharing of the burden of law-abidingness.

Another aspect of the principle of fairness is not reproachable in itself but is important in weakening or defusing the implications of that principle within the context of my overall discussion. Plainly, the principle of fairness is political through and through. Specifically, it is egalitarian. It presupposes that equality among people is a state of affairs in no need of justification, and that any depar-tures from equality must be justified. The view underlying the principle of fair-ness is that, unless there are specifiably significant differences among people, a situation of equality should obtain; at least in the first instance, a heavy burden of proof lies on anyone who invokes such differences rather than on anyone who presumes them to be absent. Now, although this egalitarian bias may be attractive, it remains a thoroughly political slant. Yet, since the principle which consists in that slant is an integral element of the argument which tries to derive the obliga-tion-to-obey from the basic functions of law, that argument is itself suffused with egalitarianism. It arrives at a verdict of prima-facie moral obligatoriness not on the basis of a premise about the fundamental role of law, but on the basis of that premise in combination with a premise espousing the ideal of equality. Hence, even if that argument could somehow succeed *on its own terms* in establishing the comprehensively applicable and universally borne obligation-to-obey, it would not pose any peril to legal positivism's insistence on the disjoinability of law and morality—because the argument's own terms can be rejected in favor of an inegalitarian slant that will not support the inference concerning the obligation-to-obey. In other words, even if the egalitarian argument could validly yield its conclusion, it would do so not by adverting solely to law's cardinal functions but by adverting to those functions *and also to the value of equality*. Insufficient for generating the conclusion about the obligation-to-obey, even when we treat the egalitarian argument with extravagant generosity, is the premise of that argument which affirms merely that the existence of law amounts to a precondition for the existence of any decent societal arrangements. Thus, given that legal positivists want simply to deny that law's role as a *sine qua non* of decent societal interaction is sufficient to ground the comprehensive obligation-to-obey, they have nothing to fear from any arguments in favor of that obligation which rely indispensably on the principle of fairness.

The preceding paragraph seeks to blunt the force of the principle of fairness as a weapon to be wielded against legal positivism, but does not impugn that principle in its own right. What is indeed troubling for that principle in its own right is its failure to bear persuasively on certain situations to which it might appear relevant. Let us contemplate first a brief example,[14] then a response that might be made by the defenders of the principle of fair play, and finally a modified version of the example which parries that response. Suppose that everyone in the United Kingdom decides to visit Cambridge tomorrow. In that event, there will ensue a disastrous situation of transportational congestion, unbearable and uncontrollable crowding of people, grotesque overburdening of essential services in the region of Cambridge, and general chaos. In short, if everybody in the United Kingdom tried to visit Cambridge tomorrow, catastrophic consequences would follow. It would seem, then, that any actual attempt by anyone to visit Cambridge on some particular day will be rendered morally dubious by the principle of fairness. After all, that principle indicates that our moral assessments of any mode or instance of conduct should proceed by inquiring what would happen if everyone engaged in such conduct. Since a dreadful breakdown of public order would result if everybody sought to visit Cambridge on a given day, the principle of fairness appears to disallow any such visit by anyone on any day. All the same, nobody except a fool believes that a visit to Cambridge by this or that person on some particular day is morally impermissible in any ordinary circumstances. We might thus conclude that the principle of fairness leads to absurd verdicts in many contexts, and we might therefore well ask whether the incorporation of that principle into an argument for the obligation-to-obey should cause us to doubt the soundness of that argument. (To be sure, as my earlier example of the garbage-removal scheme has shown, the principle of fairness leads to appropriate verdicts in many

---

[14] A broadly similar example is tersely presented in J. W. Harris, above, n. 7, at 232. See also Raz, *Authority*, above, n. 7, at 240. To a certain extent, my first example also resembles some of the arguments that are probed in C. D. Broad, above, n. 11.

contexts. Hence, even before we consider a possible riposte to the current paragraph's critique, we should not presume that the scenario involving visitors to
Cambridge will have warranted an outright rejection of the principle of fairness.
We have grounds for querying the extent of that principle's pertinence in numerous settings, but we should hardly gainsay its pertinence altogether.)

A defender of the principle of fair play will probably retort by pointing out that
the millions of British citizens who do not visit Cambridge tomorrow are not
bearing any real burden by declining to go there. Exquisitely beautiful though
Cambridge is, a visit to it or to any other specific city is not something which
most people wish to do every day. The vast majority of people in the United
Kingdom do not contemplate, and certainly do not attempt, a journey to
Cambridge on any particular day. Having to abstain from *ever* traveling to
Cambridge might be burdensome for many British people, but abstaining from
traveling there on this or that specific date is something to which most people do
not give the slightest thought; the absence of such traveling by them on a given
date is not even slightly onerous in their eyes and indeed is not worthy of their
attention at all, because they have concentrated their minds on countless other
things which they wish to do or need to do. By contrast, compliance with the
requirements of various legal norms is often quite onerous for most people.
Although some legal mandates may not be very burdensome, obedience to other
such mandates is a course of conduct that involves forbearance and self-denial.
Much the same is true of other situations to which the principle of fairness
applies. In the neighborhood with the trash-collection arrangement, for example,
each household's proper participation in the arrangement involves a willingness
to come up with the payment that is due. Because this element of forbearance or
self-denial (i.e., the felt bearing of a burden) is missing from the scenario of visitors to Cambridge, the inapplicability of the principle of fairness thereto is
scarcely surprising. In circumstances where that missing element is in fact
present—for instance, in circumstances relating to the demands of legal directives—the principle of fairness will be a fully suitable standard of conduct. In
short, the defenders of that principle can readily acknowledge that its focus on the
sharing of benefits and burdens will be pertinent only in contexts where burdens
are to be borne; they will simply add that any contexts marked by the operativeness of legal requirements are contexts where people do indeed bear burdens in
respect of those requirements.

There are at least two ways of deflecting the foregoing paragraph's rejoinder.
First, we can aptly question whether obedience to legal directives is always
burdensome. (Insofar as such obedience is not at all burdensome, the principle of
fair play—with its call for a correspondence between shared benefits and shared
burdens—will be beside the point. That principle will no more yield the constant
prima-facie moral obligation-to-obey than it will impose on each British person a
prima-facie moral duty to stay away from Cambridge.) Consider, for example, a
society in which homosexual intercourse is legally proscribed. If most people

view such intercourse as filthy and repellent, then they will scarcely undergo any sense of self-denial as they obey the anti-homosexuality statute. Their compliance with that prohibition is utterly effortless. There are very likely a number of mandates in virtually any legal system with which most people's compliance is comparably unburdensome, and there are almost certainly a myriad of mandates in any legal system that can each be fulfilled by *some* people with no sense of self-denial. In regard to every such legal directive, the principle of fair play cannot contribute to generating a prima-facie moral obligation of obedience that is borne by everybody.

Second, by pondering a modified version of the scenario of the visitors to Cambridge, we can behold certain inadequacies in the principle of fairness even with regard to a situation where the forgoing of something is indeed a burden. Suppose that a rural dweller moves to a distant city where he can earn much higher wages than would be on offer in the countryside. The highness of the wages is due in part to the inability of many other rural people to move to the city, where their relocated presence would expand the pool of laborers and would thereby drive down the wage rate. Those people would very much like to move to the city, but, for one reason or another, each of them is unable to do so. (Perhaps some of them are unable to amass the resources needed to cover the initial high costs of relocating themselves, just like many poor Europeans in the nineteenth century who were unable to realize their dreams of migrating to the United States. Perhaps some of the other rural dwellers have to look after relatives who are unwilling or too sickly to move along with them. Perhaps still others feel that they would be unable to acquire the skills necessary for urban work, even though they would dearly love to escape the poverty and stagnancy of rural life. And so forth.)

Now, there are three aspects of this new scenario that together might seem to trigger the principle of fairness. First, the person who moves to the distant city is plainly benefiting from the fact that most of his contemporaries in the countryside do not join him. Second, their remaining behind in the rural areas is burdensome for them. Third, if all the people from those rural areas relocated themselves to the city, then dire consequences would follow; important agricultural work would no longer get done, and the facilities of the city would be lethally overwhelmed. Both the fabric of rural life and the fabric of urban life in the region would fall apart. In light of these facets of the situation, the principle of fairness would apparently render illegitimate the move by the rural dweller to the city. Any such verdict, however, is outlandish. There is nothing morally dubious about his decision to migrate, at least in the absence of any complicating factors (such as left-behind dependents) of which we have not been told. Once again, then, the principle of fairness proves to have no purchase on a set of circumstances to which it should apply. Its status as a weighty moral principle is quite sporadic.

Let us conclude this subsection by glancing at one additional complication in the principle of fairness that will lead us back to the discussion of harmless violations of good laws. If that principle is to determine people's duties, then the following condition must obtain: the people involved are aware, or have good grounds for being aware, of the need for them to take on certain burdens in order to contribute to the production of certain benefits. We can see this point in connection with the garbage-removal scheme, for example. Suppose that a new family arrive in the neighborhood, and that they reasonably presume that the trash-collection service is funded by the town or county government through local taxes. As a result of an oversight or an instance of confusion, none of the other residents on the street apprises the new family of the actual arrangements under which the payments are made by the neighborhood's households periodically. Hence, until the new family move to a different region several years later, they avail themselves freely of a service for which the other families on the street are paying. They never become aware of their inadvertent free-riding, and—because of the remissness of the other families—they have never had any good grounds for becoming aware. In these circumstances, the members of the free-riding household cannot appositely be said to have acted unfairly. They have not deliberately taken advantage of anyone else, and the fact that they have unwittingly taken such advantage is not due to any culpable obtuseness or perverseness on their part. Far from being a product of negligence or intentional wrongdoing, their misconceptions are understandable and excusable. To be sure, even after the family have left the neighborhood, they should probably make some back-payments if they do become aware of the actual source of funding for the rubbish-removal scheme; but, so long as they remain ignorant of the situation through no fault of their own, their innocent free-riding does not run afoul of the principle of fair play.

Thus, even if we leave aside all the other difficulties, the aforementioned principle will not endow legal mandates with any morally obligatory force unless people are aware or should be aware of the requirements imposed by those mandates. Of course, with regard to many legal directives, including all of the fundamental prohibitions that must figure in any system of law, people are at fault if they fail to recognize that they are legally and morally called upon to act in the ways laid down by those directives. With regard to many other legal norms, however, the situation is not nearly as clear-cut. Especially in an advanced legal regime, where hosts of arcane regulations and statutes set forth requirements in great detail concerning virtually all aspects of human existence, most people are probably unfamiliar quite innocently with a number of their legal duties. Anybody who might try to keep himself informed of all of those duties would have very little time to do anything else; hence, if we claimed that every instance of unfamiliarity with some of those duties is unreasonable, we would ourselves be guilty of absurdly unreasonable expectations. Though people governed by benevolent regimes can quite properly be judged in courts of law by reference to their legal obligations, they are not morally bound to saddle themselves with the dreary task of attempting to keep abreast of all the esoteric intricacies of those obligations. And so the principle of fairness, which does not generate moral obligations when people are innocently unacquainted with requirements that lie upon them, cannot place on everybody a comprehensively applicable prima-facie moral obligation to comply with legal directives.

## (b) *No Harm in That*

The principle of fairness is only one of the key premises in the overall argument which is under scrutiny here. Additionally present, of course, is the premise summarizing the benefits of law's basic functions—benefits which accrue to everyone, in any decent society. The principle of fairness tells us that the burdens incurred in achieving those benefits are to be shared equally. We may grant as much *arguendo*, and we may also grant *arguendo* that everyone can abide by legal mandates with roughly the same degree of ease or difficulty as everyone else. We may therefore grant *arguendo* that the principle of fairness and the premise concerning law's beneficial functions together indicate that everybody should obey legal directives as far as is necessary for the continuation and vibrancy of law's salutary operations. Even when all these prodigiously generous concessions are made for the sake of argument, however, we need not and should not concede that there is a prima-facie moral obligation of obedience in respect of every norm within a benign regime of law. After all, even with the aid of the foregoing concessions, the argument under challenge here has produced only the conclusion that obedience is morally obligatory (prima facie) as far as is necessary for the smooth functioning of the law. Such a conclusion leaves open the possibility of entirely harmless disobedience—disobedience that poses not the slightest threat to the law's performance of its essential roles or to any other legitimate interests. Insofar as the nonfulfillment of certain legal norms by people in particular contexts is indeed thoroughly harmless, there is not even a prima-facie moral obligation for people to abide by those norms in such contexts.

In most American towns and cities, there are ordinances or by-laws against jaywalking. Those legal norms are typically framed in quite sweeping terms, with no provisions for permissible jaywalking in specified circumstances. Such norms therefore legally obligate citizens to abstain from jaywalking unconditionally. Now, suppose that a rather small and dull American town contains numerous sleepy streets on which there is almost no traffic throughout the day. (Any resemblance to my own home town is hardly coincidental.) Barely any cars go along those streets, and the few cars that do go along are invariably driven very slowly. Largely because of the virtual absence of traffic, none of those streets has any crosswalks. As a result, anyone who lives on one of those streets and who might wish to comply with the town's anti-jaywalking law must trudge quite a distance— perhaps a loop nearly two miles long—in order to get to the house of a neighbor who lives just across the street. Fortunately, even in a fairly small American town, scarcely anyone is so daft as to walk two miles rather than six or seven meters in order to reach a neighbor's house. Jaywalking on any of the town's sleepy streets is commonplace, a wholly taken-for-granted fact of everyday life.

Not only is the jaywalking a routine part of life on such streets, but, in addition, it is utterly harmless. Indeed, it is highly valuable, since it spares people from pointlessly expending their time on ludicrously circuitous journeys. When somebody crosses one of those quiescent streets in order to visit a neighbor, she does not endanger herself in any way, and she does not endanger or harm anyone else. Nor does she set a bad example—to herself or to anyone else—by breaking the law. In fact, were she to comply with the anti-jaywalking ordinance by setting out on a two-mile-long loop whenever she might want to say hello to her neighbor, she would be viewed not as an admirably upstanding citizen but as a fool. Such ridiculous adherence to legal norms could tend to bring the more general posture of law-abidingness into disrepute. Hence, far from tending to promote disrespect for the law when she violates the terms of the anti-jaywalking mandate, she is probably averting the emergence of such disrespect. At worst, her jaywalking will have no effect whatsoever on the likelihood that people will depart from the requirements of legal norms in ways that are not completely harmless. (We may assume that she and the other people on the largely untraveled streets indulge in jaywalking much less frequently when they are strolling along the town's busier streets, each of which includes several crosswalks. To these people, the distinction between jaywalking on those relatively busy streets and jaywalking on their own quiet streets is obvious. Their sensible inclination to engage in the latter practice does not lead them in any way to be foolhardy or slapdash about engaging in the former practice. Even the inhabitants of a humdrum American town are not led astray quite so easily.)

In sum, the abundant infractions of the anti-jaywalking law by the residents on the sleepy streets are devoid of any harmful effects. No one is endangered by those infractions, and no one is even slightly hurt by them. Indeed, as has been noted, the infractions valuably avert the wasting of considerable amounts of time on roundabout journeys. Moreover, they do not increase the probability that illegal acts will be undertaken in circumstances where the absence of harmfulness is far less clear. In fact, as has been observed, they may well decrease that probability by preventing the general stance or quality of law-abidingness from being brought into derision. In all these respects, the residents' disobedience is harmless. There are no moral reasons, either obligatory or supererogatory, that would militate against the disobedience at all.

At the same time, the anti-jaywalking ordinance is a commendable law that is both well-intentioned and usually beneficial (if it is neither too strictly nor too laxly enforced). Nobody could plausibly suggest that it is a wicked enactment or even that it is an undesirable enactment. We have therefore found that, in connection with an unobjectionable norm laid down by a benevolent legal regime, there is quite frequently no prima-facie moral obligation of obedience. Without having yet reached the problems posed by evil regimes, we can see that a premise adverting to the salutariness of law's fundamental functions and a premise adverting to the principle of fair play will not be sufficient to enable us to conclude validly that the obligation-to-obey does indeed obtain. We discover instead that some legal norms in some situations engender no prima-facie moral obligatoriness.

### (c) *Generality Versus Invariability*

The harmlessness of the infractions of the anti-jaywalking law on the quiet streets is paralleled by the harmlessness of violations of many other legal mandates in a variety of circumstances. Even within regimes of law that are morally worthy, there will arise numerous occasions on which no moral reasons whatsoever militate against people's transgressions of particular legal norms. Even within such regimes, then, there is clearly no obligation-to-obey. Some theorists have submitted, however, that the conception of the obligation-to-obey invoked here is too demanding and is therefore misleading.[15] While acknowledging that there will sometimes be no moral reasons for compliance with specific legal norms (even in a benign regime of law), these theorists have contended that there will *typically* be obligatory reasons for compliance with the legal mandates of a worthy regime. The fact that such reasons are typically present in a commendable legal system is enough to warrant our saying that a general prima-facie moral obligation of obedience to the law does there exist.

To a limited extent, the point of dispute here is a matter of terminological stipulation. If some theorists wish to use the phrase 'obligation-to-obey' or any similar wording to refer to a duty that is typically present rather than invariably present in a benign scheme of legal governance, then they are of course entitled to indulge their terminological preferences. For the most part, however, the points of contention here are substantive. They do not relate principally to the 'bottom line' (on which there are only a few nontrivial disagreements); they relate chiefly to the arguments through which that 'bottom line' should be reached.

Among the theorists who are my targets here, the most frequently propounded line of argument involves a claim about the unwelcome theoretical consequences that flow from one's denial of the existence of a general prima-facie moral obligation to obey the law (in a just regime). Supposedly, anyone who engages in such a denial will have logically committed himself to gainsaying also the existence of any general prima-facie moral obligation to keep promises or to forbear from the termination of human life. Let us consider this point first in connection with promise-keeping and then in connection with the ending of human life.

Insofar as the word 'general' in the first sentence of the preceding paragraph is taken to mean 'typical' or 'usually applicable' rather than 'comprehensively applicable' or 'invariable', the existence of the obligation mentioned in that

---

[15] An especially sophisticated expression of this view is in Chaim Gans, above, n. 7, at 74–8, 89–91. See also Chaim Gans, 'Comment', in Ruth Gavison (ed.), *Issues in Contemporary Legal Philosophy* (Oxford: Clarendon Press, 1987), 180, 185–9; Paul Harris, 'The Moral Obligation to Obey the Law', in Harris, *Political Obligation*, above, n. 7, at 151, 158–9, 174–5. For a less subtle version of this stance, see George Christie, 'On the Moral Obligation to Obey the Law', 1990 *Duke Law Journal* 1311, 1328–33 (1990).

sentence is perfectly compatible with everything said in this chapter. While maintaining that occasions for utterly harmless disobedience are quite common even in a society with a benevolent scheme of legal governance, we can and should allow that the legal norms of such a society do typically impose prima-facie moral obligations of obedience. Standardly, in such a society, there are binding moral reasons in favor of obedience to various legal mandates (even if those moral reasons are sometimes outweighed by conflicting considerations). Although there are numerous exceptions to that standard pattern, we should not feel any uneasiness about classifying them as exceptions. As will be argued later in this chapter, the distinction between what is standard and what is exceptional can affect crucially the assignment of the burden of proof for gauging the prima-facie moral obligatoriness of laws in a worthy regime.

Now, given that this chapter can happily endorse the notion of a general prima-facie moral obligation to obey the laws of a benign government, it can likewise happily endorse the notion of a comparable obligation to keep one's promises. Typically, the making of a promise will impose on the promisor at least a prima-facie moral duty to abide by its terms. Because of the role of promises as expressions of an agent's rational autonomy, and because of the valuableness of the institution of promising in social/economic/political life, there will usually be some binding moral reasons in favor of keeping various promises (even if those reasons are sometimes outweighed by contrary factors). None the less, there are numerous exceptions to this standard pattern, just as there are numerous exceptions to the standard pattern of prima-facie moral obligatoriness surrounding a benevolent government's laws. The breaking of some promises is thoroughly harmless—for example, when the fulfillment of an undertaking would damage the interests of both the promisor and the promisee and would serve no one else's interests—and the breaking of certain other promises is not only harmless but also morally obligatory, because of their evil substance. When the commanding officer in a German concentration camp promises a sadistic guard that the camp will select at least twenty children each day to be tortured and murdered by the guard, he has not placed himself under even a prima-facie moral duty to comply with his undertaking. Any expectations formed on the basis of such a promise are wholly illegitimate and are therefore devoid of moral weight.

Perhaps prima-facie moral prohibitions attach to all instances of some types of behavior that are fully specifiable in nonevaluative terms. For example, most forms of torture and homicide may always be prima facie wrong, even in the rare circumstances where they are justified on the whole. There may always be some binding moral reasons against such modes of conduct, notwithstanding that those reasons might be outweighed by more pressing concerns in highly unusual settings. With regard to the keeping of promises, by contrast, many situations can arise in which there are no moral reasons at all against departures from the terms of undertakings. The connections between the institution of promising and basic human interests are more tenuous than the connections between those interests and bans on murder or torture. Although any satisfactory long-term social inter-course requires promissory conventions of one sort or another, not everything that emerges from those conventions is promotive of human interests. The breaking of some promises will have not the slightest negative effect on human well-being, and the breaking of starkly evil promises will have only good effects. Hence, it is not the case that prima-facie moral prohibitions attach to all instances of promise-breaking. Though we should accept that there is a general prima-facie moral obligation to keep one's promises, the word 'general' has to be construed as it was above—to mean 'typical' or 'usually applicable' rather than 'invariable' or 'comprehensively applicable'. In other words, as has already been suggested, we should view the moral obligation of promise-keeping in much the same way that we view the moral obligation of obedience to the mandates of liberal-democratic legal regimes. In regard to each of those obligations, there is general applicabil-ity that falls well short of comprehensive applicability. Thus, the institution of promising and its attendant duties will not cast any doubt on the conclusions for which this chapter argues.

Equally untroubling, though somewhat more complicated, are theorists' invo-cations of the moral obligation to refrain from taking human life. In the first place, we might here follow the lead of my last two paragraphs in their handling of the obligation of promise-keeping. That is, we can conclude that there is indeed a general prima-facie moral duty to refrain from homicide, just as there is a general prima-facie moral duty to obey the legal mandates of worthy govern-ments. In the description of each such duty, the word 'general' once again carries the meaning specified above. For each of those duties, in other words, typical applicability does not amount to invariable applicability. Therefore, given that this chapter can comfortably accept the notion of a general prima-facie moral obligation to comply with the laws of commendable regimes, there is nothing whatever troublesome about the drawing of an analogy between that obligation and a similarly general (i.e., noncomprehensive) obligation of homicide-eschewal.

Furthermore, the arguments which invoke the obligation of homicide-eschewal are not only undamaging but also quite misleading. Perhaps unwit-tingly, those arguments trade on the fact that many people (not only devout Catholics) believe that taking a human life is *always* wrong. For someone who holds such a belief, any denial of the comprehensive applicability of the prima-facie duty to refrain from homicide will obviously be unacceptable and deeply distressing. Given that that underlying belief about human life is quite wide-spread, a denial of the comprehensiveness of the aforementioned duty will be jolt-ing for many people. Now, if we grant their underlying belief *arguendo*, we should naturally agree that there is a comprehensively applicable prima-facie duty to forbear from homicide. In that event, of course, the analogy between the prima-facie moral duty of law-abidingness (in benevolent regimes) and the prima-facie moral duty of homicide-eschewal is broken. Consequently, claims about the scope or nature of the latter duty cannot then warrantedly be advanced in support of claims about the scope or nature of the former duty. In other words, insofar as a belief about the moral value of all human life leads us to affirm the comprehensive applicability of the prima-facie moral obligation to refrain from homicide, we should avouch that the bearings and implications of that obligation are irrelevant to the topic of this chapter.

If by contrast we reject the premise asserting the moral value of *every* instance of human life—if, for example, we accept the unequivocal moral legitimacy of terminating the life of someone who is in incurably excruciating pain and who is desperate to die—then we shall also reject the notion of a comprehensively applicable prima-facie duty to forbear from homicide. Obviously, we shall not then be distressed by a rejection of that notion; and we shall have restored the broad analogy between the obligation of homicide-eschewal and the obligation of law-abidingness under a benign government. We shall have eliminated the distress and reinstated the analogy by embracing a fundamental premise (henceforth designated as '*P*') which maintains that there are sometimes no moral reasons against the taking of human life. That is, the underlying premise *P* which makes the obligation of homicide-eschewal relevant to the topic of this chapter is also what renders undisturbing the denial of that obligation's comprehensive applicability. Yet, as has already been noted, *P* is unacceptable to quite a few people. Those people therefore are highly upset by any denial of the comprehensive applicability of the prima-facie duty of homicide-eschewal. All or most of the theorists who advert to that duty when arguing for a general obligation of law-compliance are upholders of *P*, but, knowingly or unknowingly, they take advantage of the fact that *P* is quite widely abjured and that its implications are thus abhorrent to many people. Lurking in the background of those theorists' arguments, in other words, is the instinctive jolt felt by many people in the face of suggestions that the taking of human life can sometimes be unequivocally legitimate. Having embraced *P*, the theorists just mentioned do not experience that jolt, and are correct in analogizing the general obligation of homicide-avoidance and the general obligation of law-abidingness; but in effect they exploit the quite widespread aversion toward *P* in order to cast their opponents' position in an especially unappealing light. Since the opponents are (wrongly) said to be unable to acknowledge even a merely general duty of homicide-avoidance—inasmuch as the opponents perceive an analogy between the duty of homicide-avoidance and the duty of law-abidingness—their jurisprudential and political-philosophical stance must seem especially loathsome to people who view a merely general duty of homicide-avoidance as insufficient, in comparison with a comprehensive duty.

At any rate, the key point in the present discussion is that a *general* prima-facie moral obligation of law-abidingness under a benevolent government can indeed be recognized by this chapter and by any legal positivist. As has been stated, this chapter will later explicate that obligation by reference to the burden of proof for establishing the existence of prima-facie moral obligations of obedience in respect to particular legal norms; under any worthy regime, there will be a presumption (a rebuttable presumption, patently) in favor of the existence of a prima-facie moral obligation of obedience to each legal mandate. My ready acknowledgment of the general prima-facie moral duty of law-abidingness in relation to benign legal systems is perfectly consistent with the claim that the sheer status of a norm as a legal norm does not perforce confer on it any degree of prima-facie moral obligatoriness. After all, that claim is endorsed by the theorists against whom the present subsection of this chapter is directed. They contend simply that the status of a norm as a legal norm within a commendable legal system *typically* carries some prima-facie moral bindingness. Assertions about the *invariable* or *intrinsic* moral bindingness of legal requirements *qua* legal requirements have been explicitly abandoned by those theorists, even with regard to commendable legal systems. Accordingly, they are not saying anything at odds with the positions taken in this chapter.

## 3. The Problem of Wickedness

Any difficulties that undermine the obligation-to-obey for benevolent legal regimes will be multiplied and intensified when we turn our attention to wicked regimes. Not only will harmless disobedience of good laws continue to be possible frequently, but, in addition, the unalloyedly salutary violation of heinous legal mandates will have moved to the fore. Even if such mandates do not form an overwhelmingly large proportion of the entire set of laws in a particular scheme of governance, they change the whole moral balance of such a scheme. Instead of being characterized by a presumption in favor of obedience, the norms of a wicked legal system collectively generate a presumption tilting in the opposite direction—a presumption which each such norm must overcome if it is ever to be deemed to carry any prima-facie moral obligatoriness.

At the same time, we should recognize that there can arise situations wherein most of the legal dictates laid down by an evil government are accompanied by prima-facie moral obligations of obedience. As has already been suggested in this chapter and in Chapter 7, people will sometimes be morally obligated (prima facie) to comply with wicked behests in order to avert the emergence of an even worse state of affairs for their countrymen and themselves. (In such circumstances, of course, the obligation to obey the wicked demands is owed by each person to his fellows rather than to the malign officials who have imposed the demands.) Moreover, typically an evil legal system includes a number of mandates which in themselves are morally unobjectionable and indeed often morally obligatory. As Kent Greenawalt has observed:

In fact, after invasions or internal takeovers by autocratic regimes, the basic rules of criminal and civil law of previously democratic societies often do not change very much. The bulk of German criminal and civil law did not change radically under Hitler or during allied occupation, and the Communist countries of Eastern Europe still have criminal and civil codes that are not very different in their proscription of acts that threaten personal security from the codes that have long existed in civil law countries.[16]

People are of course subject to prima-facie obligations of obedience in connection with these sorts of mandates, notwithstanding that a presumption against the existence of those obligations must be overcome as everyone under the sway of a heinous government engages in the process of determining where his or her moral duty lies.

In short, we must consider both the matter of the burden of proof and the matter of focusing on an appropriate baseline-for-comparison. We must also take account of the fact that quite a few of the laws within many evil regimes (though not necessarily within all such regimes) are in themselves morally estimable. Before we ponder those factors, however, we should consider some potential variations among people in the shouldering of any prima-facie moral obligations of obedience that exist under nefarious schemes of governance.

### (a) *When Nothing is to Be Gained*

Recall again that the basic line of argument under attack throughout this chapter is composed of two chief premises: a premise maintaining that the orderliness and co-ordination promoted by law are superior (for everybody) to the chaotic turbulence that would prevail in the absence of law; and a premise asserting the principle of fairness. We have already explored some of the difficulties surrounding the second premise, and in particular we have looked briefly at the likelihood that that premise will fail to justify people's uniform shouldering of prima-facie moral duties of compliance with various legal norms. Even in respect of a benign system of law, the principle of fairness will probably yield variations among the degrees to which people fall under those duties of compliance. We shall now examine this same basic problem in connection with the first of the two chief premises. Insofar as that first premise does not accurately report the situation of some person or set of people within a particular legal regime, the argument containing that premise does not enable us to say that that person or set of people will be under any prima-facie moral duties to comply with the regime's directives. Indeed, given that the substantive conditions expressed in the two principal premises are individually necessary (as well as jointly sufficient, supposedly) for the existence of those prima-facie moral duties, the unsustainability of the first premise forces us to conclude that the specified person or people will *not* be under any such duties— at least in relation to directives whose contents are not independently in accordance with genuine moral requirements or ideals.

Let us first ponder, then, a situation in which all non-officials are worse off or no better off in circumstances of law-engendered orderliness and co-ordination than in circumstances of downright anarchy. Such situations are extremely rare— fortunately—but are by no means inconceivable. Indeed, they have occasionally

---

[16]   Kent Greenawalt, above, n. 7, at 130.

obtained. Suppose that in the days of Nazi Germany a large region is set aside for the extermination of Jews and other people whom the Nazis perceive as unfit to live. An elaborate governmental-administrative structure is erected for the purpose. Victims are brought to the chosen region, where each of them is either murdered almost immediately or kept alive for a while to perform excruciating tasks as a slave before being eventually murdered. Because the operations in the region-wide program of annihilation and brutal slavery are extensive, and because the logistics of those operations are complicated, the Nazi administrators and soldiers have to lay down numerous general mandates (while also issuing many situation-specific orders). With those numerous broadly focused directives, which instruct the victims and the soldiers themselves where to go and how to behave, the Nazis achieve the regularity and co-ordination that are essential for the carrying on of their massive program of butchery and subjugation. Their victims' compliance with those directives enables the region's governmental-administrative apparatus to function in a largely smooth and orderly way that serves the Nazis' exterminative purposes most effectively.

In the circumstances just described, the victims will clearly be better off or no worse off in conditions of outright anarchy than in the orderly conditions of the region-wide abattoir. When they submit to the general norms and specific orders laid down by the region's soldiers and administrators, they haplessly contribute to the continued operativeness of a system from which they suffer grievously. Of course, there are truly shuddersome obstacles that impede any efforts by the victims to revolt: paralyzing fear and helplessness; deluded hopefulness (cultivated by the Nazis, no doubt); unco-ordinatedness for actions outside the scope of the officially imposed requirements; and material weakness. If those obstacles can miraculously be overcome, and if the victims can launch a formidable rebellion that eventuates in wholesale anarchy throughout the region, they will all be better off or no worse off than if the program of annihilation were to proceed unabatedly. To be sure, some of the people in the insurrection will be quickly massacred by the Germans and will therefore be no better off in that respect than if the insurrection had not occurred. However, even they will be no worse off. Indeed, in some respects they will be better off, since they will have died as a consequence of resistance rather than as a consequence of submission. Furthermore, a lot of the victims will manage to escape and will therefore be much better off, even if the outbreak of anarchy throughout the region leads to continuous fighting and turbulence. Living in a dangerously battle-torn region is better than being slaughtered posthaste.

Happily, there seldom develops a situation wherein the vast majority of non-officials will be better off or no worse off if anarchic chaos erupts. In most societies, even in societies with wicked legal regimes, many non-officials will be worse off if public order descends into rampant lawlessness. Considerably more common than circumstances like those described in my last two paragraphs, however, are circumstances in which *some* innocent people will be made better

off through a descent into anarchy. Such circumstances are what Hart had in mind
when he observed that people in woefully downtrodden groups are the victims
rather than the beneficiaries of law's orderliness. Whereas programs of nation-
wide annihilation are rare, programs of subjugation or partial annihilation are
undertaken more frequently. When some people are targeted for extermination or
are brutally and ruthlessly enslaved, they will probably fare better through a
general decline of their society into anarchy than through the continuation of the
scheme of public order which gravely oppresses them. Indeed, when a government is actively seeking to annihilate all the members of subordinate groups, any
outbreak of widespread anarchic turmoil will almost certainly bring about an
improvement in the well-being of the people in those groups. They cannot really
be any worse off, and most of them will very likely be better off. Even when the
mistreatment of oppressed people falls somewhat short of out-and-out extermination, a system of harsh slavery can leave them in an abject state that would not
be worsened and might well be improved through the collapse of public order.
(Still, insofar as the governmental mistreatment of the dominated groups does
stop short of genocide, we should not too confidently presume that the members
of those groups would fare better if the government—and the orderliness brought
about by the government—were to disintegrate. When public order breaks down
altogether, some of the people in the dominant groups may well react to the
absence of constraints by slaughtering the people in the despised groups. Acting
out of fear and confusion and sheer hatred, the unleashed persecutors will have
turned the new circumstances of anarchy into an even more hellish plight for the
downtrodden than were the erstwhile circumstances of crushingly oppressive
orderliness.)

When a society does contain innocent people who would be better off under
conditions of anarchic turmoil than under the existing scheme of governance,
those people will not bear any prima-facie moral obligations of obedience. More
precisely, they will not bear any such obligations that are justified solely on the
basis of an argument which presupposes that legal governance is always preferable (for everyone) to the absence of law and government; those people will
undoubtedly still bear some prima-facie moral obligations of obedience that are
justified by reference to the contents of the legal norms to which the obligations
pertain. Now, an argument of the sort just mentioned—an argument which seeks
to demonstrate the existence of the obligation-to-obey partly on the basis of a
claim that the orderliness of a legal regime is always morally superior to the
hurly-burly of lawlessness—is the chief target of my present chapter. Moreover,
the obligation-to-obey which that argument purports to underwrite is supposed to
be universally borne as well as comprehensively applicable. Thus, we are now in
a position to see that any such argument has inadvisably overlooked the possibility of ghastly situations like those delineated in this subsection. When broached
in relation to any society where all non-officials or some non-officials are no
better off within the prevailing conditions of legally secured orderliness than they

would be within conditions of anarchy, the argument impugned by this chapter will have failed to show that such people are under any content-independent moral obligations of obedience. Ergo, it will have failed to demonstrate the existence of the obligation-to-obey.

*(b) What Are the Options?*

Henceforward we shall focus on societies wherein all innocent people would be made worse off by the onset of anarchic disorder. We have to determine whether, in such societies, a prima-facie moral obligation of obedience attaches to every legal mandate. More specifically, we must assess the soundness of the following line of argument (which, for ease of analysis and discussion, will be presented here with three premises rather than with two):

(i)   All innocent people are better off within the existing legal regime than in circumstances of anarchic frenzy.

(ii)  The sustainment of the regime requires compliance by a large proportion of citizens with the regime's authoritative directives in any circumstances to which those directives are applicable.

(iii) The principle of fairness calls for everyone to share equally the burden of compliance in order to preserve a state of affairs that is beneficial for everyone.

(iv)  Ergo, each person is under a prima-facie moral obligation of obedience that attaches to every prevailing legal mandate in every context to which the mandate is applicable.

Of the three premises in this argument, the first is here being taken as given—in that we are now concentrating our attention on societies where that first premise is true. We have already explored a number of the difficulties in the principle asserted by the third premise, and thus we need not ponder those specific difficulties further at this stage. Likewise, we have investigated a misleading and troublesome ambiguity in the second premise. On the one hand, that premise does not support the argument's conclusion unless it is advancing a claim about *all* the legal mandates within the prevailing system of law. On the other hand, if the second premise is indeed advancing such a claim, it woefully overlooks the possibility of utterly harmless disobedience of some good laws.

We shift our scrutiny here to a difficulty in the second premise that has not yet been examined in this chapter. As should be apparent from the much briefer discussion of this topic in Chapter 7, some especially dubious words in the second premise are '[t]he sustainment of the regime'—words which appear to suggest that the preservation of the existing scheme of governance is the lone alternative to the wholesale dissolution of public order. Though such preservation is indeed morally superior to such dissolution (*ex hypothesi*), those two eventualities are hardly exhaustive of the range of possible outcomes or objectives. When assessing the obligatory force of the prevailing system of law, we should not blithely assume that the pertinent baseline-for-comparison is a nightmare of anarchic unruliness; very seldom do people face a stark choice between upholding all the laws of their current regime and sliding into chaos. Much more often, they can choose between upholding the current laws and transforming some of those laws without collapsing into anarchic turbulence.

If we take for granted the truth of the first and third premises above, and if we put aside the problem of harmless noncompliance with good laws (in order to focus on the problem of evil laws), then a test for the prima-facie moral obligatoriness of legal norms should consist of two main prongs. Under that test, each particular law or set of laws will be unaccompanied by any prima-facie moral obligation of obedience, unless at least one of the following two conditions is satisfied:

(I) The particular law or set of laws is morally salutary or otherwise morally unobjectionable.

(II) The elimination/transformation of the particular law or set of laws is not reasonably attainable, and compliance with the particular law or set of laws is crucial for the prevention of widespread disorderliness or for the prevention of other nontrivial harm to legitimate interests.

Each of the two main strands of this test for prima-facie moral obligatoriness is obviously in need of elucidation.

At least in routine applications, every person in a society will always bear a prima-facie moral duty to act in accordance with each of the fundamental prohibitions on murder, unprovoked assault, and the like. (Even in a society with a grossly mistreated subordinate group of people, each member of that group will very likely always bear a *prima-facie* duty of this sort. However, each member's prima-facie duty in such circumstances will undoubtedly often be significantly outweighed by countervailing considerations.) Other morally salutary legal prohibitions, such as the prohibition on jaywalking, can sometimes be harmlessly disregarded. Indeed, the occasions for thoroughly harmless disobedience may be quite frequent—which is to say that the occasions marked by the absence of any prima-facie moral obligations of obedience may be quite frequent. None the less, because we here are assuming away the potential for harmless violations of good laws, we can accept that every morally salutary legal prohibition is always associated with a prima-facie obligation of compliance.

Among the legal mandates that should be classified as morally salutary, of course, are the norms that co-ordinate people's interaction in ways that are not markedly unfair—norms such as ordinary traffic laws, for example. Because those norms perform the morally valuable function of enabling people to live and work smoothly in proximity with one another, and because the fulfillment of that function requires conformity with the norms by a large proportion of the population, every person is morally duty-bound (prima facie) to abide by the norms' requirements. Unlike a prohibition on murder or assault, a co-ordinational legal norm partakes of salutariness and prima-facie moral bindingness not because of its sheer content but because of its operative force in a context where *some* pertinent norm or other is needed.

Given that we are now pretermitting all opportunities for the completely harmless nonfulfillment of morally legitimate legal mandates, the first prong of the test for prima-facie moral obligatoriness encompasses mandates that are merely unobjectionable as well as those which are salutary. Though the merely unobjectionable legal norms do not play any truly valuable role, they likewise do not produce any real harm (beyond a trivial level). Hence, if the existence of prima-facie moral duties of obedience to such norms is often doubtful—as indeed it is—the doubts are not precisely the same as those concerning duties of obedience to wicked laws. Consequently, since the focus of this chapter now lies exclusively on doubts of the latter type, we should presume here that the merely unharmful legal directives can be grouped together with those which are beneficial; that is, we can presume that each such directive always imposes on each of its addressees a prima-facie moral obligation of obedience.

In the present discussion, the second element of the test for prima-facie moral obligatoriness is of still greater importance than the first. Even if a legal norm is neither morally commendable nor morally permissible, it can give rise to obligations of obedience when the second condition (or second set of conditions) in the test above is satisfied. Let us look closely at that second prong of the test. In the opening portion thereof, the words 'not reasonably attainable' indicate that the process of achieving the elimination or transformation of evil legal norms should not involve morally serious costs. Perhaps the elimination or transformation is not practicable at all, or perhaps it can be attained only through the infliction of nontrivial damage to legitimate interests. Exactly what will count as 'reasonably attainable' or 'not reasonably attainable' is scarcely a matter that can be settled at a high level of abstraction, but a few brief comments are in order here.

Let us recall the example of the protection racket that was presented in Chapter 7. One key feature of that example is the absence of any acceptable alternatives to the continuation of the racket; if the perpetrators of the racket lose their dominant position, other thugs will move in and will mistreat the victims of the racket even more egregiously. Apart from the lack of preferable alternatives, however, the paramount reason for the continuation of the protection racket and its onerous dictates is that the moderating of those dictates within the prevailing scheme of power relations is not reasonably attainable. Just as there are no prospects for improvement externally, there are no prospects for relief internally. Alas, the men who operate the protection racket are obdurately impervious to any protests or blandishments or exhortations, and will not give ground unless they are forcibly removed from their posture of ascendance. As a result, the tempering of the racketeers' demands is simply impracticable from the perspective of their victims—who do not possess the means to drive the racketeers from power, and who in any event do not wish to bring on the dire consequences that would follow from the

ousting of them (i.e., consequences consisting in the seizure of power by hoodlums who are considerably more brutal).

We should now notice that the point about the absence of decent external alternatives is separable from the point about the infeasibility of internal reforms. Let
us suppose that the overthrow of the men who run the protection racket would not
eventuate in a takeover by other ruffians bent on afflicting the populace with even
worse hardships. Instead, the overthrow would lead to a general improvement in
the lot of the ordinary person. In these new circumstances, the sole obstacle to
that improvement is the tenacity of the racketeers themselves. If they oppose
change as obstinately as is suggested in my last paragraph, and if the ordinary
citizens are indeed devoid of any means for bringing about changes in the face of
such opposition, then an amelioration of the plight of those citizens is straightforwardly impracticable (for the time being). By contrast, if the citizens have the
resources to take violent measures that can overcome the intransigence of the
racketeers in regard to certain issues, then the easing of the citizens' hardships is
no longer strictly beyond their reach. However, from the mere fact that the induc-
ing of certain changes has become possible for the victims, we cannot safely infer
that those changes have become 'reasonably attainable'. If the forcing through of
modifications by way of some violent revolts will involve nontrivial harm to legitimate interests, then each victim bears a prima-facie moral duty to abstain from
participating in such maneuvers. To be sure, that duty may be vastly outweighed
by a contrary moral duty which derives from the urgent need for the reforms that
are procurable through violent rebellions; but the overridability of the duty-to-
abstain does not amount to that duty's nonexistence. In the sense defined by this
discussion, the effecting of the aforementioned reforms is not 'reasonably attainable'—even if, on the whole, those reforms clearly should be pursued.

Let us now suppose that the situation outside the sway of the racketeers is as bleak
as we had initially presumed. That is, the downfall of the protection racket would
clear the way for the grabbing of power by thugs who are more bloodily ruthless than
the gangsters who operate the racket. Consequently, the victims of the racket face an
absence of acceptable alternatives. Let us suppose as well, however, that the racketeers are not wholly impervious to exhortations and expressions of dissatisfaction by
the victims. While there are no prospects for improvement externally, there are
genuine prospects for some relief internally; moreover, the internal reforms are
'reasonably attainable', in that they can be accomplished through persuasion and
protest rather than through measures that would involve nontrivial damage to legitimate interests. Inasmuch as the nonfulfillment of some of the racketeers' dictates is
itself among the morally unobjectionable ways by which the ordinary people can
achieve the tempering of those dictates, they will not have any prima-facie moral
obligations to abstain from the noncompliance. Indeed, not only will each person be
morally at liberty to decline to conform with some of the racketeers' dictates, but he
or she will probably be morally duty-bound to decline—in order to contribute to the
alleviation of everybody's afflictions. Of course, the victims of the racket should

refrain from pushing their noncompliance too far. They will not wish to provoke any harsh backlash by the racketeers, nor will they wish to weaken the racketeers' hold on power to the point where the current arrangement gives way to a more repressive regimen imposed by more monstrous hoodlums. Within those constraints, however, the victims of the protection racket will have leeway to depart from the terms of the racketeers' demands. Within those constraints, there will not be any prima-facie moral reasons for them to submit to those demands.

My last few paragraphs' remarks about the protection racket and its victims can be extended straightforwardly, *mutatis mutandis*, to the situation of people living under a government that lays down legal requirements which are oppressive or odious. Insofar as the moderating of those requirements is reasonably attainable—insofar as it can be accomplished through methods (including noncompliance) that do not inflict any nontrivial damage on legitimate interests—the people subject to those requirements are not under any prima-facie moral obligations to abide by them. There is no moral reason for those people to fulfill those wicked requirements. Contrariwise, if the elimination or tempering of some evil law(s) is not reasonably attainable, then each addressee of the law(s) may sometimes bear a prima-facie moral duty of obedience thereto. Whether such a duty exists is a matter that will then hinge on the latter half of the second main strand in our test for the prima-facie moral obligatoriness of legal mandates.

If that duty of obedience does exist, it is of course owed by each citizen to the people whose legitimate interests would be harmed by an effort to bring about the changes that are not reasonably attainable. Typically, those people will be each citizen's fellow citizens rather than the officials who establish and administer the obnoxious directive(s); typically, the officials' expectations of obedience in regard to any such directive(s) are wholly illegitimate and are thus in themselves devoid of moral weight. Still, there can be many situations in which some officials or even all officials are not entirely culpable. They may be reluctant agents of evil, acting out of fear and duress rather than out of any genuine desire to promote heinous purposes. If in such circumstances the particular officials are not at fault for having come to occupy positions wherein they feel constrained to give effect to wicked directives, their expectations of citizens' obedience will very likely possess some moral weight (albeit probably not much weight).

Let us move now to the remaining portion of the test for prima-facie moral obligatoriness. Here we come to the problem of a baseline-for-comparison, broached in Chapter 7.[17] Even if the elimination or transformation of an odious

---

[17] As I have noted in Ch. 7, a particularly insightful recognition of this problem is in Kent Greenawalt, above, n. 7, at 192–4. For some other good statements of the problem (all of which approach it in ways quite different from my own approach), see Kent Greenawalt, above, n. 9, at 159–60, 172–3; John Horton, above, n. 7, at 93–5, 106–7; A. John Simmons, above, n. 2, at 26–7. Cf. John Dunn, 'Political Obligation', in David Held (ed.), *Political Theory Today* (Cambridge: Polity Press, 1991), 23, 34; Ronald Dworkin, *Law's Empire* (London: Fontana Press, 1986), 194; J. Roland Pennock, 'The Obligation to Obey the Law and the Ends of the State', in Hook, *Law*, above, n. 7, at 77, 80–1; John Rawls, above, n. 11, at 14–15.

legal norm is not reasonably attainable, the norm will not engender any obligations of obedience unless conformity with it is necessary for the avoidance of
widespread disturbances or of other nontrivial harm to legitimate interests. Our
inquiries into the prima-facie moral obligatoriness of flagitious legal norms
should never take for granted that the sole alternative to compliance with such
norms is the eruption of anarchic hugger-mugger (as if a lack of compliance with
those norms were equivalent to a lack of compliance with any legal norms whatsoever). Rather, each such inquiry must compare a probable state of affairs
marked by the heeding of some evil law and a probable state of affairs marked by
transgressions of that law. Seldom will we have good grounds for thinking that
the latter state of affairs is likely to consist in chaotic upheavals—especially if we
take account of the full range of circumstances to which any wicked law might
apply. Having apprehended the broad range of those circumstances, we shall have
grasped the full variety of the ways in which such a law might be violated.

A couple of examples may illuminate the abstract discussion here. Suppose
that the government in a strongly anti-Semitic society introduces a legal norm
which prohibits everyone from engaging in Jewish religious practices. Let us
suppose also that the Jews in the society are wholly unable to attain the elimination or softening of this ban on the exercise of their religion. Suppose further that,
if any Jews flout the ban conspicuously, they and their co-religionists will incur
the wrath of the numerous bigots who live alongside them. Instances of manifest
defiance of the new law will trigger pogroms not only against the Jews who are
directly involved, but also against other followers of their faith. In these circumstances, every Jew owes a prima-facie moral obligation to his fellow Jews to
abstain from such defiance. Nevertheless, even though each Jew is obligated to
eschew *manifest* transgressions of the anti-Semitic directive, the moral posture of
*furtive* transgressions is quite different. If (as is overwhelmingly likely) there are
settings in which some departures from the terms of the directive will not be
detected at all, and if the Jews in the society can accurately identify some of those
settings and the sorts of infractions that can be undertaken safely, then there are
no moral reasons against their committing of such infractions. No damage is
thereby inflicted on legitimate interests.

Thus, even when conformity with a wicked law is sometimes morally obligatory prima facie, there can be numerous occasions on which the law's
addressees are under no prima-facie moral duties to refrain from apt violations.
Deviations from the terms of the law in appropriate settings will not detract from
anything of moral value. In other words, the situation here is much the same as
the situation concerning the anti-jaywalking ordinance; just as there can be thoroughly harmless infractions of benign laws in certain contexts, so too there can
be thoroughly harmless infractions of evil laws (notwithstanding that those laws
can engender obligations of obedience in certain other contexts). Hence, the
latter half of the second prong in our test for prima-facie moral obligatoriness
will frequently turn out to be unsatisfied when we ponder the implications of

specific types of departures from wicked legal requirements. Frequently, then, no one will be under a prima-facie moral duty to eschew such departures.

In the example just presented, the addressees of the heinous legal mandate are the members of a subordinate group. Let us now contemplate an example involving a heinous mandate addressed to the members of the dominant group in a society. Suppose that an anti-Semitic regime in a largely Christian or Islamic country introduces a law requiring every Gentile adult to spit upon Jews when encountering them on sidewalks. Suppose further that the elimination of this iniquitous directive is not reasonably attainable, in that the regime will not yield to exhortations and protests. Now, although the nearly universal flouting of such a law could conceivably generate undesirable consequences—perhaps by prompting Gentile bigots to attack Jews, out of fury at seeing them walk along unsullied—the general societal circumstances may be such that the absence of undesirable consequences is virtually guaranteed. In those circumstances, the anti-Semitic mandate does not engender any prima-facie moral obligations of obedience at all. (We can safely assume that the pervasive disregard of the mandate does not have any deleterious effect on people's preparedness to comply with legal requirements that serve worthy purposes [such as the preservation of basic orderliness].) Furthermore, even if the societal circumstances are such that the nearly universal flouting of the anti-Semitic dictate would probably lead to highly undesirable consequences, and thus even if that dictate will engender obligations of obedience in some contexts, there are bound to be numerous occasions on which the nonfulfillment of the dictate will go completely and predictably undetected; hence, on those occasions, the noncompliance will predictably not trigger any untoward effects whatsoever. On each such occasion, then, there will not be any prima-facie moral obligation to engage in the legally required spitting.

What these examples help to illustrate is that the latter half of the second chief provision in our test for prima-facie moral obligatoriness will very rarely if ever be satisfied in a blanket or wholesale fashion. All of the fundamental legal prohibitions which would indeed satisfy that clause of the provision in a comprehensive manner—i.e., in a manner that leaves no exceptions for occasions of utterly harmless disobedience—are among the laws that are covered by the test's first provision, which deals with legal norms that are morally commendable or at least unobjectionable. Once we confine our focus to evil laws by moving from that first provision to the second, we do not find any legal requirements to which we can plausibly attribute prima-facie moral obligatoriness across the board. Some wicked legal norms will give rise to no prima-facie moral obligations of obedience at all, because the constant and universal breaching of those norms' requirements will not cause any ill effects. Other pernicious legal mandates will sometimes give rise to prima-facie moral obligations of obedience, because the defiance of those mandates in certain circumstances would yield deplorable consequences. All the same, there will be many occasions on which the disregard of those mandates will not pose the slightest danger of obnoxious results; on each such occasion, no one bears a prima-facie moral obligation to heed those mandates.

Near the outset of this subsection, a three-premise argument was delineated as the principal target of my discussion. Throughout this subsection, we have assumed away all the snags and weaknesses in the first and third premises of the aforementioned argument, in order to concentrate on the second premise. With regard to that second premise, we have additionally assumed away the possibility of harmless violations of benign laws. Against the background of these various simplifying assumptions—assumptions which portray the three-premise target of my discussion in a highly flattering light—we have explored the bearing of a two-pronged test for prima-facie moral obligatoriness. We have discovered that there will frequently be no moral reasons in favor of anyone's compliance with iniquitous legal dictates. Although the addressees of such dictates may at times have punishment-centered prudential reasons for conformity therewith, they will often not be under any prima-facie moral duties that would likewise point in the direction of conformity. By contrast, they will always be under prima-facie moral duties that point in the direction of *non*conformity with evil dictates.

## (c) *Adjusting the Focus*

Two salient aspects of the foregoing discussion are in need of clarification and amplification: the focus on individual norms or sets of norms rather than on overall legal systems; and the burden of proof in applying the elements of the test for prima-facie moral obligatoriness. Some theorists, especially those who have stressed the distinction between generality and invariability in regard to the obligation-to-obey, have submitted that any inquiry into the prima-facie moral obligatoriness of legal norms should appropriately focus on the level of an overarching regime of law rather than on particular norms within a regime.[18] Their line of reasoning runs as follows. By gauging the moral quality of a whole system of law, we ascertain whether the fact of a mandate's belonging to that system is a fact which will often weigh in favor of obedience to the mandate (insofar as obedience thereto can contribute to strengthening the overall system). We shall thus have discerned whether there exists a general obligation to obey legal norms within the sway of the specified system. That overarching obligation attaches to individual norms only because of their places within a regime that is morally salutary. Of course, the contents of many of the individual norms will in themselves be morally worthy and will therefore constitute standards of conduct that are morally binding (prima facie) in any event. However, that independent moral bindingness is separate from the moral bindingness which obtains by virtue of the norms' statuses as components of a commendable scheme of legal governance. Only the latter source of bindingness is the source of the general obligation to obey the law. Hence, when seeking to verify or disprove the existence of that

---

[18]  See especially Chaim Gans, above, n. 7, at 103–6. See also Paul Harris, above, n. 15, at 165–6.

general obligation, we should concentrate on the systemic level as opposed to the level of particular norms or sets of norms.

As will be seen shortly when we turn to the matter of the burden-of-proof in the application of our test for prima-facie moral obligatoriness, the systemic level is indeed of considerable importance within any adequate account of law's moral bindingness. Before moving on to that topic, however, my discussion must respond to the argument summarized in the preceding paragraph. If the obligation-to-obey which is challenged here were understood not as a comprehensively applicable and universally borne duty but as merely a general duty—i.e., a duty typically present but by no means invariably present—then of course the focus of this chapter would appropriately lie on the system-wide character of each regime of law. We would have to inquire about the moral worthiness or unworthiness of each regime, and therefore about the likelihood that most of the norms within each such regime will generate prima-facie moral obligations of obedience in most circumstances to which the norms are applicable. However, as has already been made clear, this chapter can happily concede that there is a *general* obligation to obey the law in morally worthy regimes. The existence of such an obligation in those regimes is hardly a source of embarrassment for the legal-positivist denial of necessary connections between law and morality. What is being challenged here is not a general obligation but a *comprehensively applicable and universally borne* obligation: an intrinsic obligation that attaches to every legal mandate purely by dint of the mandate's status as a legally valid norm. To refute the claim that such an obligation exists, we can warrantedly focus on the level of individual norms.

By showing that there will be no moral reasons at all for compliance with many legal norms in certain circumstances, and by showing that there will be no moral reasons at all for compliance with some legal norms in *any* circumstances, my discussion has disproved the thesis that the role of law as a necessary condition for decent societal interaction will always confer at least some degree of prima-facie moral obligatoriness on every full-fledged legal mandate. After all, if every such mandate were indeed always imbued with some degree of prima-facie obligatoriness, then there would always be some moral reasons in favor of conformity therewith. In short, by concentrating on the level of particular legal norms or sets of legal norms, we have discerned the falsity of a thesis about the moral standing of all such norms. (Let us henceforward designate that false thesis as '*T*'.) Because *T* purports to be comprehensive and universal rather than merely general, the best way of undermining it is to adduce clear counterexamples.

Now, although the undermining of *T* is most easily carried out in relation to evil regimes of law, it can also be carried out in connection with benevolent regimes. Recall, for instance, that the jaywalking ordinance is a worthy law in a benign legal system; all the same, many of the people who are subject to it will quite often have no moral reasons for complying with it. Nevertheless, we should refrain from rushing to the conclusion that the contrast between wicked legal systems and morally admirable legal systems does not bear significantly on the question whether people are morally obligated (prima facie) to comply with legal mandates. Here we come to the matter of the burden-of-proof in the application of the test for the prima-facie moral obligatoriness of legal directives. Indeed, the current topic goes beyond the two-pronged test on which we have been focused for the last several pages. It extends also to judgments about occasions for totally harmless infractions of good laws.

Among the theorists who emphasize the distinction between a general obligation of obedience and a comprehensive/universal obligation of obedience (in order to concentrate on the former), there is a natural tendency to maintain that the general obligation is present in benign legal regimes and absent in deplorable regimes.[19] Given that those theorists address themselves to the overall moral fiber of each system of law, their conclusions about the presence or absence of the general obligation of obedience in each system are bound to hinge on that overall fiber. This chapter's approach to the burden of proof is not entirely dissimilar, but both its specific implications and the degree of flexibility in its stance will be different. (Of course, since the focus of various theorists on the general duty to obey the law is perfectly consistent with this chapter's denial of the comprehensively applicable and universally borne obligation-to-obey, the approach of those theorists to the task of gauging the presence or absence of the general duty can likewise be readily accepted herein. Dissimilarities between that approach and the method adopted here are due not to outright incompatibilities but to differences of explanatory/analytical emphasis.)

Here, as has been indicated, the contrast between commendable legal regimes and evil legal regimes will affect the assignment of the burden of proof. When the test for prima-facie moral obligatoriness (formulated several pages ago) is to be applied to some particular legal norm, or when a decision is to be made concerning the probability that a violation of a worthy legal mandate will be utterly harmless, there is either a presumption *against* the existence of a prima-facie moral obligation of obedience or a presumption *in favor of* the existence of such an obligation. That is, one and only one of the following two possibilities will obtain:

($P_1$) It has to be shown that some morally binding reason calls prima facie for obedience to the particular law(s). Only such a showing will overcome an initial thesis that no such reason is present.

($P_2$) It has to be shown that there are no morally binding reasons which call

---

[19] See e.g. Chaim Gans, above, n. 7, at ch. 3; Paul Harris, above, n. 15, at 166–70. Some remarks (mostly very sketchy) in the following sources bear varying degrees of resemblance to my own analysis of the burden of proof: George Christie, above, n. 15, at 1314 n. 10; John Dunn, above, n. 17, at 44; Kent Greenawalt, above, n. 7, at 101–2; Paul Harris, above, n. 15, at 175–6; John Horton, above, n. 7, at 134; Rex Martin, 'The Character of Political Allegiance in a System of Rights', in Harris, *Political Obligation*, above, n. 7, at 184, 211-12; Donald Regan, 'Law's Halo', in Jules Coleman and Ellen Frankel Paul (eds), *Philosophy and Law* (Oxford: Basil Blackwell, 1987), 15, 25–6.

prima facie for obedience to the particular law(s). Only such a showing will overcome an initial thesis that at least one such reason is present.

An adoption of one of these stances as opposed to the other can affect not only the likelihood that a particular legal directive will be deemed to engender a prima-facie moral obligation of obedience, but also the likelihood that the presence or absence of such an obligation will become a live question at all (in connection with a particular directive as applied to a certain set of facts). If $P_1$ is the prevailing standard, and if there is virtually no chance that the burden of proof assigned by it can be met, then the absence of a prima-facie moral obligation of obedience will probably be taken for granted. Similarly, if $P_2$ is the prevailing standard, and if there is virtually no chance of meeting the burden of proof which it assigns, then the *presence* of the aforementioned obligation will probably not be doubted by anybody.

In regard to any specific legal system, the choice between $P_1$ and $P_2$ should hinge on the system's overall moral standing. Within a wicked legal regime, citizens' judgments about prima-facie moral obligations of obedience should be guided by $P_1$. Because any such regime contains numerous mandates that are pernicious in their explicit tenor or in their intended effects, and because the absence of any prima-facie obligations of obedience is especially likely in connection with such mandates, a general presumption against the existence of those obligations is warranted. Although some of the norms in any iniquitous legal system will undoubtedly be endued with prima-facie moral obligatoriness on many occasions, quite a large number of the system's norms will seldom or never partake of such obligatoriness. Citizens living within such a system, then, should adopt the distrustful posture ordained by $P_1$.

By contrast, people living within a benevolent regime of law are not similarly warranted in taking up a wary attitude. For their regime, the presumption established by $P_2$—a presumption in favor of the existence of prima-facie moral obligations of obedience—is appropriate. A morally worthy legal system contains few or no directives that are obnoxious in their explicit terms or in their intended effects; as a result, it is made up largely of norms that partake of prima-facie moral obligatoriness on many occasions. Quite a few of those norms, indeed, partake of such obligatoriness in all or nearly all circumstances to which they are applicable. Hence, a posture of initial receptiveness toward each of those norms is in keeping with the general character of the systemic matrix to which each of them belongs. To be sure, that stance of receptiveness will now and then give way to a recognition that there are no moral reasons whatsoever for obedience to certain laws in some contexts even under a commendable legal regime. Still, inasmuch as the burden of proof concerning the presence of such moral reasons must lie in one direction or the other, it should be tilted in a favorable direction whenever the moral character of a regime justifies our inferring that those reasons will indeed typically be present.

Now, although the assignment of the burden of proof should be attuned to the overall moral standing of each legal system, there is plainly room for some flexibility and variations. For example, if an otherwise morally commendable regime is seriously flawed in one or two specific areas of its scheme of legal regulation—perhaps certain aspects of racial relations, for instance—then the burden of proof for determining the prima-facie moral obligatoriness of the regime's mandates can reflect the anomalous moral status of the mandates in the dubious areas. $P_1$ can establish the appropriate burden of proof for citizens' judgments about the prima-facie moral obligatoriness of the norms in those areas, whereas $P_2$ will guide their judgments about the sundry other legal requirements which their regime imposes. Numerous alternative divisions and variations in the pertinent assignment of the burden of proof are possible. Although that assignment will typically follow the broad moral tenor of each system of law, it is sufficiently adaptable to accommodate notable aberrations within a system.

Flexibility or adjustability also turns up when we ponder the heaviness of the burden of proof. Legal systems do not fall into two neat categories of wickedness and benevolence; although all or most liberal-democratic regimes can safely be deemed benign, and although Communist or fascist regimes can safely be deemed heinous, there are numerous schemes of governance that are not so readily classifiable. In partial acknowledgment of the many possible gradations of worthiness or unworthiness that might be exhibited by sundry regimes, the burden of proof for decisions about the prima-facie moral obligatoriness of legal requirements should vary in its heaviness. Whichever way the burden of proof tilts, its stringency can be adjusted to reflect the intensity of the malevolence or benevolence of the regime under consideration. Finely tuned calibrations will not be feasible, of course, but broad adjustments should be perfectly manageable.

In response to this whole discussion of the judgments that are to be made about the prima-facie moral obligatoriness of legal norms, the reader may well wish to know exactly who will be reaching those judgments. On the one hand, the answer to such a question is evident: every citizen who is capable of moral decision-making must arrive at those judgments for himself or herself.[20] Although there are many figures of authority (clergymen, pundits, educators, and so forth) who will doubtless seek to influence people's determinations, the task of gauging the prima-facie moral obligatoriness of any law or set of laws is ultimately something to be undertaken by each mature individual. Pronouncements by figures of authority must themselves be assessed for correctness. On the other hand, as should be apparent from what has just been said, there are numerous factors that tend to steer and channel individuals' perceptions of these matters. Not only do figures of authority often succeed in swaying the opinions of many people, but,

[20] If the mind of a person has been thoroughly taken over by other people through some chemical or surgical or electronic means, then he or she is not 'capable of moral decision-making' in any sense that is relevant here.

in addition, social pressures and the power of habit will tend to ensure that individuals' stances concerning the prima-facie obligatoriness of legal norms will usually not be markedly at odds with one another. Though mature individuals must in the end decide for themselves how they should evaluate the directives that are laid down by their legal system, most people's opinions about the prima-facie moral obligatoriness or non-obligatoriness of those directives will be in general accordance. Except in the presence of a degree of social disharmony that would very likely render a legal regime unsustainable, people's opinions emerge amid currents and forces that foster uniformity more than fragmentation.

Moreover, notwithstanding that citizens must ultimately reach their own judgments about the existence or inexistence of moral reasons for compliance with legal norms, we do not have any grounds for thinking that most of the questions addressed by those judgments are insusceptible to being answered in uniquely correct ways. Albeit some of the relevant questions can probably each be answered affirmatively and negatively with equal validity, a lot of those questions will probably each be answerable in a single way that is superior to any contrary response. Of course, people will frequently be unable to achieve a thoroughgoing consensus on the correctness or incorrectness of competing judgments about the prima-facie moral obligatoriness of particular legal directives; but (in many instances) the lack of unanimity will be a consequence of the limitedness and plurality of individual vantage points, rather than an indication that no judgments about the prima-facie moral bindingness of various laws are singularly correct.

## III. CLOSING REMARKS

My final chapter has sought to bring this book as a whole to a fitting conclusion—a robustly legal-positivist conclusion—in several ways. First, while readily acknowledging the key function of law in providing the security and co-ordination that are prerequisite to the viability of human societies, this chapter has firmly resisted the notion that a recognition of law's basic function should lead us to abandon jurisprudential positivism's insistence on the separability of law and morality. Though the existence of law is a necessary condition for the attainment of certain highly desirable effects, it is likewise a necessary condition for the feasibility of any wicked oppression that is carried out by a government on a large scale over a long period. Just as the role of law in enabling such oppression does not constitute an inseparable link between legality and wickedness, so too its role in enabling the sustainability of human societies does not constitute an inseparable link between legality and moral worthiness. In particular, the mere status of a legal system as a legal system does not endow its mandates with prima-facie moral obligatoriness; insofar as those mandates do partake of such obligatoriness, that state of affairs is due to their contents and to the circumstances of their application rather than to their bare nature as legal norms. In short, the fundamental security-promoting and co-ordination-facilitating function of law can be very gladly acknowledged by a staunch legal positivist, who does not thereby concede anything that conflicts with his denial of necessary connections between law and morality.

Another way in which the final chapter has endeavored to bring this book to an apt conclusion is its complementing of the position taken in Chapter 2 (and in some of the other chapters as well). My second chapter has argued that the status of legal directives as legal directives does not in itself confer on officials any prima-facie moral liberties to enforce those directives in accordance with their terms; nor does that status *per se* impose on the officials any prima-facie moral *obligations* to engage in such enforcement. The current chapter has arrived at similar verdicts concerning the posture of citizens. Even when we leave aside all the difficulties in the principle of fair play, we find that the function of law in bringing about security and co-ordination is patently insufficient to establish the obligation-to-obey. A lot of morally worthy laws will sometimes not partake of prima-facie moral obligatoriness, and wicked laws will even more frequently fail to partake of such obligatoriness. Furthermore, in regard to many wicked laws, citizens will be under moral duties to disobey rather than obey. They will there-fore not be morally at liberty to obey. In short, the proper posture of citizens has turned out to involve no fewer morally mandatory or permissible departures from law-conformance (and probably a greater number of morally mandatory or permissible departures from law-conformance) than the proper posture of offi-cials. Thus, Chapter 2 and the present chapter together show that the jurispru-dential soundness of legal positivism is matched by its soundness within the realm of political philosophy. In regard to each of the two main groups of people whose actions affect the law and are affected by it—officials and citizens—the sheer standing of a legal mandate as a legal mandate does not perforce create for anyone either a prima-facie moral liberty or a prima-facie moral duty to abide by the mandate's terms.

Let us close by noting one additional way in which this chapter has tried to offer a conclusion that highlights the virtues of legal positivism. As should be plain from the length of this chapter and the length of this book as a whole, the legal-positivist insistence on the disjoinability of law and morality is a position that stands in need of defense and elaboration. That insistence is correct (or so this book has argued), but it is not *obviously* correct; it has to be defended on many fronts. Also unobvious are the precise implications of the legal-positivist stance. To be adequately supported and expounded, a denial of necessary connec-tions between law and morality must involve a great deal of theorizing in both jurisprudence and political philosophy. In combination with the other parts of this book, the current chapter has sought to give a sense of some of the myriad complexities that must be tackled. It has of course likewise endeavored to illus-trate the fruitfulness of legal positivism as a doctrine that can come to grips with those complexities.

# Index

acceptance:
: contrasted with mere obedience 226–7, 245
: of Rule of Recognition 134–5
adjudication, flexibility of positivism toward 149–50
agency, Fuller's view of 58–62
Alexander, Larry 173 n. 22, 177 n. 23
Alexy, Robert 92 n. 8, 103 n. 16, 108 n. 19
Allan, Trevor 53 n. 19, 58 n. 22, 92 n. 8, 113 n. 1, 173 n. 22
allegiance of officials 15–16, 216, 224–51
American law:
: Dworkin's focus on 129, 147, 161–2, 167
: Fuller's focus on 62
Anastaplo, George 65 n. 29
anti-Semitism 245, 300, 301
Aristotle 31–2, 238
Augustine 92 n. 8
Austin, John 61, 98–101, 219–20, 223
authority, positivist explication of 100–1, 216, 219–21
autonomy, Fuller's view of 41–2, 54–62

Bankowski, Zenon 113 n. 2
baselines for comparison, in moral judgements 206–9, 295–302
basic features of law 37–71, 95–101, 180–1, 232
basic prohibitions, in law 213–15, 224, 263–5, 296
Bayles, Michael 140 n. 6, 164 n. 18, 177 n. 23
Beardsley, Monroe 266 n. 7
Benditt, Theodore 42 n. 6, 43 n. 7
Bentham, Jeremy 99
Berkeley, George 154 n. 15
Beyleveld, Deryck 4 n. 3, 16, 54 n. 19, 181 n. 25, 216, 225–33, 236
Bix, Brian 3 n. 1, 50 n. 16, 54 n. 19, 65 n. 29, 113 n. 2, 128 n. 1
Blackburn, Simon 157 n. 16
Boardman, William 147 n. 11, 266 n. 7, 268 n. 8
'bottom line' 6
: officials' agreement on 143–6, 248–9, 250
Boyle, James 51 n. 18, 54 n. 19, 54 n. 20
branches of government 183–4, 186–7
Brandt, Richard 268 n. 8

Breckenridge, George 42 n. 7, 58 n. 22, 65 n. 29
Broad, C. D. 275 n. 11, 281 n. 14
Brownsword, Roger 4 n. 3, 54 n. 19, 181 n. 25, 216, 225–33, 236
Brudney, Daniel 54 n. 19, 58 n. 22, 66 n. 30
burden of proof, and obligations of obedience 168–71, 291, 304–7
: flexibility in 306
burdensomeness of law-conformance 279–80, 282–3
Burton, Steven 78 n. 1, 82 n. 4, 129 n. 2, 181 n. 25

Campbell, Tom 42 n. 6, 43 n. 7
cartel, evil law analogized to 76–7, 229–30, 233
central-case method 92 n. 7, 234–6
chess 148–9
Christie, George 287 n. 15, 304 n. 19
Cicero 92 n. 8
'citizen', definition of vii
citizens, *vis-à-vis* officials 9, 134, 248–9, 256–7, 308
claim to legitimacy 101–8
Coleman, Jules 14 n. 6, 63 n. 27, 154 n. 15
: on conventional morality 94 n. 10, 210–13
: on Dworkin 140 n. 6
: on inclusive positivism 199 n. 3, 247 n. 10
conflicts, contrasted with contradictions 52–3
constructiveness of interpretation 167–8, 170–3
contradictions, contrasted with conflicts 52–3
conventional morality, and law 15, 195, 209–15
conventions, contrasted with convictions 146–51, 191
Cotterrell, Roger 48 n. 13, 54 n. 19
counter-inclinational force of law 227–33, 236
Covell, Charles 50 n. 16, 54 n. 19
critical morality 210, 211
crossword puzzles 73, 200, 203, 232

Dan-Cohen, Meir 164 n. 18
Detmold, Michael 1, 7, 12, 92 n. 8, 189
: critique of 113–27
disagreements among officials 130–46
dispute-resolution 45–9
Duff, Antony 51 n. 18, 54 n. 19, 58 n. 22, 65 n. 29
: on acceptance of norms 71, 73–7